A·N·N·U·A·L E·D·I·T

Marriage and Family 00/01

Twenty-Sixth Edition

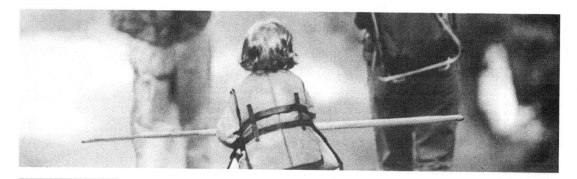

EDITOR

Kathleen R. Gilbert
Indiana University

Kathleen Gilbert is an associate professor in the Department of Applied Health Science at Indiana University. She received a B.A. in Sociology and an M.S. in Marriage and Family Relations from Northern Illinois University. Her Ph.D. in Family Studies is from Purdue University. Dr. Gilbert's primary areas of interest are loss and grief in a family context, trauma and the family, family process, and minority families. She has published several books and articles in these areas.

Dushkin/McGraw-Hill
Sluice Dock, Guilford, Connecticut 06437

Visit us on the Internet
http://www.dushkin.com/annualeditions/

Credits

1. Varied Perspectives on the Family
Unit photo—© 1999 by PhotoDisc, Inc.
2. Exploring and Establishing Relationships
Unit photo—Dushkin/McGraw-Hill photo by Pamela Carley.
3. Finding a Balance: Maintaining Relationships
Unit photo—© 2000 by Cleo Freelance Photography.
4. Crises—Challenges and Opportunities
Unit photo—Courtesy of Nick Zavalishin.
5. Families, Now and into the Future
Unit photo—© 2000 by PhotoDisc, Inc.

Copyright

Cataloging in Publication Data
Main entry under title: Annual Editions: Marriage and Family. 2000/2001.
    1. Family—United States—Periodicals. 2. Marriage—United States—Periodicals. I. Gilbert, Kathleen, *comp.*
II. Title: Marriage and family.
ISBN 0–07–236561–7   301.42'05   74–84596   ISSN 0272–7897

Twenty-Sixth Edition

Cover image © 2000 PhotoDisc, Inc.

Printed in the United States of America   1234567890BAHBAH543210   Printed on Recycled Paper

Members of the Advisory Board are instrumental in the final selection of articles for each edition of ANNUAL EDITIONS. Their review of articles for content, level, currentness, and appropriateness provides critical direction to the editor and staff. We think that you will find their careful consideration well reflected in this volume.

Editors/Advisory Board

EDITOR

Kathleen R. Gilbert
Indiana University

ADVISORY BOARD

Gloria W. Bird
Virginia Polytechnic Institute and State University

Judith Bordin
California State University, Chico

Sari G. Byrd
Suffolk Community College

Marie J. Corey
Michigan State University

Bernard Davidson
Medical College of Georgia

Preston M. Dyer
Baylor University

Linda E. Enders
Iowa State University

Anita Farel
University of North Carolina Chapel Hill

David J. Hanson
SUNY at Potsdam

Dennis Johnson
Monterey Peninsula College

Rita Krasnow
Virginia Western Community College

Marcia Lasswell
California State Polytechnic University, Pomona

William C. Marshall
Brigham Young University

Janette K. Newhouse
Radford University

N. Catherine Norris-Bush
Carson-Newman College

Florence Rose
Chaffey College

Dorothy Seiden
San Francisco State University

Robert M. Walsh
Illinois State University

Charles West
University of Mississippi

Staff

EDITORIAL STAFF

Ian A. Nielsen, Publisher
Roberta Monaco, Senior Developmental Editor
Dorothy Fink, Associate Developmental Editor
Addie Raucci, Senior Administrative Editor
Cheryl Greenleaf, Permissions Editor
Joseph Offredi, Permissions/Editorial Assistant
Diane Barker, Proofreader
Lisa Holmes-Doebrick, Program Coordinator

PRODUCTION STAFF

Brenda S. Filley, Production Manager
Charles Vitelli, Designer
Lara M. Johnson, Design/ Advertising Coordinator
Laura Levine, Graphics
Mike Campbell, Graphics
Tom Goddard, Graphics
Eldis Lima, Graphics
Juliana Arbo, Typesetting Supervisor
Marie Lazauskas, Typesetter
Kathleen D'Amico, Typesetter
Karen Roberts, Typesetter
Larry Killian, Copier Coordinator

To the Reader

In publishing ANNUAL EDITIONS we recognize the enormous role played by the magazines, newspapers, and journals of the public press in providing current, first-rate educational information in a broad spectrum of interest areas. Many of these articles are appropriate for students, researchers, and professionals seeking accurate, current material to help bridge the gap between principles and theories and the real world. These articles, however, become more useful for study when those of lasting value are carefully collected, organized, indexed, and reproduced in a low-cost format, which provides easy and permanent access when the material is needed. That is the role played by ANNUAL EDITIONS.

New to ANNUAL EDITIONS is the inclusion of related World Wide Web sites. These sites have been selected by our editorial staff to represent some of the best resources found on the World Wide Web today. Through our carefully developed topic guide, we have linked these Web resources to the articles covered in this ANNUAL EDITIONS reader. We think that you will find this volume useful, and we hope that you will take a moment to visit us on the Web at *http://www.dushkin.com* to tell us what you think.

The purpose of *Annual Editions: Marriage and Family 00/01* is to bring to the reader the latest thoughts and trends in our understanding of the family, to identify current concerns as well as problems and possible solutions, and to present alternative views of family process. The intent of this anthology is to explore intimate relationships as they are played out in marriage and family and, in doing this, to reflect the family's changing face.

The articles in this volume are taken from professional publications, semiprofessional journals, and popular lay publications aimed at both special populations and a general readership. The selections are carefully reviewed for their currency and accuracy. In some cases, contrasting viewpoints are presented. In others, articles are paired in such a way as to personalize the more impersonal scholarly information. In the current edition, a number of new articles have been added to reflect reviewers' comments. As the reader, you will note the tremendous range in tone and focus of these articles, from first-person accounts to reports of scientific discoveries as well as philosophical and theoretical writings. Some are more practical and applications-oriented, while others are more conceptual and research-oriented.

This anthology is organized to cover many of the important aspects of marriage and family. The first unit looks at varied perspectives on the family. The second unit examines the beginning steps of relationship building as individuals go through the process of exploring and establishing connections. In the third unit, means of finding and maintaining a relationship balance are examined. Unit 4 is concerned with crises and ways in which these can act as challenges and opportunities for families and their members. Finally, unit 5 takes an affirming tone as it looks at families now and into the future.

Instructors can use *Annual Editions: Marriage and Family 00/01* as a primary text for lower-level, introductory marriage and family classes, particularly when they tie the content of the readings to basic information on marriage and family. This book can also be used as a supplement to update or emphasize certain aspects of standard marriage and family textbooks. Because of the provocative nature of many of the essays in this anthology, it works well as a basis for class discussion about various aspects of marriage and family relationships.

This edition of *Annual Editions: Marriage and Family* contains *World Wide Web* sites that can be used to further explore topics addressed in the articles. These sites are cross-referenced by number in the *topic guide*.

I would like to thank everyone involved in the development of this volume. My appreciation goes to those who sent in *article rating forms* and comments on the previous edition as well as those who suggested articles to consider for inclusion in this edition. To all of the students in my Marriage and Family Interaction class who have contributed critiques of articles, I would like to say thanks.

Anyone interested in providing input for future editions of *Annual Editions: Marriage and Family* should complete and return the postage-paid *article rating form* at the end of this book. Your suggestions are much appreciated and contribute to the continuing quality of this anthology.

Kathleen R. Gilbert
Editor

Contents

UNIT 1

Varied Perspectives on the Family

Three articles explore different views on where our images of family come from and how they are influenced by our life experiences as well as societal and cultural constraints.

UNIT 2

Exploring and Establishing Relationships

Twelve articles address factors that influence the formation of close relationships, both romantic and generative.

The concepts in bold italics are developed in the article. For further expansion please refer to the Topic Guide and the Index.

The concepts in bold italics are developed in the article. For further expansion please refer to the Topic Guide and the Index.

UNIT 3

Finding a Balance: Maintaining Relationships

Seven articles consider the complex issues relating to relationships. From marriage to parent/child relationships to sibling relationships, maintaining relationships requires thought and commitment from members.

UNIT 4

Crises— Challenges and Opportunities

A wide variety of crises, normative and catastrophic, are detailed in 18 articles. From family violence, stress, and chaos to the intimate crises of infidelity, divorce, caregiving, and death, these articles provide accounts of devastation and hope.

The concepts in bold italics are developed in the article. For further expansion please refer to the Topic Guide and the Index.

The concepts in bold italics are developed in the article. For further expansion please refer to the Topic Guide and the Index.

The concepts in bold italics are developed in the article. For further expansion please refer to the Topic Guide and the Index.

UNIT 5

Families, Now and into the Future

Five articles examine ways of establishing and/or maintaining health and healthy relationships within families.

The concepts in bold italics are developed in the article. For further expansion please refer to the Topic Guide and the Index.

This topic guide suggests how the selections and World Wide Web sites found in the next section of this book relate to topics of traditional concern to marriage and family students and professionals. It is useful for locating interrelated articles and Web sites for reading and research. The guide is arranged alphabetically according to topic.

The relevant Web sites, which are numbered and annotated on pages 4 and 5, are easily identified by the Web icon (◎) under the topic articles. By linking the articles and the Web sites by topic, this ANNUAL EDITIONS reader becomes a powerful learning and research tool.

TOPIC AREA	TREATED IN	TOPIC AREA	TREATED IN
Abuse	23. Anatomy of a Violent Relationship 24. Helping Children Cope with Violence 25. Resilience in Development ◎ *1, 9, 13, 18, 19, 22, 24, 30*	**Communication**	6. Flirting Fascination 7. Back Off! 26. Sex & Marriage 38. Hard Lessons ◎ *9, 14, 19, 20, 22, 24, 28, 29*
Aging	26. Sex & Marriage 39. Harder Better Death 43. What's Ahead for Families ◎ *17, 25, 26, 27, 31, 32, 33, 34*	**Culture**	3. African American Families 15. Our Babies, Ourselves 45. Rituals for Our Times ◎ *5, 6, 7, 24, 31, 35*
Attachment	17. Healing Power of Intimacy 18. Men, Women & Money 20. Father Love and Child Development 38. Hard Lessons 42. Defining Daddy Down ◎ *13, 14, 19, 20, 22, 29*	**Dating and Mate Selection**	6. Flirting Fascination ◎ *13, 14, 19, 20, 24, 31*
		Divorce	32. Should You Leave? 33. Divorce Reform: New Directions 34. Is Divorce Too Easy? 35. Smart Plan to Save Marriages 36. Children of Divorce 37. After Divorce 43. What's Ahead for Families ◎ *19, 22, 23, 24, 28, 29*
Beliefs	15. Our Babies, Ourselves 21. Parents Speak 44. Power of Secrets 45. Rituals for Our Times ◎ *3, 4, 8, 9, 19, 24, 31*	**Family Systems**	2. Intentional Family 3. African American Families 36. Children of Divorce 42. Defining Daddy Down 44. Power of Secrets 45. Rituals for Our Times ◎ *19, 20, 22, 23, 24, 28, 29, 31*
Bereavement	37. After Divorce 38. Hard Lessons 39. Harder Better Death 40. How Kids Mourn ◎ *3, 4, 25, 26, 31, 32, 34*	**Family Therapy**	2. Intentional Family 16. Science of a Good Marriage ◎ *19, 22, 24*
Biological Issues	5. Sex Differences in the Brain 6. Flirting Fascination 8. Protecting against Unintended Pregnancy 9. Brave New World of Parenting 11. Fetal Psychology 12. Maternal Emotions 13. Fertile Minds 22. Do Parents Really Matter? ◎ *2, 10, 12, 14, 15, 16*	**Family Values**	1. New Focus on Family Values 29. Progressive Approach to Caring for Children and Community ◎ *3, 4, 5, 6, 19, 20, 22, 23, 28, 29, 31*
Children and Childcare	4. Boys Will Be Boys 13. Fertile Minds 14. Cost of Children 15. Our Babies, Ourselves 20. Father Love and Child Development 21. Parents Speak 24. Helping Children Cope with Violence 25. Resilience in Development 29. Progressive Approach to Caring for Children and Community 30. Do Working Parents Make the Grade? 36. Children of Divorce 37. After Divorce 40. How Kids Mourn ◎ *3, 4, 5, 10, 18, 20, 21, 22, 23, 24, 28, 29, 31*	**Finances, Family**	14. Cost of Children 29. Progressive Approach to Caring for Children and Community 43. What's Ahead for Families ◎ *33, 35*
		Future of the Family	1. New Focus on Family Values 9. Brave New World of Parenting 33. Divorce Reform: New Directions 41. To See Your Future Look into Your Past 42. Defining Daddy Down 43. What's Ahead for Families ◎ *19, 20, 22, 29, 31, 35*
		Gender and Gender Roles	4. Boys Will Be Boys 5. Sex Differences in the Brain 20. Father Love and Child Development 28. The Politics of Fatigue

● AE: Marriage and Family

The following World Wide Web sites have been carefully researched and selected to support the articles found in this reader. If you are interested in learning more about specific topics found in this book, these Web sites are a good place to start. The sites are cross-referenced by number and appear in the topic guide on the previous two pages. Also, you can link to these Web sites through our DUSHKIN ONLINE support site at *http://www.dushkin.com/online/*.

The following sites were available at the time of publication. Visit our Web site—we update DUSHKIN ONLINE regularly to reflect any Changes.

General Sources

1. American Psychological Association
http://www.apa.org/psychnet/
By exploring the APA's "Resources for the Public," you will be able to find links to an abundance of articles and other resources related to interpersonal relationships throughout the life span.

2. Encyclopedia Britannica
http://www.ebig.com
This huge "Britannica Internet Guide" will lead you to a cornucopia of informational sites and reference sources on such topics as family structure and other social issues.

3. Penn Library: Sociology
http://www.library.upenn.edu/resources/subject/social/ sociology/sociology.html
This site provides a number of indexes of culture and ethnic studies, population and demographics, and statistical sources that are of value in studies of marriage and the family.

4. Social Science Information Gateway
http://sosig.esrc.bris.ac.uk
This is an online catalog of Internet resources relevant to social science education and research. Sites are selected and described by a librarian or subject specialist.

Varied Perspectives on the Family

5. American Studies Web
http://www.georgetown.edu/crossroads/asw/
This eclectic site provides links to a wealth of resources on the Internet related to American studies, from gender to race and ethnicity to demography and population studies.

6. Anthropology Resources Page
http://www.usd.edu/anth/
Many cultural topics can be accessed from this site from the University of South Dakota. Click on the links to find comparisons of values and lifestyles among the world's peoples.

7. Human Rights Report—India
http://www.usis.usemb.se/human/human1998/india.html
Read this U.S. Department of State 1998 report on India's human-rights practices for an understanding into the issues that affect women's mental and physical health and well-being in different parts of the world.

8. Men's Health
http://www.menshealth.com/new/guide/index.html
Men's Health presents many links to topics about men, AIDS/STDs, impotence and infertility, and vasectomy. It includes discussions of relationship and family issues.

9. Women's Studies Resources
http://www.inform.umd.edu/EdRes/Topic/WomensStudies/
This site provides a wealth of resources related to women and their concerns. You can find links to such topics as body image, comfort (or discomfort) with sexuality, personal relationships, pornography, and more.

Exploring and Establishing Relationships

10. Ask NOAH About Pregnancy: Fertility & Infertility
http://www.noah.cuny.edu/pregnancy/fertility.html
NOAH (New York Online Access to Health) seeks to provide relevant, timely, and unbiased health information for consumers. At this site, the organization presents extensive links to a variety of resources about infertility treatments and issues.

11. Bonobos Sex and Society
http://songweaver.com/info/bonobos.html
This site, accessed through Carnegie Mellon University, contains an article explaining how a primate's behavior challenges traditional assumptions about male supremacy in human evolution. Guaranteed to generate spirited debate.

12. Go Ask Alice!
http://www.goaskalice.columbia.edu/index.html
This interactive site of the Columbia University Health Services provides discussion and insight into a number of personal issues of interest to college-age people—and those younger and older. Many questions about physical and emotional health and well-being in the modern world are answered.

13. The Kinsey Institute for Research in Sex, Gender, and Reproduction
http://www.indiana.edu/~kinsey/
The purpose of the Kinsey Institutes's Web site is to support interdisciplinary research in the study of human sexuality.

14. Mysteries of Odor in Human Sexuality
http://www.pheromones.com
Keeping in mind that this is a commercial site with the goal of selling a book by James Kohl, look here to find topics of interest to nonscientists about pheromones. Check out the diagram of "Mammalian Olfactory-Genetic-Neuronal-Hormonal-Behavioral Reciprocity and Human Sexuality" for a sense of the myriad biological influences that play a part in sexual behavior.

15. Planned Parenthood
http://www.plannedparenthood.org
Visit this well-known organization's home page for links to information on the various kinds of contraceptives (including outercourse and abstinence) and to discussions of other topics related to sexual and reproductive health.

16. The Society for the Scientific Study of Sexuality
http://www.ssc.wisc.edu/ssss/
The Society for the Scientific Study of Sexuality is an international organization dedicated to the advancement of knowledge about sexuality.

17. Sympatico: HealthyWay: Health Links
http://www.ab.sympatico.ca/Contents/Health/ GENERAL/sitemap.html

This Canadian site meant for consumers will lead you to many links related to sexual orientation. It also addresses aspects of human sexuality over the life span as well as reproductive health.

Finding a Balance: Maintaining Relationships

18. Child Welfare League of America
http://www.cwla.org
The CWLA is the United States' largest organization devoted entirely to the well-being of vulnerable children and their families. This site provides links to information about such issues as teaching morality and values.

19. Coalition for Marriage, Family, and Couples Education
http://www.smartmarriages.com
CMFCE is dedicated to bringing information about and directories of skill-based marriage education courses to the public. Nonpartisan and nonsectarian, it hopes to lower the rate of family breakdown through couple-empowering preventive education.

20. Family.com
http://www.family.com
According to this site, Family.com is an online parenting service that offers comprehensive, high-quality information and a supportive community for raising children.

21. The National Academy for Child Development
http://www.nacd.org
The NACD, dedicated to helping children and adults reach their full potential, presents links to various programs, research, and resources into a variety of family topics.

22. National Council on Family Relations
http://www.ncfr.com
This NCFR home page leads to valuable links to articles, research, and other resources on issues in family relations, such as stepfamilies, couples, and children of divorce.

23. Positive Parenting
http://www.positiveparenting.com
Positive Parenting is an organization dedicated to providing resources and information to make parenting rewarding, effective, and fun. This site provides a newsletter, an index of experts, chat groups, and links to many resources for families.

24. SocioSite
http://www.pscw.uva.nl/sociosite/TOPICS/Women.html
Open this site to gain insights into a number of issues that affect family relationships. It provides wide-ranging issues of women and men, of family and children, and more.

Crises: Challenges and Opportunities

25. Alzheimer's Association
http://www.alz.org
The Alzheimer's Association, dedicated to the prevention, cure, and treatments of Alzheimer's and related disorders, provides support to afflicted patients and their families.

26. American Association of Retired Persons
http://www.aarp.org
The AARP, a major advocacy group for older people, includes among its many resources suggested readings and Internet links to organizations that deal with social issues that may affect people and their families as they age.

27. Caregiver's Handbook
http://www.acsu.buffalo.edu/~drstall/hndbk0.html
This site is an online handbook for caregivers. Topics include medical aspects and liabilities of caregiving.

28. Children & Divorce
http://www.hec.ohio-state.edu/famlife/divorce/
Open this site to find links to articles and discussions of divorce and its effects on the family. Many bibliographical references are provided by the Ohio State University Department of Human Development & Family Science.

29. Parenting and Families
http://www.cyfc.umn.edu/Parenting/parentlink.html
By clicking on the various links, this site of the University of Minnesota's Children, Youth, and Family Consortium will lead you to many resources related to divorce, single parenting, and stepfamilies, as well as information about other topics of interest in the study of marriage and family.

30. Sexual Assault Information Page
http://www.cs.utk.edu/~bartley/saInfoPage.html
This invaluable site provides dozens of links to information and resources on a variety of sexual assault–related topics, from child sexual abuse, to date rape, to incest, to secondary victims, to offenders.

31. A Sociological Tour Through Cyberspace
http://www.trinity.edu/~mkearl/index.html
This extensive site, put together by Michael C. Kearl at Trinity University, provides essays, commentaries, data analyses, and links on such topics as death and dying, family, the sociology of time, social gerontology, and social psychology.

32. Widow Net
http://www.fortnet.org/WidowNet/
Widow Net is an information and self-help resource for and by widows and widowers. The information is helpful to people of all ages, religious backgrounds, and sexual orientation who have experienced a loss.

Families, Now and Into the Future

33. Economic Report of the President
http://www.library.nwu.edu/gpo/help/econr.html
This report includes current and anticipated trends in the United States and annual numerical goals concerning topics such as employment, income, and federal budget outlays. The database notes employment objectives for significant groups of the labor force.

34. National Institute on Aging
http://www.nih.gov/nia/
The NIA presents this home page that will take you to a variety of resources on health and lifestyle issues that are of interest to people as they grow older.

35. The North-South Institute
http://www.nsi-ins.ca/info.html
Searching this site of the North-South Institute—which works to strengthen international development cooperation and enhance gender and social equity—will lead to a variety of issues related to the family and social transitions.

We highly recommend that you review our Web site for expanded information and our other product lines. We are continually updating and adding links to our Web site in order to offer you the most usable and useful information that will support and expand the value of your Annual Editions. You can reach us at:
http://www.dushkin.com/annualeditions/.

www.dushkin.com/online/

Unit 1

Unit Selections

1. **A New Focus on Family Values,** Hara Estroff Marano
2. **The Intentional Family,** William J. Doherty
3. **African American Families: A Legacy of Vulnerability and Resilience,** Beverly Greene

Key Points to Consider

❖ If you had the power to propose a government program to support today's families, what would it be? What would be the source of background information/data you would use to structure that program? What image do you have of families that would take advantage of that program?

❖ What is the nature of your family in terms of closeness and strong ties? What might you do to strengthen your family? What would you suggest for others?

❖ Why do we seem to need to maintain stereotypes of ethnic and racial groups? How might we learn from the strengths of other groups rather than attempt to "tear down" others?

 **Links** | **www.dushkin.com/online/**

These sites are annotated on pages 4 and 5.

Our image of what family is and what it should be is a powerful combination of personal experience, family forms we encounter or observe, and attitudes we hold. Once formed, this image informs decision making and interpersonal interaction throughout our lives. It has far-reaching impacts: On an intimate level, it influences individual and family development as well as relationships both inside and outside the family. On a broader level, it affects social policy and programming.

In many ways, this image can be positive. It can act to clarify our thinking and facilitate interaction with like-minded individuals. It can also be negative, because it can narrow our thinking and limit our ability to see that other ways of carrying out the functions of family have value. Their very differentness can make them seem "bad." In this case, interaction with others can be impeded because of contrasting views.

This unit is intended to meet several goals with regard to perspectives on the family: (1) to sensitize the reader to sources of beliefs about the "shoulds" of the family—what the family should be and the ways in which family roles should be carried out, (2) to show how different views of the family can influence attitudes toward community responsibility and family policy, and (3) to show how views that dominate one's culture can influence awareness of ways of structuring family life.

The first reading, "A New Focus on Family Values," asks us to step away from the use of the narrow, personal perspective on family and look to research for information on how we approach the family values debate. Next, William Doherty, in "The Intentional Family," explores a model of family life that is intended to build strong ties among family members. In "African American Families: A Legacy of Vulnerability and Resilience," Beverly Greene debunks the stereotype of African American families as uniformly dysfunctional, presenting a picture of resilience and adaptive coping instead.

Varied Perspectives on the Family

A NEW FOCUS ON
Family
VALUES

"Family is important because it is the only institution
in contemporary society that is unabashedly
committed to love and caring as its primary function."
–Michael Lerner in *The Politics of Meaning*

By HARA ESTROFF MARANO

FAMILY ISSUES HAVE LONG BEEN HELD PRISONER BY POLITICS, and a particularly narrow cell of politics at that. To care about families is to have "family values," a term that has been co-opted by ideologues, especially those on the political right. Conservatives have not simply dominated public discourse on family issues; they have framed the debate. And for some time now, to be "pro-family" has largely boiled down to one thing: being against divorce.

Certainly there have been great changes in the American family over the past several decades. One child in four is now born to unmarried parents. The number of couples who live together outside of marriage has increased sevenfold since 1970. Divorce has been epidemic for some 25 years. And families with children are feeling particularly burdened these days, as more and more kids grow up poor.

The political right insists that such problems are fallout from the liberalization of divorce laws which occurred throughout the 1970s and early 80s, and it has begun a campaign to rewrite or repeal laws that allow easy-to-obtain, no-fault divorces. In late June, Louisiana marked the first legislative success of a nationwide movement led by conservative Christians: the state now permits couples who are tying the knot to choose a particularly binding marital contract called "covenant marriage" (a biblical-sounding term for the covenant with God embodied in Christian marriage). Couples can still opt for a standard marriage, dissolvable by no-fault divorce, but if they choose a covenant marriage the relationship can be ended only if one spouse can prove that the other has committed adultery, abandoned the home, been imprisoned for a felony, or abused their spouse or children. A separation of at least two years is required before the marriage can end.

But independent thinkers around the country are beginning to alter the nature of the family values debate. They believe that family issues and family policy have been defined too narrowly for too long. They see a much broader array of actions—by government and business as well as by individuals—that affect families and their problems. These factors include the role economic policies play, subtly or overtly, in influencing family composition; the availability of jobs and job training; the supply of suitable men; and numerous others.

The "M" Word

One of the new thinkers is Theodora Ooms, M.S.W., executive director of the Family Impact Seminar, a Washington-based think tank. She contends that while politicians and government officials have vowed to strengthen and support families, they have left out the primary ingredient. "Programs and services designed to support families in fact focus only on mothers and children," she says. But "the cornerstone of the family—the relationship of the couple, whether married or unmarried—has been essentially ignored."

At a recent two-day round table in Washington, D.C., Ooms invited scholars to shift the center of family-values discussion from ideology to research-based information. The ultimate goal: to broaden family policy so that it is informed by all the facts, takes into account the needs of all the members of a family, and supports the relationship that is the family foundation—without condemning those women (or men) who are raising children on their own.

Ooms believes that making marriages harder to dissolve is not the best way to support families. That has the effect of trapping unhappy families in their misery and, perhaps, of exposing abused women and men to danger. And by raising the "cost" of marriage, it could well push more couples into cohabitation, where legal protection exists neither for partners nor for any children they may have.

The most sensible approach is not to make marriage harder to get out of, but to make marriage better to be in. After all, Ooms points out, marriage remains a goal for the vast majority of Americans. Ninety percent marry—and, of course, want their marriages to work. "It's puzzling," she says, "that policy-makers have invested so little in finding out what, if anything, can be done to help marriages succeed." In "tribute" to their avoidance, Ooms often refers to marriage as "the M-word."

Better SEX

One reason marriage is desirable is that when it works well, it has emotional payoffs for partners. But Linda Waite, Ph.D., a sociologist at the University of Chicago, has marshaled evidence that marriage also has substantial benefits for health and well-being. Among the findings Waite reports:

• Married men drink less, live more safely, and live longer. Especially for men, marriage supplies a crucial network of emotional support.

• Married women have better health, and live in better material circumstances, than single or cohabiting women.

• Married people lead more active sex lives. While cohabiting couples have similarly high levels of sex, married men and women report more satisfaction in the bedroom. That's because married people know the tastes of their partner better and can safely cater to them, while the emotional investment in the relationship can boost the thrill.

• In addition to having more sex, the married have more money. Two can live, if not as cheaply as one, then certainly as cheaply as one and a half; they spend less to maintain the same lifestyle than if they lived separately. Further, married partners are more productive around the home than single people because each spouse can afford to develop some skills and neglect others, thereby increasing efficiency. Married couples also save more of their earnings than do single people at the same level of income.

• Marriage leads to higher wages for men; it gives them an incentive to work harder. While married motherhood lowers women's wages on average, they often use their husband's support to give them time with their kids, a benefit generally unavailable to the unmarried.

• Children do better in two-parent families. Children in single-parent households are twice as likely to drop out of high school, and they are more likely to become teenage parents. They are also far more likely to grow up poor. They may suffer from the lack of access to the time and attention of two adults; when fathers are married to the mothers of their children, the fathers' involvement in their children's life tends to be far greater. Children of single-parent families also move more often, thereby losing such important sources of support as neighbors and other community members.

Unfortunately, since the 1950s black men and women have been less likely to share in the benefits of marriage than whites, Waites notes. Although marriage rates have dropped for both blacks and whites, the decline among blacks is far steeper: currently, six in 10 black adults are not married.

Moreover, while rates of cohabitation have increased, the evidence clearly shows that "living together" is qualitatively different from marriage. For one thing, the commitment of marriage makes specialization in chores and responsibilities sensible; spouses count on their partners to fill in for them where they are weak. By contrast, cohabitation is unstable, easy to get out of, and makes specialization less rational. Second, marriage is far superior at connecting people to others—work acquaintances, in-laws—who are a source of support and benefits. It links married people to a world larger than themselves.

Waite believes the evidence supports a public health approach to marriage: make the evidence of its emotional and physical benefits widely available. Some folks who have been skeptical of marriage, she believes, will then reconsider.

Love's LOSS to Labor

In addition to the private aspirations of two partners, there are many forces in the culture that affect marriage. One of the most important is work.

Business has an important stake in shaping family policy, observes Dana Friedman, Ph.D., who heads Corporate Solutions, a New York consulting firm. She notes that marital status is absolutely critical in companies' promotion decisions; a *Business Week* survey, for example, found that 98 percent of top male corporate executives were married and had kids. Yet many companies do nothing to support marriage. Although companies now know that family issues—like finding child care—carry over into work performance, they have yet to recognize that work issues carry over into the home. In fact, reports Friedman, there are many aspects of work that actively impede good family relationships and place great strains on marriages:

• Work is more stressful today. At many companies, people are working longer hours at a faster pace, cutting into family time and making it more difficult to shift from work mode to family mode. And lowered work morale is generally dispiriting, affecting not just on-the-job performance but home life as well.

• As a result of corporate restructuring, there is no longer a guarantee of lifelong employment, adding an element of uncertainty to couples' long-term plans.

• While some companies have become aware of the link between work and family and have implemented policies such as paternity leave, companies are less likely to promote workers who actually use these policies.

• Important as company policies are to the balance between work and home life, a study at Johnson & Johnson identified other elements of the work environment as even more crucial: control over work hours, particularly during a crunch time; a sensitive supervisor; and a generally supportive work atmosphere.

The impact of work issues on home life is three times greater than the impact of home life on work, Friedman reports. Yet companies fail to take responsibility for this, even though surveys show that achieving balance between home and life is a leading concern of employees, and that those who achieve this work-life balance become the most motivated workers.

"Being a family-friendly company is no longer just about programs and policies," says Friedman. "It's about the culture of work and changing the relationships among co-workers." Work/life balance must be a strategy that's totally integrated with missions and business goals.

IT'S THE ECONOMY, STUPID

It's not just the nature of the workplace that can wreak havoc on families. It's also whether there's a workplace to go to at all. And for African-Americans, especially, job uncertainty not only has an impact on families, but may determine whether marriages occur at all.

Contrary to conventional wisdom, moral values or individual inclinations are not the main factors that influence African-Americans' decisions to marry, reports M. Belinda Tucker, Ph.D., professor of psychiatry and biobehavioral sciences at UCLA. The single most crucial factor is the climate of economic uncertainty in their particular community.

Tucker is in the midst of a 21-city survey of factors that influence family formation. So far, results show that African-Americans still value marriage and raising kids in marriage. In fact, she has found that in general, African-Americans hold more traditional values than whites. African-American women hold particularly traditional expectations for male roles. Simply put, they expect husbands to work. And when men don't work, women don't marry. Like many women, African-American women say they don't want to take on a mate with lower economic prospects than their own. The trouble is that the economic prospects of the available men often do not come close to meeting their expectations.

Furthermore, unemployment creates enormous instability within the marriages that do occur. In those cities where unemployment rates are lowest, relationship satisfaction is greatest and marriages are most stable.

In Tucker's view, a rational family policy must address economic insecurity. To be pro-family, then, is to be pro-job, especially for African-Americans. Indeed, other panelists suggested, one way government policy can be family-friendly is to open up the economic prospects for low-income men, perhaps by giving them priority in job training and welfare-to-work programs.

THE SHADOW OF DIVORCE

The law also influences the actions of couples. No-fault divorce, for example, unwittingly enforces gender inequality, because men typically have less to lose than women in leaving a relationship, according to Amy Wax, M.D., J.D., an associate professor at the University of Virginia School of Law. For example, women over the age of 40 face a much lower remarriage rate than their ex-husbands, in part because of their limited reproductive lives. And women are generally worth far less on the labor market, especially if they stopped working full-time to have kids. These advantages increase men's bargaining power within marriages. In short, the "threat factor is higher for men," Wax says.

That's why toughening divorce laws doesn't help women: it leaves untouched men's disproportionate power within marriage. And since marriages, even successful ones, "are always conducted in the shadow of divorce," Wax insists that "any discussion of the methods, costs, and benefits of keeping marriages together must take into account the gender asymmetries—in remarriage prospects, roles, and earning power—that strengthen men's bargaining power."

Participants at the Washington round table agreed that efforts at the beginning of marriage, such as marital education programs that change the way people negotiate, can give women more power. In fact, because marital education increases the benefits of staying together for both parties, it was called "the most promising reform." Also singled out was the creation of tax policies that favor married couples. And state governments should consider restructuring welfare programs that penalize married couples by providing higher benefits to single women with children.

A GROUP EFFORT

The burden of making marriage work, Ooms concludes, can't be left just for couples to shoulder by themselves. It's something policy-makers, communities, and public officials have a hand in. What binds flesh-and-blood couples is not love alone, or sheer determination, or morality. Real family values must take into account the fact that programs and policies are always making and remaking the marital bed.

The Intentional Family

William J. Doherty, Ph.D.

W E REINVENTED FAMILY LIFE in the twentieth century but never wrote a user's manual. Have no doubt about the reinvention. This century has witnessed a revolution in the structures and expectations of family life. The changes in family structures are by now familiar: A child is as likely to grow up in a single-parent family or stepfamily as in a first-married family; an adult is likely to cohabitate, marry, divorce, and remarry; and most mothers are in the paid labor force.

The revolution in expectations of family life is less widely recognized. A scene from the 1971 film *Lovers and Other Strangers* captures this cultural shift. Richie, the adult son of Italian immigrant parents, tells them that he and his wife are divorcing. The stunned parents want to know "What's the story, Richie?" When he tells them he is not "happy," the answer does not compute. "Happy?" the father retorts, "What? Do you think your mother and I are happy?" A startled Richie asks, "You mean you and Mom aren't happy?" The parents look at each other, shrug, and with one voice respond, "No. We're content." Richie storms off with the testimonial of his generation: "Well, if I'm not going to be happy, I'm not going to stay married." But the memorable line from this vignette comes from the mother, played by Beatrice Arthur: "Don't look for happiness, Richie; it'll only make you miserable."

These fictional immigrant parents represented the remnants of the Institutional Family, the traditional family based on kinship, children, community ties, economics, and the father's authority. For the Institutional Family, the primary goals for family life were stability and security; happiness was secondary. Ending a marriage because you were not "happy" made no sense. An elderly British lord expressed the values of the Institutional Family when, upon learning that I was a family therapist he commented: "A frightful mistake so many people are making these days [is] throwing away a perfectly good marriage simply because they fall in love with somebody else."

The Institutional Family was suited to a world of family farms, small family businesses, and tight communities bound together by a common religion. The dominant form of family life for many centuries, it began to give way during the Industrial Revolution of the nineteenth century, when individual freedom and the pursuit of personal happiness and achievement began to be more important than kinship obligations, and when small farms and villages started to give way to more impersonal cities. During the 1920s, American sociologists began noting how an historically new kind of family—what I term the Psychological Family—was replacing the Institutional Family of the past. This new kind of family was based on personal achievement and happiness more than on family obligations and tight community bonds. In the early twentieth century, Americans turned a corner in family life, never to go back.[1]

By the 1950s, the Psychological Family had largely replaced the Institutional Family as the cultural norm in America. In ideal form, the Psychological Family was a nuclear unit headed by a stable married couple with close emotional ties, good communication, and an effective partnership in rearing children in a nurturing atmosphere. The chief goals of this kind of family life were no longer stability and security. Instead, the overarching goal was the satisfaction of individual family members. Men's and women's roles ideally were "separate but equal," with men being experts on the "world" and women being experts on the home.

Current social debates about the Traditional Family generally center around this Psychological Family, which did not come into full flower until the 1950s. Its supporters praise its traditional values, while its critics decry its conformity and unequal gender roles. Both sides miss an important point: the Psychological Family was radical in its own right when it supplanted the Institutional Family as the dominant family form. Its emergence threatened historical family values by reversing the importance of the individual and the family. The family's main job now was to promote the happiness and achievement of individual family members, rather than individual family members' main job being to promote the well-being of the family unit. To paraphrase: Ask not what you can do for your family; ask what your family can do for you. No more radical idea ever entered family life, but it is one we now take for granted in mainstream American culture.

If you doubt this shift in family values, try to imagine a contemporary American man choosing a wife because his family thinks the match would be good for the family. Or imagine a young woman announcing that she will never marry in order to stay home to care for her aging parents. Or a young adult deciding not to have sex before marriage in order not to bring embarrassment to his or her family. Most of us would assume that there was much more to these stories; someone was not telling the truth, or there was some personal or family pathology at work. We would have trouble imagining that a healthy adult would sacrifice important personal goals for the sake of family duties. Although most Americans continue to assume that parents, especially mothers, should place family needs over personal needs while the children are being raised, all bets are off for young people's obligations to their parents and extended family. And the perceived absence of happiness in marriage is a widely acceptable reason to divorce and try again for the kind

of satisfying intimate relationship that has become a cultural birthright.

From its beginning, the Psychological Family was germinating the seeds of its own destruction. It harbored a profound contradiction: the value of individual happiness for both men and women, coupled with the value of family stability. For marriage, this meant commitment based on getting one's personal needs met in an equal relationship—a dicey combination for couples that lacked the skills required for such unions. When the feminist and sexual revolutions exploded in the late 1960s and later joined with the "Me Generation" of the 1970s, the Psychological Family began to fracture. The power of high expectations for marriage overwhelmed couples' abilities to cope at a time when divorce was losing its social stigma. The divorce rate skyrocketed along with non-marital births and single-parent and stepfamilies. The cultural image of the two-parent nuclear family from cradle to grave splintered into a montage of family forms.

We now have the first society in human history without a clear social consensus about what constitutes a "real" family and "good" family. And I don't see one emerging anytime soon.

The eclipse of the shared cultural ideal of the Psychological Family gave rise to the Pluralistic Family, which has dominated the last three decades of the twentieth century. Unlike the Institutional and Psychological Families, the Pluralistic Family does not offer an ideal for what constitutes a good family. Instead, the working assumption is that people create, or find themselves in, a wide variety of family configurations. No family form is inherently better than another, and all should be supported by the broader society. The traditional two-parent family becomes one lifestyle alternative among others, including cohabitation, single parenting, remarriage, and gay and lesbian families. The Pluralistic Family ideal is to let a thousand family forms bloom as families creatively respond to the modern world.

The Pluralistic Family carries forward the Psychological Family's emphasis on personal satisfaction but adds the new value of *flexibility:* to be a successful sailor in the seas of contemporary family life requires the ability to shift with the winds that come your way and the willingness to change boats when necessary. Essentially, you can never tell which kind of family structure you or your children may end up in, so be flexible.[2]

There is intense debate over the merits of the Pluralistic Family ideal in contemporary society. These cultural debates reflect a struggle between adherents to the Psychological Family and the Pluralistic Family. (Hardly anyone wants to go back to the Institutional Family because the value of personal satisfaction in family life ranks high among virtually all groups in American society, with the exception of recent immigrants.) But the very existence of the cultural debate shows the strength of the idea of the Pluralistic Family: the two-parent Psychological Family competes as just one lifestyle ideal among others. We now have the first society in human history without a clear social consensus about what constitutes a "real" family and "good" family. And I don't see one emerging anytime soon.

Following these staggering twentieth-century changes in family life, we now live in the best and worst of times for families. The worst of times because families have historically followed the guidance of their community and culture in shaping marriage, childrearing, and the countless other elements of family living; and now the

The natural drift of family life in contemporary America is toward slowly diminishing connection, meaning, and community.

community and culture are unable to provide a coherent vision or set of tools and supports. Families are left to struggle on their own. We also live in the best of times because we understand better what makes families work, and because now we have unprecedented freedom to shape the kind of family life we want, to be *intentional* about our families.

DEFINING THE INTENTIONAL FAMILY

Sometimes with my therapy clients, I use an analogy of the Mississippi River, which flows just a couple of miles from my office. I say that family life is like putting a canoe into that great body of water. If you enter the water at St. Paul and don't do anything, you will head south toward New Orleans. If you want to go north, or even stay at St. Paul, you have to work hard and have a plan. In the same way, if you get married or have a child without a working plan for your family's journey, you will likely head "south" toward less closeness, less meaning, and less joy over time. A family, like a canoe, must be steered or paddled, or it won't take you where you want to go.

The natural drift of family life in contemporary America is toward slowly diminishing connection, meaning,

Only an Intentional Family has a fighting chance to maintain and increase its sense of connection, meaning, and community over the years.

and community. You don't have to be a "dysfunctional" couple to feel more distant as the years go by, or a particularly inept parent to feel that you spend more time disciplining your children than enjoying them. You are not unusual if you feel you have too little time for meaningful involvement with your community. Lacking cultural support and tools for shaping the kinds of families we want, most of us end up hoping the river currents carry us to somewhere we want to go. In the "anything goes" world of the Pluralistic Family, where specifically do we want to go, and how in the world do we get there?

Only an Intentional Family has a fighting chance to maintain and increase its sense of connection, meaning, and community over the years. An Intentional Family is one whose members create a working plan for maintaining and building family ties, and then implement the plan as best they can. An Intentional Family rows and steers its boat rather than being moved only by the winds and the current.

At heart, the Intentional Family is a ritualizing family. It creates patterns of connecting through everyday family rituals, seasonal celebrations, special occasions, and community involvement. An Intentional Family does not let mealtimes deteriorate into television watching. It does not let adolescents "do their own thing" at the expense of all family outings. It is willing to look at how it handles Christmas or bar mitzvahs in order to make them work better for everyone. It has the discipline to stick with good rituals, and the flexibility to change them when they are not working anymore.

The Entropic Family

The opposite of the Intentional Family is the Entropic Family. Entropy is the term for the tendency of a physical system to lose energy and coherence over time, such as a gas that expands and dissipates until there is little trace left. Similarly, the Entropic Family, through lack of conscious attention to its inner life and community ties, gradually loses a sense of cohesion over the years. Its maintenance rituals such as meals and birthdays lose their spark, and then degenerate. Individual family members may have active lives in the world, but the energy of the family itself slowly sweeps away.

Contemporary society creates Entropic Families by two means. First is our lack of support for couples to make marriage work and for parents to make childrearing work. We generate the highest expectations of family life of any generation in human history, but provide the least guidance as to how to achieve success in our contemporary family forms. We struggle as a society over the most basic kinds of family support, such as unpaid leave for caring for babies and sick family members. And we have barely begun to face our joint responsibility to help families learn the skills for parenting, partnership, and intimacy that most of us expect of family life. No wonder that the odds of a happy lifetime marriage are probably no more than one in four—half of new couples divorce and another quarter are probably not very happy.

The second way that we collectively create Entropic Families is by putting up barriers to sustaining family rituals. Cars, televisions, busy work schedules, consumerism, and a host of other forces propel family members along fast-moving, diverging tracks. Family meals become casualties of soccer practice, violin lessons, work demands, and the lure of a favorite television rerun. Tired parents lack energy to focus the family on reconnecting at the end of the workday. The Christmas holidays appear before family plans are in place, and vacations are patched together at the last minute.

In Entropic Families, there is no less love, no less desire for meaning and connection than in Intentional Families. But their members gradually drift apart because they lack the infusions of bonding, intimacy, and community that only well-maintained family rituals can give. In the end, most families that are not intentional will follow the currents of entropy toward less closeness than they had hoped for when they started their family journey; the forces pulling on families are just too strong in the modern world. Ultimately, we must decide either to steer or go where the river takes us. The key to successful steering is to be intentional about our family rituals.

FAMILY RITUALS

When you recall your favorite memories of childhood, probably they center around family rituals such as bedtime, an annual vacation, Thanksgiving, Christmas, or the weekly Sabbath meal. Your worst memories might also be connected with these family rituals. Interestingly, many family researchers and family therapists have learned only recently how significant a component family rituals are to the glue that holds families together.[3] Previously, most researchers and therapists emphasized *talk:* how couples communicate, how parents verbally praise and discipline children. But as important as talking is, what professionals weren't considering was how we *enact* our family relationships.

Family rituals are repeated and coordinated activities that have significance for the family.[4] To be a ritual, the activity has to have *meaning* or *significance;* otherwise, it is a routine but not a ritual. For example, most families' bathroom activities are routines rather than rituals because they do not have much symbolic importance, although such an activity can become a ritual. For

example, one of my clients and his new wife took a shower together every morning, which became a ritual for them. To be a ritual, then, the activity must also be *repeated;* an occasional, unplanned trip to a cabin would not make for a family ritual, whereas an annual trip that family members look forward to would. Finally, a ritual activity must be *coordinated;* a meal that each person fixes and eats alone would not qualify as a family ritual, whereas a meal that everyone gathers deliberately together to eat would, if done regularly and with meaning.

A goal of this book is to show you how to transform some family routines into family rituals. Family rituals give us four important things:

Predictability. The sense of regularity and order that families require, especially those with children. Knowing that the father will talk to his child and read a story every night makes bedtime something to look forward to and savor. If bedtime talks and stories have to be negotiated every night—if there is no predictability—then the ritual loses its power.

Connection. The bedtime ritual may be the primary one-to-one time shared between a father and his child. For couples, bedtime rituals may also be an important opportunity to connect emotionally and perhaps sexually after a busy, distracted day. Couples who value rituals of connection generally make sure they coordinate their evening plans so as to go to bed together. Those who generally go to bed at different times are apt to lose connection over time, unless they have strong alternative rituals of connection.

Identity. A sense of who belongs to the family and what is special about the family. You may know who your core family members are by who is invited to the Thanksgiving meal; including nonrelatives in core family rituals makes them "family," too. Families who take interesting vacations together acquire the self-image of a fun-loving family. They will say "We are campers" or "We are hikers." For some couples, shopping for antiques becomes a ritual outing that helps form a couple identity as antique lovers.

A way to enact values. Values demonstrate what we believe and hold dear. Religious rituals are a good example, as is a family volunteering together for community work; or ensuring that the children join in regular family visits to a grandparent in a nursing home, thereby teaching that it is important to honor and support this elderly family member.[5]

Types of Family Rituals

Family rituals by definition involve more than one family member, but not all family rituals necessarily involve the whole family. Some rituals involve just two members;

say, a married couple going out to dinner or a parent reading to a child. Some involve subgroups, as when my father took my sister and me to Philadelphia Phillies baseball games. Some involve the larger extended family, such as family reunions and holiday rituals. Others include close friends of the family, and still others, a larger community such as a church or synagogue or a volunteer group to support the local children's museum. It is important to think of the different combinations of participants in family rituals. Successful Intentional Families learn to ritualize everything from pairs to communities.[6]

I like to classify family rituals by the *function* they play for families; that is, by the needs they serve. Thus, there are rituals for connection or bonding, rituals for showing love to individual family members, and rituals that bind the family to the larger community.

Connection rituals offer everyday opportunities for family bonding, such as family meals, morning and bedtime routines, and the comings and goings of family members to and from work and school. They also involve family outings, from small trips to the ice cream store to major family vacations. The goal is a sense of family bonding.

Love rituals focus on developing one-to-one intimacy and making individual family members feel special. They can be subdivided into couple rituals and special-person rituals. Examples of couple love rituals are anniversaries, Valentine's Day, "dating," and sexual relations. Special-person rituals generally center around birthdays, Mother's Day, and Father's Day.

Community rituals have a more public dimension than connection and love rituals. They include major family events such as weddings and funerals that link families to their communities, as well as religious activities in churches, synagogues, or mosques. In addition, community rituals include conscious efforts to connect with a wider social network than the family, to both give and gain support. Too much writing about family life has ignored the public face of families and concentrated narrowly on the internal hearth and home. The healthiest families give to their communities and receive support back in good measure.

Thanksgiving and Christmas have evolved into a special category of family ritual, involving all three functions of rituals: connection, love, and community. They are the grand rituals of the calendar year for the majority of American families, Christian and non-Christian alike. And for many people, holiday rituals hold both the fondest and most depressing memories of childhood.

Historians have learned recently that community rituals, not "home" rituals, formed the linchpin of family life in the era of the Institutional Family. Before the mid-nineteenth century in Europe and America, family rituals hardly existed as we know of them today. Ritual activities occurred mostly in community settings such as churches and public commons, not inside the family itself. Families had daily routines, of course, but apparently they did not regard them as significant sources of family connection. They ate meals, but they did not think of family dinners as a special time separate from other times. Indeed, families prior to the late nineteenth century did not dwell much on their interior life. Christmas was celebrated with community festivals, not with family rituals of celebration and gift-giving. Families did not have birthday parties, and couples did not celebrate anniversaries. It was only with the passing of the Institutional Family and the gradual emergence of the Psychological Family after the Industrial Revolution that families began to think of themselves as separate from their communities and in need of special family rituals. As their urban environment grew more alien and as fathers went into the workforce away from home, families began to cultivate their inner world through special rituals. When communities broke up, families had to become intentional about their own rituals.[7]

There is no universal yardstick for measuring family rituals for all of our diverse contemporary families. Remarried families have different needs from first-married families, as do single-parent families from two-parent families. Different ethnic traditions require different degrees of flexibility or structure in family rituals. Some families are tied closely to their ethnic origins and to their extended families, and some have more independent lifestyles. Some families have young children, some have adolescents, and some have no children. Some families are experiencing peaceful periods in their life, and thus feel free to be creative with their rituals, while others are undergoing tremendous stress and need to just hang on to what they have. There is no ritual formula that applies to all this diversity. Indeed, the idea of the Intentional Family is encourage families to use their own values, histories, religions, and cultures to consciously plan their life together and in community.

TAMING TIME AND TECHNOLOGY

Becoming a ritualizing Intentional Family means learning to manage the two principal drains on the energy of most American families: time demands outside the home and electronic technology inside the home.

Now that most mothers are employed, and fathers are working as much or more than ever, there is a net decrease in the amount of time parents have to spend with their children and with each other. Add to that the fact that jobs for teenagers are plentiful, and many of them are also employed during family dinner hours and on weekends. And middle-class families in particular now spend a huge amount of time driving their children to various lessons and practices, on top of attending their games and events. If time is the raw material of family rituals, we are suffering from its shortage. Many American families feel starved for time.[8]

How can we become more intentional about family life in the face of this time shortage? Let's say you are already an overwhelmed single parent, or a married person who barely has time to talk to your spouse. Will thinking about enhancing your family rituals just serve to make you feel even more guilty than you already do? Two general strategies will be exemplified throughout this book. First is to make better use of the time you already spend on family activities. You have to feed your children, so start with improving the quality of those feeding rituals, without lengthening the time. You have to put your kids to bed; work on making it more pleasurable. You probably have birthday parties, holiday celebrations, and countless other family activities. You can enhance their quality while not adding to their number or extending their time requirements.

Disconnecting the Wires

The second general strategy is to experiment with carving out time from another activity that occupies more than its fair share of your attention. I recommend taming technology. We live in an era of the wired American family. The average American family has 2.5 television sets, and the average American spends over four hours per day watching television. That means television watching consumes half of our nonsleep, nonwork time. You can't tell me there is no surplus family ritual time to be carved out there! Add in CD players, telephones, and, increasingly, computers and the Internet. When we are in our cars, there is the radio and tape player. When we are out for walks, there are head phones. When we are running errands, more of us talk on cellular phones. We are always interruptible and distractible, two conditions that work against family rituals and intentional family life.[9]

Believe me, I am not a Luddite, rejecting all modern technology. When my daughter was in Europe, the telephone and e-mail kept us in contact. And television watching can be a relaxing way for family members to unwind. But, for many of us, electronic technology is the pet that has taken over the house. That's the bad news. The good news is that taming it even a little, such as by turning off the television during meals, can free up time for family rituals. We trained our dog to stay out of our bedrooms, and we banned television from there as well. No one, including the dog, has suffered for it.

The idea behind the Intentional Family is that families can decide for themselves, based on their own traditions, values, and circumstances, how best to ritualize their lives. Most families have some rituals they enjoy, some they don't enjoy but feel stuck with, and some they could benefit from creating or refurbishing. As you read this book, I encourage you to develop an agenda of current rituals you might want to remodel and new ones you might want to try. But hold off on trying anything new on your family until you read the last chapter, where I discuss specific strategies for creating and modifying family rituals. Moving too quickly or unilaterally in the domain of family rituals is sure to result in your family members saying "No way!" to your creative ideas. Changing family rituals requires sensitivity, tact, timing, and diplomatic skills—the very talents necessary to survive as an Intentional Family in an era of both unprecedented confusion and opportunity for families.

NOTES

1. See Steven Mintz and Susan Kellogg, *Domestic Revolutions: A Social History of American Family Life* (New York: The Free Press), 1988, pp. 107–131.
2. For background on changes in family norms from the Psychological Family to the Pluralistic Family in the twentieth century, see William J. Doherty, "Private Lives, Public Values," *Psychology Today*, 25 (May–June, 1990), pp. 32–37, 82; and Judith Stacey, *Brave New Families: Stories of Domestic Upheaval in Late Twentieth-Century America* (New York: Basic Books), 1990.
3. For academic and clinical background on family rituals, see James H. S. Bossard and Eleanor S. Boll, *Ritual in Family Living* (Philadelphia: University of Pennsylvania Press), 1950; Evan Imber-Black, Janine Roberts, and Richard Whiting (eds.), *Rituals in Families and Family Therapy* (New York: W.W. Norton), 1988; Evan Imber-Black and Janine Roberts, *Rituals for Our Times* (New York: Harper-Collins), 1992; Mara Selvini Palazzoli, Luigi Boscolo, Gianfranco Cecchin, Giuliana Prata, "Family Rituals: A Powerful Tool in Family Therapy," *Family Process* 16 (1977): pp. 445–454; Steven J. Wolin and Linda A. Bennett, "Family Rituals," *Family Process* 23 (1984): pp. 401–420.
4. This definition is my version of Wolin and Bennett's (1984) definition of a family ritual: "a symbolic form of communication that, owing to the satisfaction that family members experience through its repetition, is acted out in a systematic fashion over time." "Family Rituals," *Family Process*, 23 (1984), p. 401.
5. See Wolin and Bennett, "Family Rituals," *Family Process* 23 (1984), pp. 401–420; Evan Imber-Black, "Ritual Themes in Families and Family Therapy," in Imber-Black, Roberts, and Whiting, pp. 47–83.
6. The popular author Robert Fulghum has written about family and community rituals. However, he also refers to certain individual activities, such as personal morning routines, as rituals. I am using the term ritual in the more traditional social science sense to refer only to social, not private activities. See Robert Fulghum, *From Beginning to End: The Rituals of Our Lives* (New York: Viking), 1995.
7. See John R. Gillis, "Ritualization of Middle-Class Family Life in Nineteenth-Century Britain," *International Journal of Politics, Culture, and Society* 3 (1989): pp. 213–235; John Gillis, "Making Time for Family: The Invention of Family Time(s) and the Reinvention of Family History," *Journal of Family History* 21 (1996): pp. 4–21; Penne L. Restad, *Christmas in America: A History* (New York: Oxford University Press), 1995.
8. For data on parents' spending less time with children, see Joseph Pleck, "Paternal Involvement: Levels, Sources, and Consequences," in Michael E. Lamb (ed.), *The Role of the Father in Child Development.* Third edition. (Hillsdale, New Jersey: Erlbaum), 1996; for documentation of the amount of time spent working, see Juliet B. Schor, *The Overworked American* (New York: Basic Books), 1991.
9. George Gallup Jr., and Frank Newport, "Gallup Survey Finds More Viewers Are Getting Pickier," *Minneapolis-St. Paul Star Tribune,* October 7, 1990, pp. 1F, 7F.

African American Families

A Legacy of Vulnerability and Resilience

African Americans, despite a legacy of stigmatizing psychological folklore and an antagonistic environment manifested in centuries of racial discrimination, display an undeniable development of adaptive coping strategies and resilience. Understanding the realities in the lives of contemporary African American families requires an examination of the history of African Americans in the United States.

Beverly Greene

African Americans are one of the oldest and largest groups of persons of color in the United States. The first census in 1790 counted 760,000 African Americans. By 1990, over 30,000,000 were counted. African Americans are descendants of people who belonged to the tribes of the West African coast and were the primary objects of the U.S. slave trade. Many African Americans have Native American and European ancestry as well.

They are perhaps the only ethnic group in the United States whose immigration was wholly involuntary. Entry into the United States was not, as it was for members of white ethnic groups and other groups of persons of color, the result of an effort to better their circumstances or find a more advantageous political climate than their homeland could offer. Instead of bettering their circumstances, their forced departure from the West African coast resulted in pervasive losses. Aside from the loss of life for many, there was a loss of community, the loss of original languages, and the loss of status as human beings for those who survived the Atlantic Passage.

As slaves, literally deprived of all human rights, they were to provide free labor and were bought and sold as any other commodity. Their children were salable commodities as well. In this system, family attachments were routinely ignored as slaves were transported, sold, and regarded as livestock with no regard for their family or important emotional ties. In this context, slave families came to place less emphasis on the role of biological parents because most children were separated from and not raised by them. Rather, children were informally "adopted" and raised by other people in their immediate community in extended rather than nuclear family arrangements. These extended family arrangements are still a prominent feature of contemporary African American families and may be considered a major survival tool.

The struggles of African Americans are often viewed as if they ended with emancipation. This belief ignores over a century more of legal racial discrimination that led to the civil rights struggles which reached a peak in the 1950s and 1960s. Even in the wake of legislation designed to make racial discrimination illegal, discrimination in more subtle, institutionalized forms still operates to this day in ways that continue to challenge the optimal physical, psychological, and economic well-being of African Americans.

Characteristics of African American Families

Characteristics of contemporary African American families represent an interaction of African cultural derivatives, the need to adapt to a racially antagonistic environment, and the influence of American cultural imperatives. They include extended networks of kinship between family members and persons who are not blood-related in complex networks of obligation and support. African Americans as a group are geographically and socioeconomically diverse. However, they share both cultural origins and the need to manage the anxieties and prejudices of a dominant group that is culturally different and that discriminates against African Americans both

... all African Americans must make psychological sense out of their disparaged condition, deflect hostility from the dominant group, and negotiate racial barriers under a wide range of circumstances.

actively and passively on the basis of race. In some form, all African Americans must make psychological sense out of their disparaged condition, deflect hostility from the dominant group, and negotiate racial barriers under a wide range of circumstances. If the group is to survive, the members must teach their children to do so as well.

In this regard, African American parents have a special task and a unique stressor that are not shared by their white counterparts. These consist of the special things they must do to prepare their children to function in an adaptive fashion without internalizing the dominant culture's negative messages about African American people. In *Children of Color*, Allen and Majidi-Ahi note that teaching African American children how to cope with racism represents a socialization issue that exemplifies all that is distinct about the African American experience in America. A major component of this experience entails the task of communicating to African American children the racial realities and dangers of the world, how to correctly identify and cope with the resulting barrier, and how to seek support for the feelings evoked when confronting these barriers.

Succeeding Against Odds

Despite many historical and contemporary obstacles, African Americans have succeeded against many overwhelming odds in every generation. African American families are an important source of socialization and support for their members and can be an important translator of the dominant culture for African American children. At its best, this system teaches African American children to imitate and function in the dominant culture

without believing that its demeaning images of African Americans are true.

Another role of the family is to pass along different kinds of successful coping strategies against racism. One strategy, the heightened sensitivity to the potential for exploitation by white persons, has been referred to by Grier and Cobbs in *Black Rage* as cultural paranoia. While this heightened sensitivity often has been pathologized by the dominant culture, it is a realistic and adaptive way of approaching situations that have frequently been antagonistic. Hopson and Hopson in *Different and Wonderful* suggest that another important coping strategy and a major source of psychological resilience is reflected in the sharing of African cultural derivatives with children while encouraging them to take pride in their ancestry. In *Long Memory*, Mary Berry and John Blassinngame note that each generation of African Americans prepares the next for survival in a society that

devalues them by passing along "searing vignettes" about what has preceded them. They view this process as a long collective memory that is in and of itself an instrument of survival.

African American families must do all of these things in addition to providing the normal range of basic necessities that all families must provide for their children. In the context of a racist society, however, African American families' ability to do this may be compromised by the institutional barriers that providers in the family invariably confront. In these scenarios there may be a drain on the family's emo-

tional and material resources, making the extended family structure an important resource in this regard. Sharing the burden of child care and child rearing helps to ease this burden in many families and can be seen as an example of resilience.

Multiple Mothering

In *Black Families*, Nancy Boyd-Franklin gives one example of this in what she describes as "multiple mothering." "Multiple mothers" refers to grandmothers, aunts, cousins, close friends, or people considered "kin" to a child's mother. They need not be biologically related. These multiple mothers provide emotional safety valves, sounding boards, and alternative role models to children while often providing their real mothers with important tangible support in the form of child care. These arrangements also emphasize the important role for elder members of the family and the importance of their connection to members of the next generation. It is important to remember this extended family structure when viewing "single-parent families." The fact that African American families may deviate in structure from the White Anglo Saxon Protestant norm does

The single-parent family as a large and diverse group among African Americans is not synonymous with teenaged or underaged mothers.

not warrant pathologizing them or presuming that this deviation accounts for family problems.

In what appear to be many single-parent families, extensive networks of other family members, family friends, neighbors, and others are routinely involved in the caretaking of children. Hence, the unmarried status of the mother does not automatically tell us what the rest of the family structure is like. The single-parent family as a large and diverse group among African Americans is not synonymous with teenaged or underaged mothers. Becoming a parent before one is biologically and emotionally mature, or when it interferes with important developmental tasks of the parent, is certainly not what is recommended. Rather, I suggest that African American family structures be viewed as perhaps having a wider range of flexibility in what is available to its members, reflected in a wider range of persons, in addition to biological parents, involved in parenting roles.

Gender Role Flexibility

Robert Hill, in *The Strengths of Black Families,* identifies major characteristics of African American families: strong kinship bonds, a strong achievement motivation, a strong religious and spiritual orientation, and a strong work orientation. Hill views these characteristics as strengths that have helped African Americans survive and function under difficult circumstances. He further cites gender-role flexibility as an important and adaptive characteristic of African American families. This flexibility in gender role is explained in part as a derivative of the value of interdependence among group members, typical of Western African precolonial cultures, that is unlike the value of rugged individualism of the West. It is also a function of the need to adapt to racism in the United States in many different ways.

One of the features that distinguished African American women from their white counterparts was their role as workers. Aside from being brought into the country as slaves whose primary function was to work, the status of African American women as slaves superseded their status as women. Hence they were not given the courtesies of femininity that were routinely accorded white women. Conventions of femininity considered many forms of labor that were routine for white males inappropriate for white females. Slavery deprived African American women of this protection, and as such their roles as workers did not differ from those of African American males. Hence at the very outset, rigid gender-role stratification among African Americans was not permitted. Later, because African American men faced significant racial barriers in the workplace and could not fit the idealized image of the Western male provider, women were forced to work to help support the home. Thus, the dominant cultural norm of women remaining in the home while men worked outside the home was never a practical reality for African American families.

This does not mean that there is no sexism within African American families. Tensions are often produced when African American men internalize the dominant culture's value of male domination and female subordination. Working women become the targets of African American male frustration rather than institutional racism. Despite such occurrences, flexibility in gender roles represents another example of an adaptive strategy that has contributed to the survival of African American families.

Summary

African American families have functioned under a legacy of challenges to their survival, beginning with slavery when families were not allowed to exist and when they were continually disrupted by abrupt and permanent separations. Surviving these disruptions, African American families have continued to demonstrate their flexibility and resilience under many adverse circumstances. It is not surprising that many African American families would be in crisis, given the range of routine assaults they face. What is more surprising is that many of these families display a remarkable legacy of adaptive strengths. James Comer, in *Maggie's American Dream,* reminds us that what we learn from survivors will tell us more about the circumvention of problems than will an exclusive focus on victims. African Americans are, if anything, survivors of historical and contemporary circumstances that may increase their vulnerability. However, as survivors they have much to teach us about resilience.

Beverly Greene is a professor of psychology at St. Johns' University and a clinical psychologist in private practice in New York City. A Fellow of the American Psychological Association and the recipient of national awards for her distinguished professional contributions, she is a coeditor of *Women of Color: Integrating Ethnic and Gender Identities in Psychotherapy.*

Unit 2

Unit Selections

Key Points to Consider

❖ What do you think is the role of flirtation in the formation of relationships? What is the biological function of flirtation?

❖ What do you look for in a mate? Would you be willing to settle for less? Why or why not?

❖ Have you thought about your own use of contraceptives? How would you advise a friend if he or she came to you and asked about the most appropriate contraceptive to use?

❖ Does it surprise you to learn that sex during pregnancy may be highly enjoyable?

❖ Do you see children as a part of your life? Why or why not? How do children enrich a relationship? What are the drawbacks of having children? What are the responsibilities associated with parenthood? If you do have children, how do you think it will affect you and your relationship with your partner? What are your attitudes and beliefs about parenthood?

 **Links** www.dushkin.com/online/

10. **Ask NOAH About Pregnancy: Fertility & Infertility**
    http://www.noah.cuny.edu/pregnancy/fertility.html
11. **Bonobos Sex and Society**
    http://songweaver.com/info/bonobos.html
12. **Go Ask Alice!**
    http://www.goaskalice.columbia.edu/index.html
13. **The Kinsey Institute for Research in Sex, Gender, and Reproduction**
    http://www.indiana.edu/~kinsey/
14. **Mysteries of Odor in Human Sexuality**
    http://www.pheromones.com
15. **Planned Parenthood**
    http://www.plannedparenthood.org
16. **The Society for the Scientific Study of Sexuality**
    http://www.ssc.wisc.edu/ssss/
17. **Sympatico: HealthyWay: Health Links**
    http://www.ab.sympatico.ca/Contents/Health/GENERAL/sitemap.html

These sites are annotated on pages 4 and 5.

By and large, humans are social animals, and as such, we seek out meaningful connections with other humans. John Bowlby, Mary Ainsworth, and others have proposed that this drive toward connection is biologically based and is at the core of what it means to be human. However it plays out in childhood and adulthood, the need for connection, to love and be loved, is a powerful force moving us to establish and maintain close relationships. At the same time, our biology influences the way in which we relate to each other and the way in which we create and maintain relationships.

As we explore various possibilities, we engage in the complex business of relationship building. In this business, many processes occur simultaneously: Messages are sent and received; differences are negotiated; assumptions and expectations are or are not met. The ultimate goals are closeness and continuity.

How we feel about others and what we see as essential to these relationships play an important role in our establishing and maintaining relationships. In this unit, we look at factors that underlie the establishment of relationships as well as the beginning stages of relationships.

The first subsection explores gender differences and their influences in relationships and on how we relate to the world. The first article, "Boys Will Be Boys," explores the results of a growing interest in the essential nature of boys. Among the topics discussed are parental responsibilities and techniques for recognizing unique characteristics of boys and ways of socializing them toward healthy relationships, in childhood and beyond. "Sex Differences in the Brain" addresses the biological differences between male and female brains and their impact on relationship building and maintenance.

The second subsection takes a broad look at factors that influence the building of meaningful relationships and at the beginning stages of adult relationships. The first essay, "Flirting Fascination," describes biological explanations for flirtatious behavior. In "Back Off!" Geraldine Piorkowski suggests that, just as time together is important for a relationship, so too is time for individuals to be alone.

In the third subsection, important aspects of adult relationships are explored: sexuality and pregnancy.

Particular attention is given to the idea of responsibility to oneself and others in acting out our sexuality. "Protecting against Unintended Pregnancy" is a fact-filled guide to the selection of a contraceptive. The next article, "The Brave New World of Parenting," explores the result of successful efforts to overcome infertility and the problems that parents may face once they have had a child through extraordinary means. The final article in this subsection, "Pregnant Pleasures" addresses the nature of sexual relations during pregnancy, and some of the information may surprise the reader.

In the final subsection, the creation of a new generation and the costs and joys of doing so are explored. The first three articles, "Fetal Psychology," "Maternal Emotions May Influence Fetal Behaviors," and "Fertile Minds," look at the nature of fetal and infant development. Readers of "The Cost of Children" may find themselves amazed at the high cost of rearing a child. Cross-cultural variations in maternal attitudes and beliefs are presented in "Our Babies, Ourselves."

Exploring and Establishing Relationships

a

Boys will be Boys

Developmental research has been focused on girls; now it's their brothers' turn. Boys need help, too, but first they need to be understood.
BY BARBARA KANTROWITZ AND CLAUDIA KALB

IT WAS A CLASSIC MARS-VENUS ENCOUN-ter. Only in this case, the woman was from Harvard and the man—well, boy—was a 4-year-old at a suburban Boston nursery school. Graduate student Judy Chu was in his classroom last fall to gather observations for her doctoral dissertation on human development. His greeting was startling: he held up his finger as if it were a gun and pretended to shoot her. "I felt bad," Chu recalls. "I felt as if he didn't like me." Months later and much more boy-savvy, Chu has a different interpretation: the gunplay wasn't hostile—it was just a way for him to say hello. "They don't mean it to have harsh consequences. It's a way for them to connect."

Researchers like Chu are discovering new meaning in lots of things boys have done for ages. In fact, they're dissecting just about every aspect of the developing male psyche and creating a hot new field of inquiry: the study of boys. They're also producing a slew of books with titles like "Real Boys: Rescuing Our Sons From the Myths of Boyhood" and "Raising Cain: Protecting the Emotional Life of Boys" that will hit the stores in the next few months.

What some researchers are finding is that boys and girls really are from two different planets. But since the two sexes have to live together here on Earth, they should be raised with special consideration for their distinct needs. Boys and girls have different "crisis points," experts say, stages in their emotional and social development where things can go very wrong. Until recently, girls got all the attention. But boys need help, too. They're much more likely than girls to have discipline problems at school and to be diagnosed with attention deficit disorder (ADD). Boys far outnumber girls in special-education classes. They're also more likely to commit violent crimes and end up in jail. Consider the headlines: Jonesboro, Ark.; Paducah, Ky.; Pearl, Miss. In all these school shootings, the perpetrators were young adolescent boys.

Even normal boy behavior has come to be considered pathological in the wake of the feminist movement. An abundance of physical energy and the urge to conquer—these are normal male characteristics, and in an earlier age they were good things, even essential to survival. "If Huck Finn or Tom Sawyer were alive today," says Michael Gurian, author of "The Wonder of Boys," "we'd say they had ADD or a conduct disorder." He says one of the new insights we're gaining about boys is a very old one: boys will be boys. "They are who they are," says Gurian, "and we need to love them for who they are. Let's not try to rewire them."

Indirectly, boys are benefiting from all the research done on girls, especially the landmark work by Harvard University's Carol Gilligan. Her 1982 book, "In a Different Voice: Psychological Theory and Women's Development," inspired Take Our Daughters to Work Day, along with best-selling spinoffs like Mary Pipher's "Reviving Ophelia." The traditional, unisex way of looking at child development was profoundly flawed, Gilligan says: "It was like having a one-dimensional perspective on a two-dimensional scene." At Harvard, where she chairs the gender-studies department, Gilligan is now supervising work on males, including Chu's project. Other researchers are studying mental illness and violence in boys.

While girls' horizons have been expanding, boys' have narrowed, confined to rigid ideas of acceptable male behavior no matter how hard their parents tried to avoid stereotypes. The macho ideal still rules. "We gave boys dolls and they used them as guns," says Gurian. "For 15 years, all we heard was that [gender differences] were all about socialization. Parents who raised their kids through that period said in the end, 'That's not true. Boys and girls can be awfully different.' I think we're awakening to the biological realities and the sociological realities."

But what exactly is the essential nature of boys? Even as infants, boys and girls behave differently. A recent study at Children's Hospital in Boston found that boy babies are more emotionally expressive; girls are more reflective. (That means boy babies tend to cry when they're unhappy; girl babies suck their thumbs.) This could indicate that girls

The Wonder (and Worry) Years

There may be no such thing as *child* development anymore. Instead, researchers are now studying each gender's development separately and discovering that boys and girls face very different sorts of challenges. Here is a rough guide to the major phases in their development.

Boys

0–3 years At birth, boys have brains that are 5% larger than girls' (size doesn't affect intelligence) and proportionately larger bodies—disparities that increase with age.

4–6 years The start of school is a tough time as boys must curb aggressive impulses. They lag behind girls in reading skills, and hyperactivity may be a problem.

Age 1	2	3	4	5	6	7

Girls

0–3 years Girls are born with a higher proportion of nerve cells to process information. More brain regions are involved in language production and recognition.

4–6 years Girls are well suited to school. They are calm, get along with others, pick up on social cues, and reading and writing come easily to them.

are innately more able to control their emotions. Boys have higher levels of testosterone and lower levels of the neurotransmitter serotonin, which inhibits aggression and impulsivity. That may help explain why more males than females carry through with suicide, become alcoholics and are diagnosed with ADD.

The developmental research on the impact of these physiological differences is still in the embryonic stage, but psychologists are drawing some interesting comparisons between girls and boys (chart). For girls, the first crisis point often comes in early adolescence. Until then, Gilligan and others found, girls have an enormous capacity for establishing relationships and interpreting emotions. But in their early teens, girls clamp down, squash their emotions, blunt their insight. Their self-esteem plummets. The first crisis point for boys comes much earlier, researchers now say. "There's an outbreak of symptoms at age 5, 6, 7, just like you see in girls at 11, 12, 13," says Gilligan. Problems at this age include bed-wetting and separation anxiety. "They don't have the language or experience" to articulate it fully, she says, "but the feelings are no less intense." That's why Gilligan's student Chu is studying preschoolers. For girls at this age, Chu says, hugging a parent goodbye "is almost a nonissue." But little boys, who display a great deal of tenderness, soon begin to bury it with "big boy" behavior to avoid being called sissies. "When their parents drop them off, they want to be close and want to be held, but not in front of other people," says Chu. "Even as early as 4, they're already aware of those masculine stereotypes and are negotiating their way around them."

It's a phenomenon that parents, especially mothers, know well. One morning last month, Lori Dube, a 37-year-old mother of three from Evanston, Ill., visited her oldest son, Abe, almost 5, at his nursery school, where he was having lunch with his friends. She kissed him, prompting another boy to comment scornfully: "Do you know what your mom just did? She kissed you!" Dube acknowledges, with some sadness, that she'll have to be

more sensitive to Abe's new reactions to future public displays of affection. "Even if he loves it, he's getting these messages that it's not good."

There's a struggle—a desire and need for warmth on the one hand and a pull toward independence on the other. Boys like Abe are going through what psychologists long ago declared an integral part of growing up: individualization and disconnection from parents, especially mothers. But now some researchers think that process is too abrupt. When boys repress normal feelings like love because of social pressure, says William Pollack, head of the Center for Men at Boston's McLean Hospital and author of the forthcoming "Real Boys," "they've lost contact with the genuine nature of who they are and what they feel. Boys are in a silent crisis. The only time we notice it is when they pull the trigger."

No one is saying that acting like Rambo in nursery school leads directly to tragedies like Jonesboro. But researchers do think that boys who are forced to shut down positive emotions are left with only one socially acceptable outlet: anger. The cultural ideals boys are exposed to in movies and on TV still emphasize traditional masculine roles—warrior, rogue, adventurer—with heavy doses of violence. For every Mr. Mom, there are a dozen Terminators. "The feminist movement has done a great job of convincing people that a woman can be nurturing and a mother and a tough trial lawyer at the same time," says Dan Kindlon, an assistant professor of psychiatry at Harvard Medical School. "But we haven't done that as much with men. We're afraid that if they're too soft, that's all they can be."

And the demands placed on boys in the early years of elementary school can increase their overall stress levels. Scientists have known for years that boys and girls develop physically and intellectually at very different rates (time-line). Boys' fine motor skills—the ability to hold a pencil, for example—are usually considerably behind girls. They often learn to read later. At the same time, they're much more active—not the best combination for academic advance-

ment. "Boys feel like school is a game rigged against them," says Michael Thompson, co-author with Kindlon of "Raising Cain." "The things at which they excel—gross motor skills, visual and spatial skills, their exuberance—do not find as good a reception in school" as the things girls excel at. Boys (and girls) are also in academic programs at much younger ages than they used to be, increasing the chances that males will be forced to sit still before they are ready. The result, for many boys, is frustration, says Thompson: "By fourth grade, they're saying the teachers like girls better."

A second crisis point for boys occurs around the same time their sisters are stumbling, in early adolescence. By then, say Thompson and Kindlon, boys go one step further in their drive to be "real guys." They partake in a "culture of cruelty," enforcing male stereotypes on one another. "Anything tender, anything compassionate or too artistic is labeled gay," says Thompson. "The homophobia of boys in the 11, 12, 13 range is a stronger force than gravity."

Boys who refuse to fit the mold suffer. Glo Wellman of the California Parenting Institute in Santa Rosa has three sons, 22, 19 and 12. One of her boys, she says, is a "non-typical boy: he's very sensitive and caring and creative and artistic." Not surprisingly, he had the most difficulty growing up, she says. "We've got a long way to go to help boys . . . to have a sense that they can be anything they want to be."

In later adolescence, the once affectionate toddler has been replaced by a sulky stranger who often acts as though torture would be preferable to a brief exchange of words with Mom or Dad. Parents have to try even harder to keep in touch. Boys want and need the attention, but often just don't know how to ask for it. In a recent national poll, teenagers named their parents as their No. 1 heroes. Researchers say a strong parental bond is the most important protection against everything from smoking to suicide.

For San Francisco Chronicle columnist Adnir Lara, that message sank in when she was traveling to New York a few years ago with her son, then 15. She sat next to a woman who told her that until recently she

7-10 years While good at gross motor skills, boys trail girls in finer control. Many of the best students but also nearly all of the poorest ones are boys.

11-13 years A mixed bag. Dropout rates begin to climb, but good students start pulling ahead of girls in math skills and catching up some in verbal ones.

14-16 years Entering adolescence, boys hit another rough patch. Indulging in drugs, alcohol and aggressive behavior are common forms of rebellion.

	8	9	10		11	12	13		14	15	16

7-10 years Very good years for girls. On average, they outperform boys at school, excelling in verbal skills while holding their own in math.

11-13 years The start of puberty and girls' most vulnerable time. Many experience depression; as many as 15% may try to kill themselves.

14-16 years Eating disorders are a major concern. Although anorexia can manifest itself as early as 8, it typically afflicts girls starting at 11 or 12; bulimia at 15.

SOURCES: DR. MICHAEL THOMPSON, BARNEY BRAWER. RESEARCH BY BILL YOURVOULIAS —NEWSWEEK

Trouble Spots: Where Boys Run Into Problems

Not all boys are the same, of course, but most rebel in predictable patterns and with predictable weapons: underachievement, aggression and drug and alcohol use. While taking chances is an important aspect of the growth process, it can lead to real trouble.

When Johnny Can't Read

Girls have reading disorders nearly as often as boys, but are able to overcome them. Disability rates, as identified by:

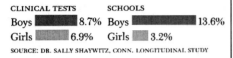

CLINICAL TESTS   SCHOOLS
Boys 8.7%   Boys 13.6%
Girls 6.9%   Girls 3.2%

SOURCE: DR. SALLY SHAYWITZ, CONN. LONGITUDINAL STUDY

Suicidal Impulses

While girls are much more likely to try to kill themselves, boys are likelier to die from their attempts.

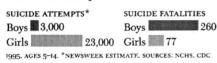

SUICIDE ATTEMPTS*   SUICIDE FATALITIES
Boys 3,000   Boys 260
Girls 23,000   Girls 77

1995, AGES 5–14. *NEWSWEEK ESTIMATE. SOURCES: NCHS, CDC

Binge Drinking

Boys binge more on alcohol. Those who had five or more drinks in a row in the last two weeks:

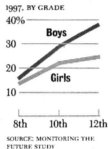

1997, BY GRADE
40%
30
Boys
20
Girls
10
8th   10th   12th

SOURCE: MONITORING THE FUTURE STUDY

Aggression That Turns to Violence

Boys get arrested three times as often as girls, but for some nonviolent crimes the numbers are surprisingly even.

Arrests of 10- to 17-year-olds: ■ Boys ▨ Girls

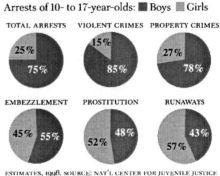

TOTAL ARRESTS — 25% / 75%
VIOLENT CRIMES — 15% / 85%
PROPERTY CRIMES — 27% / 78%
EMBEZZLEMENT — 45% / 55%
PROSTITUTION — 52% / 48%
RUNAWAYS — 57% / 43%

ESTIMATES, 1996. SOURCE: NAT'L CENTER FOR JUVENILE JUSTICE

Eating Disorders

Boys can also have eating disorders. Kids who used laxatives or vomited to lose weight:

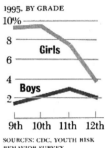

1995, BY GRADE
10%
8
Girls
6
4
Boys
2
9th   10th   11th   12th

SOURCES: CDC, YOUTH RISK BEHAVIOR SURVEY

would have had to change seats because she would not have been able to bear the pain of seeing a teenage son and mother together. The woman's son was 17 when his girlfriend dumped him; he went into the garage and killed himself. "This story made me aware that with a boy especially, you have to keep talking because they don't come and talk to you," she says. Lara's son is now 17; she also has a 19-year-old daughter. "My daughter stalked me. She followed me from room to room. She was yelling, but she was in touch. Boys don't do that. They leave the room and you don't know what they're feeling." Her son is now 6 feet 3. "He's a man. There are barriers. You have to reach through that and remember to ruffle his hair."

With the high rate of divorce, many boys are growing up without any adult men in their lives at all. Don Elium, coauthor of the best-selling 1992 book "Raising a Son," says that with troubled boys, there's often a common theme: distant, uninvolved fathers, and mothers who have taken on more responsibility to fill the gap. That was the case with Raymundo Infante Jr., a 16-year-old high-school junior, who lives with his mother, Mildred, 38, a hospital administrative assistant in Chicago, and his sister, Vanessa, 19. His parents divorced when he was a baby and he had little contact with his father until a year ago. The hurt built up—in sixth grade, Raymundo was so depressed that he told a classmate he wanted to kill himself. The classmate told the teacher, who told a counselor, and Raymundo saw a psychiatrist for a year. "I felt that I just wasn't good enough, or he just didn't want me," Raymundo says.

Last year Raymundo finally confronted his dad, who works two jobs—in an office and on a construction crew—and accused him of caring more about work than about his son. Now the two spend time together on weekends and sometimes go shopping, but there is still a huge gap of lost years.

Black boys are especially vulnerable, since they are more likely than whites to grow up in homes without fathers. They're often on their own much sooner than whites. Black leaders are looking for alternatives. In Atlanta, the Rev. Tim McDonald's First Iconium Baptist Church just chartered a Boy Scout troop. "Gangs are so prevalent because guys want to belong to something," says McDonald. "We've got to give them something positive to belong to." Black educators like Chicagoan Jawanza Kunjufu think mentoring programs will overcome the bias against academic success as "too white." Some cities are also experimenting with all-boy classrooms in predominantly black schools.

Researchers hope that in the next few years, they'll come up with strategies that will help boys the way the work of Gilligan and others helped girls. In the meantime, experts say, there are some guidelines. Parents can channel their sons' energy into constructive activities, like team sports. They should also look for "teachable moments" to encourage qualities such as empathy. When Diane Fisher, a Cincinnati-area psychologist, hears her 8- and 10-year-old boys talking about "finishing somebody," she knows she has mistakenly rented a violent videogame. She pulls the plug and tells them: "In our

house, killing people is not entertainment, even if it's just pretend."

Parents can also teach by example. New Yorkers Dana and Frank Minaya say they've never disciplined their 16-year-old son Walter in anger. They insist on resolving all disputes calmly and reasonably, without yelling. If there is a problem, they call an official family meeting "and we never leave without a big hug," says Frank. Walter tries to be open with his parents. "I don't want to miss out on any advice," he says.

Most of all, wise parents of boys should go with the flow. Cindy Lang, 36, a full-time mother in Woodside, Calif., is continually amazed by the relentless energy of her sons, Roger Lloyd, 12, and Chris, 9. "You accept the fact that they're going to involve themselves in risky behavior, like skateboarding down a flight of stairs. As a girl, I certainly wasn't skateboarding down a flight of stairs." Just last week, she got a phone call from school telling her that Roger Lloyd was in the emergency room because he had fallen backward while playing basketball and school officials thought he might have a concussion. He's fine now, but she's prepared for the next emergency: "I have a cell phone so I can be on alert." Boys will be boys. And we have to let them.

With KAREN SPRINGEN *in Chicago,*
PATRICIA KING *in San Francisco,*
PAT WINGERT *in Washington,* VERN E. SMITH
in Atlanta and ELIZABETH ANGELL *in New York*

by Doreen Kimura

Sex Differences in the Brain

Men and women display patterns of behavioral and cognitive differences that reflect varying hormonal influences on brain development

Men and women differ not only in their physical attributes and reproductive function but also in many other characteristics, including the way they solve intellectual problems. For the past few decades, it has been ideologically fashionable to insist that these behavioral differences are minimal and are the consequence of variations in experience during development before and after adolescence. Evidence accumulated more recently, however, suggests that the effects of sex hormones on brain organization occur so early in life that from the start the environment is acting on differently wired brains in boys and girls. Such effects make evaluating the role of experience, independent of physiological predisposition, a difficult if not dubious task. The biological bases of sex differences in brain and behavior have become much better known through increasing numbers of behavioral, neurological and endoctinological studies.

We know, for instance, from observations of both humans and nonhumans that males are more aggressive than females, that young males engage in more rough-and-tumble play than females and that females are more nurturing. We also know that in general males are better at a variety of spatial or navigational tasks. How do these and other sex differences come about? Much of our information and many of our ideas about how sexual differentiation takes place derive from research on animals. From such investigations, it appears that perhaps the most important factor in the differentiation of males and females is the level of exposure to various sex hormones early in life.

In most mammals, including humans, the developing organism has the potential to be male or female. Producing a male, however, is a complex process. When a Y chromosome is present, testes, or male gonads, form. This development is the critical first step toward becoming a male. When no Y chromosome is present, ovaries form.

Testes produce male hormones, or androgens (testosterone chief among them), which are responsible not only for transformation of the genitals into male organs but also for organization of corresponding male behaviors early in life. As with genital formation, the intrinsic tendency that occurs in the absence of mascu-linizing hormonal influence, according to seminal studies by Robert W. Goy of the University of Wisconsin, is to develop female genital structures and behavior. Female anatomy and probably most behavior associated with females are thus the default modes in the absence of androgens.

If a rodent with functional male genitals is deprived of androgens immediately after birth (either by castration or by the administration of a compound that blocks androgens), male sexual behavior, such as mounting, will be reduced, and more female sexual behavior, such as lordosis (arching of the back when receptive to coitus), will be expressed. Similarly, if androgens are administered to a female directly after birth, she will display more male sexual behavior and less female behavior in adulthood. These lifelong effects of early exposure to sex hormones are characterized as "organizational" because they appear to alter brain function permanently during a critical period in prenatal or early postnatal development. Administering the same sex hormones at later stages or in the adult has no such effect.

Not all the behaviors that categorize males are organized at the same time, however. Organization by androgens

Reprinted with permission from *Scientific American Presents*, Vol. 10, Issue 2, Summer 1999, pp. 26-31. © 1999 by Scientific American, Inc. All rights reserved.

of the male-typical behaviors of mounting and of rough-and-tumble play, for example, occur at different times prenatally in rhesus monkeys.

The area in the brain that regulates female and male reproductive behavior is the hypothalamus. This tiny structure at the base of the brain connects to the pituitary, the master endocrine gland. It has been shown that a region of the hypothalamus is visibly larger in male rats than in females and that this size difference is under hormonal control. Scientists have also found parallel sex differences in a clump of nerve cells in the human brain—parts of the interstitial nucleus of the anterior hypothalamus—that is larger in men than in women. Even sexual orientation and gender identity have been related to anatomical variation in the hypothalamus. In 1991, while at the Salk Institute for Biological Studies in San Diego, Simon Levay reported that one of the interstitial nuclei of the anterior hypothalamus that is usually larger in human males than in females is smaller in homosexual than in heterosexual men. Other researchers, Jiang-Ning Zhou of the Netherlands Institute of Brain Research and his colleagues there and at Free University in Amsterdam, observed another part of the hypothalamus to be smaller in male-to-female transsexuals than in a male control group. These findings are consistent with suggestions that sexual orientation and gender identity have a significant biological component.

Hormones and Intellect

What of differences in intellectual function between men and women? Major sex differences in function seem to lie in patterns of ability rather than in overall level of intelligence (measured as IQ), although some researchers, such as Richard Lynn of the University of Ulster in Northern Ireland, have argued that there exists a small IQ difference favoring human males. Differences in intellectual pattern refer to the fact

that people have different intellectual strengths. For example, some people are especially good at using words, whereas others are better at dealing with external stimuli, such as identifying an object in a different orientation. Individuals may have the same overall intelligence but differing abilities.

Sex differences in problem solving have been systematically studied in adults in laboratory situations. On average, men perform better than women at certain spatial tasks. In particular, men seem to have an advantage in tests that require the subject to imagine rotating an object or manipulating it in some other way. They also outperform women in mathematical reasoning tests and in navigating their way through a route. Further, men exhibit more accuracy in tests of target-directed motor skills—that is, in guiding or intercepting projectiles.

Women, on average, excel on tests that measure recall of words and on tests that challenge the person to find words that begin with a specific letter or fulfill some other constraint. They also tend to be better than men at rapidly identifying matching items and performing certain precision manual tasks, such as placing pegs in designated holes on a board.

In examining the nature of sex differences in navigating routes, one study found that men completed a computer simulation of a maze or labyrinth task more quickly and with fewer errors than women did. Another study by different researchers used a path on a tabletop map to measure route learning. Their results showed that although men learned the route in fewer trials and with fewer errors, women remembered more of the landmarks, such as pictures of different types of buildings, than men did. These results and others suggest that women tend to use landmarks as a strategy to orient themselves in everyday life more than men do.

Other findings seemed also to point to female superiority in landmark memory. Researchers tested the ability of individuals to recall ob-

jects and their locations within a confined space—such as in a room or on a tabletop. In these studies, women were better able to remember whether items had changed places or not. Other investigators found that women were superior at a memory task where they had to remember the locations of pictures on cards that were turned over in pairs. At this kind of object location, in contrast to other spatial tasks, women appeared to have the advantage.

It is important to keep in mind that some of the average sex differences in cognition vary from slight to quite large and that men and women overlap enormously on many cognitive tests that show average differences. For example, whereas women perform better than men in both verbal memory (recalling words from lists or paragraphs) and verbal fluency (finding words that begin with a specific letter), there was a large difference in memory ability but only a small disparity for the fluency tasks. On the whole, variation between men and women tends to be smaller than deviations within each sex, but very large differences between the groups do exist —in men's high level of visual-spatial targeting ability, for one.

Although it used to be thought that sex differences in problem solving did not appear until puberty, the accumulated evidence now suggests that some cognitive and skill differences are present much earlier. For example, researchers have found that three- and four-year-old boys were better at targeting and mentally rotating figures within a clock face than girls of the same age were. Prepubescent girls, however, excelled at recalling lists of words.

Male and female rodents have also been found to solve problems differently. Christina L. Williams of Duke University has shown that female rats have a greater tendency to use landmarks in spatial learning tasks, as it appears women do. In Williams's experiment, female rats used landmark cues, such as pictures on the wall, in preference to

Problem-Solving Tasks Favoring
Men

Men tend to perform better than women on certain spatial tasks. They do well on tests that involve mentally rotating an object or manipulating it in some fashion, such as imagining turning this three-dimensional object

or determining where the holes punched in a folded piece of paper will fall when the paper is unfolded:

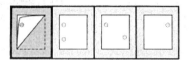

Men also are more accurate than women at target-directed motor skills, such as guiding or intercepting projectiles:

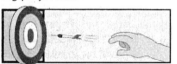

They do better at matching lines with identical slopes:

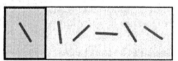

And men tend to do better than women on tests of mathematical reasoning:

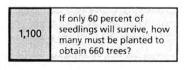

| 1,100 | If only 60 percent of seedlings will survive, how many must be planted to obtain 660 trees? |

Problem-Solving Tasks Favoring
Women

Women tend to perform better than men on tests of perceptual speed in which subjects must rapidly identify matching items—for example, pairing the house on the far left with its twin:

In addition, women remember whether an object, or a series of objects, has been displaced:

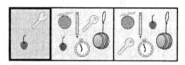

When read a story, paragraph or a list of unrelated words, women demonstrate better recall:

Dog, shadow, hamburger, cloud, flower, eyelash, pencil, paper, water, light, fork, road, building....

Women do better on precision manual tasks—that is, those involving fine-motor coordination—such as placing the pegs in holes on a board:

And women do better than men on mathematical calculation tests:

| 77 | 14 x 3 – 17 + 52 |
| 43 | $2(15+3) + 12 - \frac{15}{3}$ |

DOREEN KIMURA AND JOHN MENGEL

Depriving newborn males of sex hormones by castrating them or administering hormones to newborn females resulted in a complete reversal of sex-typed behaviors in the adult animals. Treated males behaved like females and treated females like males.

Structural differences may parallel behavioral ones. Lucia F. Jacobs, then at the University of Pittsburgh, discovered that the hippocampus—a region thought to be involved in spatial learning in both birds and mammals–is larger in several male species of rodents than in females. At present, there are insufficient data on possible sex differences in hippocampal size in human subjects.

One of the most compelling areas of evidence for hormonally influenced sex differences in humans comes from studies of girls exposed to excess androgens in the prenatal or neonatal stage. The production of abnormally large quantities of adrenal androgens can occur because of a genetic defect in a condition called congenital adrenal hyperplasia (CAH). Before the 1970s a similar condition also unexpectedly appeared in the offspring of pregnant women who took various synthetic steroids. Although the consequent masculinization of the genitals can be corrected by surgery and drug therapy can stop the overproduction of androgens, the effects of prenatal exposure on the brain cannot be reversed.

Sheri A. Berenbaum of Southern Illinois University at Carbondale and Melissa Hines of the University of California at Los Angeles observed the play behavior of CAH girls and compared it with that of their male and female siblings. Given a choice of transportation and construction toys, dolls and kitchen supplies, or books and board games, the CAH girls preferred the more typically masculine toys—for example, they played with cars for the same amount of time that boys did. Both the CAH girls and the boys differed from unaffected girls in their patterns of choice. Berenbaum also found that CAH girls had greater

geometric cues: angles and the shape of the room, for instance. If no landmarks were available, however, females used the geometric cues. In contrast, males did not use landmarks at all, preferring geometric cues almost exclusively.

Williams also found that hormonal manipulation during the critical period could alter these behaviors.

*TESTOSTERONE LEVELS can affect perfor-
mance on some tests (see boxes for example
of tests). Women with high levels of testosterone perform better on spatial tasks (top) than
women with low levels do, but men with low
levels outperform men with high levels. One
a mathematical reasoning test (middle), low
testosterone corresponds to better performance in men; in women there is no such relation. On a test of perceptual speed in which
women usually excel (bottom), no relation is
found between testosterone and performance.*

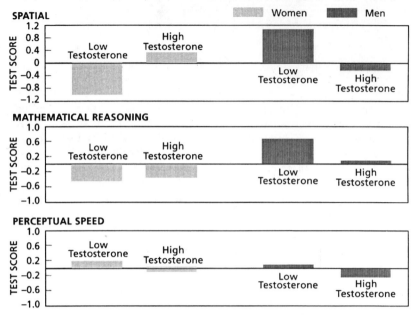

DOREEN KIMURA

interest in male-typical activities and careers. Because there is every reason to think parents would be at least as likely to encourage feminine preferences in their CAH daughters as in their unaffected daughters, these findings suggest that these preferences were actually altered in some way by the early hormonal environment.

Other researchers also found that spatial abilities that are typically better in males are enhanced in CAH girls. But the reverse was reported in one study of CAH-affected boys–they performed worse than unaffected boys on the spatial tests males usually excel at.

Such studies suggest that although levels of androgen relate to spatial ability, it is not simply the case that the higher the levels, the better the spatial scores. Rather studies point to some optimal level of androgen (in the low male range) for maximal spatial ability. This finding may also be true with men and mathematical reasoning; low-androgen men tested higher. There was no obvious correlation between hormone levels and women's math scores, however.

These findings are relevant to the suggestion by Camilla P. Benbow of Iowa State University that high mathematical ability has a significant biological determinant. Benbow and her colleagues have reported consistent sex differences in mathematical reasoning ability that favor males. In mathematically talented youth, the differences were especially sharp at the upper end of the distribution, where males outnumbered females 13 to one. Benbow argues that these differences are not readily explained by socialization.

It is important to keep in mind that the relation between natural hormone levels and problem solving is based on correlational data. Although some form of connection between the two measures exists, we do not necessarily know how the association is determined nor what its causal basis is. We also know little at present about the relation between adult levels of hormones and those in early life, when abilities appear to become organized in the nervous system.

Hormonal Highs and Lows

One of the most intriguing findings in adults is that cognitive patterns may remain sensitive to hormonal fluctuations throughout life. Elizabeth Hampson of the University of Western Ontario showed that women's performances at certain tasks changed throughout the menstrual cycle as levels of estrogen varied. High levels of the hormone were associated not only with relatively depressed spatial ability but also with enhanced speech and manual skill tasks. In addition, I have observed seasonal fluctuations in spatial ability in men: their performance improves in the spring, when testosterone levels are lower. Whether these hormonally

linked fluctuations in intellectual ability represent useful evolutionary adaptations or merely highs and lows of an average test level remains to be seen through further research endeavors.

A long history of studying people with damage to one half of their brain indicates that in most people the left hemisphere of the brain is critical for speech and the right for certain perceptual and spatial functions. Researchers studying sex differences have widely assumed that the right and left hemispheres of the brain are more asymmetrically organized for speech and spatial functions in men than in women.

This belief rests on several lines of research. Parts of the corpus callosum, a major neural system connecting the two hemispheres, as well as another connector, the anterior commissure, appear to be larger in women, which may permit better communication between hemispheres. Perceptual techniques that measure brain asymmetry in normal-functioning people sometimes show smaller asymmetries in women than in men, and damage to one brain hemisphere sometimes has a lesser effect in women than the comparable injury in men does. My own data on patients with damage to one hemisphere of the brain suggest that

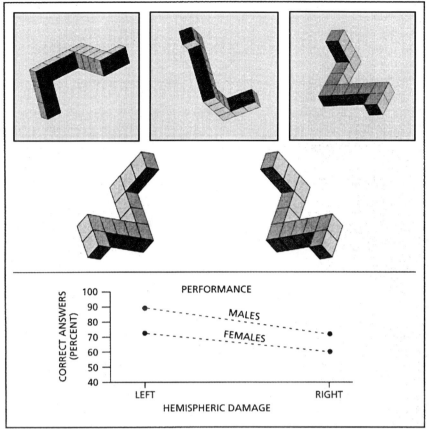

DOREEN KIMURA

RIGHT HEMISPHERIC DAMAGE affects spatial ability to the same degree in both sexes (graph at bottom), suggesting that women and men rely equally on that hemisphere for certain spatial tasks. In one test of spatial-rotation performance, photographs of a three-dimensional object must be matched to one of two mirror images of the same object.

for functions such as basic speech and spatial ability, there are no major sex differences in hemispheric asymmetry, although there may be such disparities in certain more abstract abilities, such as defining words.

If the known overall differences between men and women in spatial ability were related to differing dependence on the right brain hemisphere for such functions, then damage to that hemisphere might be expected to have a more devastating effect on spatial performance in men. My laboratory has studied the ability of patients with damage to one hemisphere of the brain to visualize the rotation of certain objects. As expected, for both sexes, those with damage to the right hemisphere got lower scores on these tests than those with damage to the left hemisphere did. Also, as anticipated, women did less well than

men on this test. Damage to the right hemisphere, however, had no greater effect on men than on women.

The results of this study and others suggest that the normal differences between men and women on rotational and line orientation tasks need not be the result of different degrees of dependence on the right hemisphere. Some other brain systems may be mediating the higher performance by men.

Another brain difference between the sexes has been shown for speech and certain manual functions. Women incur aphasia (impairment of the power to produce and understand speech) more often after anterior damage than after posterior damage to the brain. In men, posterior damage more often affects speech. A similar pattern is seen in apraxia, difficulty in selecting appropriate hand movements, such as

showing how to manipulate a particular object or copying the movements of the experimenter. Women seldom experience apraxia after left posterior damage, whereas men often do.

Men also incur aphasia from left hemisphere damage more often than women do. One explanation suggests that restricted damage within a hemisphere after a stroke more often affects the posterior region of the left hemisphere. Because men rely more on this region for speech than women do, they are more likely to be affected. We do not yet understand the effects on cognitive differences of such divergent patterns of speech and manual functions.

Although my laboratory has not found evidence of sex differences in functional brain asymmetry with regard to basic speech, movement or spatial-rotation abilities, we have found slight differences in some verbal skills. Scores on a vocabulary test and on a verbal fluency test, for instance, were slightly affected by damage to either hemisphere in women, but such scores were affected only by left hemisphere damage in men. These findings suggest that when using some more abstract verbal skills, women do use their hemispheres more equally than men do. But we have not found this to be true for all word-related tasks; for example, verbal memory appears to depend just as much on the left hemisphere in women as in men.

In recent years, new techniques for assessing the brain's activity—including functional magnetic resonance imaging (fMRI) and positron emission tomography (PET), when used during various problem-solving activities—have shown promise for providing more information about how brain function may vary among normal, healthy individuals. The research using these two techniques has so far yielded interesting, yet at times seemingly conflicting, results.

Some research has shown greater differences in activity between the hemispheres of men than of women during certain language tasks, such as judging if two words rhyme and cre-

APHASIA, or speech disorders, occur most often in women when damage is sustained in the anterior of the brain. In men, they occur more frequently when damage is in the posterior region. The data presented at the right derive from one set of patients.

INCIDENCE OF APHASIA

■ FEMALES

▨ MALES

MOTOR CORTEX

65%

29%

60%

12%

ANTERIOR

VISUAL CORTEX

POSTERIOR

LEFT HEMISPHERE

JARED SCHNEIDMAN

ating past tenses of verbs. Other research has failed to find sex differences in functional asymmetry. The different results may be attributed in part to different language tasks being used in the various studies, perhaps showing that the sexes may differ in brain organization for some language tasks but not for others.

The varying results may also reflect the complexity of these techniques. The brain is always active to some degree. So for any activity, such as reading aloud, the comparison activity—here, reading silently—is intended to be very similar. We then "subtract" the brain pattern that occurs during silent reading to find the brain pattern present while reading aloud. Yet such methods require dubious assumptions about what the subject is doing during either activity. In addition, the more complex the activity, the more difficult it is to know what is actually being measured after subtracting the comparison activity.

Looking Back

To understand human behavior—how men and women differ from one another, for instance–we must look beyond the demands of modern life. Our brains are essentially like those of our ancestors of 50,000 and more years ago, and we can gain some insight into sex differences by studying the differing roles men and women have played in evolutionary history. Men were responsible for hunting and scavenging, defending the group against predators and enemies, and shaping and using weapons. Women gathered food near the home base, tended the home, prepared food and clothing, and cared for small children. Such specialization would put different selection pressures on men and women.

Any behavioral differences between individuals or groups must somehow be mediated by the brain. Sex differences have been reported in brain structure and organization, and studies have been done on the role of sex hormones in influencing human behavior. But questions remain regarding how hormones act on human brain systems to produce the sex differences we described, such as in play behavior or in cognitive patterns.

The information we have from laboratory animals helps to guide our explanations, but ultimately these hypotheses must be tested on people. Refinements in brain-imaging techniques, when used in conjunction with our knowledge of hormonal influences and with continuing studies on the behavioral deficits after damage to various brain regions, should provide insight into some of these questions.

The Author

DOREEN KIMURA studies the neural and hormonal basis of human intellectual functions. She is professor of psychology at Simon Fraser University. Until recently, she was professor of psychology and honorary lecturer in the department of clinical neurological sciences at the University of Western Ontario. Kimura is a fellow of the Royal Society of Canada.

Further Reading

SEX ON THE BRAIN; THE BIOLOGICAL DIFFERENCES BETWEEN MEN AND WOMEN. Deborah Blum. Viking Press, 1997.

THE TROUBLE WITH TESTOSTERONE; AND OTHER ESSAYS ON THE BIOLOGY OF THE HUMAN PREDICAMENT. Robert M. Sapolsky. Scribner, 1997.

SEX AND COGNITION. Doreen Kimura. MIT Press, 1999.

EXACTLY how do we signal our amorous interest and intent in each other?

FLIRTING Fascination

It's been trivialized, even demonized, but the coquettish behavior indulged in by men and women alike is actually a vital silent language exchanging critical—and startling—information about our general health and reproductive fitness.

By Joann Ellison Rodgers

She was," he proclaimed, "so extraordinarily beautiful that I nearly laughed out loud. She... [was] famine, fire, destruction and plague... the only true begetter. Her breasts were apocalyptic, they would topple empires before they withered... her body was a miracle of construction... She was unquestionably gorgeous. She was lavish. She was a dark, unyielding largesse. She was, in short, too bloody much.... Those huge violet blue eyes... had an odd glint.... Aeons passed, civilizations came and went while these cosmic headlights examined my flawed personality. Every pockmark on my face became a crater of the moon."

So Richard Burton described his first sight of a 19-year-old Elizabeth Taylor. He didn't record what happened next, but a growing cadre of scientists would bet their lab coats and research budgets that sometime after that breathcatching, gut-gripping moment of instant mutual awareness, Liz tossed her hair, swayed her hips, arched her feet, giggled, gazed wide-eyed, flicked her tongue over her lips and extended that apocalyptic chest, and that Dick, for his part, arched his back, stretched his pecs, imperceptibly swayed his pelvis in a tame Elvis performance, swaggered, laughed loudly, tugged his tie and clasped the back of his neck, which had the thoroughly engaging effect of stiffening his stance and puffing his chest.

What eventually got these two strangers from across the fabled crowded room to each other's side was what does it for all of us—in a word, flirtation, the capacity to automatically turn our actions into sexual semaphores signaling interest in the opposite sex as predictably and instinctively as peacocks fan their tails, codfish thrust their pelvic fins or mice twitch their noses and tilt their backs to draw in the object of their attention.

WE SIGNAL our interest in the OPPOSITE SEX as instinctively as PEACOCKS flare their TAILS or FISH their FINS.

Long trivialized and even demonized, flirtation is gaining new respectability thanks to a spate of provocative studies of animal and human behavior in many parts of the world. The capacity of men and women to flirt and to be receptive to flirting turns out to be a remarkable set of behaviors embedded deep in our psyches. Every come-

Reprinted with permission from *Psychology Today*, January/February 1999, pp. 36-41, 64-70. © 1999 by Sussex Publishers, Inc.

hither look sent and every sidelong glance received are mutually understood signals of such transcendent history and beguiling sophistication that only now are they beginning to yield clues to the psychological and biological wisdom they encode.

This much is clear so far: flirting is nature's solution to the problem every creature faces in a world full of potential mates–how to choose the right one. We all need a partner who is not merely fertile but genetically different as well as healthy enough to promise viable offspring, provide some kind of help in the hard job of parenting and offer some social compatibility.

Our animal and human ancestors needed a means of quickly and safely judging the value of potential mates without "going all the way" and risking pregnancy with every possible candidate they encountered. Flirting achieved that end, offering a relatively risk-free set of signals with which to sample the field, try out sexual wares and exchange vital information about candidates' general health and reproductive fitness.

Flirting is a negotiation process that takes place after there has been some initial attraction," observes Steven W. Gangestad, Ph.D., an evolutionary psychologist at the University of New Mexico in Albuquerque who is currently studying how people choose their mates. "Two people have to share with each other the information that they are attracted, and then test each other" on an array of attributes. Simply announcing, 'I'm attracted to you, are you attracted to me?' doesn't work so well. "It works much better to reveal this and have it revealed to you in smaller doses," explains Gangestad. "The flirting then becomes something that enhances the attraction."

It is an axiom of science that traits and behaviors crucial to survival– such as anything to do with attraction and sex–require, and get, a lot of an animal's resources. All mammals and most animals (including birds, fish,

even fruit flies) engage in complicated and energy-intensive plots and plans for attracting others to the business of sex. That is, they flirt.

From nature's standpoint, the goal of life is the survival of our DNA. Sex is the way most animals gain the flexibility to healthfully sort and mix their genes. Getting sex, in turn, is wholly dependent on attracting attention and being attracted. And flirting is the way a person focuses the attention of a specific member of the opposite sex. If our ancestors hadn't done it well enough, we wouldn't be around to discuss it now.

SCIENCE has calculated just how CURVY a woman has to be to GARNER male appreciation.

A silent language of elaborate visual and other gestures, flirting is "spoken" by intellect-driven people as well as instinct-driven animals. The very universality of flirting, preserved through evolutionary history from insects to man, suggests that a flirting plan is wired into us, and that it has been embedded in our genes and in our brain's operating system the same way and for the same reasons that every other sexual trait has been–by trial and error, with conservation of what works best.

Like any other language, flirting may be deployed in ways subtle or coarse, adolescent or suave. Nevertheless, it has evolved just like pheasant spurs and lion manes: to advertise ourselves to the opposite sex.

Flirtation first emerged as a subject of serious scrutiny a scant 30 years ago. Irenäus Eibl-Eibesfeldt, now honorary director of the Ludwig-Boltzmann Institute

for Urban Ethology in Vienna, was already familiar with the widespread dances and prances of mate-seeking animals. Then he discovered that people in dozens of cultures, from the South Sea islands to the Far East, Western Europe, Africa and South America, similarly engage in a fairly fixed repertoire of gestures to test sexual availability and interest.

Having devised a special camera that allowed him to point the lens in one direction while actually photographing in another, he "caught" couples on film during their flirtations, and discovered, for one thing, that women, from primitives who have no written language to those who read *Cosmo* and *Marie Claire,* use nonverbal signals that are startlingly alike. On Eibl-Eibesfeldt's screen flickered identical flirtation messages: a female smiling at a male, then arching her brows to make her eyes wide, quickly lowering her lids and, tucking her chin slightly down and coyly to the side, averting her gaze, followed within seconds, almost on cue, by putting her hands on or near her mouth and giggling.

Regardless of language, socioeconomic status or religious upbringing, couples who continued flirting placed a palm up on the table or knees, reassuring the prospective partner of harmlessness. They shrugged their shoulders, signifying helplessness. Women exaggeratedly extended their neck, a sign of vulnerability and submissiveness.

FLIRTING is self PROMOTION—but nature DEMANDS a certain amount of TRUTH in advertising.

For Eibl-Eibesfeldt, these gestures represented primal behaviors driven by the old parts of our brain's evolutionary memory. A woman presenting her extended neck to a man she wants is not much different, his work suggested, than a gray female wolf's submissiveness to a dominant male she's after.

Since then, researchers have turned up the intensity, looking, for example, at compressed bouts of flirting and courtship in their natural habitat–hotel bars and cocktail lounges. From observations at a Hyatt hotel cocktail lounge, researchers documented a set of signals that whisks a just-met man and woman from barroom to bedroom. Her giggles and soft laughs were followed by hair twirling and head-tossing; he countered with body arching, leaning back in the chair and placing his arms behind head, not unlike a pigeon puffing his chest.

If all went well, a couple would invariably progress from touching themselves to touching each other. The first tentative contacts could be termed "lint-picking." She would lift an imaginary mote from his lapel; he would brush a real or imaginary crumb from her lips. Their heads moved closer, their hands pressed out in front of them on the table, their fingers inches from each other's, playing with salt shakers or utensils. Whoops! An "accidental" finger touch, then perhaps some digital "dirty dancing," more touching and leaning in cheek to cheek. By body language alone, the investigators could predict which pairs would ride up the elevators together.

Social psychologist Timothy Perper, Ph.D., an independent scholar and writer based in Philadelphia, and anthropologist David Givens, Ph.D., spent months in dimly lit lounges documenting these flirtation rituals. Like the ear wiggles, nose flicks and back arches that signal "come hither" in rodents, the women smiled, gazed, swayed, giggled, licked their lips, and aided and abetted by the wearing of high heels, they swayed their backs, forcing their buttocks to tilt out and up and their chests to thrust forward.

The men arched, stretched, swiveled, and made grand gestures of whipping out lighters and lighting up cigarettes. They'd point their chins in the air with a cigarette dangling in their mouth, then loop their arms in a wide arc to put the lighter away. Their swaggers, bursts of laughter and grandiose gestures were an urban pantomime of the prancing and preening indulged in by male baboons and gorillas in the wild. Man or monkey, the signals all said, "Look at me, trust me, I'm powerful, but I won't hurt you." And "I don't want anything much . . . yet."

The sequence FLIRTATION takes is ALWAYS the same; LOOK, talk, touch, kiss, do the DEED.

All the silent swaying, leaning, smiling, bobbing and gazing eventually brought a pair into full frontal alignment. Face to face, they indulged in simultaneous touching of everything from eyeglasses to fingertips to crossed legs. Says Perper, "This kind of sequence–attention, recognition, dancing, synchronization–is fundamental to courtship. From the Song of Songs until today, the sequence is the same: look, talk, touch, kiss, do the deed."

The fact that flirting is a largely nonexplicit drama doesn't mean that important information isn't being delivered in those silent signals. By swaying her hips, or emphasizing them in a form-fitting dress, a flirtatious woman is riveting attention on her pelvis, suggesting its ample capacity for bearing a child. By arching her brows and exaggerating her gaze, her eyes appear large in her face, the way a child's eyes do, advertising, along

with giggles, her youth and "submissiveness." By drawing her tongue along her lips, she compels attention to what many biologists believe are facial echoes of vaginal lips, transmitting sexual maturity and her interest in sex. By coyly averting her gaze and playing "hard to get," she communicates her unwillingness to give sex to just anyone or to someone who will love her and leave her.

For his part, by extending a strong chin and jaw, expanding and showing off pectoral muscles and a hairy chest, flashing money, laughing loudly or resonantly, smiling, and doing all these things without accosting a woman, a man signals his ability to protect offspring, his resources and the testosterone-driven vitality of his sperm as well as the tamer side of him that is willing to stick around, after the sex, for fatherhood. It's the behavioral equivalent of "I'll respect you in the morning."

I can't tell you why I was attracted to her the instant she walked into my office," recalls a 32-year-old screenwriter. "It was chemistry. We both flirted and we both knew it would lead nowhere. I'm happily married." The statement is almost stupefyingly commonplace, but also instructive. Each of us "turns on" not to mankind or womankind but to a particular member of the opposite sex. Certain stances, personal styles, gestures, intimations of emotional compatibility, perhaps even odors, automatically arouse our interest because they not only instantly advertise genetic fitness but they match the template of Desired Mate we all carry in our mind's eye.

As with Dick and Liz, or any couple, the rational, thinking part of their brains got them to the place where girl met boy; they had the event on their calendars, planned what they would wear, arranged for transportation. But in that first meeting, their capacity to react with their instinct and hearts, not their heads, overrode their cognitive brains. Otherwise, they might not have had the nerve to look at each other.

The rational brain is always on the lookout for dangers, for complexities, for reasons to act or not act. If every time man and woman met they immediately considered all the possible risks and vulnerabilities they might face if they mated or had children, they'd run screaming from the room.

The instant of ATTRACTION in fact MIMICS a kind of BRAIN DAMAGE.

It's no secret that the brain's emotionally loaded limbic system sometimes operates independently of the more rational neocortex, such as in the face of danger, when the fight-or-flight response is activated. Similarly, when the matter is sex—another situation on which survival depends—we also react without even a neural nod to the neocortex. Instead, the flirtational operating system appears to kick in without conscious consent. If, at the moment they had met, Dick and Liz had stopped to consider all the possible outcomes of a relationship, they both would have been old before they got close enough to speak.

The moment of attraction, in fact, mimics a kind of brain damage. At the University of Iowa, where he is professor and head of neurology, Antonio Damasio, M.D., has found that people with damage to the connection between their limbic structures and the higher brain are smart and rational—but unable to make decisions. They bring commitment phobia to a whole new level. In attraction, we don't stop and think, we react, operating on a "gut" feeling, with butterflies, giddiness, sweaty palms and flushed faces brought on by the reactivity of the

emotional brain. We suspend intellect at least long enough to propel us to the next step in the mating game—flirtation.

Somewhere beyond flirtation, as a relationship progresses, courtship gets under way, and with it, intellectual processes resume. Two adults can then evaluate potential mates more rationally, think things over and decide whether to love, honor and cherish. But at the moment of attraction and flirtation, bodies, minds and sense are temporarily hostage to the more ancient parts of the brain, the impulsive parts that humans share with animals.

If flirting is a form of self promotion, nature demands a certain amount of truth in advertising. "For a signaling system to convey something meaningful about a desirable attribute, there has to be some honesty," explains Gangestad, "so that if you don't have the attribute you can't fake it." Just as the extravagant colors of birds that figure so prominently in their flirting rituals proclaim the health of animals so plumed, humans have some signals that can't be faked.

Waist-hip ratio is likely one of them. It's no secret that men snap to attention and even go dry at the mouth at the sight of a shapely woman. Science has now calculated just how curvy a woman has to be to garner such appreciation: the waist must measure no more than 60 to 70% of her hip circumference. It is a visual signal that not only figures powerfully in attraction, but is a moving force in flirtation. And unless steel-boned corsets stage a comeback, it is an attribute that just can't be put into play unless it is real.

In simplest terms, says Gangestad, waist-hip ratio is an honest indicator of health. Studies have shown that hourglass-shaped women are less likely than other women to get diabetes and cardiac disease. They are also most likely to bear children, as hips take their shape at puberty from the feminizing hormone estrogen.

"The literature shows that women with a 0.7 waist-hip ratio have a sex-typical hormone profile in the relationship of estrogen to testosterone, and that women with a straighter torso, meaning a waist-hip ratio closer to 1:1, indeed have lower fertility," Gangestad reports. "It appears that males have evolved to pay attention to this cue that ancestrally was related to fertility."

The virtually visceral responsiveness to physical features in flirtation may also be as good a guarantee as one can get that a potential partner shapes up on a hidden but crucial aspect of health: immunity to disease. Scientists know that the testosterone that gives men jutting jaws, prominent noses and big brows, and, to a lesser extent, the estrogen that gives women soft features and curving hips, also suppresses the ability to fight disease. But looks have their own logic, and bodies and faces that are exemplars of their gender signal that their bearer has biological power to spare; after all, he or she has survived despite the hormonal "handicap."

Take the case of such elaborate male ornamentation as peacock tails and stag antlers. In the 1980s, evolutionary biologists William Hamilton and Marlena Zuk linked such features to inborn resistance to disease parasites. Antlers and tail feathers are known to be attractive to females of their species and are major machinery of flirtation. But developing and maintaining such extravagant equipment is costly, taking huge nutritional resources and even slowing the animals down, making them more vulnerable to predators.

The only animals that can afford such ornamentation are those with tip-top constitutions. So, like big bones, big horns, big tails and big spurs in animals, jutting jaws are honest markers for a healthy immune system. Scientists point out that such features are in fact respected by other men as well as attractive to women. Studies show that tall, square-jawed men achieve higher ranks in the military than do those with weak chins, and that taller men are over-represented in boardrooms as well as bedrooms.

Whatever specific physical features men and women are primed to respond to, they all have a quality in common–symmetry That is, attributes deemed attractive have an outward appearance of evenness and right-left balance. Unlike the color and condition of tail feathers, symmetry serves not so much as an honest marker of current health status, but as a signal of a general capacity to be healthy. Symmetry, says Gangestad, is "a footprint left by your whole developmental history." It alone explains why Elizabeth Taylor, Denzel Washington and Queen Nefertiti are universally recognized as beautiful–and full of sex appeal.

> Women prefer men with symmetrical features, and they prefer them at a very specific time—when they are most fertile.

"Bilateral symmetry is a hot topic these days," beams Albert Thornhill, a biologist at the University of New Mexico and a pioneer in the study of symmetry in attraction and flirtation. He and Gangestad believe it is a marker of "developmental precision," the extent to which a genetic blueprint is realized in the flesh despite all the environmental and other perturbations that tend to throw development off course.

Recent studies conducted by the two demonstrate not only that women prefer symmetrical men, they prefer them at a very specific time–when they are most fertile. "We found that female preferences change across the menstrual cycle," Gangestad reports. "We think the finding says something

about the way female mate preferences are designed. Because the preference for male symmetry is specific to the time of ovulation, when women are most likely to conceive, we think women are choosing a mate who is going to provide better genes for healthy babies. It's an indirect benefit, rather than a direct or material benefit to the female herself."

In their study, 52 women rated the attractiveness of 42 men–by their smell. Each of the men slept in one T-shirt for two nights, after which the women were given a whiff of it. Prior to the smell test, all the men had undergone careful calipered measurement of 10 features, from ear width to finger length. Those whose body features were the most symmetrical were the ones whose smells were most preferred, but only among women who were in the ovulatory phase of their menstrual cycle. At other times in their cycle, women had no preference either for symmetrical or asymmetrical males.

The preference for symmetry is not limited to humans. Thornhill first stumbled upon symmetry two decades ago, during experiments with scorpion flies in Australia, Japan and Europe. He noticed that females chose particular male flies on the basis of the level and quality of "nuptial gifts," nutrients passed to the female during courtship and mating.

"That was the first inkling I had that insects were very sophisticated about their mating strategies," Thornhill recalls. But the more time he spent recording the sexual lives of scorpion flies, the more he realized that the females were selecting partners long before they sampled any gifts, and they were reckoning by the symmetry of the males' wings. "I discovered that males and females with the most symmetrical wings had the most mating success and that by using wing symmetry, I–and presumably the fly–could predict reproductive fitness better than scent or any other factor."

Since then, Thornhill and colleagues around the world have conducted more than 20 separate tests of

symmetry of everything from eyes, ears and nostrils to limbs, wrists and fingers. Even if they never speak a word or get closer than a photograph, women view symmetrical men as more dominant, powerful, richer and better sex and marriage material. And symmetrical men view themselves the same way! Men, for their part, rate symmetrical women as more fertile, more attractive, healthier and better sex and marriage material, too–just as such women see themselves as having a competitive edge in the mating sweepstakes.

Flirtation, it turns out, is most successful among the most symmetrical. Men's bodily symmetry matches up with the number of lifetime sex partners they report having. Symmetrical men also engage in more infidelity in their romantic relationships–"extra-pair copulations" in the language of the lab. And they get to sex more quickly after meeting a romantic partner compared to asymmetrical men. They lose their virginity earlier in life, too.

When women flirt with symmetrical men, what their instincts are reading might once have been banned in Boston. Male symmetry is also shorthand for female sexual satisfaction. Gangestad and Thornhill surveyed 86 couples in 1995 and found that symmetrical men "fire off more female copulatory orgasms than asymmetrical men." Women with symmetrical partners were more than twice as likely to climax during intercourse. Thrills are only a short-term payoff, however; female orgasm is really a shill for fertilization, pulling sperm from the vagina into the cervix.

Successful as symmetrical men are at flirtation, it's only their presumably better genes that women really want. Women definitely do not prefer symmetrical men for long-term relationships. There's a definite downside to getting someone with really good DNA. Symmetry, Gangestad explains, affords those men who possess it to take a dastardly mating strategy. His studies show that symmetrical men invest less in any one romantic relationship–less time, less attention, less money. And less fidelity. They're too busy spreading around their symmetry. "They also tend to sexualize other women more," Gangestad reports. "It may be that males who can have the most access without giving a lot of investment take advantage of that."

A guy who will stick around and help out with parenting is on most women's wish list of qualities in a mate, Gangestad concedes. "I wouldn't exclude the possibility that men have been doing some direct parental care for some time, and so a preference for that might also have an evolutionary basis." But also on a woman's wish list from an evolutionary standpoint would be someone who is going to provide good genes for healthy babies. Unfortunately, says the Albuquerque researcher, "what can and does happen in a mating market is that those things don't all come in the same package."

Although the signals and semaphores of flirting are largely devoid of explicit content, the style with which one flirts can be downright revelatory. "*How* a person flirts honestly reveals some important qualities about an individual," says Gangestad. Symmetry isn't everything; there are signals of more subtle skills.

In some species, the females watch the males fight each other and then choose the one who can hold the central territory. But we humans are more differently evolved creatures with more complex lives in which our higher faculties presumably contribute something to success, whether it's surviving in primitive equatorial caves or sophisticated urban ones.

Enter creativity, humor and intelligence. Deployed in flirting, they disclose more about an individual person than all the antlers do about leching animals. "They are likely saying something important about our very viability," says Gangestad. "When we can engage in humor and creativity, they

act as an honest signal that we've got a reasonably well put together nervous system. They may indicate there's some developmental integrity underneath our brain." And a certain ability to withstand whatever challenges life throws a person's way.

Symmetrical men give women more orgasms, but they also are more likely to be unfaithful to their partners.

What's more, our basic social ability to "read" another's facial gestures and emotional expressions acts as a fact-checking system in flirtation. It enables us to glimpse the tone of a prospective mate's inner life and to check for the presence or absence of psychological weakness. And in fact, women are pretty good at doping out information about such important attributes—even when they get very little time to make a judgment.

In a recent set of studies, Gangestad and a colleague extracted one-minute segments from more extensive videotaped interviews with men not in committed relationships. The brief segments were then shown to women who were asked to rate the men on a variety of characteristics, including how attractive they'd be in a pair relationship. The women were able to make judgments about each man's intelligence, ability to be caring and how nice he seemed. They also paid attention to another set of characteristics—how effective a man was likely to be with other males, how socially influential he was.

The men who were rated most attractive for long-term relationships scored high on both sets of charac-

teristics. But what may be most notable about the study was that women's observations, from a mere snippet of videotape, were remarkably accurate. They correlated closely with the men's ratings of their own personality.

After two people share the information that they are attracted, then, through the way they flirt, they may unwittingly let on more about themselves. "It becomes a testing ground as well as an information-revealing process," says Gangestad.

Thus, while we appear to be pre-programmed with an urge to wile or wiggle our way onto another's mental radar screen, we also seem psychologically constituted to pay rapt attention to looks and actions intended to be sexually appealing. Otherwise, neither Liz and Dick nor any two contenders would have a reliable, safe or peaceful means of communicating attraction and getting to the more durable business of courtship, mating and commitment to the offspring that will carry our DNA into the next generation.

JOANN RODGERS wishes that people were less squeamish about sex. "It's unfortunate," she says, since "sex is the most important aspect of the survival of our species," a view she espouses both in her upcoming book on the natural science of sex and in her article on flirting. Especially tragic, she says, "is how difficult it is to find funding for sex research in this P.C. era." Director of media relations at the Johns Hopkins Medical Institutions in Baltimore, Maryland, Rodgers has also written on medicine and life science for numerous magazines. She is a former President of the National Association of Science Writers.

BACK OFF!

We're putting way too many expectations on our closest relationships. It's time to retreat a bit. Consider developing same-sex friendships. Or cultivating a garden. Whatever you do, take a break from the relentless pursuit of intimacy.

Geraldine K. Piorkowski, Ph.D.

You can't miss it. It's the favorite topic of Oprah and all the other talks shows. It's the suds of every soap opera. And I probably don't have to remind you that it's the subject of an extraordinary number of self-help books. Intimate relationships. No matter where we tune or turn, we are bombarded with messages that there is a way to do it right, certainly some way of doing it better—if only we could find it. There are countless books simply on the subject of how to communicate better. Or, if it's not working out, to exit swiftly.

We are overfocused on intimate relationships, and I question whether our current preoccupation with intimacy isn't unnatural, not entirely in keeping with the essential physical and psychological nature of people. The evidence suggests that there is a limit to the amount of closeness people can tolerate and that we need time alone for productivity and creativity. Time alone is necessary to replenish psychological resources and to solidify the boundaries of the self.

All our cultural focus on relationships ultimately has, I believe, a negative impact on us. It causes us to look upon intimate relationships as a solution to all our ills. And that only sets us up for disappointment, contributing to the remarkable 50 percent divorce rate.

Our overfocus on relationship leads us to demand too much of intimacy. We put all our emotional eggs in the one basket of intimate romantic relationships. A romantic partner must be all things to us—lover, friend, companion, playmate, and parent.

We approach intimate relationships with the expectation that this new love will make up for past letdowns in life and love. The expectation that this time around will be better is bound to disappoint, because present-day lovers feel burdened by demands with roots in old relationships.

We expect unconditional love, unfailing nurturance, and protection. There is also the expectation that the new partner will make up for the characteristics we lack in our own personality—for example, that he or she will be an outgoing soul to compensate for our shyness or a goal-oriented person to provide direction in our messy life.

If the personal ads were rewritten to emphasize the emotional expectations we bring to intimacy, they would sound like this. "WANTED: Lively humorous man who could bring joy to my gloomy days and save me from a lifetime of depression." Or, "WANTED: Women with self-esteem lower than mine. With her, I could feel superior and gain temporary boosts of self-confidence from the comparison."

From my many years as a clinical psychologist, I have come to recognize that intimacy is not an unmitigated good. It is not only difficult to achieve, it is treacherous in some fundamental ways. And it can actually harm people.

The potential for emotional pain and upset is so great in intimate relationships because we are not cloaked in the protective garb of maturity. We are unprotected, exposed, vulnerable to hurt; our defenses are down. We are wide open to pain.

Intuitively recognizing the dangers involved, people normally erect elaborate barriers to shield themselves from closeness. We may act superior, comical, mysterious, or super independent because we fear that intimacy will bring criticism, humiliation, or betrayal—whatever an earlier relationship sensitized us to. We develop expectations based on what has happened in our lives with parents, with friends, with a first love. And we often act in anticipation of these expectations, bringing about the result we most want to avoid.

The closer we get to another person, the greater the risks of intimacy. It's not just that we are more vulnerable and defenseless. We are also more emotionally unstable, childish, and less intelligent than in any other situation. You may be able to run a large company with skill and judgment, but be immature, ultrasensitive, and needy at home. Civilized rules of conduct often get suspended. Intimacy is both unnerving and baffling.

HEALTHY RETREATS

Once our fears are aroused in the context of intimacy, we tend to go about calming them in unproductive ways. We make excessive demands of our partner, for affection, for unconditional regard. The trouble is, when people feel demands are being made of them, they tend to retreat and hide in ways that hurt their partner. They certainly do not listen.

Fears of intimacy typically limit our vulnerability by calling defensive strategies into play. Without a doubt, the defense of choice against the dangers of intimacy is withdrawal. Partners tune out. One may retreat into work. One walks out of the house, slamming the door. Another doesn't call for days. Whatever the way, we spent a great deal of time avoiding intimacy.

When one partner unilaterally backs off, it tends to be done in a hurtful manner. The other partner feels rejected, uncared about, and unloved. Typically, absolutely nothing gets worked out.

However, avoidance is not necessarily unhealthy. Partners can pursue a time out, where one or both work through their conflict in a solitary way that is ultimately renewing. What usually happens, however, is that when partners avoid each other, they are avoiding

> *After many years of working with all kinds of couples, I have come to believe that human nature dictates that intimate relationships have to be cyclical.*

open warfare but doing nothing to resolve the underlying conflicts.

Fears of intimacy can actually be pretty healthy, when they're realistic and protective of the self. And they appear even in good relationships. Take the fears of commitment that are apt to surface in couples just before the wedding. If they can get together and talk through their fears, then they will not scare one another or themselves into backing off permanently.

After many years of working with all kinds of couples, I have come to believe that human nature dictates that intimate relationships have to be cyclical. There are limitations to intimacy and I think it is wise to respect the dangers. Periods of closeness have to be balanced with periods of distance. For every two steps forward, we often need to take one step back.

An occasional retreat from intimacy gives individuals time to recharge. If offers time to strengthen your sense of who you are. Think of it as constructive avoidance. We need to take some emphasis off what partners can do for us and put it on what we can do for ourselves and what we can do with other relationships. Developing and strengthening same-sex friendships, even opposite-sex friendships, has its own rewards and aids the couple by reducing the demands and emotional expectations we place on partners.

In our culture, our obsession with romantic love relationships has led us to confuse all emotional bonds with sexual bonds, just as we confuse infatuation with emotional intimacy. As a result, we seem to avoid strong but deeply rewarding emotional attachments with others of our own sex. But having recently lost a dear friend of several decades, I am personally sensitive to the need for emotionally deep, same-sex relationships. They can be shared as a way of strengthening gender identity and enjoying rewarding companionship. We need to put more energy into nonromantic relationships as well as other activities.

One of the best ways of recharging oneself is to take pleasure in learning and spiritual development. And there's a great deal to be said for spending time solving political, educational, or social ills of the world.

Distance and closeness boundaries need to be calibrated and constantly readjusted in every intimate relationship. Such boundaries not only vary with each couple, they change as the relationship progresses. One couple may maintain their emotional connection by spending one evening together a week, while another couple needs daily coming together of some sort. Problems arise in relationships when partners cannot agree on the boundaries. These boundaries must be jointly negotiated or the ongoing conflict will rob the relationship of its vitality.

S.O.S. SIGNALS

When you're feeling agitated or upset that your partner is not spending enough time with you, consider it a signal to step back and sort out internally what is going on. Whether you feel anxiety or anger, the emotional arousal should serve as a cue to back off and think through where the upset is coming from, and to consider whether it is realistic.

That requires at least a modest retreat from a partner. It could be a half hour, or two hours. Or two days—whenever internal clarity comes. In the grip of emotion, it is often difficult to discriminate exactly which emotion it is and what its source is. "What is it I am concerned about? Is this fear realistic considering Patrick's behavior in the present? He's never done this to me before, and he's been demonstrating his trustworthiness all over the place, so what am I afraid of? Is it coming from my early years of neglect with two distant parents who never had time for me? Or from my experiences with Steve, who dumped me two years ago?"

Introspective and self-aware people already spend their time thinking about how they work, their motives, what their feelings mean. Impulsive people will have a harder time with the sorting-out process. The best way to sort things out is to pay attention to the nature of the upset. Exactly what you are upset about suggests what your unmet need is, whether it's for love, understanding, nurturance, protection, or special status. And

once you identify the need, you can figure out its antecedents.

The kinds of things we get upset about in intimacy tend to follow certain themes. Basically, we become hurt or resentful because we're getting "too much" or "too little" of something. Too many demands, too much criticism, too much domination. Or the converse, too little affectional, conversational, or sexual attention (which translates into "you don't feel I'm important" or "you don't love me"). Insufficient empathy is usually voiced as "you don't understand me," and too little responsibility translates into failure to take on one's share of household and/or financial tasks. All these complaints require some attention, action, or retreat.

SHIFTING GEARS

It's not enough to identify the source of personal concern. You have to present your concerns in a way your partner can hear. If I say directly to my partner, "I'm afraid you're going to leave me," he has the opportunity to respond, "Darling, that's not true. What gave you that idea?" I get the reassurance I need. But if I toss it out in an argument, in the form of "you don't care about me," then my partner's emotional arousal keeps him from hearing me. And he is likely to back away—just when I need reassurance most.

If people were aware that intimate relationships are by nature characterized by ambivalence, they would understand the need to negotiate occasional retreats. They wouldn't feel so threatened by the times when one partner says, "I have to be by myself because I need to think about my life and where I'm going." Or "I need to be with my friends and spend time playing." If people did more backing off into constructive activities, including time to meditate or to play, intimate relationships would be in much better shape today.

If couples could be direct about what they need, then the need for retreat would not be subject to the misrepresentation that now is rampant. The trouble is, we don't talk to each other that openly and honestly. What happens is, one partner backs off and doesn't call and the partner left behind doesn't know what the withdrawal means. But he or she draws on a personal history that provides room for all sorts of negative interpretations, the most common being "he doesn't care about me."

No matter how hard a partner ties to be all things to us, gratifying all of another's needs is a herculean task—beyond the human calling. Criticism, disappointment, and momentary rejection are intrinsic parts of intimate life; developing a thicker skin can be healthy. And maintaining a life apart from the relationships is necessary. Energy invested in other people and activities provides a welcome balance.

GOOD-ENOUGH INTIMACY

Since our intimate partner will never be perfect, what is reasonable to expect? The late British psychiatrist D. W. Winnicott put forth the idea of "good-enough mothering." He was convinced that mothering could never be perfect because of the mother's own emotional needs. "Good-enough mothering" refers to imperfect, though adequate provision of emotional care that is not damaging to the children.

In a similar vein, I believe there is a level of imperfect intimacy that is good enough to live and grow on. In good-enough intimacy, painful encounters occasionally occur, but they are balanced by the strength and pleasures of the relationship. There are enough positives to balance the negatives. People who do very well in intimate relationships don't have a perfect relationship, but it is good enough.

The standard of good-enough intimacy is essentially subjective, but there are some objective criteria. A relationship must have enough companionship, affection, autonomy, connectedness, and separateness, along with some activities that partners engage in together and that they both enjoy. The relationship meets the needs of both partners reasonably well enough, both feel reasonably good about the relationship. If one person is unhappy in the relationship, then by definition it is not good enough for them.

People looking for good-enough intimacy are bound to be happier than those seeking perfect intimacy. Their expectations are lower and more realistic. Time and time again, those who examine the intricacies of happiness have found the same thing—realistic expectations are among the prime contributors to happiness.

Protecting Against
Unintended Pregnancy
A Guide To Contraceptive Choices

by Tamar Nordenberg

I am 20 and have never gone to see a doctor about birth control.
My boyfriend and I have been going together for a couple of years and have
been using condoms. So far, everything is fine. Are condoms alone safe enough,
or is something else safe besides the Pill? I do not want to go on the Pill.
—Letter to the Kinsey Institute for Research in Sex, Gender, and Reproduction

This young woman is not alone in her uncertainty about contraceptive options. A 1995 report by the National Academy of Sciences' Institute of Medicine, *The Best Intentions: Unintended Pregnancy and the Well-being of Children and Families,* attributed the high rate of unintended pregnancies in the United States, in part, to Americans' lack of knowledge about contraception. About 6 of every 10 pregnancies in the United States are unplanned, according to the report.

Being informed about the pros and cons of various contraceptives is important not only for preventing unintended pregnancies but also for reducing the risk of illness or death from sexually transmitted diseases (STDs), including AIDS.

The Food and Drug Administration has approved a number of birth control methods, ranging from over-the-counter male and female condoms and vaginal spermicides to doctor-pre-

1994 by Photodisc, Inc.

From *FDA Consumer,* April 1997, pp. 20-26. Reprinted by permission of *FDA Consumer,* the magazine of the U.S. Food and Drug Administration.

scribed birth control pills, diaphragms, intrauterine devices (IUDs), injected hormones, and hormonal implants. Other contraceptive options include fertility awareness and voluntary surgical sterilization.

"On the whole, the contraceptive choices that Americans have are very safe and effective," says Dennis Barbour, president of the Association of Reproductive Health Professionals, "but a method that is very good for one woman may be lousy for another."

The choice of birth control depends on factors such as a person's health, frequency of sexual activity, number of partners, and desire to have children in the future. Effectiveness rates, based on statistical estimates, are another key consideration (see "Birth Control Guide"). FDA is developing a more consumer-friendly table to be added to the labeling of all contraceptive drugs and devices.

Barrier Methods

• **Male condom.** The male condom is a sheath placed over the erect penis before penetration, preventing pregnancy by blocking the passage of sperm.

A condom can be used only once. Some have spermicide added, usually nonoxynol-9 in the United States, to kill sperm. Spermicide has not been scientifically shown to provide additional contraceptive protection over the condom alone. Because they act

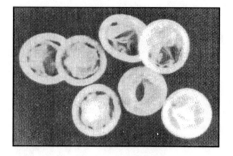

Photos from: Planned Parenthood Federation

as a mechanical barrier, condoms prevent direct vaginal contact with semen, infectious genital secretions, and genital lesions and discharges.

Most condoms are made from latex rubber, while a small percentage are made from lamb intestines (sometimes called "lambskin" condoms). Condoms made from polyurethane have been marketed in the United States since 1994.

Except for abstinence, latex condoms are the most effective method for reducing the risk of infection from the viruses that cause AIDS, other HIV-related illnesses, and other STDs.

Some condoms are prelubricated. These lubricants don't provide more birth control or STD protection. Non-oil-based lubricants, such as water or KY jelly, can be used with latex or lambskin condoms, but oil-based lubricants, such as petroleum jelly (Vaseline), lotions, or massage or baby oil, should not be used because they can weaken the material.

• **Female condom.** The Reality Female Condom, approved by FDA in April 1993, consists of a lubricated polyurethane sheath shaped similarly to the male condom. The closed end, which has a flexible ring, is inserted

into the vagina, while the open end remains outside, partially covering the labia.

The female condom, like the male condom, is available without a prescription and is intended for one-time use. It should not be used together with a male condom because they may not both stay in place.

• **Diaphragm.** Available by prescription only and sized by a health professional to achieve a proper fit, the diaphragm has a dual mechanism to prevent pregnancy. A dome-shaped rubber disk with a flexible rim covers the cervix so sperm can't reach the uterus, while a spermicide applied to the diaphragm before insertion kills sperm.

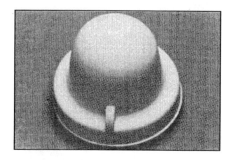

The diaphragm protects for six hours. For intercourse after the six-hour period, or for repeated intercourse within this period, fresh spermicide should be placed in the vagina with the diaphragm still in place. The diaphragm should be left in place for at least six hours after the last intercourse but not for longer than a total of 24 hours because of the risk of toxic shock syndrome (TSS), a rare but potentially fatal infection. Symptoms of TSS include sudden fever, stomach upset, sunburn-like rash, and a drop in blood pressure.

• **Cervical cap.** The cap is a soft rubber cup with a round rim, sized by a health professional to fit snugly around the cervix. It is available by prescription only and, like the diaphragm, is used with spermicide.

It protects for 48 hours and for multiple acts of intercourse within this time. Wearing it for more than 48 hours is not recommended because of the risk, though low, of TSS. Also, with prolonged use of two or more days, the cap may cause an unpleasant vaginal odor or discharge in some women.

• **Sponge.** The vaginal contraceptive sponge has not been available since the sole manufacturer, Whitehall Laboratories of Madison, N.J., voluntarily stopped selling it in 1995. It remains an approved product and could be marketed again.

The sponge, a donut-shaped polyurethane device containing the spermicide nonoxynol-9, is inserted into the vagina to cover the cervix. A woven polyester loop is designed to ease removal.

The sponge protects for up to 24 hours and for multiple acts of intercourse within this time. It should be left in place for at least six hours after intercourse but should be removed no more than 30 hours after insertion because of the risk, though low, of TSS.

Vaginal Spermicides Alone

Vaginal spermicides are available in foam, cream, jelly, film, suppository, or tablet forms. All types contain a sperm-killing chemical.

Studies have not produced definitive data on the efficacy of spermicides alone, but according to the authors of *Contraceptive Technology*, a leading resource for contraceptive information, the failure rate for typical users may be 21 percent per year.

Package instructions must be carefully followed because some spermicide products require the couple to wait 10 minutes or more after inserting the spermicide before having sex. One dose of spermicide is usually effective for one hour. For repeated intercourse, additional spermicide must be applied. And after intercourse, the spermicide has to remain in place for at least six to eight hours to ensure that all sperm are killed. The woman should not douche or rinse the vagina during this time.

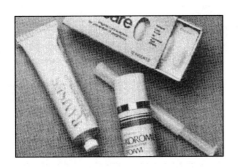

Hormonal Methods

• *Combined oral contraceptives.* Typically called "the pill," combined oral contraceptives have been on the market for more than 35 years and are the most popular form of reversible birth control in the United States. This form of birth control suppresses ovulation (the monthly release of an egg from the ovaries) by the combined actions of the hormones estrogen and progestin.

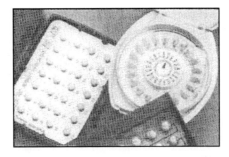

If a woman remembers to take the pill every day as directed, she has an extremely low chance of becoming pregnant in a year. But the pill's effectiveness may be reduced if the woman is taking some medications, such as certain antibiotics.

Besides preventing pregnancy, the pill offers additional benefits. As stated in the labeling, the pill can make periods more regular. It also has a protective effect against pelvic inflammatory disease, an infection of the fallopian tubes or uterus that is a major cause of infertility in women, and against ovarian and endometrial cancers.

The decision whether to take the pill should be made in consultation with a health professional. Birth control pills are safe for most women—safer even than delivering a baby—but they carry some risks.

Current low-dose pills have fewer risks associated with them than earlier versions. But women who smoke—especially those over 35—and women with certain medical conditions, such as a history of blood clots or breast or endometrial cancer, may be advised against taking the pill. The pill may contribute to cardiovascular disease, including high blood pressure, blood clots, and blockage of the arteries.

One of the biggest questions has been whether the pill increases the risk of breast cancer in past and current pill users. An international study published in the September 1996 journal *Contraception* concluded that women's risk of breast cancer 10 years after going off birth control pills was no higher than that of women who had never used the pill. During pill use and for the first 10 years after stopping the pill, women's risk of breast cancer was only slightly higher in pill users than non-pill users.

Side effects of the pill, which often subside after a few months' use, include nausea, headache, breast tenderness, weight gain, irregular bleeding, and depression.

Doctors sometimes prescribe higher doses of combined oral contraceptives for use as "morning after" pills to be taken within 72 hours of unprotected intercourse to prevent the possibly fertilized egg from reaching the uterus. In a Feb. 25, 1997, *Federal Register* notice, FDA stated its conclusion that, on the basis of current scientific evidence, certain oral contraceptives are safe and effective for this use.

• *Minipills.* Although taken daily like combined oral contraceptives, minipills contain only the hormone progestin and no estrogen. They work by reducing and thickening cervical mucus to prevent sperm from reaching the egg. They also keep the uterine lining from thickening, which prevents a fertilized egg from implanting in the uterus. These pills are generally less effective than combined oral contraceptives.

Minipills can decrease menstrual bleeding and cramps, as well as the risk of endometrial and ovarian cancer and pelvic inflammatory disease. Because they contain no estrogen, minipills don't present the risk of blood clots associated with estrogen in combined pills. They are a good option for women who can't take estrogen because they are breast-feeding or because estrogen-containing prod-

Birth Control Guide

Efficacy rates in this chart are based on Contraceptive Technology (16th edition, 1994). They are yearly estimates of effectiveness in typical use, which refers to a method's reliability in real life, when people don't always use a method properly. For comparison, about 85 percent of sexually active women using no contraception would be expected to become pregnant in a year.

This chart is a summary; it is not intended to be used alone. All product labeling should be followed carefully, and a health-care professional should be consulted for some methods.

Type	Male Condom	Female Condom	Diaphragm with Spermicide	Cervical Cap with Spermicide	Sponge with Spermicide (not currently marketed)	Spermicides Alone
Estimated Effectiveness	88%[a]	79%	82%	64–82%[b]	64–82%[b]	79%
Some Risks[d]	Irritation and allergic reactions (less likely with polyurethane)	Irritation and allergic reactions	Irritation and allergic reactions, urinary tract infection	Irritation and allergic reactions, abnormal Pap test	Irritation and allergic reactions, difficulty in removal	Irritation and allergic reactions
Protection from Sexually Transmitted Diseases (STDs)	Except for abstinence, latex condoms are the best protection against STDs, including herpes and AIDS.	May give some STD protection; not as effective as latex condom.	Protects against cervical infection; spermicide may give some protection against chlamydia and gonorrhea; otherwise unknown.	Spermicide may give some protection against chlamydia and gonorrhea; otherwise unknown.	Spermicide may give some protection against chlamydia and gonorrhea; otherwise unknown.	May give some protection against chlamydia and gonorrhea; otherwise unknown.
Convenience	Applied immediately before intercourse; used only once and discarded.	Applied immediately before intercourse; used only once and discarded.	Inserted before intercourse and left in place at least six hours after; can be left in place for 24 hours, with additional spermicide for repeated intercourse.	May be difficult to insert; can remain in place for 48 hours without reapplying spermicide for repeated intercourse.	Inserted before intercourse and protects for 24 hours without additional spermicide; must be left in place for at least six hours after intercourse; must be removed within 30 hours of insertion; used only once and discarded.	Instructions vary: usually applied no more than one hour before intercourse and left in place at least six to eight hours after.
Availability	Non-prescription	Non-prescription	Prescription	Prescription	Nonprescription; not currently marketed.	Nonprescription

a Effectiveness rate for polyurethane condoms has not been established.
b Less effective for women who have had a baby because the birth process stretches the vagina and cervix, making it more difficult to achieve a proper fit.
c Based on perfect use, when the woman takes the pill every day as directed.
d Serious medical risks from contraceptives are rare.

Oral Contraceptives—combined pill	Oral Contraceptives—progestin-only minipill	Injection (Depo-Provera)	Implant (Norplant)	IUD (Intrauterine Device)	Periodic Abstinence	Surgical Sterilization—female or male
Over 99%[c]	Over 99%[c]	Over 99%	Over 99%	98–99%	About 80% (varies, based on method)	Over 99%
Dizziness; nausea; changes in menstruation, mood, and weight; rarely, cardiovascular disease, including high blood pressure, blood clots, heart attack, and strokes	Ectopic pregnancy, irregular bleeding, weight gain, breast tenderness	Irregular bleeding, weight gain, breast tenderness, headaches	Irregular bleeding, weight gain, breast tenderness, headaches, difficulty in removal	Cramps, bleeding, pelvic inflammatory disease, infertility, perforation of uterus	None	Pain, bleeding, infection, other minor postsurgical complications
None, except some protection against pelvic inflammatory disease.	None, except some protection against pelvic inflammatory disease.	None	None	None	None	None
Must be taken on daily schedule, regardless of frequency of intercourse.	Must be taken on daily schedule, regardless of frequency of intercourse.	One injection every three months	Implanted by health-care provider—minor outpatient surgical procedure; effective for up to five years.	After insertion by physician, can remain in place for up to one or 10 years, depending on type.	Requires frequent monitoring of body functions (for example, body temperature for one method).	One-time surgical procedure
Prescription	Prescription	Prescription	Prescription	Prescription	Instructions from health-care provider	Surgery

ucts cause them to have severe head-aches or high blood pressure.

Side effects of minipills include menstrual cycle changes, weight gain, and breast tenderness.

• *Injectable progestins.* Depo-Provera, approved by FDA in 1992, is injected by a health professional into the buttocks or arm muscle every three months. Depo-Provera prevents pregnancy in three ways: It inhibits ovulation, changes the cervical mucus to help prevent sperm from reaching the egg, and changes the uterine lining to prevent the fertilized egg from implanting in the uterus. The progestin injection is extremely effective in preventing pregnancy, in large part because it requires little effort for the woman to comply: She simply has to get an injection by a doctor once every three months.

The benefits are similar to those of the minipill and another progestin-only contraceptive, Norplant. Side effects are also similar and can include irregular or missed periods, weight gain, and breast tenderness.

(See "Depo-Provera: The Quarterly Contraceptive" in the March 1993 *FDA Consumer.*)

• *Implantable progestins.* Norplant, approved by FDA in 1990, and the newer Norplant 2, approved in 1996, are the third type of progestin-only contraceptive. Made up of match-stick-sized rubber rods, this contraceptive is surgically implanted under the skin of the upper arm, where it steadily releases the contraceptive steroid levonorgestrel.

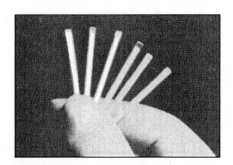

The six-rod Norplant provides protection for up to five years (or until it is removed), while the two-rod Norplant 2 protects for up to three years.

Norplant failures are rare, but are higher with increased body weight.

Some women may experience inflammation or infection at the site of the implant. Other side effects include menstrual cycle changes, weight gain, and breast tenderness.

Intrauterine Devices

An IUD is a T-shaped device inserted into the uterus by a health-care professional. Two types of IUDs are available in the United States: the Paragard CopperT 380A and the Progestasert Progesterone T. The Paragard IUD can remain in place for 10 years, while the Progestasert IUD must be replaced every year.

It's not entirely clear how IUDs prevent pregnancy. They seem to prevent sperm and eggs from meeting by either immobilizing the sperm on their way to the fallopian tubes or changing the uterine lining so the fertilized egg cannot implant in it.

IUDs have one of the lowest failure rates of any contraceptive method. "In the population for which the IUD is appropriate—for those in a mutually monogamous, stable relationship who aren't at a high risk of infection—the IUD is a very safe and very effective method of contraception," says Lisa Rarick, M.D., director of FDA's division of reproductive and urologic drug products.

The IUD's image suffered when the Dalkon Shield IUD was taken off the market in 1975. This IUD was associated with a high incidence of pelvic infections and infertility, and some deaths. Today, serious complications from IUDs are rare, although IUD users may be at increased risk of developing pelvic inflammatory disease. Other side effects can include perforation of the uterus, abnormal bleeding, and cramps. Complications occur most often during and immediately after insertion.

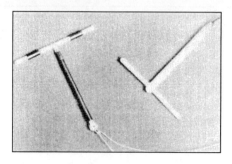

Traditional Methods

• *Fertility awareness.* Also known as natural family planning or periodic abstinence, fertility awareness entails not having sexual intercourse on the days of a woman's menstrual cycle when she could become pregnant or using a barrier method of birth control on those days.

Because a sperm may live in the female's reproductive tract for up to seven days and the egg remains fertile for about 24 hours, a woman can get pregnant within a substantial window of time—from seven days before ovulation to three days after. Methods

to approximate when a woman is fertile are usually based on the menstrual cycle, changes in cervical mucus, or changes in body temperature.

"Natural family planning can work," Rarick says, "but it takes an extremely motivated couple to use the method effectively."

• *Withdrawal.* In this method, also called *coitus interruptus,* the man withdraws his penis from the vagina before ejaculation. Fertilization is prevented because the sperm don't enter the vagina.

Effectiveness depends on the male's ability to withdraw before ejaculation. Also, withdrawal doesn't provide protection from STDs, including HIV.

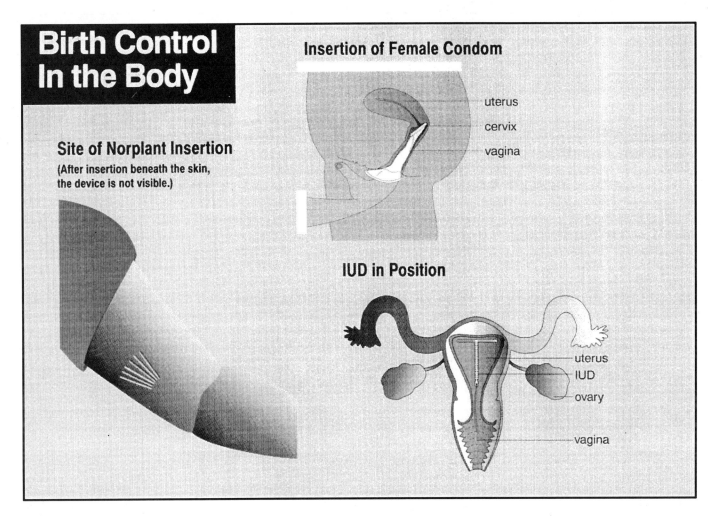

Birth Control In the Body

Site of Norplant Insertion
(After insertion beneath the skin, the device is not visible.)

Insertion of Female Condom

- uterus
- cervix
- vagina

IUD in Position

- uterus
- IUD
- ovary
- vagina

Infectious diseases can be transmitted by direct contact with surface lesions and by pre-ejaculatory fluid.

Surgical Sterilization

Surgical sterilization is a contraceptive option intended for people who don't want children in the future. It is considered permanent because reversal requires major surgery that is often unsuccessful.

- *Female sterilization.* Female sterilization blocks the fallopian tubes so the egg can't travel to the uterus. Sterilization is done by various surgical techniques performed under general anesthesia.

Complications from these operations are rare and can include infection, hemorrhage, and problems related to the use of general anesthesia.

- *Male sterilization.* This procedure, called a vasectomy, involves sealing, tying or cutting a man's vas deferens, which otherwise would carry the sperm from the testicle to the penis.

Vasectomy involves a quick operation, usually under 30 minutes, with possible minor postsurgical complications, such as bleeding or infection.

Research continues on effective contraceptives that minimize side effects. One important research focus, according to FDA's Rarick, is the development of birth control methods that are both spermicidal and microbicidal to prevent not only pregnancy but also transmission of HIV and other STDs.

Tamar Nordenberg is a staff writer for FDA Consumer.

THE BRAVE NEW
WORLD OF PARENTING

More and more couples who might never have
been able to conceive are now giving birth, thanks
to high-tech infertility treatments. But as parents,
they face unexpected emotional challenges

BY JESSICA SNYDER SACHS

LAURA BENCIVENGA GETS LIVID WHEN HER HUSBAND GRUMBLES
about their toddler waking them in the night. "He'll mutter
something under his breath, and I'll say, 'How can you
say that? We worked so hard for this,' " she says. "I guess
I don't feel we have the right to complain."

Infertility is a heartache shared by over five million
couples in this country. Thanks to advances in technology,
however, pregnancy and parenthood are now possible for
more than half of these families.

Possible, perhaps, but seldom easy. Infertility treatment
can involve years of powerful drugs, hormone injections,
and an alphabet soup of such invasive procedures as IVF
(in vitro fertilization), GIFT (gamete intrafallopian transfer), and ZIFT (zygote intrafallopian transfer). Many couple also grapple with difficult decisions about whether to
use donor sperm or eggs, or even a surrogate mother.

These high-tech routes to parenthood, collectively known as assisted reproductive technology (ART), often don't work, but they do result in more than 16,000 babies each year in the U.S. alone. Studies show that ART babies are as healthy as those conceived "the easy way." It's their parents who have the experts concerned.

"Infertility and years of aggressive treatment can leave wounds that don't entirely heal," says therapist Ellen Glazer, coauthor of *Choosing Assisted Reproductions: Social, Emotional, and Ethical Considerations* and the mother of two daughters, 14 and 17, one through adoption and the other with the help of fertility treatments. "You make promises to yourself like, If I'm ever a parent, I'll never complain, I'll always be patient, I'll never take my child for granted."

Such unrealistic expectations aren't restricted to the previously infertile, of course; nor are separation anxiety or worries about a baby's health or one's competence as a parent. But years of fertility treatments can dramatically inflate not only expectations but also insecurities and fears.

Midnight grumblings aside, Barrett Bencivenga, of Short Hills, New Jersey, admits to a painfully intense protectiveness for his 2½-year-old daughter, Caroline: "We're so lucky to have her, I feel I have to make sure nothing happens to her." When Caroline was learning to walk, Daddy became her shadow, his outstretched arms trying to keep gravity at bay. "At work, I find myself worrying about where she is and what she's doing," he says. Not just once in a while, but many times throughout the day. "I don't want to be stifling," he says. "I know she needs to explore her world."

Acknowledging such feelings can be tremendously helpful, according to infertility and adoption educator Patricia Irwin-Johnston, author of *Taking Charge of Infertility.* "Parents who have worked through the medical as well as emotional ramifications of infertility, and who understand how their losses can continue to play a role in their lives, are among the best parents I know," she says.

THE ROYAL TREATMENT?

Six years ago, an article in *The New York Times Magazine* posed the question "What does it feel like being a $100,000 baby?" The assumption was that any child conceived at such great expense and effort was bound to be spoiled rotten and to fail the impossible task of justifying her cost in the eyes of her parents.

Michael and Pamela Stevinson, of Madera, California, confess to giving their in vitro twins anything they want. "When their second birthday came around, our house had more toys than Toys 'R' Us," says their mom.

Once-infertile couples need to free themselves of the self-imposed obligation to be superparents

Adding fuel to the Stevinsons' overindulgence is the fact that they underwent a procedure called fetal reduction. Like hundreds of other couples who've used in vitro fertilization, they had agreed to the implantation of multiple embryos, four of which took. Eighteen weeks into the pregnancy, specialists urged reducing the pregnancy to twins to improve the odds of healthy births. (Quadruplets are more than 13 times likelier to die within the first year than single-birth children. Twins face five times the risk.) "Our joy came with a bittersweet reminder of those we lost," says Pamela. "How can we help but overindulge?"

Still, most experts say that the stereotype of the spoiled "test-tube baby" is inaccurate. "We just don't find the His-Majesty-the-Baby stuff among the families we've studied," says Dorothy Greenfeld, director of psychological services at the Yale Center for Reproductive Medicine. "As a group, these children aren't any more spoiled than others."

Part of the reason may be that the long ordeal of infertility treatment inspires many parents to invest extra effort in disciplining their kids. "All those years of waiting gave us plenty of time to see how we didn't want our children to behave," says Pat Kotsakis, of Palatine, Illinois, now the mother of a 5-, a 7-, and a 9-year-old. "It bothered us to see other kids acting bratty and spoiled."

Still, discipline *can* involve an inner struggle, according to Tom and Margaret Potter, of Bridgewater, New Jersey. "Sometimes I feel guilty after raising my voice to my older daughter," says Margaret. "I think, How could I? She's such an incredible gift!" The Potters' two children—Sarah, 4, and Brooke, 1½—were born with the help of in vitro fertilization and a gestational surrogate. Margaret's uterus, but not her ovaries, had been removed due to cervical cancer.

"WHERE DID I COME FROM?"

Kids delight in hearing the story of their birth, but the telling can fluster a parent who has traveled the high-tech route to pregnancy.

Making the project easier are two helpful guidebooks: *The Long-Awaited Stork: A Guide to Parenting After Infertility,* by therapist Ellen Glazer (Jossey-Bass); and *Flight of the Stork: What Children Think (and When) About Sex and Family Building,* by family psychologist Anne Bernstein (Perspective Press).

IN THE BEGINNING Around age 3 or 4, according to Bernstein, kids become curious about where they came from. Their questions are a natural opportunity to broach the subject, but parents need to be careful not to overwhelm their children with technical details. "When conception involves the mother's egg and father's sperm, I see no need to tell the child how that egg and sperm got together," says Bernstein. "After all, if your child was conceived in bed, you wouldn't discuss sexual positions."

EXTRA EXPLANATIONS Kids born through sperm or egg donation need more information. Bernstein gives this example of what a parent might say:

"Babies grow in the mother's uterus. To start the baby, a woman's egg and a man's sperm must join together. But sometimes, when a woman and a man try to start a baby, a baby doesn't grow. There are lots of reasons why that can happen. Sometimes, the father's sperm/mother's egg isn't strong or healthy. If the man and woman really want to grow a baby, they may get sperm/eggs from a man/woman who wants to help."

CALMING WORDS Some kids may need reassurance that the donor was not a parent who rejected them:

Child: "Why didn't the man/woman who gave the sperm/eggs want to be my daddy/mommy?"

Parent: "This person didn't know you. He/she gave his sperm/egg because he/she wanted to help, not because he/she was ready to be a daddy/mommy."

"The concepts take time for children to assimilate," says Bernstein. "Encourage questions, and let them know you're open to their concerns without making them feel like they're different." —J.S.S.

GREAT EXPECTATIONS

Sometimes the long, arduous course of infertility treatment and waiting can result in parents who become demanding, as if their children have some kind of debt to pay, says Diane Clapp, a counselor with RESOLVE, a national infertility support and advocacy group. But by expecting brilliance or perfect behavior all the time, they place an unfair burden on the kids. "Such parents need to remember that the infertility treatment was something they did themselves," she says. Children should never have to carry any burden because of the mechanics of their conception.

More common are the overblown expectations that once-infertile parents place on *themselves*. "It's as if they don't feel deserving if they're anything less than perfect," says Glazer. Laura Bencivenga, for example, recalls her extreme dismay at Caroline's first diaper rash, which developed two weeks after she was born. "I felt totally incompetent, like I couldn't even put on a diaper right," she says. Fortunately, Bencivenga's sister assured her that such ailments are common and are not a reflection of a person's ability to raise a child. Experts advise parents like Bencivenga to try to free themselves of self-imposed obligations to be superparents.

Also common is the assumption that child rearing will be nothing but a joy, says Clapp. Parents may fantasize about how perfect life will be when their baby finally arrives. Then, when the reality of midnight crying and endless diapers finally hits, normal feelings of resentment can stir up guilt.

Previously infertile parents need to give themselves permission occasionally to resent the day-to-day drudgery and strain of parenthood—and even to complain, the way other parents do, says Clapp.

A IS FOR ANXIETY

Infertility can shake a person's self-confidence to the core. "Many of the couples I see had been very successful in their lives," says Judith Kottick, counseling coordinator for the department of reproductive medicine at Saint Barnabas Medical Center, in Livingston, New Jersey. "Then infertility hit them and shattered their rosy view. Many struggle with feelings that they're somehow incapable and that they were never meant to be parents." Admits Laura Bencivenga: The experience of infertility has never left me. I still second-guess myself on everything that has to do with being a parent."

Some parents who've been through a series of infertility treatments become overanxious about their baby's health. Janet Moller (not her real name), of Boston, confesses to steering her 9-month-old son clear of playgroups and crowded restaurants, where germs may abound. "The prospect of any-

Some expectant parents feel so vulnerable that they refuse to embrace the pregnancy or birth for fear of tempting fate

thing happening to this baby is too terrible to imagine," she says. After eight years of trying, Moller and her husband had a child with the help of a surrogate, who donated her egg and also carried the baby to term. "It's as if years of miscarriages and failed attempts at pregnancy have robbed these parents of their naïveté that things will be okay," says Judith Lewis, Ph.D., a nurse researcher at Virginia Commonwealth University. "They expect things to go wrong."

It may be no surprise, then, that midnight finds more than a few such parents checking to make sure their baby is still breathing. "I know all parents do it occasionally," says Margo Rush, of Shelton, Connecticut. "But I do it a lot more than most." Rush's son, Jonathan (now 20 months), was born after five miscarriages and four years of infertility treatment. "I think it's still in the back of my mind that I might lose him, that this is too good to be true."

After two years of infertility treatment and a heart-wrenching experience with fetal reduction, Michael Stevinson found himself afraid to hold his newborn twins, Douglas and Michelle. "He never talked about it," says his wife, Pamela. "But I know he was scared to get attached, afraid that they might die too."

In a recent study of previously infertile mothers, Lewis found that 90 percent brought babies home to nurseries so sparsely furnished, some didn't even have a crib. She calls it "vulnerable parent syndrome." It's as if these parents fear they'd be tempting fate if they let themselves embrace the reality of pregnancy and birth.

In many cases, feelings of fear and denial begin to subside in the first days or weeks after birth. Occasionally, Lewis says, they linger longer.

For some, a feeling of impending doom magnifies separation anxiety. "Other parents tend to look back on their childless days with an easy fondness," says Glazer. "They look forward to having time to themselves again, if only for an occasional night out.

But for infertile couples, revisiting the feeling of being 'without child' can be terribly painful."

Glazer encourages such parents to be patient with themselves. "There will be times when it will feel easier to let go and others when you'll need to hold on," she says. "It's part of a process that will go on for years."

TOO MUCH TOO SOON?

Infertile couples sometimes feel compelled to jump back on the treatment treadmill soon after their baby's arrival, before it's too late to conceive again. Within seven months of giving birth, Laura Bencivenga, then 41, was back on fertility drugs and preparing for another cycle of in vitro fertilization. She was almost relieved when her doctors told her that her ovaries were no longer responding. "I knew I didn't want to put my body and my family through this anymore," she says with resignation.

There are no easy answers to the question of when new parents should resume infertility treatment, but experts advise that they give themselves a hefty dose of compassion. "Realize that you may be emotionally exhausted from your first go-around with new parenthood," says Clapp. Parents should weigh the importance of rushing back into treatment against the need to savor their baby and recoup their inner strength. What can help: close friends and family, or even a secondary infertility support group through a local chapter of RESOLVE or an infertility clinic.

WHEN DONOR MAKES THREE

Over 300,000 children in this country have been born through donor insemination. And though not as common, babies born through egg donation are rapidly increasing in number, from a few hundred per year in the 1980s to several thousand annually today.

Since one parent will lack genetic ties to the child, counselors at fertility clinics urge prospective parents to carefully explore their feelings before pursuing this route to conception. Still, they shouldn't be surprised if certain issues resurface after birth, says Anne Bernstein, Ph.D., a psychologist in Berkeley, California. Sometimes the parent without a genetic link ends up feeling less legitimate than the other, and retreats emotionally.

Many parents worry that a child born through the help of a donor may feel stigmatized or may someday reject them as "real" parents. For these and other reasons, parents may choose not to reveal that the conception was donor-aided, even to their own child.

But psychologists caution about the effects of such secrecy. "There will be times when the child will pick up that something

MINDING YOUR MARRIAGE

Infertility treatment can take a terrible toll on a couple's sex life. Feelings of failure can taint the intimacy and passion between partners. Years of scheduled intercourse can wear down their sense of spontaneity and fun. And the stigma of infertility can warp a woman's image of herself, says Judith Lewis, Ph.D., of Virginia Commonwealth University's School of Nursing.

Men commonly suffer sexual dysfunction after infertility treatment. Though seldom required to undergo invasive surgical procedures, men can be affected by the cold, mechanical nature of supplying sperm for in vitro fertilization into a cup.

And the transition to parenthood—a stress on any marriage—can add further strain.

Experts emphasize that talking about your feelings is essential, giving each other some room to grumble, as well as lots of love and support.

Make an effort to revive dating too. "Within a few months after the birth, you need to get out, just the two of you," says Peter Kaplan, M.D., a clinical instructor of psychiatry at the New York University School of Medicine.

"Now that you're launched as a family," says therapist Ellen Glazer, "it's time to begin reexperiencing the pleasure and passion that were part of your relationship and inspired you to have a family."

—J. S. S.

is wrong," says Bernstein. "It may be a pinched expression when someone tells the parent, 'Oh, he looks just like you,' or an awkward silence when the pediatrician asks about family medical history."

Like many mental health workers, Bernstein urges parents to be open with their children. "The question is, do you want to spring this potentially mind-blowing information on a child when he's a teenager, or introduce it naturally, early on, as part of the story of his birth?"

For better or worse, secrecy isn't an option for the thousands of single women who become mothers through donor insemination. Linda Gerhart, of Plano, Texas, is already anticipating the day when 9-month-old Brandon asks, "Where's Daddy?" Among the things that Gerhart will share with her son is an audiotape of his biological father, in which he talks about himself and the altruistic reasons that he chose to become a sperm donor.

"It would be dishonest to say that I didn't want my genes to be carried on, that I didn't want my children to look like me, be like me," admits Mark Sullivan (not his real name), of suburban Maryland. His and his wife's two children, 3 and 5, were conceived through donor insemination.

Sullivan feels comfortable as a father today, he says, because he acknowledged his loss. "There's a residue of sadness," he says. "But I know that I'm not less of a father." He and his wife have formed a support group for parents of children conceived with donor sperm or eggs. "Now, as we tell the kids the story of their birth, we can point out friends born in a similar way."

Janet Moller and her husband have chosen to stay in contact with the egg donor, who also carried their son to term. (Janet has legally adopted the child.) "He will know that he's special because he has two mommies who love him," she says. He will also know that he has a half-brother by his birth mom. "If and how a relationship evolves remains to be seen," she says.

Whatever the circumstances of their birth, what kids need most is a sense of confidence. "Both parents and children need to come to believe that they are entitled to and deserving of one another and that they belong together," says Irwin-Johnston. The biggest gift moms and dads can give their children, she adds, is to fully embrace their wonderful new role as parents.

Contributing editor JESSICA SNYDER SACHS *is a science and health writer and the former editor of* Science Digest.

Pregnant *pleasures*

Your sex life will change . . . maybe for the better.

By Caren Osten Gerszberg

The question of whether a woman is sexy during pregnancy was never debated on CNN—until actress Hunter Tylo sued the makers of *Melrose Place* for pregnancy discrimination last year. The actress had been fired after becoming pregnant; the producers felt that she couldn't realistically play the role of a seductress (even if her belly was hidden from view). A jury of ten women and two men sided with Tylo, awarding her almost $5 million.

Although Tylo felt confident about the fact that she was as alluring as ever, it's hard for most pregnant women to feel like sex symbols. Plagued by fatigue and morning sickness in her first trimester, Trish Ratliff, of Fort Eustis, Virginia, for example, says that making love was the last thing on her mind. She also had visible stretch marks on her breasts, hips, and thighs, which made her feel self-conscious about her body. On the other hand, Laurie Greenberg, of New York City, was surprised to find that she constantly seemed to be in the mood. Everything seems to take on a new shape during pregnancy—your body, your future, and, inevitably, your sex drive.

It would be remarkable, in fact, if pregnancy had no effect on sexual desire, because your libido is linked to both the physical and emotional changes you're experiencing, notes Christiane Northrup, M.D, assistant clinical professor of obstetrics and gynecology at the University of Vermont, in Burlington. In a normal pregnancy, sexual intercourse is safe and healthy right until the very end, even in a slightly modified version of the man on top. Many women actually find that it's the most enjoyable sex they've ever had, according to Northrup, who is the author of *Women's Bodies, Women's Wisdom* (Bantam).

For many expectant mothers, pregnancy is a rare opportunity to have spontaneous sex. "It's very exciting not having to worry about birth control or trying to get pregnant," says Lee Dannay, of New York City. "Without either concern, I can just relax and enjoy the moment."

When your partner takes delight in your changing appearance, it can help alleviate anxiety you may feel about your burgeoning body. Once her morning sickness subsided, Trish Ratliff liked the way her husband watched her as she dressed or undressed. "He wanted to make love as much as he always had, and he particularly loved touching my breasts, because they were twice as big as they used to be."

Laurie Greenberg's husband, Ira, however, admitted that he was less turned on, even though he responded whenever she initiated lovemaking. "It didn't really bother me," says Laurie, "because the thought of a beautiful baby growing inside of me made me feel very good about my body."

Of course, in addition to raising emotional issues in bed, your changing shape also poses physical ones. Nausea can make any sexual position uncomfortable if pressure is placed on your abdomen. And your size may keep you from feeling either agile or alluring.

However, sexual desire returns to normal for most women during the middle trimester, when their bodies have adjusted to pregnancy and size isn't a major obstacle. In fact, increased blood flow to the pelvic area caused by hormonal changes can produce a heightened sensitivity, explains Northrup, allowing some pregnant women to experience orgasm more easily and more frequently—or maybe even for the first time in their life.

Don't worry—you won't hurt the baby

Both of you may be concerned that intercourse could harm the baby, but it is well protected by the amniotic sac and the mucous plug, which blocks the cervix and guards against infection. Some couples even have the irrational notion that the baby seems to be "watching" them.

As your pregnancy progresses, you may have to experiment with different positions. Some doctors suggest having vaginal intercourse facing each other side by side, or in the spooning position, in which your partner lies behind you; this prevents excess pressure from being placed on your belly.

"Positions that might be dangerous are going to be very uncomfortable," says Linda Hughey Holt, M.D., director of the Institute for Women's Health at Evanston Northwestern Healthcare, in Evanston, Illinois, and coauthor of *The Pregnancy Book* (Little, Brown & Co.). "A woman in her ninth month, for example, shouldn't lie with her full weight on her belly, but she wouldn't be able to anyway." Similarly, a man should use his arms to support himself when he's lying on top.

Sex has been shown to speed up labor only when a woman is at term or past her due date. In normal pregnancies, there is no direct link between intercourse earlier on and the start of labor. Sometimes, however, a doctor may rec-

Reprinted with permission from *Parents* magazine, April 1998, pp. 89-90, a publication of Gruner & Jahr USA Publishing. © 1998 by Caren Osten Gerszberg.

Too embarrassed to ask your doctor?

Q: Sometimes urine trickles out during sex. Is this normal?
A: Yes. This can happen during intercourse if there's pressure put on your belly. The muscles in the bladder also tend to relax during pregnancy, causing small amounts of urine to leak in some women when they laugh, cough, or sneeze.

Q: Is it okay for my partner to perform oral sex on me?
A: Generally, yes. In very rare instances, forcefully blowing air into the vagina can cause an amniotic fluid embolism—air enters the uterus and forces amniotic fluid into the mother's circulatory system—which could be fatal to both mother and baby.

Q: Why do my breasts leak when my husband touches them?
A: When the nipples are stimulated during the last weeks of pregnancy, they may leak colostrum, a protein-filled liquid produced for the baby before the milk comes in. (Nipple stimulation also can cause the uterus to contract, but there's no reason to avoid it in a healthy pregnancy.)

Q: In my last pregnancy, I was overdue, and having sex finally started my labor. I'm worried that sex may cause me to go into labor early this time. Is that possible?
A: Although sexual intercourse can trigger uterine contractions that may lead to labor, it's not a cause of premature labor. However, if you are at risk for preterm labor because of a prior history, if you're carrying twins, or if your cervix has started to dilate, your doctor may suggest that you abstain.

ommend limiting or abstaining from sex after a certain point if you have a prior history of early contractions or preterm labor, since nipple stimulation and orgasm may trigger contractions. Sex also should be avoided by women who have placenta previa, a condition in which the placenta covers the cervix.

If you've had a prior miscarriage, your doctor may suggest abstaining from sex during the first trimester, just to be on the safe side. Although there is no causal connection between intercourse and miscarriage, it's possible that your uterus may be especially sensitive. Lynn Gallop, of Wilmington, North Carolina, had six first-trimester miscarriages before getting pregnant with her son, Jack. "My doctor told us we could start having sex after four months, but I was always too scared," she says. If you notice any spotting or bleeding, have pain during intercourse, or if your water breaks, stop having sex immediately and call your doctor.

This is also the perfect time to experiment with alternative ways to express your affection, from foot rubs to taking baths together. Your comfort level—both physical and emotional—should determine how often you have sex and when. Whether it's a question of general anxiety or a specific technique, communication is the best way for you and your partner to maintain a healthy sex life. "Once I explained to my husband that my nipples were very sensitive but I still enjoyed it when he touched the rest of my breast, he changed his technique, and it felt good," says Ratliff. And if the two of you can talk openly about your sex life now, you'll also feel more comfortable discussing it after the baby arrives.

Caren Oslen Gerszberg is a freelance writer in Larchmont, New York.

pFsEyTcAHLOLOGY

Behaviorally speaking, there's little difference between a newborn baby and a 32-week-old fetus. A new wave of research suggests that the fetus can feel, dream, even enjoy *The Cat in the Hat*. The abortion debate may never be the same.

By Janet L. Hopson

The scene never fails to give goose bumps: the baby, just seconds old and still dewy from the womb, is lifted into the arms of its exhausted but blissful parents. They gaze adoringly as their new child stretches and squirms, scrunches its mouth and opens its eyes. To anyone watching this tender vignette, the message is unmistakable. Birth is the beginning of it all, ground zero, the moment from which the clock starts ticking. Not so, declares Janet DiPietro. Birth may be a grand occasion, says the Johns Hopkins University psychologist, but "it is a trivial event in development. Nothing neurologically interesting happens."

Armed with highly sensitive and sophisticated monitoring gear, DiPietro and other researchers today are discovering that the real action starts weeks earlier. At 32 weeks of gestation—two months before a baby is considered fully prepared for the world, or "at term"—a fetus is behaving almost exactly as a newborn. And it continues to do so for the next 12 weeks.

As if overturning the common conception of infancy weren't enough, scientists are creating a startling new picture of intelligent life in the womb. Among the revelations:

• By nine weeks, a developing fetus can hiccup and react to loud noises. By the end of the second trimester it can hear.

• Just as adults do, the fetus experiences the rapid eye movement (REM) sleep of dreams.

• The fetus savors its mother's meals, first picking up the food tastes of a culture in the womb.

A fetus spends hours in the rapid eye movement sleep of dreams.

• Among other mental feats, the fetus can distinguish between the voice of Mom and that of a stranger, and respond to a familiar story read to it.

• Even a premature baby is aware, feels, responds, and adapts to its environment.

• Just because the fetus is responsive to certain stimuli doesn't mean that it should be the target of efforts to enhance development. Sensory stimulation of the fetus can in fact lead to bizarre patterns of adaptation later on.

The roots of human behavior, researchers now know, begin to develop early—just weeks after conception, in fact. Well before a woman typically knows she is pregnant, her embryo's brain has already begun to bulge. By five weeks, the organ that looks like a lumpy inchworm has already embarked on the most spectacular feat of human development: the creation of the deeply creased and convoluted cerebral cortex, the part of the brain that will eventually allow the growing person to move, think, speak, plan, and create in a human way.

At nine weeks, the embryo's ballooning brain allows it to bend its body, hiccup, and react to loud sounds. At week ten, it moves its arms, "breathes" amniotic fluid in and out, opens its jaw, and stretches. Before the first trimester is over, it yawns, sucks, and swallows as well as feels and smells. By the end of the second trimester, it can hear; toward the end of pregnancy, it can see.

FETAL ALERTNESS

Scientists who follow the fetus' daily life find that it spends most of its time not exercising these new abilities but sleeping. At 32 weeks, it drowses 90 to 95% of the day. Some of these hours are spent in deep sleep, some in REM sleep, and some in an indeterminate state, a product of the fetus' immature brain that is different from sleep in a baby, child, or adult. During REM sleep, the fetus' eyes move back and forth just as an adult's eyes do, and many researchers believe that it is dreaming. DiPietro speculates that fetuses dream about what they know—the sensations they feel in the womb.

Closer to birth, the fetus sleeps 85 to 90% of the time, the same as a newborn. Between its frequent naps, the fetus seems to have "something like an awake alert period," according to developmental psychologist William Fifer, Ph.D., who with his Columbia University colleagues is monitoring these sleep and wakefulness cycles in order to identify patterns of normal and abnormal brain development, including potential predictors of

sudden infant death syndrome. Says Fifer, "We are, in effect, asking the fetus: 'Are you paying attention? Is your nervous system behaving in the appropriate way?' "

FETAL MOVEMENT

Awake or asleep, the human fetus moves 50 times or more each hour, flexing and extending its body, moving its head, face, and limbs and exploring its warm wet compartment by touch. Heidelise Als, Ph.D., a developmental psychologist at Harvard Medical School, is fascinated by the amount of tactile stimulation a fetus gives itself. "It touches a hand to the face, one hand to the other hand, clasps its feet, touches its foot to its leg, its hand to its umbilical cord," she reports.

Als believes there is a mismatch between the environment given to preemies in hospitals and the environment they would have had in the womb. She has been working for years to change the care given to preemies so that they can curl up, bring their knees together, and touch things with their hands as they would have for weeks in the womb.

Along with such common movements, DiPietro has also noted some odder fetal activities, including "licking the uterine wall and literally walking around the womb by pushing off with its feet." Laterborns may have more room in the womb for such maneuvers than first babies. After the initial pregnancy, a woman's uterus is bigger and the umbilical cord longer, allowing more freedom of movement. "Second and subsequent children may develop more motor experience in utero and so may become more active infants," DiPietro speculates.

Fetuses react sharply to their mother's actions. "When we're watching the fetus on ultrasound and the mother starts to laugh, we can see the fetus, floating upside down in the womb, bounce up and down on its head, bum-bum-bum, like it's bouncing on a trampoline," says DiPietro. "When mothers watch this on the screen, they laugh harder, and the fetus goes up and down even faster. We've wondered whether this is why people grow up liking roller coasters."

FETAL TASTE

Why people grow up liking hot chilies or spicy curries may also have something to do with the fetal environment. By 13 to 15 weeks a fetus' taste buds already look like a mature adult's, and doctors know that the amniotic fluid that surrounds it can smell strongly of curry, cumin,

By 15 weeks, a fetus has an adult's taste buds and may be able to savor its mother's meals.

What's the Impact on Abortion?

Though research in fetal psychology focuses on the last trimester, when most abortions are illegal, the thought of a fetus dreaming, listening and responding to its mother's voice is sure to add new complexity to the debate. The new findings undoubtedly will strengthen the convictions of right-to-lifers—and they may shake the certainty of pro-choice proponents who believe that mental life begins at birth.

Many of the scientists engaged in studying the fetus, however, remain detached from the abortion controversy, insisting that their work is completely irrelevant to the debate.

"I don't think that fetal research informs the issue at all," contends psychologist Janet DiPietro of Johns Hopkins University. "The essence of the abortion debate is: When does life begin? Some people believe it begins at conception, the other extreme believes that it begins after the baby is born, and there's a group in the middle that believes it begins at around 24 or 25 weeks, when a fetus can live outside of the womb, though it needs a lot of help to do so.

"Up to about 25 weeks, whether or not it's sucking its thumb or has personality or all that, the fetus cannot survive outside of its mother. So is that life, or not? That is a moral, ethical, and religious question, not one for science. Things

can behave and not be alive. Right-to-lifers may say that this research proves that a fetus is alive, but it does not. It cannot."

"Fetal research only changes the abortion debate for people who think that life starts at some magical point," maintains Heidelise Als, a psychologist at Harvard University. "If you believe that life begins at conception, then you don't need the proof of fetal behavior." For others, however, abortion is a very complex issue and involves far more than whether research shows that a fetus hiccups. "Your circumstances and personal beliefs have much more impact on the decision," she observes.

Like DiPietro, Als realizes that "people may use this research as an emotional way to draw people to the pro-life side, but it should not be used by belligerent activists." Instead, she believes, it should be applied to helping mothers have the healthiest pregnancy possible and preparing them to best parent their child. Columbia University psychologist William Fifer, Ph.D., agrees. "The research is much more relevant for issues regarding viable fetuses—preemies."

Simply put, say the three, their work is intended to help the babies that live—not to decide whether fetuses should.—*Camille Chatterjee*

garlic, onion and other essences from a mother's diet. Whether fetuses can taste these flavors isn't yet known, but scientists have found that a 33-week-old preemie will suck harder on a sweetened nipple than on a plain rubber one.

"During the last trimester, the fetus is swallowing up to a liter a day" of amniotic fluid, notes Julie Mennella, Ph.D., a biopsychologist at the Monell Chemical Senses Center in Philadelphia. She thinks the fluid may act as a "flavor bridge" to breast milk, which also carries food flavors from the mother's diet.

FETAL HEARING

Whether or not a fetus can taste, there's little question that it can hear. A very premature baby entering the world at 24 to 25 weeks responds to the sounds around it, observes Als, so its auditory apparatus must already have been functioning in the womb. Many pregnant women report a fetal jerk or sudden kick just after a door slams or a car backfires.

Even without such intrusions, the womb is not a silent place. Researchers who have inserted a hydrophone into the uterus of a pregnant woman have picked up a noise level "akin to the background noise in an apartment," according to DiPietro. Sounds include the whooshing of blood in the mother's vessels, the gurgling and rumbling of her stomach and intestines, as well as the tones of her voice filtered through tissues, bones, and fluid, and the

voices of other people coming through the amniotic wall. Fifer has found that fetal heart rate slows when the mother is speaking, suggesting that the fetus not only hears and recognizes the sound, but is calmed by it.

FETAL VISION

Vision is the last sense to develop. A very premature infant can see light and shape; researchers presume that a fetus has the same ability. Just as the womb isn't completely quiet, it isn't utterly dark, either. Says Fifer: "There may be just enough visual stimulation filtered through the mother's tissues that a fetus can respond when the mother is in bright light," such as when she is sunbathing.

Japanese scientists have even reported a distinct fetal reaction to flashes of light shined on the mother's belly. However, other researchers warn that exposing fetuses (or premature infants) to bright light before they are ready can be dangerous. In fact, Harvard's Als believes that retinal damage in premature infants, which has long been ascribed to high concentrations of oxygen, may actually be due to overexposure to light at the wrong time in development.

A six-month fetus, born about 14 weeks too early, has a brain that is neither prepared for nor expecting signals from the eyes to be transmitted into the brain's visual cortex, and from there into the executive-branch frontal lobes, where information is integrated. When the fetus

A fetus prefers hearing Mom's voice over a stranger's—speaking in her native, not a foreign tongue—and being read aloud familiar tales rather than new stories.

is forced to see too much too soon, says Als, the accelerated stimulation may lead to aberrations of brain development.

FETAL LEARNING

Along with the ability to feel, see, and hear comes the capacity to learn and remember. These activities can be rudimentary, automatic, even biochemical. For example, a fetus, after an initial reaction of alarm, eventually stops responding to a repeated loud noise. The fetus displays the same kind of primitive learning, known as habituation, in response to its mother's voice, Fifer has found.

But the fetus has shown itself capable of far more. In the 1980s, psychology professor Anthony James DeCasper, Ph.D., and colleagues at the University of North Carolina at Greensboro, devised a feeding contraption that allows a baby to suck faster to hear one set of sounds through headphones and to suck slower to hear a different set. With this technique, DeCasper discovered that within hours of birth, a baby already prefers its mother's voice to a stranger's, suggesting it must have learned and remembered the voice, albeit not necessarily consciously, from its last months in the womb. More recently, he's found that a newborn prefers a story read to it repeatedly in the womb—in this case, *The Cat in the Hat*—over a new story introduced soon after birth.

DeCasper and others have uncovered more mental feats. Newborns can not only distinguish their mother from a stranger speaking, but would rather hear Mom's voice, especially the way it sounds filtered through amniotic fluid rather than through air. They're xenophobes, too: they prefer to hear Mom speaking in her native language than to hear her or someone else speaking in a foreign tongue.

By monitoring changes in fetal heart rate, psychologist Jean-Pierre Lecanuet, Ph.D., and his colleagues in Paris have found that fetuses can even tell strangers' voices apart. They also seem to like certain stories more than others. The fetal heartbeat will slow down when a familiar French fairy tale such as *"La Poulette"* ("The Chick") or *"Le Petit Crapaud"* ("The Little Toad"), is read near the mother's belly. When the same reader delivers another unfamiliar story, the fetal heartbeat stays steady.

The fetus is likely responding to the cadence of voices and stories, not their actual words, observes Fifer, but the conclusion is the same: the fetus can listen, learn, and remember at some level, and, as with most babies

and children, it likes the comfort and reassurance of the familiar.

FETAL PERSONALITY

It's no secret that babies are born with distinct differences and patterns of activity that suggest individual temperament. Just when and how the behavioral traits originate in the womb is now the subject of intense scrutiny.

In the first formal study of fetal temperament in 1996, DiPietro and her colleagues recorded the heart rate and movements of 31 fetuses six times before birth and compared them to readings taken twice after birth. (They've since extended their study to include 100 more fetuses.) Their findings: fetuses that are very active in the womb tend to be more irritable infants. Those with irregular sleep/wake patterns in the womb sleep more poorly as young infants. And fetuses with high heart rates become unpredictable, inactive babies.

"Behavior doesn't begin at birth," declares DiPietro. "It begins before and develops in predictable ways." One of the most important influences on development is the fetal environment. As Harvard's Als observes, "The fetus gets an enormous amount of 'hormonal bathing' through the mother, so its chronobiological rhythms are influenced by the mother's sleep/wake cycles, her eating patterns, her movements."

The hormones a mother puts out in response to stress also appear critical. DiPietro finds that highly pressured mothers-to-be tend to have more active fetuses—and more irritable infants. "The most stressed are working pregnant women," says DiPietro. "These days, women tend to work up to the day they deliver, even though the implications for pregnancy aren't entirely clear yet. That's our cultural norm, but I think it's insane."

Als agrees that working can be an enormous stress, but emphasizes that pregnancy hormones help to buffer both mother and fetus. Individual reactions to stress also matter. "The pregnant woman who chooses to work is a different woman already from the one who chooses not to work," she explains.

She's also different from the woman who has no choice but to work. DiPietro's studies show that the fetuses of poor women are distinct neurobehaviorally—less active, with a less variable heart rate—from the fetuses of middle-class women. Yet "poor women rate themselves as less stressed than do working middle-class women," she notes. DiPietro suspects that inadequate nutrition and exposure to pollutants may significantly affect the fetuses of poor women.

Stress, diet, and toxins may combine to have a harmful effect on intelligence. A recent study by biostatistician Bernie Devlin, Ph.D., of the University of Pittsburgh, suggests that genes may have less impact on IQ than previously thought and that the environment of the womb may account for much more. "Our old notion of nature influencing the fetus before birth and nurture after birth needs an update," DiPietro insists. "There is an antenatal environment, too, that is provided by the mother."

Parents-to-be who want to further their unborn child's mental development should start by assuring that the antenatal environment is well-nourished, low-stress, drug-free. Various authors and "experts" also have suggested poking the fetus at regular intervals, speaking to it through a paper tube or "pregaphone," piping in classical music, even flashing lights at the mother's abdomen.

Does such stimulation work? More importantly: Is it safe? Some who use these methods swear their children are smarter, more verbally and musically inclined, more physically coordinated and socially adept than average. Scientists, however, are skeptical.

"There has been no defended research anywhere that shows any enduring effect from these stimulations," asserts Fifer. "Since no one can even say for certain when a fetus is awake, poking them or sticking speakers on the mother's abdomen may be changing their natural sleep patterns. No one would consider poking or prodding a newborn baby in her bassinet or putting a speaker next to her ear, so why would you do such a thing with a fetus?"

Als is more emphatic: "My bet is that poking, shaking, or otherwise deliberately stimulating the fetus might alter its developmental sequence, and anything that affects the development of the brain comes at a cost."

Gently talking to the fetus, however, seems to pose little risk. Fifer suggests that this kind of activity may help parents as much as the fetus. "Thinking about your fetus, talking to it, having your spouse talk to it, will all help prepare you for this new creature that's going to jump into your life and turn it upside down," he says—once it finally makes its anti-climactic entrance.

Maternal emotions may influence fetal behaviors

One psychologist has shown that fetal behavior may predict infant temperament.

By Beth Azar
Monitor staff

Researchers are beginning to see behavioral effects of the uterine environment on fetal behavior. And they're finding that such behaviors in utero may predict behaviors in the newborn.

"While most people assume that the constitutional nature of infant temperament reflects genetic influences, I'm convinced that the intrauterine hormonal milieu, moderated by the mother's level of stress and other psychological characteristics, make an equally significant contribution," says Johns Hopkins University psychologist Janet DiPietro, PhD.

In a series of studies, she has found that fetal measures, such as movement and heart rate, may predict 20 percent to 60 percent of variation in temperament. In the first study to test this link, DiPietro and her colleagues examined 31 fetuses at six points during gestation and then mothers reported on their temperaments at 3 and 6 months after birth.

The babies who were more active prenatally were perceived by their mothers as being more irritable and more active at 3 and 6 months. And babies with higher heart rates in utero were less active and less predictable than babies with lower in-utero heart

rates. Also, babies who never developed a regular sleep-wake pattern in the womb woke more at night at age 3 months than infants who began to regulate their sleep-wake pattern prenatally. DiPietro and her colleagues have begun a study to replicate these findings using a larger sample and laboratory-based observations of temperament.

Certain environmental factors, such as maternal stress and socioeconomic status, seem to affect the same fetal behaviors—heart rate and movement— that DiPietro finds help predict infant temperament.

For example, in a study of 103 infants and their mothers, now in press at *Developmental Psychobiology,* she finds that, prenatally, babies of women of low socioeconomic status were less active and had less heart-rate variability than babies of middle-class women. All of the fetuses fell within normal clinical values, but the differences between the two groups were consistent, says DiPietro.

Data collected on maternal perceptions of stress suggest that fetuses of women who report a lot of stress—regardless of socioeconomic status— have different patterns of movement and heart rate than fetuses of women

under less stress. It's still unclear whether this difference affects postnatal development, says DiPietro.

But even small changes in mood seem to directly affect the fetus, according to preliminary data from a study by Columbia University psychologist William Fifer, PhD, and his colleagues. They showed pregnant women a videotape of a woman breast-feeding her baby. During the film, the women's heart rates and respiration increased, and as they did so did the heart rates of their fetuses. It's unclear how the change in heart rate is transmitted from mother to fetus, says Fifer. The fetus could be responding to movements, hormonal changes or simply the sound of its mother's increased heart rate.

An abundance of research shows that infant behavior is affected by the substances mothers consume during pregnancy. Now studies in the fetus find that the effects begin prenatally. For example, Emory University psychologist Eugene K. Emory, PhD, and his colleagues find that if a woman smokes, her fetus does not habituate to a vibrating stimulus but the fetuses of non-smokers do. This may indicate a difference in the stress response of fetuses of women who smoke, says Emory.

FERTILE MINDS

From birth, a baby's brain cells proliferate wildly,
making connections that may shape a lifetime of experience.
The first three years are critical

By J. MADELEINE NASH

RAT-A-TAT-TAT. RAT-A-TAT-TAT. RAT-A-tat-tat. If scientists could eavesdrop on the brain of a human embryo 10, maybe 12 weeks after conception, they would hear an astonishing racket. Inside the womb, long before light first strikes the retina of the eye or the earliest dreamy images flicker through the cortex, nerve cells in the developing brain crackle with purposeful activity. Like teenagers with telephones, cells in one neighborhood of the brain are calling friends in another, and these cells are calling their friends, and they keep calling one another over and over again, "almost," says neurobiologist Carla Shatz of the University of California, Berkeley, "as if they were autodialing."

But these neurons—as the long, wiry cells that carry electrical messages through the nervous system and the brain are called—are not transmitting signals in scattershot fashion. That would produce a featureless static, the sort of noise picked up by a radio tuned between stations. On the contrary, evidence is growing that the staccato bursts of electricity that form those distinctive rat-a-tat-tats arise from coordinated waves of neural activity, and that those pulsing waves, like currents shifting sand on the ocean floor, actually change the shape of the brain, carving mental circuits into patterns that over time will enable the newborn infant to perceive a father's voice, a mother's touch, a shiny mobile twirling over the crib.

Of all the discoveries that have poured out of neuroscience labs in recent years, the finding that the electrical activity of brain cells changes the physical structure of the brain is perhaps the most breathtaking. For the rhythmic firing of neurons is no longer assumed to be a by-product of building the brain but essential to the process, and it begins, scientists have established, well before birth. A brain is not a computer. Nature does not cobble it together, then turn it on. No, the brain begins working long before it is finished. And the same processes that wire the brain before birth, neuroscientists are finding, also drive the explosion of learning that occurs immediately afterward.

At birth a baby's brain contains 100 billion neurons, roughly as many nerve cells as there are stars in the Milky Way. Also in place are a trillion glial cells, named after the Greek word for glue, which form a kind of honeycomb that protects and nourishes the neurons. But while the brain contains virtually all the nerve cells it will ever have, the pattern of wiring between them has yet to stabilize. Up to this point, says Shatz, "what the brain has done is lay out circuits that are its best guess about what's required for vision, for language, for whatever." And now it is up to neural activity—no longer spontaneous, but driven by a flood of sensory experiences—to take this rough blueprint and progressively refine it.

During the first years of life, the brain undergoes a series of extraordinary changes. Starting shortly after birth, a baby's brain, in a display of biological exuberance, produces trillions more connections between neurons than it can possibly use. Then, through a process that resembles Darwinian competition, the brain eliminates connections, or synapses, that are seldom or never used. The excess synapses in a child's brain undergo a draconian pruning, starting around the age of 10 or earlier, leaving behind a mind whose patterns of emotion and thought are, for better or worse, unique.

Deprived of a stimulating environment, a child's brain suffers. Researchers at Baylor College of Medicine, for example, have found that children who don't play much or are rarely touched develop brains 20% to 30% smaller than normal for their age. Laboratory animals provide another provocative parallel. Not only do young rats reared in toy-strewn cages exhibit more complex behavior than rats confined to sterile, uninteresting boxes, researchers at the University of Illinois at Urbana-Champaign have found, but the brains of these rats contain as many as 25% more synapses per neuron. Rich experiences, in other words, really do produce rich brains.

The new insights into brain development are more than just interesting science. They have profound implications for parents and policymakers. In an age when mothers and fathers are increasingly pressed for time—and may already be feeling guilty about how many hours they spend away from their children—the results coming out of the labs are likely to increase concerns about leaving very young children in the care of others. For the data underscore the importance of

 From *Time*, February 3, 1997, pp. 48-56. © 1997 by Time Inc. Magazine Company. Reprinted by permission.

hands-on parenting, of finding the time to cuddle a baby, talk with a toddler and provide infants with stimulating experiences.

The new insights have begun to infuse new passion into the political debate over early education and day care. There is an urgent need, say child-development experts, for preschool programs designed to boost the brain power of youngsters born into impoverished rural and inner-city households. Without such programs, they warn, the current drive to curtail welfare costs by pushing mothers with infants and toddlers into the work force may well backfire. "There is a time scale to brain development, and the most important year is the first," notes Frank Newman, president of the Education Commission of the States. By the age of three, a child who is neglected or abused bears marks that, if not indelible, are exceedingly difficult to erase.

But the new research offers hope as well. Scientists have found that the brain during the first years of life is so malleable that very young children who suffer strokes or injuries that wipe out an entire hemisphere can still mature into highly functional adults. Moreover, it is becoming increasingly clear that well-designed preschool programs can help many children overcome glaring deficits in their home environment. With appropriate therapy, say researchers, even serious disorders like dyslexia may be treatable. While inherited problems may place certain children at greater risk than others, says Dr. Harry Chugani, a pediatric neurologist at Wayne State University in Detroit, that is no excuse for ignoring the environment's power to remodel the brain. "We may not do much to change what happens before birth, but we can change what happens after a baby is born," he observes.

Strong evidence that activity changes the brain began accumulating in the 1970s. But only recently have researchers had tools powerful enough to reveal the precise mechanisms by which those changes are brought about. Neural activity triggers a biochemical cascade that reaches all the way to the nucleus of cells and the coils of DNA that encode specific genes. In fact, two of the genes affected by neural activity in embryonic fruit flies, neurobiologist Corey Goodman and his colleagues at Berkeley reported late last year, are identical to those that other studies have linked to learning and memory. How thrilling, exclaims Goodman, how intellectually satisfying that the snippets of DNA that embryos use to build their brains are the very same ones that will later allow adult organisms to process and store new information.

As researchers explore the once hidden links between brain activity and brain structure, they are beginning to construct a sturdy bridge over the chasm that previously separated genes from the environment. Experts now agree that a baby does not come into

Wiring Vision

WHAT'S GOING ON Babies can see at birth, but not in fine-grained detail. They have not yet acquired the knack of focusing both eyes on a single object or developed more sophisticated visual skills like depth perception. they also lack hand-eye coordination.
WHAT PARENTS CAN DO There is no need to buy high-contrast black-and-white toys to stimulate vision. But regular eye exams, starting as early as two weeks of age, can detect problems that, if left uncorrected, can cause a weak or unused eye to lose its functional connections to the brain.
WINDOW OF LEARNING Unless it is exercised early on, the visual system will not develop.

AGE (in years)	Birth	1	2	3	4	5	6	7	8	9	10
Visual acuity											
Binocular vision											

the world as a genetically preprogrammed automaton or a blank slate at the mercy of the environment, but arrives as something much more interesting. For this reason the debate that engaged countless generations of philosophers—whether nature or nurture calls the shots—no longer interests most scientists. They are much too busy chronicling the myriad ways in which genes and the environment interact. "It's not a competition," says Dr. Stanley Greenspan, a psychiatrist at George Washington University. "It's a dance."

THE IMPORTANCE OF GENES

THAT DANCE BEGINS AT AROUND THE THIRD week of gestation, when a thin layer of cells in the developing embryo performs an origami-like trick, folding inward to give rise to a fluid-filled cylinder known as the neural tube. As cells in the neural tube proliferate at the astonishing rate of 250,000 a minute, the brain and spinal cord assemble themselves in a series of tightly choreographed steps. Nature is the dominant partner during this phase of development, but nurture plays a vital supportive role. Changes in the environment of the womb—whether caused by maternal malnutrition, drug abuse or a viral infection—can wreck the clockwork precision of the neural assembly line. Some forms of epilepsy, mental retardation, autism and schizophrenia appear to be the results of developmental processes gone awry.

But what awes scientists who study the brain, what still stuns them, is not that things occasionally go wrong in the devel-

oping brain but that so much of the time they go right. This is all the more remarkable, says Berkeley's Shatz, as the central nervous system of an embryo is not a miniature of the adult system but more like a tadpole that gives rise to a frog. Among other things, the cells produced in the neural tube must migrate to distant locations and accurately lay down the connections that link one part of the brain to another. In addition, the embryonic brain must construct a variety of temporary structures, including the neural tube, that will, like a tadpole's tail, eventually disappear.

What biochemical magic underlies this incredible metamorphosis? The instructions programmed into the genes, of course. Scientists have recently discovered, for instance, that a gene nicknamed "sonic hedgehog" (after the popular video game Sonic the Hedgehog) determines the fate of neurons in the spinal cord and the brain. Like a strong scent carried by the wind, the protein encoded by the hedgehog gene (so called because in its absence, fruit-fly embryos sprout a coat of prickles) diffuses outward from the cells that produce it, becoming fainter and fainter. Columbia University neurobiologist Thomas Jessell has found that it takes middling concentrations of this potent morphing factor to produce a motor neuron and lower concentrations to make an interneuron (a cell that relays signals to other neurons, instead of to muscle fibers, as motor neurons do).

Scientists are also beginning to identify some of the genes that guide neurons in their long migrations. Consider the problem faced by neurons destined to become part of the cerebral cortex. Because they arise relatively late in the development of the mammalian brain, billions of these cells must push and shove their way through dense colonies established by earlier migrants. "It's as if the entire population of the East Coast decided to move en masse to the West Coast," marvels Yale University neuroscientist Dr. Pasko Rakic, and marched through Cleveland, Chicago and Denver to get there.

But of all the problems the growing nervous system must solve, the most daunting is posed by the wiring itself. After birth, when the number of connections explodes, each of the brain's billions of neurons will forge links to thousands of others. First they must spin out a web of wire-like fibers known as axons (which transmit signals) and dendrites (which receive them). The objective is to form a synapse, the gap-like structure over which the axon of one neuron beams a signal to the dendrites of another. Before this can happen, axons and dendrites must almost touch. And while the short, bushy dendrites don't have to travel very far, axons—the heavy-duty cables of the nervous system—must traverse distances that are the microscopic equivalent of miles.

What guides an axon on its incredible voyage is a "growth cone," a creepy, crawly sprout that looks something like an amoeba. Scientists have known about growth cones since the turn of the century. What they didn't know until recently was that growth cones come equipped with the molecular equivalent of sonar and radar. Just as instruments in a submarine or airplane scan the environment for signals, so molecules arrayed on the surface of growth cones search their surroundings for the presence of certain proteins. Some of these proteins, it turns out, are attractants that pull the growth cones toward them, while others are repellents that push them away.

THE FIRST STIRRINGS

UP TO THIS POINT, GENES HAVE CONTROLLED the unfolding of the brain. As soon as axons make their first connections, however, the nerves begin to fire, and what they do starts to matter more and more. In essence, say scientists, the developing nervous system has strung the equivalent of telephone trunk lines between the right neighborhoods in the right cities. Now it has to sort out which wires belong to which house, a problem that cannot be solved by genes alone for reasons that boil down to simple arithmetic. Eventually, Berkeley's Goodman estimates, a human brain must forge quadrillions of connections. But there are only 100,000 genes in human DNA. Even though half these genes—some 50,000—appear to be dedicated to constructing and maintaining the nervous system, he observes, that's not enough to specify more than a tiny fraction of the connections required by a fully functioning brain.

In adult mammals, for example, the axons that connect the brain's visual system arrange themselves in striking layers and columns that reflect the division between the left eye and the right. But these axons start out as scrambled as a bowl of spaghetti, according to Michael Stryker, chairman of the physiology department at the University of California at San Francisco. What sorts out the mess, scientists have established, is neural activity. In a series of experiments viewed as classics by scientists in the field, Berkeley's Shatz chemically blocked neural activity in embryonic cats. The result? The axons that connect neurons in the retina of the eye to the brain never formed the left eye–right eye geometry needed to support vision.

But no recent finding has intrigued researchers more than the results reported in October by Corey Goodman and his Berkeley colleagues. In studying a deceptively simple problem—how axons from motor neurons in the fly's central nerve cord establish connections with muscle cells in its limbs—the Berkeley researchers made an

Wiring Feelings

WHAT'S GOING ON Among the first circuits the brain constructs are those that govern the emotions. Beginning around two months of age, the distress and contentment experienced by newborns start to evolve into more complex feelings: joy and sadness, envy and empathy, pride and shame.
WHAT PARENTS CAN DO Loving care provides a baby's brain with the right kind of emotional stimulation. Neglecting a baby can produce brainwave patterns that dampen happy feelings. Abuse can produce heightened anxiety and abnormal stress responses.
WINDOW OF LEARNING Emotions develop in layers, each more complex than the last.

AGE (in years)	Birth 1 2 3 4 5 6 7 8 9 10
Stress Response	
Empathy, Envy	

unexpected discovery. They knew there was a gene that keeps bundles of axons together as they race toward their muscle-cell targets. What they discovered was that the electrical activity produced by neurons inhibited this gene, dramatically increasing the number of connections the axons made. Even more intriguing, the signals amplified the activity of a second gene—a gene called CREB.

The discovery of the CREB amplifier, more than any other, links the developmental processes that occur before birth to those that continue long after. For the twin processes of memory and learning in adult animals, Columbia University neurophysiologist Eric Kandel has shown, rely on the CREB molecule. When Kandel blocked the activity of CREB in giant snails, their brains changed in ways that suggested that they could still learn but could remember what they learned for only a short period of time. Without CREB, it seems, snails—and by extension, more developed animals like humans—can form no long-term memories. And without long-term memories, it is hard to imagine that infant brains could ever master more than rudimentary skills. "Nurture is important," says Kandel. "But nurture works through nature."

EXPERIENCE KICKS IN

WHEN A BABY IS BORN, IT CAN SEE AND HEAR and smell and respond to touch, but only dimly. The brain stem, a primitive region that controls vital functions like heartbeat and breathing, has completed its wiring. Elsewhere the connections between neurons are wispy and weak. But over the first few months of life, the brain's higher centers ex-

plode with new synapses. And as dendrites and axons swell with buds and branches like trees in spring, metabolism soars. By the age of two, a child's brain contains twice as many synapses and consumes twice as much energy as the brain of a normal adult.

University of Chicago pediatric neurologist Dr. Peter Huttenlocher has chronicled this extraordinary epoch in brain development by autopsying the brains of infants and young children who have died unexpectedly. The number of synapses in one layer of the visual cortex, Huttenlocher reports, rises from around 2,500 per neuron at birth to as many as 18,000 about six months later. Other regions of the cortex score similarly spectacular increases but on slightly different schedules. And while these microscopic connections between nerve fibers continue to form throughout life, they reach their highest average densities (15,000 synapses per neuron) at around the age of two and remain at that level until the age of 10 or 11.

This profusion of connections lends the growing brain exceptional flexibility and resilience. Consider the case of 13-year-old Brandi Binder, who developed such severe epilepsy that surgeons at UCLA had to remove the entire right side of her cortex when she was six. Binder lost virtually all the control she had established over muscles on the left side of her body, the side controlled by the right side of the brain. Yet today, after years of therapy ranging from leg lifts to math and music drills, Binder is an A student at the Holmes Middle School in Colorado Springs, Colorado. She loves music, math and art—skills usually associated with the right half of the brain. And while Binder's recuperation is not 100%—for example, she has never regained the use of her left arm—it comes close. Says UCLA pediatric neurologist Dr. Donald Shields: "If there's a way to compensate, the developing brain will find it."

What wires a child's brain, say neuroscientists—or rewires it after physical trauma—is repeated experience. Each time a baby tries to touch a tantalizing object or gazes intently at a face or listens to a lullaby, tiny bursts of electricity shoot through the brain, knitting neurons into circuits as well defined as those etched onto silicon chips. The results are those behavioral mileposts that never cease to delight and awe parents. Around the age of two months, for example, the motor-control centers of the brain develop to the point that infants can suddenly reach out and grab a nearby object. Around the age of four months, the cortex begins to refine the connections needed for depth perception and binocular vision. And around the age of 12 months, the speech centers of the brain are poised to produce what is perhaps the most magical moment of childhood: the first word that marks the flowering of language.

When the brain does not receive the right information—or shuts it out—the result can be devastating. Some children who display early signs of autism, for example, retreat from the world because they are hypersensitive to sensory stimulation, others because their senses are underactive and provide them with too little information. To be effective, then, says George Washington University's Greenspan, treatment must target the underlying condition, protecting some children from disorienting noises and lights, providing others with attention-grabbing stimulation. But when parents and therapists collaborate in an intensive effort to reach these abnormal brains, writes Greenspan in a new book, *The Growth of the Mind* (Addison-Wesley, 1997), three-year-olds who begin the descent into the autistic's limited universe can sometimes be snatched back.

Indeed, parents are the brain's first and most important teachers. Among other things, they appear to help babies learn by adopting the rhythmic, high-pitched speaking style known as Parentese. When speaking to babies, Stanford University psychologist Anne Fernald has found, mothers and fathers from many cultures change their speech patterns in the same peculiar ways. "They put their faces very close to the child," she reports. "They use shorter utterances, and they speak in an unusually melodious fashion." The heart rate of infants increases while listening to Parentese, even Parentese delivered in a foreign language. Moreover, Fernald says, Parentese appears to hasten the process of connecting words to the objects they denote. Twelve-month-olds, directed to "look at the ball" in Parentese, direct their eyes to the correct picture more frequently than when the instruction is delivered in normal English.

In some ways the exaggerated, vowel-rich sounds of Parentese appear to resemble the choice morsels fed to hatchlings by adult birds. The University of Washington's Patricia Kuhl and her colleagues have conditioned dozens of newborns to turn their heads when they detect the *ee* sound emitted by American parents, vs. the *eu* favored by doting Swedes. Very young babies, says Kuhl, invariably perceive slight variations in pronunciation as totally different sounds. But by the age of six months, American babies no longer react when they hear variants of *ee,* and Swedish babies have become impervious to differences in *eu.* "It's as though their brains have formed little magnets," says Kuhl, "and all the sounds in the vicinity are swept in."

TUNED TO DANGER

EVEN MORE FUNDAMENTAL, SAYS DR. BRUCE Perry of Baylor College of Medicine in Houston, is the role parents play in setting

Wiring Language

WHAT'S GOING ON Even before birth, an infant is tuning into the melody of its mother's voice. Over the next six years, its brain will set up the circuitry needed to decipher—and reproduce—the lyrics. A six-month-old can recognize the vowel sounds that are the basic building blocks of speech.

WHAT PARENTS CAN DO Talking to a baby a lot, researchers have found, significantly speeds up the process of learning new words. The high-pitched, singsong speech style known as Parentese helps babies connect objects with words.

WINDOW OF LEARNING Language skills are sharpest early on but grow throughout life.

AGE (in years)	Birth	1	2	3	4	5	6	7	8	9	10
Recognition of speech											
Vocabulary											

up the neural circuitry that helps children regulate their responses to stress. Children who are physically abused early in life, he observes, develop brains that are exquisitely tuned to danger. At the slightest threat, their hearts race, their stress hormones surge and their brains anxiously track the nonverbal cues that might signal the next attack. Because the brain develops in sequence, with more primitive structures stabilizing their connections first, early abuse is particularly damaging. Says Perry: "Experience is the chief architect of the brain." And because these early experiences of stress form a kind of template around which later brain development is organized, the changes they create are all the more pervasive.

Emotional deprivation early in life has a similar effect. For six years University of Washington psychologist Geraldine Dawson and her colleagues have monitored the brain-wave patterns of children born to mothers who were diagnosed as suffering from depression. As infants, these children showed markedly reduced activity in the left frontal lobe, an area of the brain that serves as a center for joy and other lighthearted emotions. Even more telling, the patterns of brain activity displayed by these children closely tracked the ups and downs of their mother's depression. At the age of three, children whose mothers were more severely depressed or whose depression lasted longer continued to show abnormally low readings.

Strikingly, not all the children born to depressed mothers develop these aberrant brain-wave patterns, Dawson has found. What accounts for the difference appears to be the emotional tone of the exchanges be-

tween mother and child. By scrutinizing hours of videotape that show depressed mothers interacting with their babies, Dawson has attempted to identify the links between maternal behavior and children's brains. She found that mothers who were disengaged, irritable or impatient had babies with sad brains. But depressed mothers who managed to rise above their melancholy, lavishing their babies with attention and indulging in playful games, had children with brain activity of a considerably more cheerful cast.

When is it too late to repair the damage wrought by physical and emotional abuse or neglect? For a time, at least, a child's brain is extremely forgiving. If a mother snaps out of her depression before her child is a year old, Dawson has found, brain activity in the left frontal lobe quickly picks up. However, the ability to rebound declines markedly as a child grows older. Many scientists believe that in the first few years of childhood there are a number of critical or sensitive periods, or "windows," when the brain demands certain types of input in order to create or stabilize certain long-lasting structures.

For example, children who are born with a cataract will become permanently blind in that eye if the clouded lens is not promptly removed. Why? The brain's visual centers require sensory stimulus—in this case the stimulus provided by light hitting the retina of the eye—to maintain their still tentative connections. More controversially, many linguists believe that language skills unfold according to a strict, biologically defined timetable. Children, in their view, resemble certain species of birds that cannot master their song unless they hear it sung at an early age. In zebra finches the window for acquiring the appropriate song opens 25 to 30 days after hatching and shuts some 50 days later.

WINDOWS OF OPPORTUNITY

WITH A FEW EXCEPTIONS, THE WINDOWS OF opportunity in the human brain do not close quite so abruptly. There appears to be a series of windows for developing language. The window for acquiring syntax may close as early as five or six years of age, while the window for adding new words may never close. The ability to learn a second language is highest between birth and the age of six, then undergoes a steady and inexorable decline. Many adults still manage to learn new languages, but usually only after great struggle.

The brain's greatest growth spurt, neuroscientists have now confirmed, draws to a close around the age of 10, when the balance between synapse creation and atrophy abruptly shifts. Over the next several years, the brain will ruthlessly destroy its weakest synapses, preserving only those that have been magically transformed by experience. This magic, once again, seems to be encoded in the genes. The ephemeral bursts of electricity that travel through the brain, creating everything from visual images and pleasurable sensations to dark dreams and wild thoughts, ensure the survival of synapses by stimulating genes that promote the release of powerful growth factors and suppressing genes that encode for synapse-destroying enzymes.

By the end of adolescence, around the age of 18, the brain has declined in plasticity but increased in power. Talents and latent tendencies that have been nurtured are ready to blossom. The experiences that drive neural activity, says Yale's Rakic, are like a sculptor's chisel or a dressmaker's shears, conjuring up form from a lump of stone or a length of cloth. The presence of extra material expands the range of possibilities, but cutting away the extraneous is what makes art. "It is the overproduction of synaptic connections followed by their loss that leads to patterns in the brain," says neuroscientist William Greenough of the University of Illinois at Urbana-Champaign. Potential for greatness may be encoded in the genes, but whether that potential is realized as a gift for mathematics, say, or a brilliant criminal mind depends on patterns etched by experience in those critical early years.

Wiring Movement

WHAT'S GOING ON At birth babies can move their limbs, but in a jerky, uncontrolled fashion. Over the next four years, the brain progressively refines the circuits for reaching, grabbing, sitting, crawling, walking and running.
WHAT PARENTS CAN DO Give babies as much freedom to explore as safety permits. Just reaching for an object helps the brain develop hand-eye coordination. As soon as children are ready for them, activities like drawing and playing a violin or piano encourage the development of fine motor skills.
WINDOW OF LEARNING Motor-skill development moves from gross to increasingly fine.

AGE (in years)	Birth 1 2 3 4 5 6 7 8 9 10
Basic motor skills	
Fine motor ability	
Musical fingering	

Psychiatrists and educators have long recognized the value of early experience. But their observations have until now been largely anecdotal. What's so exciting, says Matthew Melmed, executive director of Zero to Three, a nonprofit organization devoted to highlighting the importance of the first three years of life, is that modern neuroscience is providing the hard, quantifiable evidence that was missing earlier. "Because you can see the results under a microscope or in a PET scan," he observes, "it's become that much more convincing."

What lessons can be drawn from the new findings? Among other things, it is clear that foreign languages should be taught in elementary school, if not before. That remedial education may be more effective at the age of three or four than at nine or 10. That good, affordable day care is not a luxury or a fringe benefit for welfare mothers and working parents but essential brain food for the next generation. For while new synapses continue to form throughout life, and even adults continually refurbish their minds through reading and learning, never again will the brain be able to master new skills so readily or rebound from setbacks so easily.

Rat-a-tat-tat. Rat-a-tat-tat. Rat-a-tat-tat. Just last week, in the U.S. alone, some 77,000 newborns began the miraculous process of wiring their brains for a lifetime of learning. If parents and policymakers don't pay attention to the conditions under which this delicate process takes place, we will all suffer the consequences—starting around the year 2010.

THE COST OF CHILDREN

Of course they're cute. But have you any idea how much one will set you back? A hardheaded inquiry

By Phillip J. Longman

To examine in coldly economic terms a parent's decision to have children is widely thought to be in bad taste. A child, after all, isn't precisely akin to a consumer product such as a dishwasher, a house, a car, or a personal computer–any one of which, of course, is cheaper to acquire and usually easier to return. A child is a font of love, hope for the future, continuation of one's bloodline, and various other intangible pleasures, and it is these sentimental considerations (along with some earthier imperatives) that prevail when parents bring a child into this world.

But let's face it: Children don't come free. Indeed, their cost is rising. According to one government calculation, the direct cost of raising a child to age 18 has risen by 20 percent since 1960 (adjusted for inflation and changes in family size). And this calculation doesn't take into account the forgone wages that result from a parent taking time off to raise children–an economic cost that has skyrocketed during the last generation as women have entered the work force in unprecedented numbers. "It's become much more expensive to raise children while the economic returns to parents have diminished," notes feminist economist Shirley Burggraf. "The family can't survive on romance."

Knowing the real cost of children is critical to a host of financial questions, such as how much house one can afford, how much one should be saving for college tuition, and how much one must earn to have a larger family. To help answer such questions, *U.S. News* has undertaken to identify and add up as best it can all the costs of raising a child from birth to college graduation. (For the purposes of this calculation, we're assuming these children will pay for any advanced degrees they may want out of their own pockets.)

Our starting point is data from the United States Department of Agriculture, which every year publishes estimates of how much families in different income brackets spend on raising children to age 18. To these calculations we have added the cost of a college education and wages forgone because of the rigors of child-rearing. (There's plenty we haven't counted: soccer camp, cello lessons, SAT prep., and other extra-cost options.) What we've found is that the typical child in a middle-income family requires a 22-year investment of just over $1.45 million. That's a pretty steep price tag in a country where the median income for families with children is just $41,000. The child's unit cost rises to $2.78 million for the top-third income bracket and drops to $761,871 for the bottom-third income bracket.

Tut tut, you say. Surely this is another case of newsmagazine hyperbole. All right, then, let's take it from the top:

■ **Acquisition costs.** In most cases, conceiving a child biologically is gloriously cost free. But not for all: An estimated 6.1 percent of women ages 15–24, and 11.2 percent of women ages 25–34, suffer from what health statisticians refer to as "impaired fecundity." Serving this huge market are some 300 infertility clinics nationwide that performed 59,142 treatment "cycles" in 1995, according to a recently released study by the Centers for Disease Control and Prevention. The cost of treatments–only 19 percent of which actually produced a take-home baby–averaged around $8,000 a try. It's not uncommon for infertile couples to spend $50,000 or more in pursuit of pregnancy. Though most insurance policies will pay for some form of infertility treatment, insurers are cutting back rapidly in the total bills they'll cover. For the purposes of our tally, we'll ignore fertility treatments, but this can be a significant cost.

For most people, the meter starts running with pregnancy. Costs vary dramatically from hospital to hospital, from region to region, and according to how complicated the pregnancy is. Out-of-pocket costs, obviously, will also vary depending on how much health insurance you have. But here's an idea of what your bills might be.

For an uneventful normal pregnancy, 12 prenatal care visits are usually recommended–the cost of which varies according to one's insurance plan. According to HCIA Inc., a Baltimore health care information company, the cost to insured patients of a normal delivery in a hospital averages about $2,800. (Twins are cheaper on a per-head basis: typical total delivery cost: $4,115.)

For parents without insurance, direct costs are clearly much higher. According to a 1994 study, the cost of an uncomplicated "normal" delivery averages $6,400 nationally. Caesarean delivery costs an average of $11,000, and more complicated births may range up to $400,000. Premature babies requiring neonatal intensive care will cost $1,000 to $2,500 for every day they stay in the hospital. Though most people can count on insurance to cover a majority of such costs, there are many people who can't. According to a report issued in March by the U.S. government's Agency for Health Care Policy and Research, 17 percent of Hispanic children, 12.6 percent of black children, and 6 percent of white ones lack any health in-

surance coverage whatsoever, including coverage by Medicaid or other public programs.

An alternative path to acquiring a child is through adoption. Of the roughly 30,000 adoptions of healthy infants in the United States each year, most involve expenses of $10,000 to $15,000. These include the cost of paying for a social worker to perform a "home study" to vouchsafe the adoptive parents' suitability, agency fees, travel expenses (many adoptions these days cross national boundaries), medical and sometimes living expenses for the birth mother, and legal fees. Offsetting these costs for parents who adopt is a new $5,000 federal tax credit. Since most people don't adopt, these costs, too, are excluded from *U.S. News*'s tally.

THREADS.
To clothe a child to age 18 costs **$22,063.** And yes, girls cost 18 percent more than boys.

■ **Child care.** The Department of Agriculture calculates that the middle-class parents of a 3-to-5-year-old spend just over $1,260 a year on average for child care. (According to the Census Bureau, fully 56 percent of American families with children use paid child care.) Wealthier families are more likely to opt for the pricier nanny. Irish Nanny Services of Dublin advertises Irish nannies "with good moral standards" who are "renowned for their expertise with children." The price for U.S. parents begins at $250 per week; plus 1.5 paid holidays for every month

worked; plus a nonrefundable finder's fee equal to 10 percent of the yearly salary payable upfront.

The average cost for all families using child care is $74.15 a week, or about 7.5 percent of average pretax family income, which is roughly equal to most workers' employee-contribution rate for Social Security. The rate is much steeper, of course, at the low end of the income scale; families making less than $1,200 a month who use day care spend an average 25.1 percent of their income on day-care expenses.

■ **Food.** Middle-class families spend an average $990 a year feeding a child under 2. (Breast-feeding helps: One serving of infant formula can cost as much as $3.29.) As kids get bigger, so do their appetites: Feeding a middle-class 15-year-old currently costs $1,920 a year on average. A middle-class only child born in 1997 can be expected to consume a total of $54,795 in food by age 18.

■ **Housing.** The bigger your family, the bigger the house you need. Families with children also often pay a premium to live in safe, leafy neighborhoods with good schools. USDA estimates that the average middle-class, husband-wife family with one child will spend, on a per capita basis, an additional $97,549 to provide the child with shelter.

■ **Transportation.** Priced a minivan lately? The added transportation cost of having one middle-class child totals $46,345, according to the USDA. This does not include the cost of commuting to jobs parents must hold in order to support their children. Predictably, as children get older, the cost of driving them around grows. Parents with teenagers spend over 70 percent more on transportation than families with infants. Just the cost of providing teenage drivers with auto insurance can run into the thousands.

■ **Health care.** Obviously, this cost varies tremendously, depending largely on the health of the child. The lifetime health costs of a child born with cerebral palsy, for instance, average $503,000; with Down's syndrome, $451,000; and with spina bifida,

$294,000, according to the March of Dimes.

Again, out-of-pocket costs for health care will depend largely on whether the parents have good (or any) health insurance. In 1996, nearly 11 million American children, or 15.4 percent of the population under 18, had none. Deductibles, copayments, and specific coverages also vary widely even among those with insurance. Taking all these variables into account, and including the cost of insurance, the USDA estimates that the average cost of keeping a middle-class child born in 1997 healthy to age 18 will be more than $20,757.

■ **Clothing.** Even after allowing for hand-me-downs and gifts from doting grandparents, keeping an only child properly dressed to age 18 will cost an average total of $22,063, according to the USDA. Predictably, in this realm, daughters cost more than sons: According to the Bureau of Labor Statistics, husband-wife families with children spend nearly 18 percent more on girls' clothes than on those for boys.

■ **Primary and secondary education.** Fully 89 percent of all school-age kids in the United States attend public schools. Public education costs American society more than $293 billion per year, but for the purposes of this tally, we'll exclude taxes (which, after all, are paid by parents and nonparents alike) and consider public education to be free.

For the roughly 5 million grade-school students now enrolled in private schools, costs vary widely. About 50 percent of these students attend parochial schools, where tuition averaged $1,934 in 1993–94, the last school year for which data are available. By contrast, parents earning over $125,000 a year who send a child to the elite Deerfield Academy in Deerfield, Mass., and who manage to qualify for financial aid, are expected to contribute $10,600 a year in tuition. Overall, the U.S. Department of Education reports, private-school tuition in 1993–94 averaged $2,200 a year in elementary schools and $5,500 in secondary schools, with

schools for children who are handicapped or have "special needs" charging an average $15,189. These costs have been rising quickly. Reflecting increasing demand, the average tuition of private schools increased by more than double the overall rate of inflation between 1990 and 1996.

■ **Toys and other miscellaneous expenses.** The USDA doesn't break out spending on toys by income group or the age of children. But for all husband-and-wife families with children, the average amount spent on pets, toys, and playground equipment in 1995 was $485.

TUMBLES.
Children are usually quite healthy, but they'll still run you **$20,757** to keep fit till age 18.

What do all these bills come to? USDA calculates that a typical middle-class, husband-wife family will spend a total of $301,183 to raise an only child born in 1997 to age 18 (table, "Cost of children born in 1997). More affluent parents (with income over $59,700 a year) will spend an average of $437,869 on an only child. The average figure for lower-income families (with income below $35,500 a year) is $221,750.

Certain economies of scale are available to larger families. As family size increases, food costs per person go down the most. (Just feed everyone stew.) Per capita housing and transportation costs also decrease, but not by as much. All told, for middle-class families, the marginal cost of raising a second child will be approximately 24

percent less than the cost of a single child. The marginal unit cost continues to drop for each successive child.

Now let's consider two costs the USDA calculation leaves out. The first is college. From the start of the 1990s through September of 1997, average tuition at the nation's colleges increased by more than 75 percent, while overall prices in the economy inflated by little more than 26 percent. Common sense would suggest that this rate of tuition inflation cannot possibly sustain itself over the long term, especially if real family income remains flat or grows only slowly. Sooner or later, some combination of new technology and organizational reform will surely render higher education less costly. Still, who would have imagined that the price of a college education would ever have risen to where it is today? With an undergraduate education becoming ever more necessary to guarantee a middle-class lifestyle, perhaps its price will rise even faster in the future. Given these imponderables, we'll assume college costs will continue to rise at the average annual rate of the 1990s, or 7.45 percent, and that the cost of room, board, and books grows at 5 percent, which is the annual inflation rate of the past 20 years.

Now, let's do some illustrative arithmetic. Say you had a child in September 1997. Let's forget straight off about sending him to Harvard or Princeton, or any other private college, and aim for a top state school, the University of Michigan–Ann Arbor. Tuition, fees, plus room and board for in-state students there currently amount to $11,694 a year. Under the inflation assumptions described above, it turns out you'll need a total of $157,831 to see a child born last year through graduation at Ann Arbor (assuming you are a Michigan resident; tuition is more than three times higher for out-of-state residents).

Ok, now let's figure out how to pay for that tuition. Assuming an average annual 7 percent total return on savings, you'll have put away more than $319 each month, starting on your child's date

Cost of children born in 1997

Higher income (one-child family; 1997 before-tax family income: more than $59,700)

Age	Housing	Food	Transportation	Clothing	Health care	Day care and education	Misc.	College (Princeton)	Forgone wages	Total for year
0	$5,915	$1,624	$1,885	$719	$744	$2,120	$1,860		$44,650	$59,518
1	$6,211	$1,706	$1,979	$755	$781	$2,226	$1,953		$48,669	$64,279
2	$6,521	$1,791	$2,078	$793	$820	$2,338	$2,051		$53,049	$69,440
3	$6,804	$2,124	$2,139	$818	$833	$2,670	$2,168		$57,823	$75,379
4	$7,144	$2,231	$2,246	$859	$874	$2,803	$2,276		$63,027	$81,461
5	$7,501	$2,342	$2,358	$902	$918	$2,944	$2,390		$41,047	$60,402
6	$7,760	$2,974	$2,675	$1,030	$1,097	$2,127	$2,576		$45,847	$66,087
7	$8,148	$3,123	$2,809	$1,082	$1,152	$2,233	$2,704		$52,033	$73,285
8	$8,556	$3,279	$2,950	$1,136	$1,209	$2,345	$2,840		$57,900	$80,214
9	$8,599	$4,001	$3,232	$1,308	$1,366	$1,712	$3,039		$65,315	$88,572
10	$9,029	$4,201	$3,393	$1,373	$1,434	$1,798	$3,191		$72,460	$96,880
11	$9,480	$4,411	$3,563	$1,442	$1,506	$1,888	$3,351		$64,402	$90,042
12	$10,444	$4,855	$3,986	$2,494	$1,581	$1,537	$3,897		$72,230	$101,024
13	$10,966	$5,097	$4,185	$2,619	$1,660	$1,613	$4,092		$82,517	$112,750
14	$11,514	$5,352	$4,395	$2,750	$1,743	$1,694	$4,296		$92,118	$123,863
15	$11,008	$5,929	$5,620	$2,629	$1,933	$3,119	$3,944		$104,460	$138,642
16	$11,558	$6,226	$5,901	$2,761	$2,030	$3,275	$4,141		$116,188	$152,080
17	$12,136	$6,537	$6,196	$2,899	$2,132	$3,439	$4,348		$130,979	$168,665
18								$103,574	$145,257	$248,831
19								$110,831	$140,766	$251,597
20								$118,605	$156,987	$275,592
21								$126,935	$177,732	$304,667
Total	$159,294	$67,805	$61,589	$28,370	$23,813	$41,881	$55,117	$459,945	$1,885,454	$2,783,268

Middle income (one child family; 1997 before-tax family income: $35,500 to $59,700)

Age	Housing	Food	Transportation	Clothing	Health care	Day care and education	Misc.	College (Univ. of Michigan)	Forgone wages	Total for year
0	$3,720	$1,228	$1,352	$546	$645	$1,401	$1,104		$23,600	$33,594
1	$3,906	$1,289	$1,419	$573	$677	$1,471	$1,159		$25,724	$36,218
2	$4,101	$1,353	$1,490	$602	$711	$1,545	$1,217		$28,039	$39,058
3	$4,263	$1,636	$1,522	$617	$718	$1,809	$1,306		$30,563	$42,434
4	$4,476	$1,718	$1,598	$648	$754	$1,899	$1,372		$33,313	$45,778
5	$4,700	$1,804	$1,678	$681	$791	$1,994	$1,440		$21,695	$34,783
6	$4,819	$2,426	$1,961	$798	$947	$1,346	$1,579		$24,233	$38,108
7	$5,060	$2,547	$2,059	$838	$995	$1,413	$1,658		$27,502	$42,072
8	$5,313	$2,675	$2,162	$879	$1,044	$1,484	$1,740		$30,603	$45,901
9	$5,194	$3,289	$2,405	$1,020	$1,193	$1,020	$1,885		$34,523	$50,527

(continued on next page)

of birth, to have enough money on hand to pay for four years of college as each semester's tuition bill comes due. If you wait until the child is in kindergarten to start saving, your monthly savings requirement will jump to $524. If you wait until the child reaches freshman year of high school, the number will jump to $1,957 a month.

Or here's another way to look at the challenge. Take a middle-class fam-

Age	Housing	Food	Transportation	Clothing	Health care	Day care and education	Misc.	College (Florida A&M)	Forgone wages	Total for year
10	$5,454	$3,454	$2,525	$1,071	$1,252	$1,071	$1,979		$38,299	**$55,104**
11	$5,726	$3,627	$2,651	$1,124	$1,315	$1,124	$2,078		$34,040	**$51,685**
12	$6,502	$3,852	$3,029	$1,982	$1,381	$868	$2,539		$38,178	**$58,331**
13	$6,828	$4,045	$3,180	$2,081	$1,450	$912	$2,666		$43,615	**$64,776**
14	$7,169	$4,247	$3,339	$2,185	$1,522	$957	$2,799		$48,690	**$70,908**
15	$6,445	$4,950	$4,434	$2,037	$1,701	$1,701	$2,372		$55,213	**$78,852**
16	$6,767	$5,197	$4,656	$2,138	$1,786	$1,786	$2,490		$61,412	**$86,233**
17	$7,105	$5,457	$4,888	$2,245	$1,876	$1,876	$2,615		$69,230	**$95,292**
18								$35,821	$76,777	**$112,598**
19								$38,140	$74,402	**$112,543**
20								$40,614	$82,976	**$123,591**
21								$43,255	$93,941	**$137,196**
Total	**$97,549**	**$54,795**	**$46,345**	**$22,063**	**$20,757**	**$25,678**	**$33,996**	**$157,832**	**$996,567**	**$1,455,581**

Lower income (one-child family; 1997 before-tax family income: less than $35,500)

Age	Housing	Food	Transportation	Clothing	Health care	Day care and education	Misc.	College (Florida A&M)	Forgone wages	Total for year
0	$2,753	$1,029	$905	$459	$496	$856	$719		$11,050	**$18,267**
1	$2,890	$1,081	$950	$482	$521	$898	$755		$12,045	**$19,622**
2	$3,035	$1,135	$998	$506	$547	$943	$793		$13,129	**$21,085**
3	$3,144	$1,321	$1,005	$517	$545	$1,120	$847		$14,310	**$22,808**
4	$3,301	$1,387	$1,055	$543	$573	$1,176	$889		$15,598	**$24,521**
5	$3,466	$1,456	$1,108	$570	$601	$1,234	$934		$10,158	**$19,527**
6	$3,523	$1,977	$1,363	$681	$731	$764	$1,047		$11,346	**$21,433**
7	$3,699	$2,076	$1,431	$715	$768	$803	$1,099		$12,877	**$23,468**
8	$3,884	$2,180	$1,502	$751	$806	$843	$1,154		$14,329	**$25,450**
9	$3,674	$2,732	$1,712	$866	$923	$539	$1,270		$16,164	**$27,879**
10	$3,858	$2,868	$1,798	$909	$970	$566	$1,333		$17,932	**$30,233**
11	$4,051	$3,012	$1,888	$954	$1,018	$594	$1,400		$15,938	**$28,854**
12	$4,743	$3,318	$2,227	$1,692	$1,069	$445	$1,826		$17,876	**$33,196**
13	$4,980	$3,484	$2,338	$1,777	$1,122	$468	$1,917		$20,421	**$36,508**
14	$5,229	$3,658	$2,455	$1,866	$1,178	$491	$2,013		$22,797	**$39,689**
15	$4,434	$4,150	$3,480	$1,727	$1,315	$851	$1,547		$25,852	**$43,355**
16	$4,656	$4,358	$3,654	$1,814	$1,380	$893	$1,624		$28,754	**$47,133**
17	$4,888	$4,576	$3,837	$1,904	$1,449	$938	$1,705		$32,415	**$51,713**
18								$16,783	$35,948	**$52,731**
19								$17,802	$34,837	**$52,639**
20								$18,886	$38,851	**$57,737**
21								$20,038	$43,985	**$64,023**
Total	**$70,208**	**$45,797**	**$33,705**	**$18,732**	**$61,013**	**$14,421**	**$22,873**	**$73,508**	**$466,613**	**$761,871**

Note: Numbers may not add up because of rounding

ily earning, say, $47,200 in 1998. Assume that inflation will average 5 percent over the next 18 years and that this family's income will grow 4 per- cent above inflation. Assume finally that this family will earn a 7 percent annual average return on its savings. Now suppose this family had a new child last year, and the parents want to prefund the likely cost of sending this child to a top-rank state school. What percent of family income do they need to put away each year toward the child's college expenses? Answer: about 4 percent.

So far, this accounting puts the cost of raising and educating a middle-class, only child at roughly $459,014 ($301,183 in direct expenditures to age 18 plus $157,831 for college costs). Now suppose you're considering having a child and want to have enough money in the bank by the day the child is born to be able to cover all of his or her direct future costs to you. No one actually does this, of course, but as any chief financial officer knows, this is a useful way to calculate the real burden of long-term liabilities. Assume you can earn 7 percent on your investments after your child is born. In that case, you'll need to build a nest egg of $204,470 by delivery day. Assuming you want to raise your child with a middle-class standard of living, this is the approximate present value of your liabilities for future expenses related to that child.

Or, suppose you want to have a child 10 years from now and want to start a regular savings plan that will allow you just enough money by the child's date of birth to cover all future child-related expenses as they occur. What you need to start saving today is $1,181 a month. Again, nobody actually does this, but amortizing the cost of children in this way provides a useful benchmark in figuring how "affordable" children are. Could you "afford" to pay an extra $1,181 every month for the next 10 years servicing your credit-card debt? Failing to prefund future liabilities, such as the future cost of a child, is financially equivalent to borrowing. If your family income goes up substantially in the future, you may be able to afford your child-related "unfunded liabilities," but if it remains stagnant or grows only slowly, as real family income has for decades, then these unfunded liabilities will hurt.

A final expenditure to add to our tally is a bit more abstract but no less real: forgone family income. People who have children tend to have less time on their hands to make money.

Consider first the forgone income for an unwed teenage mother who rears her child alone. Researchers at the University of Michigan have compared the earning power, over 20 years, of women who did and did not have children out of wedlock as teenagers. Interestingly, at ages 19 and 20, women who had given birth to illegitimate children actually had slightly higher incomes on average than women who remained childless during their teenage years; this presumably reflected the effect of welfare payments, which can boost short-term income above what the average childless full-time student earns. But by age 21, unmarried women who refrained from having become pregnant as teenagers, or who had abortions, began to pull well ahead of those who did not. By age 29, women who did not have the burden of raising a child alone as teenagers could expect to have earned a total of $72,191 more than women who did carry this burden.

What does it cost a married woman to have children? The answer depends crucially on her opportunities. Obviously, a woman who gives up a career as a nurse's aide to have a baby does not forgo as much income as a woman who gives up a law partnership. But for both there is an "opportunity cost," which can be roughly estimated. As economist Burggraf points out in her recent book, *The Feminine Economy and Economic Man,* people tend to take marriage partners of similar educational backgrounds and aspirations (social scientists label this "assortive mating"). For example, college-educated men are 15 times more likely to marry college-educated women than are men who never completed high school. This means that the opportunity cost of either spouse taking time off to raise a child is often 50 percent of a family's potential income.

That's exactly the trade-off faced by Colette Hochstein and her husband, Michael Lingenfelter. Both are librarians who work extensively with computer-information retrieval systems. Her position is with the National Institutes of Health in Bethesda,

Md.; he works in the White House library. Together, they spend more money on day care for their 2-year-old daughter, Miranda—about 17 percent of their household income—than on any other expense except their mortgage. Yet since they both earn roughly the same salary, the only way to avoid paying for day care would be to sacrifice half their household income. If either of them were to quit work to take care of Miranda full time, says Hochstein, the economic cost would extend beyond Miranda's childhood years: "In this rapidly changing, high-tech time, there are few professions in which one could take even a year's leave of absence without falling seriously behind."

Given the career opportunities now available to women, virtually all parents face some opportunity cost in having children, and it usually adds up to serious money. Consider this hypothetical middle-class, husband-wife family. They met in college and soon after married. Two years into their marriage, they each were earning $23,600, but then came Junior. She immediately quit her job to stay home with the baby, causing their family income to fall by half. After their child reaches kindergarten, she hopes to begin working half time; by the time the child reaches age 11, she hopes to be able to boost her work hours to 30 a week. But remembering her own escapades while home alone during high school, she does not plan to return to full-time work until the child goes off to college.

What's the opportunity cost of these life choices? Assume, as the USDA does, that inflation averages 5 percent over her working life. Further assume that, because of her "mommy track," her average annual real wage increases come to 2 percent instead of a possible 4 percent she could have earned as a childless and fully committed full-time professional. In that event, she'll sacrifice $996,567 in forgone income over just the next 21 years. Adjusting for inflation, that's equal in today's dollars to roughly $548,563.

Where does this leave the total bill? Combine $996,567 in forgone wages with the USDA's estimates of a typical middle-class family's direct child-related expenses for an only child ($301,183); add in the likely cost of sending a child born last year to a first-rank, in-state public university ($157,831), and the total cost of one typical middle-class child born in 1997 comes in at $1,445,581. Even after adjusting for inflation, the cost of a middle-class child born last year is still $799,913 in today's dollars.

To be sure, parents also receive some direct subsidies for their child-care costs. Being able to claim a dependent is worth $2,650 in federal taxes due this year, for example. And under current law, families are eligible to take a tax credit for child-care expenses, with a maximum credit of $720 for one child in a low-income family and up to $1,440 for two or more children. President Clinton recently proposed making this credit more generous, so that a family of four making $35,000 and saddled with high child-care bills would no longer owe any federal income taxes. But even if Clinton's plan is approved, parents who stay home with their kids will continue to receive no compensation for their lost income, and even those taking the credits will find themselves far worse off financially, in most cases, than if they had decided to remain childless.

Given current economic incentives, it is hardly surprising that the "smartest" people in our society end up being those least likely to have children. Middle-aged women with graduate degrees are more than three times more likely to be childless than those who dropped out of high school. Similarly, two-income married-couple families earning over $75,000 are 70 percent more likely to be childless than those earning between $10,000 and $19,999. You don't have to be an economic materialist to see the financial reality behind these numbers. Highly educated, high-income people have a higher opportu-

nity cost, in the form of lost income, if they decide to have children.

Government policy makers are forever talking about the need for society to "invest" in today's youth, if for no other reason than to pay for the huge, largely socialized cost of supporting the growing ranks of the elderly. It's a noble goal, but at the individual family level, a child, financially speaking, looks more like a high-priced consumer item with no warranty. It's the decision to remain childless that offers the real investment opportunity.

TUMMIES. Feeding a middle-class 15-year-old costs **$1,920** a year on average. Hide the Cheez-Its!

Imagine a middle-class, college-age, sexually active woman who is contemplating whether to spend $5,000 to have her tubes tied so she'll never have to worry about getting pregnant. We've already seen how the cost of giving birth to just one child could easily exceed $1.4 million over the next 22 years. Even though many of those costs could be well down the road, a typical middle-class young woman paying $5,000 for such an operation could expect that "investment" to compound at a rate of fully 680 percent over the next 22 years alone. (The return on a vasectomy, which is even cheaper, would be much high-

er.) It will be a long time before anyone finds a deal that lucrative on Wall Street.

But wait a minute. Isn't this an absurd conclusion? Children aren't just a bundle of liabilities. If they were, the way for society to become richer would be for everyone to stop having kids, but of course that wouldn't work. Without a rising new generation of workers, there will be nobody around to assume our debts, and before long, even the store shelves will be empty. So why does our accounting suggest the opposite?

Because society's economic interests and those of parents as individuals don't perfectly coincide. The financial sacrifice a parent makes to have and raise children creates enormous wealth for society as a whole. But the modern reality is that everyone shares in much of that wealth regardless of what role he or she played in creating it. If, for example, you don't choose to have children, or you treat your children badly, you still won't have to give up any of your Social Security pension.

Historically, support in old age did depend, almost entirely, on how many children you had, and on how well your investment in them turned out. Even before parents grew old, they could usually count on their children to perform economically useful tasks around the farm or shop. This made children economic assets—from the point of view of both society at large and parents.

Now the economic returns of parenting mostly bypass parents, and a proper accounting has to reflect that. For economic man in the late 20th century, child-rearing has become a crummy financial bargain. Fortunately, as Mom always said, there's more to life than money.

Amy Graham contributed to this article.

Our Babies, Ourselves

By Meredith F. Small

During one of his many trips to Gusiiland in southwestern Kenya, anthropologist Robert LeVine tried an experiment: he showed a group of Gusii mothers a videotape of middle-class American women tending their babies. The Gusii mothers were appalled. Why does that mother ignore the cries of her unhappy baby during a simple diaper change? And how come that grandmother does nothing to soothe the screaming baby in her lap? These American women, the Gusii concluded,

are clearly incompetent mothers. In response, the same charge might be leveled at the Gusii by American mothers. What mother hands over her tiny infant to a six-year-old sister and expects the older child to provide adequate care? And why don't those Gusii women spend more time talking to their babies, so that they will grow up smart?

Both culture—the traditional way of doing things in a particular society—and individual experience guide parents in their tasks. When a father chooses to

pick up his newborn and not let it cry, when a mother decides to bottle-feed on a schedule rather than breast-feed on demand, when a couple bring the newborn into their bed at night, they are prompted by what they believe to be the best methods of caregiving.

For decades, anthropologists have been recording how children are raised in different societies. At first, the major goals were to describe parental roles and understand how child-rearing practices and rituals helped to generate adult per-

---

Gusii Survival Skills

By Robert A. LeVine

Farming peoples of subSaharan Africa have long faced the grim reality that many babies fail to survive, often succumbing to gastrointestinal diseases, malaria, or other infections. In the 1970s, when I lived among the Gusii in a small town in southwestern Kenya, infant mortality in that nation was on the decline but was still high—about eighty deaths per thousand live births during the first years, compared with about ten in the United States at that time and six to eight in Western Europe.

The Gusii grew corn, millet, and cash crops such as coffee and tea. Women handled the more routine tasks of cultivation, food processing, and trading, while men were supervisors or entrepreneurs. Many men worked at jobs outside the village, in urban centers or on plantations. The soci-

ety was polygamous, with perhaps 10 percent of the men having two or more wives. A woman was expected to give birth every two years, from marriage to menopause, and the average married women bore about ten live children—one of the highest fertility rates in the world.

Nursing mothers slept alone with a new infant for fifteen months to insure its health. For the first three to six months, the Gusii mothers were especially vigilant for signs of ill health or slow growth, and they were quick to nurture unusually small or sick infants by feeding and holding them more often. Mothers whose newborns were deemed particularly at risk—including twins and those born prematurely—entered a ritual seclusion for several weeks, staying with their infants in a hut with a constant fire.

Mothers kept infants from crying in the early months by holding them constantly and being quick to comfort them. After three to six months—if the baby was growing normally—mothers began to entrust the baby to the care of other children (usually six to twelve years old) in order to pursue tasks that helped support the family. Fathers did not take care of infants, for this was not a traditional male activity.

Because they were so worried about their children's survival, Gusii parents did not explicitly strive to foster cognitive, social, and emotional development. These needs were not neglected, however, because from birth Gusii babies entered an active and responsive interpersonal environment, first with their mothers and young caregivers, and later as part of a group of children.

An Infant's Three Rs

By Sara Harkness and Charles M. Super

You are an American visitor spending a morning in a pleasant middle-class Dutch home to observe the normal routine of a mother and her six-month-old baby. The mother made sure you got there by 8:30 to witness the morning bath, an opportunity for playful interaction with the baby. The baby was then dressed in cozy warm clothes, her hair brushed and styled with a tiny curlicue atop her head. The mother gave her the midmorning bottle, then sang to her and played patty-cake for a few minutes before placing her in the playpen to entertain herself with a mobile while the mother attended to other things nearby. Now, about half an hour later, the baby is beginning to get fussy.

The mother watches for a minute, then offers a toy and turns away. The baby again begins to fuss. "Seems bored and in need of attention," you think. But the mother looks at the baby sympathetically and in a soothing voice says, "Oh, are you tired?" Without further ado she picks up the baby, carries her upstairs, tucks her into her crib, and pulls down the shades. To your surprise, the baby fusses for only a few more moments, then is quiet. The mother returns looking serene. "She needs plenty of sleep in order to grow," she explains. "When she doesn't have her nap or go to bed on time, we can always tell the difference—she's not so happy and playful."

Different patterns in infant sleep can be found in Western societies that seem quite similar to those of the United States. We discovered the "three R's" of Dutch child rearing—*rust* (rest), *regelmaat* (regularity) and *reinheid* (cleanliness)—while doing research on a sample of sixty families with infants or young children in a middle-class community near Leiden and Amsterdam, the sort of community typical of Dutch life styles in all but the big cities nowadays. At six months, the Dutch babies were sleeping more than a comparison group of American babies—a total of fifteen hours per day compared with thirteen hours for the Americans. While awake at home, the Dutch babies were more often left to play quietly in their playpens or infant seats. A daily ride in the baby carriage provided time for the baby to look around at the passing scene or to doze peacefully. If the mother needed to go out for a while without the baby, she could leave it alone in bed for a short period or time her outing with the baby's nap time and ask a neighbor to monitor with a "baby phone."

To understand how Dutch families manage to establish such a restful routine by the time their babies are six months old, we made a second research visit to the same community. We found that by two weeks of age, the Dutch babies were already sleeping more than same-age American babies. In fact, a dilemma for some Dutch parents was whether to wake the baby after eight hours, as instructed by the local health care providers, or let them sleep longer. The main method for establishing and maintaining this pattern was to create a calm, regular, and restful environment for the infant throughout the day.

Far from worrying about providing "adequate stimulation," these mothers were conscientious about avoiding overstimulation in the form of late family outings, disruptions in the regularity of eating and sleeping, or too many things to look at or listen to. Few parents were troubled by their babies' nighttime sleep routines. Babies's feeding schedules were structured following the guidelines of the local baby clinic (a national service). If a baby continued to wake up at night when feeding was no longer considered necessary, the mother (or father) would most commonly give it a pacifier and a little back rub to help it get back to sleep. Only in rare instances did parents find themselves forced to choose between letting the baby scream and allowing too much night waking.

Many aspects of Dutch society support the three Rs throughout infancy and childhood—for example, shopping is close to home, and families usually have neighbors and relatives nearby who are available to help out with child care. The small scale of neighborhoods and a network of bicycle paths provide local play sites and a safe way for children to get around easily on their own (no "soccer moms" are needed for daily transportation!). Work sites for both fathers and mothers are also generally close to home, and there are many flexible or part-time job arrangements.

National policies for health and other social benefits insure universal coverage regardless of one's employment status, and the principle of the "family wage" has prevailed in labor relations so that mothers of infants and young children rarely work more than part-time, if at all. In many ways, the three Rs of Dutch child rearing are just one aspect of a calm and unhurried life style for the whole family.

sonality. In the 1950s, for example, John and Beatrice Whiting, and their colleagues at Harvard, Yale, and Cornell Universities, launched a major comparative study of childhood, looking at six varied communities in different regions: Okinawa, the Philippines, northern India, Kenya, Mexico, and New England. They showed that communal expectations play a major role in setting parenting styles, which in turn play a part in shaping children to become accepted adults.

More recent work by anthropologists and child-development researchers has shown that parents readily accept their society's prevailing ideology on how babies should be treated, usually because it makes sense in their environmental or social circumstances. In the United States, for example, where individualism is valued, parents do not hold babies as much as in other cultures, and they place them in rooms of their own to sleep. Pediatricians and parents alike often say this fosters independence and self-reliance. Japanese parents, in contrast, believe that individuals should be well integrated into society, and so they "indulge" their babies: Japanese infants are held more often, not left to cry, and sleep with their parents. Efe parents in Congo believe even more in a communal life, and their infants are regularly nursed, held, and comforted by any number of group members, not just parents. Whether such practices help form the anticipated adult personality traits remains to be shown, however.

Recently, a group of anthropologists, child-development experts, and pediatricians have taken the cross-cultural approach in a new direction by investigating how differing parenting styles affect infant health and growth. Instead of emphasizing the development of adult personality, these researchers, who call themselves ethnopediatricians, focus

Doctor's Orders

By Edward Z. Tronick

In Boston, a pediatric resident is experiencing a vague sense of disquiet as she interviews a Puerto Rican mother who has brought her baby in for a checkup. When she is at work, the mother explains, the two older children, ages six and nine, take care of the two younger ones, a two-year-old and the three-month-old baby. Warning bells go off for the resident: young children cannot possibly be sensitive to the needs of babies and toddlers. And yet the baby is thriving; he is well over the ninetieth percentile in weight and height and is full of smiles.

The resident questions the mother in detail: How is the baby fed? Is the apartment safe for a two-year-old? The responses are all reassuring, but the resident nonetheless launches into a lecture on the importance of the mother to normal infant development. The mother falls silent, and the resident is now convinced that something is seriously wrong. And something is—the resident's model of child care.

The resident subscribes to what I call the "continuous care and contact" model of parenting, which demands a high level of contact, frequent feeding, and constant supervision, with almost all care provided by the mother. According to this model, a mother should also enhance cognitive development with play and verbal engagement. The pediatric resident is comfortable with this formula—she is not even conscious of it—because she was raised this way and treats her own child in the same manner. But at the Child Development Unit of Children's Hospital in Boston, which I direct, I want residents to abandon the idea that there is only one way to raise a child. Not to do so may interfere with patient care.

Many models of parenting are valid. Among Efe foragers of Congo's Ituri Forest, for example, a newborn is routinely cared for by several people. Babies are even nursed by many women. But few individuals ever play with the infant; as far as the Efe are concerned, the baby's job is to sleep.

In Peru, the Quechua swaddle their infants in a pouch of blankets that the mother, or a child caretaker, carries on her back. Inside the pouch, the infant cannot move, and its eyes are covered. Quechua babies are nursed in a perfunctory fashion, with three or four hours between feedings.

As I explain to novice pediatricians, such practices do not fit the continuous care and contact model; yet these babies grow up just fine. But my residents see these cultures as exotic, not relevant to the industrialized world. And so I follow up with examples closer to home: Dutch parents who leave an infant alone in order to go shopping, sometimes pinning the child's shirt to the bed to keep the baby on its back; or Japanese mothers who periodically wake a sleeping infant to teach the child who is in charge. The questions soon follow. "How could a mother leave her infant alone?" "Why would a parent ever want to wake up a sleeping baby?"

The data from cross-cultural studies indicate that child-care practices vary, and that these styles aim to make the child into a culturally appropriate adult. The Efe make future Efe. The resident makes future residents. A doctor who has a vague sense that something is wrong with how someone cares for a baby may first need to explore his or her own assumptions, the hidden "shoulds" that are based solely on tradition. Of course, pediatric residents must make sure children are cared for responsibly. I know I have helped residents broaden their views when their lectures on good mothering are replaced by such comments as "What a gorgeous baby! I can't imagine how you manage both work and three others at home!"

on the child as an organism. Ethnopediatricians see the human infant as a product of evolution, geared to enter a particular environment of care. What an infant actually gets is a compromise, as parents are pulled by their offspring's needs and pushed by social and personal expectations.

Compared with offspring of many other mammals, primate infants are dependent and vulnerable. Baby monkeys and apes stay close to the mother's body, clinging to her stomach or riding on her back, and nursing at will. They are protected in this way for many months, until they develop enough motor and cognitive skills to move about. Human infants are at the extreme: virtually helpless as newborns, they need twelve months just to learn to walk and years of social learning before they can function on their own.

Dependence during infancy is the price we pay for being hominids, members of the group of upright-walking primates that includes humans and their extinct relatives. Four million years ago, when our ancestors became bipedal, the hominid pelvis underwent a necessary renovation. At first, this new pelvic architecture presented no problem during birth because the early hominids, known as australopithecines, still had rather small brains, one-third the present size. But starting about 1.5 million years ago, human brain size ballooned. Hominid babies now had to twist and bend to pass through the birth canal, and more important, birth had to be triggered before the skull grew too big.

As a result, the human infant is born neurologically unfinished and unable to coordinate muscle movement. Natural selection has compensated for this by favoring a close adult-infant tie that lasts years and goes beyond meeting the needs of food and shelter. In a sense, the human baby is not isolated but is part of a physiologically and emotionally entwined dyad of infant and caregiver. The adult might be male or female, a birth or adoptive parent, as long as at least one person is attuned to the infant's needs.

The signs of this interrelationship are many. Through conditioning, a mother's breast milk often begins to flow at the sound of her own infant's cries, even before the nipple is stimulated. New mothers also easily recognize the cries (and smells) of their infants over those of other babies. For their part, newborns recognize their own mother's voice and prefer it over others. One experiment showed that a baby's heart rate quickly synchronizes with Mom's or Dad's, but not with that of a friendly stranger. Babies are also predisposed

The Crying Game

By Ronald G. Barr

All normal human infants cry, although they vary a great deal in how much. A mysterious and still unexplained phenomenon is that crying tends to increase in the first few weeks of life, peaks in the second or third month, and then decreases. Some babies in the United States cry so much during the peak period—often in excess of three hours a day—and seem so difficult to soothe that parents come to doubt their nurturing skills or begin to fear that their offspring is suffering from a painful disease. Some mothers discontinue nursing and switch to bottle-feeding because they believe their breast milk is insufficiently nutritious and that their infants are always hungry. In extreme cases, the crying may provoke physical abuse, sometimes even precipitating the infant's death.

A look at another culture, the !Kung San hunter-gatherers of southern Africa, provides us with an opportunity to see whether caregiving strategies have any effect on infant crying. Both the !Kung San and Western infants escalate their crying during the early weeks of life, with a similar peak at two or three months. A comparison of Dutch, American, and !Kung San infants shows that the number of individual crying episodes are virtually identical. What differs is their length: !Kung San infants cry about half as long as Western babies. This implies that caregiving can influence only some aspects of crying, such as duration.

What is particularly striking about child-rearing among the !Kung San is that infants are in constant contact with a caregiver; they are carried or held most of the time, are usually in an upright position, and are breast-fed about four times an hour for one to two minutes at a time. Furthermore, the mother almost always responds to the smallest cry or fret within ten seconds.

I believe that crying was adaptive for our ancestors. As seen in the contemporary !Kung San, crying probably elicited a quick response, and thus consisted of frequent but relatively short episodes. This pattern helped keep an adult close by to provide adequate nutrition as well as protection from predators. I have also argued that crying helped an infant forge a strong attachment with the mother and—because new pregnancies are delayed by the prolongation of frequent nursing—secure more of her caregiving resources.

In the United States, where the threat of predation has receded and adequate nutrition is usually available even without breast-feeding, crying may be less adaptive. In any case, caregiving in the United States may be viewed as a cultural experiment in which the infant is relatively more separated—and separable—from the mother, both in terms of frequency of contact and actual distance.

The Western strategy is advantageous when the mother's employment outside of the home and away from the baby is necessary to sustain family resources. But the trade-off seems to be an increase in the length of crying bouts.

to be socially engaged with caregivers. From birth, infants move their bodies in synchrony with adult speech and the general nature of language. Babies quickly recognize the arrangement of a human face—two eyes, a nose, and a mouth in the right place—over other more Picasso-like rearrangements. And mothers and infants will position themselves face-to-face when they lie down to sleep.

Babies and mothers seem to follow a typical pattern of play, a coordinated waltz that moves from attention to inattention and back again. This innate social connection was tested experimentally by Jeffrey Cohn and Edward Tronick in a series of three-minute laboratory experiments at the University of Massachusetts, in which they asked mothers to act depressed and not respond to baby's cues. When faced with a suddenly unresponsive mother, a baby repeatedly reaches out and flaps around, trying to catch her eye. When this tactic does not work, the baby gives up, turning away and going limp. And when the mother begins to respond again, it takes thirty seconds for the baby to reengage.

Given that human infants arrive in a state of dependency, ethnopediatricians have sought to define the care required to meet their physical, cognitive, and emotional needs. They assume there must be ways to treat babies that have proved adaptive over time and are therefore likely to be most appropriate. Surveys of parenting in different societies reveal broad patterns. In almost all cultures, infants sleep with their parents in the same room and most often in the same bed. At all other times, infants are usually carried. Caregivers also usually respond quickly to infant cries; mothers most often by offering the breast. Since most hunter-gatherer groups also follow this overall style, this is probably the ancestral pattern. If there is an exception to these generalizations, it is the industrialized West.

Nuances of caretaking, however, do vary with particular social situations. !Kung San mothers of Botswana usually carry their infants on gathering expeditions, while the forest-living Ache of Paraguay, also hunters and gatherers, usually leave infants in camp while they gather. Gusii mothers working in garden plots leave their babies in the care of older children, while working mothers in the West may turn to unrelated adults. Such choices have physiological or behavioral consequences for the infant. As parents navigate between infant needs and the constraints of making a life, they may face a series of trade-offs that set the caregiver-infant dyad at odds. The areas of greatest controversy are breast-feeding, crying, and sleep—the major preoccupations of babies and their parents.

Strapped to their mothers' sides or backs in traditional fashion, human infants have quick access to the breast. Easy access makes sense because of the nature of human milk. Compared with that of other mammals, primate milk is relatively low in fat and protein but high in carbohydrates. Such milk is biologically suitable if the infant can nurse on a frequent basis. Most Western babies are fed in a somewhat different way. At least half are bottle-fed from birth, while

When to Wean

By Katherine A. Dettwyler

Breast-feeding in humans is a biological process grounded in our mammalian ancestry. It is also an activity modified by social and cultural constraints, including a mother's everyday work schedule and a variety of beliefs about personal autonomy, the proper relationship between mother and child (or between mother and father), and infant health and nutrition. The same may be said of the termination of breast-feeding, or weaning.

In the United States, children are commonly bottle-fed from birth or weaned within a few months. But in some societies, children as old as four or five years may still be nursed. The American Academy of Pediatrics currently advises breast-feeding for a minimum of one year (this may be revised upward), and the World Health Organization recommends two years or more. Amid conflicting advice, many wonder how long breast-feeding should last to provide an infant with optimal nutrition and health.

Nonhuman primates and other mammals give us some clues as to what the "natural" age of weaning would be if humans were less bound by cultural norms. Compared with most other orders of placental mammals, primates (including humans) have longer life spans and spend more time at each life stage, such as gestation, infant dependency, and puberty. Within the primate order itself, the trend in longevity increases from smaller-bodied, smaller-brained, often solitary prosimians through the larger-bodied, larger-brained, and usually social apes and humans. Gestation, for instance, is eighteen weeks in lemurs, twenty-four weeks in macaques, thirty-three weeks in chimpanzees, and thirty-eight weeks in humans.

Studies of nonhuman primates offer a number of different means of estimating the natural time for human weaning. First, large-bodied primates wean their offspring some months after the young have quadrupled their birth weight. In modern humans, this weight milestone is passed at about two and a half to three years of age. Second, like many other mammals, primate offspring tend to be weaned when they have attained about one third of their adult weight; humans reach this level between four and seven years of age. Third, in all species studied so far, primates also wean their offspring at the time the first permanent molars erupt; this occurs at five and a half to six years in modern humans. Fourth, in chimpanzees and gorillas, breast-feeding usually lasts about six times the duration of gestation. On this basis, a human breast-feeding would be projected to continue for four and a half years.

Taken together, these and other projections suggest that somewhat more than two and a half years is the natural minimum age of weaning for humans and seven years the maximum age, well into childhood. The high end of this range, six to seven years, closely matches both the completion of human brain growth and the maturation of the child's immune system.

In many non-Western cultures, children are routinely nursed for three to five years. Incidentally, this practice inhibits ovulation in the mother, providing a natural mechanism of family planning. Even in the United States, a significant number of children are breast-fed beyond three years of age. While not all women are able or willing to nurse each of their children for many years, those who do should be encouraged and sup-ported. Health care professionals, family, friends, and nosy neighbors should be reassured that "extended" breast-feeding, for as long as seven years, appears physiologically normal and natural.

Substantial evidence is already available to suggest that curtailing the duration of breast-feeding far below two and a half years—when the human child has evolved to expect more—can be deleterious. Every study that includes the duration of breast-feeding as a variable shows that, on average, the longer a baby is nursed, the better its health and cognitive development. For example, breast-fed children have fewer allergies, fewer ear infections, and less diarrhea, and their risk for sudden infant death syndrome (a rare but devastating occurrence) is lower. Breast-fed children also have higher cognitive test scores and lower incidence of attention deficit hyperactivity disorder.

In many cases, specific biochemical constituents of breast milk have been identified that either protect directly against disease or help the child's body develop its own defense system. For example, in the case of many viral diseases, the baby brings the virus to the mother, and her gut-wall cells manufacture specific antibodies against the virus, which then travel to the mammary glands and go back to the baby. The docosahesanoic acid in breast milk may be responsible for improved cognitive and attention functions. And the infant's exposure to the hormones and cholesterol in the milk appears to condition the body, reducing the risk of heart disease and breast cancer in later years. These and other discoveries show that breast-feeding serves functions for which no simple substitute is available.

others are weaned from breast to bottle after only a few months. And most—whether nursed or bottle-fed—are fed at scheduled times, waiting hours between feedings. Long intervals in nursing disrupt the manufacture of breast milk, making it still lower in fat and thus less satisfying the next time the nipple is offered. And so crying over food and even the struggles of weaning result from the infant's unfulfilled expectations.

Sleep is also a major issue for new parents. In the West, babies are encouraged to sleep all through the night as soon as possible. And when infants do not do so, they merit the label "sleep problem" from both parents and pediatricians. But infants seem predisposed to sleep rather lightly, waking many times during the night. And while sleeping close to an adult allows infants to nurse more often and may have other beneficial effects, Westerners usually expect babies to sleep alone. This practice has roots in ecclesiastical laws enacted to protect against the smothering of infants by "lying over"—often a thinly disguised cover for infanticide—which was a concern in Europe beginning in the Middle Ages. Solitary sleep is reinforced by the rather recent notion of parental privacy. Western parents are also often convinced that solitary sleep will mold strong character.

Infants' care is shaped by tradition, fads, science, and folk wisdom. Cross-cultural and evolutionary studies provide a useful perspective for parents and pediatricians as they sift through the alternatives. Where these insights fail to guide us, however, important clues are provided by the floppy but interactive

Bedtime Story

By James J. McKenna

For as far back as you care to go, mothers have followed the protective and convenient practice of sleeping with their infants. Even now, for the vast majority of people across the globe, "cosleeping" and nighttime breast-feeding remain inseparable practices. Only in the past 200 years, and mostly in Western industrialized societies, have parents considered it normal and biologically appropriate for a mother and infant to sleep apart.

In the sleep laboratory at the University of California's Irvine School of Medicine, my colleagues and I observed mother-infant pairs as they slept both apart and together over three consecutive nights. Using a polygraph, we recorded the mother's and infant's heart rates, brain waves (EEGs), breathing, body temperature, and episodes of nursing. Infrared video photography simultaneously monitored their behavior.

We found that bed-sharing infants face their mothers for most of the night and that both mother and infants are highly responsive to each other's movements, wake more frequently, and spend more time in lighter stages of sleep than they do while sleeping alone. Bed-sharing infants nurse almost twice as often, and three times as long per bout, than they do when sleeping alone. But they rarely cry. Mothers who routinely sleep with their infants get at least as much sleep as mothers who sleep without them.

In addition to providing more nighttime nourishment and greater protection, sleeping with the mother supplies the infant with a steady stream of sensations of the mother's presence, including touch, smell, movement, and warmth. These stimuli can perhaps even compensate for the human infant's extreme neurological immaturity at birth.

Cosleeping might also turn out to give some babies protection from sudden infant death syndrome (SIDS), a heartbreaking and enigmatic killer. Cosleeping infants nurse more often, sleep more lightly, and have practice responding to maternal arousals. Arousal deficiencies are suspected in some SIDS deaths, and long periods in deep sleep may exacerbate this problem. Perhaps the physiological changes induced by cosleeping, especially when combined with nighttime breast-feeding, can benefit some infants by helping them sleep more lightly. At the same time, cosleeping makes it easier for a mother to detect and respond to an infant in crisis. Rethinking another sleeping practice has already shown a dramatic effect: In the United States, SIDS rates fell at least 30 percent after 1992, when the American Academy of Pediatrics recommended placing sleeping babies on their backs, rather than face down.

The effect of cosleeping on SIDS remains to be proved, so it would be premature to recommend it as the best arrangement for all families. The possible hazards of cosleeping must also be assessed. Is the environment otherwise safe, with appropriate bedding materials? Do the parents smoke? Do they use drugs or alcohol? (These appear to be the main factors in those rare cases in which a mother inadvertently smothers her child.) Since cosleeping was the ancestral condition, the future for our infants may well entail a borrowing back from ancient ways.

babies themselves. Grinning when we talk to them, crying in distress when left alone, sleeping best when close at heart, they teach us that growth is a cooperative venture.

A professor of anthropology at Cornell University, **Meredith F. Small** became interested in "ethnopediatrics" in 1995, after interviewing anthropologist James J. McKenna on the subject of infant sleep. Trained as a primate behaviorist, Small has observed female mating behavior in three species of macaque monkeys. She now writes about science for a general audience; her book *Our Babies, Ourselves* is published by Anchor Books/Doubleday (1998). Her previous contributions to *Natural History* include "These Animals Think, Therefore . . ." (August 1996) and "Read in the Bone" (June 1997).

RECOMMENDED READING

Parents' Cultural Belief Systems: Their Origins, Expressions, and Consequences, by Sara Harkness and Charles M. Super (Guilford Press, 1996)

Child Care and Culture: Lessons from Africa, by Robert A. LeVine et al. (Cambridge University Press, 1994)

Our Babies, Ourselves, by Meredith F. Small (Anchor Books/Doubleday, 1998)

Breastfeeding: Biocultural Perspectives, edited by Patricia Stuart-Macadam and Katherine A. Dettwyler (Aldine de Gruyler, 1995)

The Family Bed: An Age Old Concept in Childrearing, by Tine Thevenin (Avery Publishing Group, 1987)

Human Birth: An Evolutionary Perspective, by Wenda R. Trevathan (Aldine de Gruyter, 1987)

Six Cultures: Studies of Child Rearing, edited by Beatrice B. Whiting (John Wiley, 1963)

Unit 3

Unit Selections

Key Points to Consider

❖ When you think of a marriage, what do you picture? What are your expectations of your (future) spouse? What are your expectations of yourself? What and how much are you willing to give to your marriage? Who, in your opinion, should get married? How is your experience of committed relationships influenced by those you saw while growing up? How do those relationships affect your own willingness to enter a committed relationship?

❖ How should each spouse behave in a marriage? How are men's and women's roles the same or different?

❖ What do you expect parenthood to be like? What have you learned in talking with your parents or other parents about their expectations and experiences? Why should you share parenting tasks with your spouse or partner? Why would you want or not want to have a child by yourself? Do you believe that fathers and mothers should have different roles? How would you contrast the views of parents and children? Do they see their relationship in radically different ways?

 **Links** | **www.dushkin.com/online/**

These sites are annotated on pages 4 and 5.

And they lived happily ever after . . . The romantic image conjured up by this well-known final line from fairy tales is not reflective of the reality of family life and relationship maintenance. The belief that somehow love alone should carry us through is pervasive. In reality, maintaining a relationship takes dedication, hard work, and commitment.

We come into relationships, regardless of their nature, with fantasies about how things ought to be. Spouses, parents, children, siblings, and others—all family members have at least some unrealistic expectations about each other. It is through the negotiation of their lives together that they come to work through these expectations and replace them with other, it is hoped, more realistic ones. By recognizing and acting on their own contribution to the family, members can set and attain realistic family goals. Tolerance and acceptance of differences can facilitate this process as can competent communication skills. Along the way, family members need to learn new skills and develop new habits of relating to each other. This will not be easy, and, try as they may, not everything will be controllable. Factors both inside and outside the family may impede their progress.

From the start, the expectations both partners have of their relationship have an impact, and the need to negotiate differences is a constant factor. Adding a child to the family affects the lives of parents in ways that they could previously only imagine. Feeling under siege, many parents struggle to know the right way to rear their children. These factors can all combine to make child rearing more difficult than it might otherwise have been. Other family relationships also evolve, and in our nuclear family–focused culture, it is possible to forget that family relationships extend beyond those between spouses and parents and children.

The initial subsection presents a number of aspects regarding marital and other committed, long-term relationships and ways of balancing multiple and often competing roles played by today's couples, who hope to fulfill individual as well as couple needs. It is a difficult balancing act to cope with the expectations and pressures of work, home, children, and relational intimacy. In "The Science of a Good Marriage," the work done by John Gottman on what makes a good marriage

is detailed. What is presented may surprise the reader, as some forms of good marriages contradict previously held ideas. Relationships benefit us in more ways than mere social contact, and Bill Thomson, in "The Healing Power of Intimacy," identifies several ways in which we benefit, physically, from intimate relationships. In the last article in this subsection of unit 3, Olivia Mellan, in "Men, Women & Money," suggests ways in which couples can put money, an emotionally loaded topic, in its place.

The next subsection examines the parent/child relationship. The first article, "Parental Rights: An Overview," is a provocative piece on the rights of parents to make decisions about their children's welfare. The next reading, "Father Love and Child Development: History and Current Evidence" offers a look at how father love affects child development as much as mother love. The next two articles look at the parent-child relationship from both ends. The first, "Parents Speak: Zero to Three's Findings from Research on Parents' Views of Early Childhood Development," is from the parents' perspective and the second, "Do Parents Really Matter? Kid Stuff" is from the children's viewpoint.

The Science of a Good Marriage

Psychology is unlocking the secrets of happy couples.

BY BARBARA KANTROWITZ AND PAT WINGERT

THE MYTH OF MARRIAGE GOES LIKE this: somewhere out there is the perfect soul mate, the yin that meshes easily and effortlessly with your yang. And then there is the reality of marriage, which, as any spouse knows, is not unlike what Thomas Edison once said about genius: 1 percent inspiration and 99 percent perspiration. That sweaty part, the hard work of keeping a marriage healthy and strong, fascinates John Gottman. He's a psychologist at the University of Washington, and he has spent more than two decades trying to unravel the bewildering complex of emotions that binds two humans together for a year, a decade or even (if you're lucky) a lifetime.

Gottman, 56, comes to this endeavor with the best of qualifications: he's got the spirit of a scientist and the soul of a romantic. A survivor of one divorce, he's now happily married to fellow psychologist Julie Schwartz Gottman (they run couples workshops together). His daunting task is to quantify such intangibles as joy, contempt and tension. Ground zero for this research is the Family Research Laboratory on the Seattle campus (nicknamed the Love Lab). It consists of a series of nondescript offices equipped with video cameras and pulse, sweat and movement monitors to read the hearts and minds of hundreds of couples who have volunteered to be guinea pigs in longitudinal studies of the marital relationship. These volunteers have opened up their lives to the researchers, dissecting everything from the frequency of sex to who takes out the garbage. The results form the basis of Gottman's new book, "The Seven Principles for Making Marriage Work," which he hopes will give spouses a scientific road map to happiness.

Among his unexpected conclusions: anger is not the most destructive emotion in a marriage, since both happy and miserable couples fight. Many popular therapies aim at defusing anger between spouses, but Gottman found that the real demons (he calls them "the Four Horsemen of the Apocalypse") are criticism, contempt, defensiveness and stonewalling. His research shows that the best way to keep these demons at bay is for couples to develop a "love map" of their spouse's dreams and fears. The happy couples all had such a deep understanding of their partner's psyche that they could navigate roadblocks without creating emotional gridlock.

Gottman's research also contradicts the Mars-Venus school of relationships, which holds that men and women come from two very different emotional worlds. According to his studies, gender differences may contribute to marital problems, but they don't cause them. Equal percentages of both men and women he interviewed said that the quality of the spousal friendship is the most important factor in marital satisfaction.

Gottman says he can predict, with more than 90 percent accuracy, which couples are likely to end up in divorce court. The first seven years are especially precarious; the average time for a divorce in this group is 5.2 years. The next danger point comes around 16 to 20 years into the marriage, with an average of 16.4 years. He describes one couple he first met as newlyweds: even then they began every discussion of their problems with sarcasm or criticism, what Gottman calls a "harsh start-up." Although they professed to be in love and committed to the relationship, Gottman correctly predicted that they were in trouble. Four years later they were headed for divorce, he says.

An unequal balance of power is also deadly to a marriage. Gottman found that a husband who doesn't share power with his wife has a much higher risk of damaging the relationship. Why are men singled out? Gottman says his data show that most wives, even those in unstable marriages, are likely to accept their husband's influence. It's the men who need to shape up, he says. The changes can be simple, like turning off the football game when she needs to talk. Gottman says the gesture proves he values "us" over "me."

Gottman's research is built on the work of many other scientists who have focused on emotion and human interaction. Early studies of marriage relied heavily on questionnaires filled out by couples, but these were often inaccurate. In the 1970s several psychology labs began using direct observation of couples to study marriage. A big boon was a relatively new tool for psychologists: videotape. Having a visual record that could be endlessly replayed made it much easier to study the emotional flow between spouses. In 1978 researchers Paul Ekman and Wallace Freisen devised a coding system for the human face (see, "Facing Your Problems") that eventually provided another way to measure interchange between spouses.

Although early studies focused on couples in trouble, Gottman thought it was also important to study couples whose marriages work; he thinks they're the real experts. The Love Lab volunteers are interviewed about the history of their marriage. They then talk in front of the cameras about subjects that cause conflict between them. One couple Gottman describes in the book, Tim and Kara, argued constantly about his friend Buddy, who often wound up spending the night on Tim and Kara's couch. The researchers take scenes like this and break down every second of interaction to create a statistical pattern of good and bad moments. How many times did she roll her eyes (a sign of contempt) when he spoke? How often did he fidget (indicating tension or stress)? The frequency of negative and positive expressions, combined with the data collected by the heart, sweat and other monitors, provides a multidimensional view of the relationship. (Tim and Kara ultimately decided Buddy could stay, only not as often.)

Gottman and other researchers see their work as a matter of public health. The average couple who seek help have been having problems for six years—long enough to have done serious damage to their relationship. That delay, Gottman says, is as dangerous as putting off regular mammograms. The United States has one of the highest divorce rates in the industrialized world, and studies have shown a direct correlation between marriage and well-being. Happily married people are healthier; even their immune systems work better than those of people who are unhappily married or divorced. Kids suffer as well; if their parents split, they're more likely to have emotional or school problems.

But going to a marriage counselor won't necessarily help. "Therapy is at an impasse," Gottman says, "because it is not based on solid empirical knowledge of what real couples do to keep their marriages happy and stable." In a 1995 Consumer Reports survey, marriage therapy ranked at the bottom of a poll of patient satisfaction with various psychotherapies. The magazine said part of the problem was that "almost anyone can hang out a shingle as a marriage counselor." Even credentialed therapists may use approaches that have no basis in research. Several recent studies have shown that many current treatments produce few long-term benefits for couples who seek help.

One example: the process called "active listening." It was originally used by therapists to objectively summarize the complaints of a patient and validate the way the patient is feeling. ("So, I'm hearing that you think your father always liked your sister

Know Your Spouse

Test the strength of your marriage in this relationship quiz prepared especially for NEWSWEEK by John Gottman.

TRUE/FALSE

		T	F
1	I can name my partner's best friends	☐	☐
2	I can tell you what stresses my partner is currently facing	☐	☐
3	I know the names of some of the people who have been irritating my partner lately	☐	☐
4	I can tell you some of my partner's life dreams	☐	☐
5	I can tell you about my partner's basic philosophy of life	☐	☐
6	I can list the relatives my partner likes the least	☐	☐
7	I feel that my partner knows me pretty well	☐	☐
8	When we are apart, I often think fondly of my partner	☐	☐
9	I often touch or kiss my partner affectionately	☐	☐
10	My partner really respects me	☐	☐
11	There is fire and passion in this relationship	☐	☐
12	Romance is definitely still a part of our relationship	☐	☐
13	My partner appreciates the things I do in this relationship	☐	☐
14	My partner generally likes my personality	☐	☐
15	Our sex life is mostly satisfying	☐	☐
16	At the end of the day my partner is glad to see me	☐	☐
17	My partner is one of my best friends	☐	☐
18	We just love talking to each other	☐	☐
19	There is lots of give and take (both people have influence) in our discussions	☐	☐
20	My partner listens respectfully, even when we disagree	☐	☐
21	My partner is usually a great help as a problem solver	☐	☐
22	We generally mesh well on basic values and goals in life	☐	☐

Scoring: GIVE YOURSELF ONE POINT FOR EACH "TRUE" ANSWER. ABOVE 12: YOU HAVE A LOT OF STRENGTH IN YOUR RELATIONSHIP. CONGRATULATIONS. BELOW 12: YOUR RELATIONSHIP COULD STAND SOME IMPROVEMENT AND COULD PROBABLY BENEFIT FROM SOME WORK ON THE BASICS, SUCH AS IMPROVING COMMUNICATION.

better and you're hurt by that.") In recent years this technique has been modified for marital therapy—ineffectively, Gottman says. Even highly trained therapists would have a hard time stepping back in the middle of a fight and saying, "So, I'm hearing that you think I'm a fat, lazy slob."

Happily married couples have a very different way of relating to each other during disputes, Gottman found. The partners make frequent "repair attempts," reaching out to each other in an effort to prevent negativity from getting out of control in the midst of conflict. Humor is often part of a successful repair attempt. In his book, Gottman describes one couple arguing about the kind of

car to buy (she favors a minivan; he wants a snazzier Jeep). In the midst of yelling, the wife suddenly puts her hand on her hip and sticks out her tongue—mimicking their 4-year-old son. They both start laughing, and the tension is defused.

In happy unions, couples build what Gottman calls a "sound marital house" by working together and appreciating the best in each other. They learn to cope with the two kinds of problems that are part of every marriage: solvable conflicts and perpetual problems that may represent underlying conflicts and that can lead to emotional gridlock. Gottman says 69 percent of marital conflicts fall into the latter category. Happy spouses

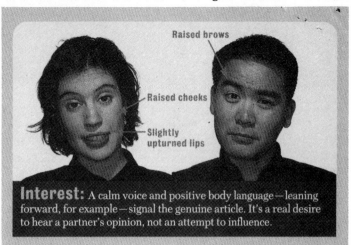

Raised brows

Raised cheeks

Slightly upturned lips

Interest: A calm voice and positive body language—leaning forward, for example—signal the genuine article. It's a real desire to hear a partner's opinion, not an attempt to influence.

Facing Your Problems

IN THE LAB, THE WAY A MARRIED COUPLE FIGHTS CAN OFTEN tell psychologists more than *what* they fight about. The expressions and underlying emotions displayed during a conflict may reveal the strength or weakness of the marriage. During a couple's 15-minute conversation—on a topic known to be a sore point—researchers at the University of Washington measure physiological responses (below) and facial expressions, which can reveal true feelings even when words don't. Videotapes also show how long the partners' emotional responses last—even the happiest of couples has fleeting moments of bad feeling, but if the negative indicators tend to endure, it can signal a marriage in trouble.

Photos by Andrew Brusso.

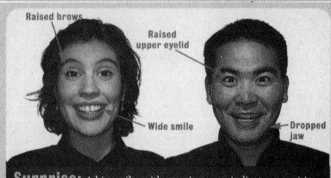

Raised brows

Raised upper eyelid

Wide smile

Dropped jaw

Surprise: A big smile, with popping eyes, indicates a positive surprise. Something unexpected but unpleasant yields the eye-pop only. Either way, a short-lived state.

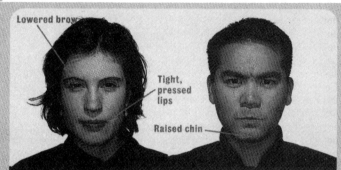

Lowered brow

Tight, pressed lips

Raised chin

Anger: The tone is cold or loud, the wording staccato. But honest anger, an internal state, is different from contempt, directed at the spouse. A fake smile, without raised cheeks, may mask anger.

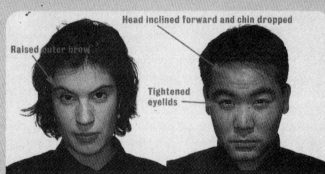

Head inclined forward and chin dropped

Raised outer brow

Tightened eyelids

Domineering: A "low and slow" voice often signals that one partner is trying to force the other to his or her view. Ranges from lawyerly cross-examination to blatant threats.

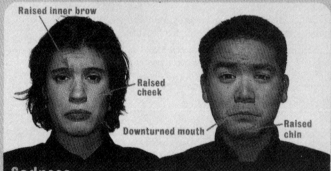

Raised inner brow

Raised cheek

Downturned mouth

Raised chin

Sadness: Passivity and sulking can look like stonewalling or disengaging from a fight, but sad people maintain more eye contact than stonewallers.

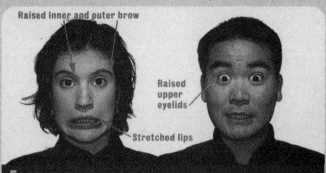

Raised inner and outer brow

Raised upper eyelids

Stretched lips

Fear: Outright fear is rare; a lower-grade version—tension— is more common. And a wife's tension, if pronounced, can be a predictor for divorce down the road.

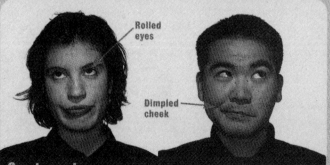

Rolled eyes

Dimpled cheek

Contempt: If prolonged, this expression is a red alert. Especially when accompanied by sarcasm and insults, it suggests a marriage in serious trouble.

deal with these issues in a way that strengthens the marriage. One couple Gottman studied argued constantly about order in their household (she demanded neatness, and he couldn't care less). Over the years they managed to accommodate their differences, acknowledging that their affection for each other was more important than newspapers piled up in the corner of the living room.

As psychologists learn more about marriage, they have begun devising new approaches to therapy. Philip Cowan and Carolyn Pape-Cowan, a husband-and-wife team (married for 41 years) at the University of California, Berkeley, are looking at one of the most critical periods in a marriage: the birth of a first child. (Two thirds of couples experience a "precipitous drop" in marital satisfaction at this point, researchers say.) "Trying to take two people's dreams of a perfect family and make them one is quite a trick," Pape-Cowan says. The happiest couples were those who looked on their spouses as partners with whom they shared household and child-care duties. The Cowans say one way to help spouses get through the transition to parenting would be ongoing group sessions with other young families to provide the kind of support people used to get from their communities and extended families.

Inside the Love Lab

In the laboratory, video cameras record facial expressions. Motion-sensing jiggle-ometers register fidgeting, and a cluster of sensors reads physiological data.

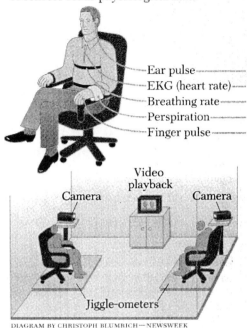

- Ear pulse
- EKG (heart rate)
- Breathing rate
- Perspiration
- Finger pulse

Video playback

Camera   Camera

Jiggle-ometers

DIAGRAM BY CHRISTOPH BLUMRICH—NEWSWEEK

Two other researchers—Neil Jacobson at the University of Washington and Andrew Christensen at UCLA—have developed what they call "acceptance therapy" after studying the interactions of couples in conflict. The goal of their therapy is to help people learn to live with aspects of their spouse's characters that simply can't be changed. "People can love each other not just for what they have in common but for things that make them complementary," says Jacobson. "When we looked at a clinical sample of what predicted failure in traditional behavior therapy, what we came upon again and again was an inability to accept differences."

Despite all these advances in marital therapy, researchers still say they can't save all marriages—and in fact there are some that *shouldn't* be saved. Patterns of physical abuse, for example, are extremely difficult to alter, Gottman says. And there are cases where the differences between the spouses are so profound and long-standing that even the best therapy is futile. Gottman says one quick way to test whether a couple still has a chance is to ask what initially attracted them to each other. If they can recall those magic first moments (and smile when they talk about them), all is not lost. "We can still fan the embers," says Gottman. For all the rest of us, there's hope.

THE HEALING POWER
of **Intimacy**

Healthy long-term relationships offer big rewards—better health, longer life, even more sex than the single life offers. But less than 50 percent of couples stick together for the long haul. Here's how some therapists are teaching couples to use their relationship "hot spots" for greater intimacy and lasting love.

BILL THOMSON

Bill Thomson is Senior Features Editor of Natural Health.

Joe and Martha came to see couples therapist Seymour Boorstein when their relationship was in crisis. They'd been married many years but were locked in a terrible battle over the renovations of their guest cottage. Martha wanted a much bigger refrigerator and stove than Joe wanted. He was interested in aesthetics and insisted on less intrusive appliances. She became outraged at his refusal to go along with her plan. Caught in a deadlock, they went to Boorstein.

A psychiatrist and editor of a textbook on transpersonal psychology, Boorstein looks at marriage from a mind/body perspective. His wife and co-teacher, Sylvia, teaches meditation and has a new book out, *IT'S EASIER THAN YOU THINK: THE BUDDHIST WAY TO HAPPINESS* (HarperSan Francisco, 1995). They've been together forty-three years.

In his work, Seymour has found that the majority of problems in couple relationships are caused when our primitive instinct for survival is triggered. When you or your partner get angry—whether you're peeved at him for burning the toast or outraged at her for wrecking the car—it is because the mind has perceived a threat and sent the body into a fight-or-flight mode.

"It's important for the couple to see that although they are disagreeing about the size of a stove, they really aren't," says Boorstein. "It's an issue of survival. What's upsetting Martha is not so much the now, but what she's projected from the past into the now."

In therapy sessions with Boorstein, Martha learned that as a child she had not been fed regularly and needed to scream for food. As a woman, she had always been more comfortable with a well-stocked, large refrigerator.

"The instant she got that awareness," Boorstein says, "her rage disappeared." She saw the unreasonableness of her demand and was more comfortable with smaller appliances. Joe felt compassion for his wife. He sincerely told her to renovate the cottage and install appliances in a way that made her comfortable.

Because the parts of the brain that perceive threats, the limbic and reptilian brains, are the more "primitive" ones, which respond as if survival were at stake, our automatic tendency when we perceive a threat is to fight or flee—the two classic reactions during relationship struggles. A third part of the human brain, the neocortex, is the relational part of the brain which Boorstein believes is where our lovingness originates. The neocortex is able to distinguish between true threats to our survival and imposters, while the primitive parts of the brain (which develop in children before the relational part does) respond swiftly to anything even resembling a threat. "When we get frightened on any primitive level," Boorstein explains, "the primitive brain overrides the neocortex and does what's necessary for survival. These are very different from the strategies we need to make a relationship work."

When two people—whether married, long-term heterosexual, or same-sex couples—begin to understand one another in this way, it becomes easier to override the primitive brain. As a couple learns to examine what's triggering their feelings, they slowly pull away from living in survival mode. Not only does this enable them to get along, they stop subjecting their bodies to the chronic stress that accompanies repeated fight-or-flight reactions.

Numerous studies have confirmed the effects of chronic stress, from high blood pressure to immune disorders to depression. From a health standpoint, in other words, the brain that's loving wins out over the brain that's stressing, every time. This explains, in part, why couples who work out their problems are likely to be healthier (*see* box "Marriage Will Make You Healthier, Wealthier, and Sexier").

Couples can learn strategies to understand their "hot spots"—the areas of conflict within their marriage or long-term relationship—and use them to strengthen bonds and build trust.

Indeed, the Boorsteins and other innovative therapists are now helping couples access issues from the past that set off the primitive brain and cause ranting and raving or splitting. Their work is proving to help couples not only stick it out, but in the long run, make each of the partners stronger and healthier.

MARRIAGE WILL MAKE YOU HEALTHIER, WEALTHIER, AND SEXIER

While our national divorce rate—50 percent—might make you think marriage doesn't have much to offer, Linda J. Waite, Ph.D., a researcher at the University of Chicago, recently assembled some impressive data on the fate of unmarried versus married people. Consider the following evidence:

■ **Being single lowers life expectancy more than cancer.** For both men and women, being unmarried eats into life expectancy more than the risks of being overweight and getting cancer. For single men, bachelorhood is a greater risk factor than heart disease. They pay for their freedom with 3,500 days of their life (almost ten years) while heart disease, on average, takes only 2,100 days off their life. On average, the single life takes 1,600 days off a woman's life while cancer takes 980 days.

■ **Married men have fewer alcohol problems.** Married men have about half the alcohol-related troubles as their party-going single counterparts. In other words, the wedded average one-half incident per month while singles are getting into pickles one time a month. (Regardless of marital status, women have one-tenth the booze problems of men.)

■ **Married families save more money.** The median household wealth of marrieds is $132,000. It's less than one-third that for divorced, widowed, and the never married—around $40,000.

■ **Marriage reduces risk-taking behavior.** Both divorced men and women take risks—driving too fast, getting into fights, and practicing unhealthy lifestyle habits—at a higher rate than marrieds do (about 30 percent higher for men and 45 percent for women).

■ **Married people have sex twice as often.** If you're an average married man, you're having sex 6.84 times a month; if you're a woman, you're having sex 6.11 times a month. (These different figures raise questions about where men are getting the additional sex that the women aren't getting. But rest assured, this is a "statistical anomaly.") Single people have sex only about half as much—women, 3.23 times a month, and men, 3.63 times.

■ **Married men get more physical pleasure from sex.** Fifty-four percent of married men report being physically satisfied from sex with their wives while 43 percent of single men say they're satisfied with their sex. Married women, however, are only barely "statistically" happier than unmarried women.

■ **Married men and women are more emotionally pleased with sex.** Fifty-one percent of married men report emotional satisfaction from sex versus 36 percent of single men. For women, 44 percent of the marrieds are emotionally gratified with their love-making versus 33 percent of the single women.

"Women, when they're ready to give up say the same thing—'I've given and I've given and I've given, and no matter how much I give, I don't get back. I feel empty. I have nothing left to give.'"

"TILL DISSATISFACTION DO US PART"

"We are at a turning point in the history of couple consciousness," says John Welwood, Ph.D., a psychologist from Mill Valley, California, and author of several books on intimacy, including *JOURNEY OF THE HEART* (HarperCollins, 1990) and one to be released in January, *LOVE AND AWAKENING* (HarperCollins).

"In the past, marriage was a functional business that maintained the family and society," states Welwood. "During the last half century, people in the West have begun to look to marriage simply as a source of personal pleasure and need gratification. That's very new and we're seeing the limits of it."

Indeed, instead of "till death do us part," couples often stay together only "till dissatisfaction do us part." Also, divorce laws in the last several decades have been relaxed. Couples don't need to claim grounds of cruelty or abuse to get out of marriage. They can end it due to "irretrievable breakdown of the marriage," which can mean your spouse's sloppiness drives you crazy, or else you're just bored.

"The problem with basing marriage purely on pleasure and having your needs met is that those things come and go," Welwood says.

The problem with basing marriage purely on pleasure and having your needs met is that those things come and go.

MARRIED, AMERICAN STYLE

Every fifteen minutes in America, sixty married couples untie the knot and opt for life alone, and untold others in relationships walk away from them. At the turn of the century, one out of fourteen marriages ended in divorce; today, every other one does. According to Census Bureau data, since 1970, the percentage of married Americans (among all adults eighteen and over) has declined 15 percent, while the number of divorced has risen 300 percent.

Why aren't people staying together? John Gray, Ph.D, couples therapist and author of *MEN ARE FROM MARS, WOWEN ARE FROM VENUS* (HarperCollins, 1992), offers at least some insight.

Marital malcontent, he says, stems from a colossal shake-up in men's and women's roles. "Women don't need men the way they once did," says Gray, a forty-four-year-old former celibate monk who is now married with three kids. "A woman today doesn't need a protector—she can carry her Mace; she's got police forces; she's got lawyers; what does she need a guy for?"

Gray recalls, "I had one woman yelling at me on a radio show recently, 'I don't need a man. I've got a sperm bank!'

"Women are having careers to support themselves and be independent. They're feeling the same responsibilities their fathers felt, but they also want to create a beautiful relationship and have children and a home. Women are carrying a weight that is heavier than any woman in history has ever carried. Naturally, they are going to be unhappy."

Men, for their part, don't know what women want to make them happy. "After listening to couples again and again," Gray says, "right before they're about to get a divorce, the message I hear from men is 'I've given and I've given and I've given and no matter how much I give, it's not enough to maker her happy.'

And when they go, disappointed partners look for insights on magazine racks and in bookstores—making books such as Gray's and Thomas Moore's *SOUL MATES* behemoth best-sellers. Alas, the popular newsstand solutions (often running along the lines of how to have "hotter, happier sex") are less than satisfying. Even Gray sometimes offers questionable cures. His advice that men must make women feel they're being heard (even if the guy has to *pretend* that he hears her) and that women must make men feel appreciated (however hard it is for her to imagine *why*) may win temporary peace in a relationship, but lasting love?

Welwood believes we need a new vision of intimate relationships if we are going to find lasting love. "There is a much deeper kind of happiness—which goes far beyond immediate gratification—that comes from realizing who you are and sharing that with someone you love," says Welwood. "*This* is the basis for healthy and satisfying relationships."

Welwood's definition of a healthy relationship involves working with the obstacles that arise when the going gets rough between partners. Indeed, hard times are the catalyst for healing emotional wounds that go back to childhood and that threaten not only our marriages but other arenas of our lives as well. In fact, recognizing and dealing with each partner's psychological wounds is necessary for a successful relationship.

As these wounds heal, instead of putting the blame for our marital difficulties on our partners, we learn to take responsibility for them, to "own them," the psychoanalyst would say. When we work to make this happen, we become less stressed and the relationship—instead of dying out—grows into a trusting intimacy that we value both in spite of its troubles, and because of them.

FINDING A SOUL CONNECTION

Welwood's explanation of how relationship conflicts arise is different than Boorstein's, though he, like Boorstein, looks to the couple's past. Often as children, Welwood explains, we built a psychological shell around us to protect ourselves from feeling pain. Born open and loving, as children we are often taught that some aspect of ourself is unacceptable. Maybe our exuberance was squelched or our creativity was dampened. Or, maybe we were taught we had to behave a certain way in order to be good.

"No matter how much our parents love us," Welwood writes in *LOVE AND AWAKENING*, "they generally see their version of who we are, reflecting their own hopes, fears, expectations, and unmet needs." Instead of suffering the pain of rejection by our parents, we often develop a personality that will win their acceptance.

This adaptation, which is necessary for a child's psychic survival and integration into the family, forces children to build a false personality that they struggle to maintain throughout their lives. "The young child is like an open hand that gradually contracts and closes," says Welwood. "Eventually, we learn to shut ourselves down."

This protective tightening gets installed in our body and mind as a rigid set of defenses. "In this way," he says, "we inflict on ourselves the core wound that will haunt us

the rest of our lives—we separate from our deeper spiritual nature, which is an openness to life."

Falling in love provides a glimpse of this spiritual nature. As Welwood details in *LOVE AND AWAKENING*, in love's early stages, feelings such as openness, peace, and expansiveness simply emerge, unbidden. We become inspired to commit ourselves to a new partner who is able to generate such feelings in us. When people are truly in love, which Welwood calls a "soul connection," they see behind the false facade of one another and connect on a deeper level. They connect with one another's "essential nature," which brings out the feelings of openness and peace. One of the most complimentary things you can say about a partners is "I feel I can be myself with him." Or, simply, "He understands me. He gets who I am." This, says Welwood, is because when someone loves you in this way, they see through your facade and see who you really are. Being seen in this manner, however, can also bring about conflicts.

"If, for example, we harbor an image of ourselves as unlovable, then when the opportunity arises to be loved for who we really are, we won't know how to handle it," Welwood says. "Even though this is what we truly long for, it will also frighten us to death—because it threatens our whole identity." To let love enter, we have to give up who we think we are.

"I don't know any couples who have not suffered this fall from grace at some point, losing touch with the original bright presence that first drew them together," says Welwood. The longer we avoid these old psychological wounds and our rigid set of defenses, the greater becomes their hold on us. If left unresolved, we wind up living an exhausting charade, as Welwood calls it.

The antidote, Welwood says, is to let ourselves open to the feelings we fear the most. When people learn to open to their pain—within the context of an intimate relationship—there results a softening, a relaxation, and greater self-acceptance; it also deepens their connection with themselves and with each other, and can provide them a lifelong mutual path and direction.

"That's the real work of the relationship—and the real opportunity to develop deeper, lasting intimacy," says Welwood.

Of course, facing the challenges on this path takes great courage. As Welwood discusses in *LOVE AND AWAKENING*, in many ways, having a soul connection is like finding a worthy opponent. We have met our match, someone who won't let us get away with anything that is false or diminishes our being. This is often apparent in the first few years of a relationship, as the partners challenge each other, saying, in effect, "Why are you so stuck in your ways?"

If two partners confront each other like this in order to prove something or to get

their own way, it will only result in a power struggle between two egos. Often we resist our partner's confrontations because they threaten to blow our cover, exposing parts of us we have a hard time acknowledging. Yet in blowing our cover, our partner is actually doing us a favor. This is what happened to Keith and Melissa, whose relationship Welwood describes in *LOVE AND AWAKENING*.

SACRED COMBAT

Keith was first attracted to Melissa because of her generosity of spirit. Everything about her—her warmth, her smile, her capacity to lavish affection, her emotional expressiveness—expressed this abundance. Although Keith loved these qualities in her, he felt threatened by them since he felt that these qualities were lacking in himself. In truth, Keith was very unexpressive because he had closed down his feelings as a child in order not to be overwhelmed by his emotionally intrusive mother.

In their typical conflict, Melissa would be unhappy about Keith's austerity and constrictedness while he became defensive, reacting in an angry, controlling manner. He would try to tone her down, while she remained intent on loosening him up. As the conflict between their different strategies escalated, their fights grew more fierce.

We resist our partner's confrontations because they threaten to blow our cover. But actually they're doing us a favor.

In examining the deeper source of their conflict, Keith eventually saw that Melissa was forcing him—by her very presence in his life—to confront ways in which he remained constricted. Melissa also saw that because she had grown up in a repressive family, she had come to believe that any self-restraint or detachment was a form of death. However, her emotional extravagance often veered into self-indulgence. When she was swept up in her feelings, she would exaggerate their significance, and this often left both of them feeling hurt and confused. Melissa had something important to learn from Keith in this regard—about not always acting out her feelings. By confronting Melissa's emotional tyrannies, Keith had a grounding effect on her; in learning to reflect

IN A LOVE CRISIS?

That's good! Use your relationship's "hot spots" to learn more about yourself and your partner. Here are nine ideas for dealing with love's day-to-day trials, taken from talks and writings by psychotherapists who specialize in working with couples: Seymour and Sylvia Boorstein, John Gray, and John and Jennifer Welwood.

1. Shut up. One thing that makes Gray's *MEN ARE FROM MARS, WOMEN ARE FROM VENUS* so popular is that he tells men a hundred different ways, LISTEN! This happens to be the single most powerful tool either sex has for averting trouble. If your partner wants to talk, let him or her talk. Don't interrupt. Don't vacuum. Don't answer the phone. Don't look to see what's on TV later. Listen.

2. Good happens. Students of Buddhism learn to observe that *everything* arises and passes. If you are angry or lonely or hurt and are distraught over your feelings and can't seem to get them resolved, allow them to pass before you act on them. They usually will pass. Your anger will somehow get soothed. Bad stuff happens. So does good.

3. Avoid the "67th argument." Every couple has had some particular discussion about sixty-seven times a year that *always* leads to an argument. You can see it coming. He says this, you say that, he says this again, and you know what's coming after you say that again: Mount Saint Helens erupts. So, change the script. It doesn't work. Do something else. Order a pizza, walk to the mail box, or watch the squirrels outside.

4. What are you afraid of? Beneath all anger is fear. If you understand this, then the next time you're so angry that you're ready to throw your plate of spaghetti at your lover's face, stop for a minute. Ask yourself, what am I so afraid of that I've gotten this mad? Or, if it's your partner who is brewing up a storm, try to feel empathy for the fear. What's he or she so afraid of? Compassion melts anger.

5. Feel lust, don't feed it. President Jimmy Carter made news when he confessed in *PLAYBOY* magazine that he had lusted in his heart. As he described his lusting, he had responded as a true Buddhist. He didn't act on his lust. He just felt it. Lust, like any powerful appetite, can never be fed enough. If you feed your lustful feelings in inappropriate ways, they will just want to be refed. Don't feed lust, feel it.

6. "Don't feed your lover a 150-pound burger." Boorstein says when you want to get a point across to your partner, you have to watch both the timing and the dosage of your efforts. Harping becomes nagging, which is counterproductive. Boorstein says, "You can't take a 150-pound hamburger and stuff it into a baby and get an adult. You have to put a little bit in. They chew a while, spit some out, swallow some. After a while, they grow a little."

7. The cure is in the poison. If your jealousy—or any strong emotion—is too much to bear, the most potent way of dealing with it is to walk right up to it and look it right in the eye. Say to yourself, "That's me. I am jealous." You feel the part of your body where it hurts. Your belly? Your neck? Your chest? Wherever it is, feel it and acknowledge it. Welwood and others say this is the entry point to meeting painful emotions head-on. If you confront them like this, they often back down.

8. It's up to you. One of the hardest things for people to accept and understand is that even in love, they're on their own when it comes to finding happiness. "Being responsible" means that you have to look at *your* issues and work them out with yourself. You may think the other person is the cause of the, or can be, the answer. But that's generally not the case. What partners can do is *support* one another's struggles.

9. Pretty good is perfect. A woman in her late seventies, married for fifty years, heard another woman say, "My relationship is pretty good, but it isn't perfect." The older woman said, "Listen, when you're talking about relationships, 'pretty good' is perfect."

on her feelings before rushing into action, she was able to settle into herself in a new way.

As Keith and Melissa come to appreciate how they were each other's teachers, this helped them see their conflict in a new light—

as part of a creative and fruitful "sacred combat"—rather than just a divisive struggle. This, says Welwood, is what a soul connection is about—two people joining together to nurture, stimulate, and provoke important steps in each other's unfolding.

RECOGNIZE YOUR SHADOW

Psychotherapists Kathleen Hendricks, Ph.D., ADTR, and Gay Hendricks, Ph.D., have counselled thousands of people with relationships problems over a fifteen-year period. One thing they say you can count on a relationship to do is to pull this kind of "unconscious stuff"—what psychoanalysts call your shadow—to the surface.

Robert A. Johnson, the author of many books on Jungian analysis, explains the shadow concept in *OWNING YOUR OWN SHADOW*. He writes, "We are born whole, but early on our way, we begin the shadow-making process; we divide our lives. We sort out our God-given characteristics into those that are acceptable to our society and those that we have to put away."

Johnson says we can hide these parts of ourselves, but they do not go away. "They only collect in the dark corners of our personality," he says. "When they have hidden long enough, they take on a life of their own." Our shadow can gain power over years. "If it accumulates more energy than our ego, it erupts as an overpowering rage or some indiscretion," says Johnson.

To remedy the problem, Hendricks explains, we teach couples to tell the "microscopic truth." Say, "my stomach is tight," or "I'm scared. I'm afraid of losing you when you do that." This is what psychoanalysts call "owning your shadow."

Johnson says, "The shadow is very important in marriage, and we can make or break a relationship depending on how conscious we are of this. We must come to terms with what we find annoying and distasteful—even downright intolerable—in the other and also in ourselves. Yet, it is precisely this confrontation that leads to our greatest growth."

Owning your shadow, say the Hendrickses, is about being truthful, with your partner and yourself. "It takes actual physical energy," says Kathleen, "to keep yourself from telling the truth. It can happen in a split second. You can suddenly be defensive without realizing a fear has come up. You can withdraw, withhold, and project in an instant and suddenly it looks like the other person's fault."

Psychotherapists such as the Hendrickses and John Welwood, and his wife of ten years, Jennifer—also a psychotherapist who counsels couples—agree that the intimate partnership is the ideal setting where two people can support one another's inquiry into the recesses of the shadow. In an honest, open relationship, each partner summons the shadow—the anger, the hurt, the pain—and owns it, takes responsibility for it as his or her own, instead of "projecting" it onto others. When we project it, we're basically trying to dish it off to someone else, to disown it. All that this accomplishes, of course, is to arouse anger and reaction from the other person.

"What we found in the early years of our relationship," says Gay, "was that we had awesome barriers to overcome in learning to tell each other the truth, even the simplest truth, like 'I was angry when you wrecked my car.' That was hard for me to say because my programming was to be Mr. Reasonable. I was angry, but it took me weeks to get past being Mr. Reasonable. It was a big breakthrough for me, to say, 'I'm angry.' "

And this process is ongoing, says Kathleen, "In relationships, taking healthy responsibility is something you will have opportunity to do over and over."

COMPASSION FOR BUGABOOS

It's much easier for partners to take responsibility for their shadows when they're extending empathy—compassion—to one another. The Boorsteins learned this lesson in their own marriage.

"If we were criticized a lot early in life," Seymour says, "as I was by my mother, we tend to project onto people around us the image of the person who was critical of us. Even though she died ten years ago, my mother still follows me." Seymour often speaks in public, but he says if he sees disapproving looks in the audience, he gets nervous. The biggest problem he's had in marriage, he says, is convincing his conscious mind that Sylvia is not his mother.

"Sylvia's not like my mother at all, but I've been sure at times that she was," he says. "It's gotten much better over the years, but I still slip up on occasion. I say to myself 'Ah-ha! I've been waiting forty-three years. I *knew* she would get like that.' "

Sylvia says she sees her mother too. But hers was approving, so she's not uncomfortable in front of audiences, she doesn't easily read criticism into innocent looks or comments, as Seymour might. Sylvia's bugaboo, however, is that she easily becomes fretful. Fifteen years ago, when their youngest daughter was studying theater dance in San Francisco, which required her commuting into the city, Sylvia could not sleep at night while worrying about the girl's safety.

"Seymour and I would be in bed and he'd fall asleep, and I'd get up at 10:45 when our daughter was to be home at 10:30 and I'd say to him, 'Get up. Worry.' He'd say, 'I have to work in the morning. I can't get up now.' He'd go back to sleep while I worried."

Couples seldom look for reasons *why* they're fretful or fearful. But doing so, says Sylvia, builds empathy, a foundation of successful relationships.

THE REASON FOR INTIMACY

Not a few people today wonder whether the struggles of a committed relationship are worth the troubles they seem to bring about. Jennifer and John Welwood have been together for ten years, and they've asked themselves what they give one another that they couldn't get on their own.

Jennifer says, "John creates an environment for me to develop as a human being. I'm very aware of needing him in my life to help me in this way. And it's mutual. That is what our relationship gives to both of us."

John adds, "When you find a larger purpose for your relationship—such as stimulating and supporting one another's deepest unfolding—that provides a bond that can hold two people together for a very long time. Then, whether things are going well this week or not, whether we're happy or not at any given moment, is secondary."

MEN WOMEN & MONEY

MONEY IS SUCH AN **EMOTIONALLY** LOADED TOPIC THAT FEW **COUPLES** DISCUSS IT DIRECTLY. **YET** IT, MORE THAN **SEX**, IS WHAT **DRIVES** PARTNERS **APART.** PSYCHOTHERAPIST **OLIVIA MELLAN** SHOWS **HOW** TO PUT **MONEY** IN ITS PLACE.

FOR MOST PEOPLE, MONEY IS never just money, a tool to accomplish some of life's goals. It is love, power, happiness, security, control, dependency, independence, freedom and more. Money is so loaded a symbol that to unload it–and I believe it must be unloaded to live in a fully rational and balanced relationship to money–reaches deep into the human psyche. Usually, when the button of money is pressed, deeper issues emerge that have long been neglected. As a result, money matters are a perfect vehicle for awareness and growth.

Most people relate to money much as they relate to a person–in an ongoing and complex way that taps deep-seated emotions. When two individuals form an enduring relationship with each other, money is always a partner, too. In these liberated times, couples discuss many things before marriage, but the meaning of money is not one of them. Money is still a taboo topic. Often, the silence is a shield for the shame, guilt and anxiety people feel about their own ways with money. I, for one, would not want to tell a date that I'm an overspender.

Many individuals have a troubled relationship with money. Then, when they get into a couple relationship, money matters get explosive. Other people may have no problem with money individually; the trouble starts after they're in the relationship.

IN TWO DECADES as a psychotherapist specializing in resolving money conflicts, I have observed that couples usually polarize around money. Partners tend to assume defense styles, or personalities, in relation to money that are direct opposites to each other. I call it Mellan's Law: If opposites don't attract right off the bat, then they will create each other eventually.

Commonly, a hoarder marries a spender. The United States is in fact a nation of overspenders. We live in a market economy and we are led to believe that we are good citizens to the degree that we go out and spend. Because of our community breakdown and spiritual alienation, many people feel a core emptiness that they try to fill up with Things. If we're not overspending, we're typically worrying about money or compulsively hoarding it.

We grow up in families where nobody talks about money. Most people will immediately protest: "Not true. My family talked about money all the time." When I ask, "How did you talk?" they reply, "My father worried about not having enough, and he yelled at my mother for spending too much."

The fact remains that people do not grow up with educational or philosophic conversations about what money is and isn't, what it can and can't do. We don't examine the societal messages telling us that gratification lies in spending or that keeping up with the

OPPOSITES ATTRACT. HOARDERS TYPICALLY PAIR WITH SPENDERS, AND WORRIERS JOIN WITH AVOIDERS.

Joneses is important. Information-based money discussions are so taboo that we usually reach adulthood without a realistic sense of our family's finances.

I ONCE MET A MAN who had no idea that he grew up in a wealthy family. He said, "We had a family restaurant and my mother was always worrying about how we were at the edge of doom. As a child I developed a stammer from all that money anxiety. As an adolescent, I worked day and night to keep the restaurant afloat. Years later, my mother was talking about the good old days when we were making so much money in the restaurant business. I started screaming at her about all the money anxiety I carried. I was outraged that it wasn't even based on a real threat. When I stopped screaming, I noticed that my stammer was gone."

And it never returned. That's a therapist's dream story: one catharsis, no symptom. But it does show how money carries a huge emotional load.

As a result of the money taboo, I grew up as most kids do: imitating my parents' way of handling money without being aware of it. My father, affected by the Depression, worried out loud about money. My mother was a shopaholic, expressing love by buying me and herself clothes. She'd hide the purchases behind a living room chair until my father was in a good mood. As an adult, whenever I felt either depressed or particularly happy, I too would go out and shop. And even if I bought everything at a thrift store, I'd hide all the items behind a chair until my husband was in a good mood. Actually, I alternated between shopping and worrying about money.

Some people do the opposite. They typically say, "My father was a hoarder and a worrier. I hated the way he made me account for every penny of my allowance. I made a vow to myself that I'd never be like that." Such people, however, are any-

thing but free of the parental attitude; their behavior is still defined by it.

In addition to irrational attitudes and beliefs about money that we internalize from our families of origin, we carry our own emotionally-charged memories of money from childhood. I remember being in a barbershop with my father when I was six, and some kid asked his father for a quarter. The father said no. The kid started to sob uncontrollably. I remember being so gripped by the child's sense of deprivation, I made a vow right then that I was never going to feel deprived like that. If you tell yourself at six that you're never going to feel deprived, you have the makings of a chronic overspender.

COUPLES POLARIZED over money engage in a balancing dance of opposites. Two spenders who come together will fight each other for the superspender role; the other, as a defense, will learn to hoard because someone has to set limits. When it comes to defense styles, there's always a pursuer (or clinger) and a withdrawer. With two withdrawers, one will become the superwithdrawer. The other will become a pursuer, because if they both withdrew there would be no connection at all.

An equally common polarity is the worrier and avoider. Avoiders don't focus on the details of their money life, such as whether they have enough money or how much interest they're paying on their credit cards; they just spend. A worrier will turn a mate into an avoider just as a way of escaping the avalanche of worry. And an avoider will turn a mate into a worrier. Two partners couldn't both avoid forever; somebody will eventually get concerned and take on the worrier role. Doubling the trouble, hoarders are usually worriers and spenders are usually avoiders.

As with all polar personality styles, hoarders and spenders live in different universes marked by opposing beliefs. What feels good to one feels horrible to the other. When not spending, a hoarder feels virtuous, in control. A spender when not spending feels anx-

DOING WHAT DOESN'T COME NATURALLY

GROWTH, CREATIVITY, INTIMACY AND FLEXIBILITY come from doing what is not automatic. For a hoarder, spending money on one's self or a loved one for immediate pleasure changes the pattern. For a spender, it's saving or investing money, or going on a slow, choreographed binge. Breaking habits doesn't happen all at once; it's a slow process. For example, I can't say, "Don't worry!" to a worrier. But I can say, "Pick one hour to worry, write down your worries for that time and give up worrying for the rest of the day."

PARTNERS CAN BEGIN to change their ingrained habits by taking the following steps:

• Do what doesn't come naturally once a week. Eventually you and your partner will have moved enough toward some middle ground that you are not locked into your roles.
• While practicing a new behavior, write down how it feels in order to monitor your progress.
• Reward yourself for that new behavior.—O.M.

PLANNERS OFTEN FIND THEMSELVES TIED TO DREAMERS, AND MONEY MONKS GET TOGETHER WITH DEDICATED AMASSERS.

ious and deprived. Indeed, spenders can't tolerate the word "budget"; financial planners have to draw up a "spending plan."

Other money personalities include planners, who are detail-oriented, and dreamers, who are global visionaries. In addition, there are money monks, often ex-hippies, political activists or spiritual souls, who feel that money corrupts and it's better to not have too much. Sometimes they marry money amassers, who believe that the guy with the most money wins. Amassers are not hoarders; they don't simply save, they invest to make their money grow. They save, spend and invest.

WHAT MAKES EACH OF the personality types is the operation of internal belief systems, what I call money myths–all the money messages, vows and emotional memories acquired from the family of origin, the peer group, the culture at large and filtered through a person's intrinsic temperament. Many spenders, for example, don't give away just money; they are effusive with feelings, words, everything. Hoarders are typically taciturn and withholding. Even in therapy, they have to be encouraged to open up.

Here is the ironic part. The longer couples are married, the more they lock into polarized roles. Then they attack each other for their differences, projecting onto the other attitudes about every other spender or hoarder

they have encountered in their life. They fail to acknowledge the positive aspects of their partner's personality type and of the balancing dance itself.

The failure of people to explore their money personalities leads to deep misunderstanding and hurt. Take the case of a man who views money as security. He does not believe in spending a great deal on gifts; he believes in saving. He's married to a woman who believes that money is both love and happiness; she's a spender. They are about to celebrate a major anniversary. He spends days in record stores searching for the song they danced to when they were dating in the '60s, "their song." When she gets his gift, she thinks he's chintzy and is insulted. He's inconsolably hurt. She, meanwhile, has bought him an expensive gift.

Money issues rarely manifest themselves openly in relationships. Instead, couples fight over what money represents. And while money issues can rear their head anytime; there are specific transition periods in relationships that force them to the surface: tax time, starting a family and buying a house. Couples may complain, "We can't agree on where we want to live." Or, "He wants to go on vacation and I want to save our money for retirement." Or, "She keeps indulging the children, getting them everything they want, and I don't think that's good for the kids."

In addition to money personalities, there are male-female differences in approaches to money that haunt many relationships. It could be said that some differences reflect men as hunters and women as gatherers. In his theater piece *Defending the Caveman*, Rob Becker describes men: they go out and buy a shirt, wear it until it dies, then go out and kill another shirt. Women, in contrast, gather. They shop for this for next Christmas for their niece and for that for their son-in-law.

OTHER PERVASIVE MONEY differences exist between the genders. First, men and women have differences of personal boundaries because

CONVERSING WITH CASH

HOW DO YOU TURN YOUR consciousness to an area that's usually in the dark? When a couple comes in fighting about money, I first have them clarify their own personal history and private relationship with money before turning to the dynamic between them.

I want people to see what money symbolizes to them. Then they can "unload" the symbol.

As an exercise at home, I ask each to engage in a dialogue with their Money, and not share the conversation until they come back. The goal is to see what money symbolizes for each person, and to recognize that money is just a tool to accomplish certain of life's goals.

In the dialogue, imagine your money is being interviewed on *Oprah*. Ask how it thinks the relationship between you two is going, how it feels about the way you treat it.

Perhaps Money will reply, "You know, you're squeezing me so tight, I can't breathe. You need to let go a little." Or, "You throw me around, but you don't treat me with respect. You need to pay more attention to me." Either speak into a tape recorder or write the conversation down on paper.

After this dialogue, draw on at least three voices in your head—mother, father and any other figure—and have them comment on what has transpired. Finally, consider what God, a Higher Power or inner wisdom might say.

Either Money or God, or both, will help you see the direction you need to move in to achieve money harmony.

Occasionally, a couple is unable to have a dialogue with Money. I then ask them to write down all their childhood memories and associations relating to money and start there.—O.M.

they are both raised largely by women. Men have to psychologically separate more rigidly from women because of the sex difference; women do not have to separate so rigidly, and therefore can afford less distinct boundaries.

MEN THINK NOTHING OF CHOOSING THE FAMILY CAR BY THEMSELVES, WHILE WOMEN THINK IT SHOULD BE A TEAM EFFORT.

Second, men are raised to see the world as hierarchical and competitive. There's always a one-up and one-down position, a winner and a loser. Women see the world as cooperative and democratic; they share. In addition, they are allowed—even encouraged—to be needy and vulnerable, while men are discouraged from such display.

The boundary and hierarchical differences between men and women lead to clashes around money decisionmaking. Men think nothing of going out alone and buying a big-screen TV, or even the family car or com-

puter, then coming home and saying, "Hi honey. I have a new car." She says, "Why didn't you consult me? I thought we were a team." And he says, "Are you my mother? Do I have to ask your permission?"

Because of their more rigid boundaries, men think of themselves as islands and withdraw when facing difficulties of intimacy. They don't see themselves as part of a team. And, of course, men and women are raised to believe different things about the way they should actually handle money. Despite many social changes, men are still bred to believe they will be good at dealing with money—although nobody tells them how to do it. In that way, money is like sex; they're just supposed to know. Women are raised to believe they won't be good at it and, if they're lucky, some man will take care of the details of money and investing.

One of the major financial houses recently canvassed high school students and asked how good they were about math and money The boys said, "We're pretty good." The girls said, "We're not very good." In fact, they both knew the same amount about money; but their confidence levels were vastly different.

Moreover, when men make money in the stock market, they

credit their own cleverness. When they lose money, they blame the incompetence of their advisors or bad luck. When women make money in the market, they credit the cleverness of their advisors, good luck or even the stars. When they lose money, they blame themselves.

This explanatory style is literally and figuratively depressing. In addition, women are still paid three-quarters of what men are paid for the same job. These events conspire to reduce women's confidence—and inspire "bag-lady" nightmares. Because of the forced dependency on men to make decisions about money, women fear being out on the street with nothing.

When men make more money than their spouse, they believe their superior earnings entitle them to greater power in decision-making. By contrast, women who make more than their mates almost always desire democratic decision-making. As a woman and a therapist, I have a definite bias towards shared decision-making and shared power. It is the only arrangement that works. I prefer to think of men's sense of money not as an entitlement but as a defense against the terrible provider-burden they carry.

Men are trained to believe that money equals power and that power is

8 TIPS TO TALKING ABOUT MONEY

NEVER TRY TO NEGOTIATE about money before airing your feelings; otherwise, negotiations will always break down.

1 Find a non-stressful time when money is not a loaded issue (not tax season, please) and when the kids are not around. Agree on some ground rules: no interrupting each other; no long tirades; after one person shares a difficult piece of information, the partner will try to mirror it back before responding.
2 Take turns sharing your childhood messages about money. How did your parents save it, spend it, talk about it? How did they deal with allowances? What specific money messages did you get and how might they be affecting you today?
3 Share your old hurts, resentments and fears about money.

4 Mention your concerns and fears about your partner's money style. Then acknowledge what you admire about their methods and what you secretly envy. Hoarders secretly admire spenders' capacity to enjoy life in the present, while spenders secretly envy hoarders' ability to set limits, to budget and delay gratification. But typically they won't tell each other because they're afraid it confers license to continue in that style. In reality, positive statements help to make partners feel safe enough to give up the negative aspects of their behavior.
5 Talk about your goals for the future, short- and long-term.
6 Share your hopes and dreams.
7 Consider making a shared budget or a spending plan together by merging the hopes and the goals that have come up on your list more than once.
8 Set a time to have the next money talk. Aim for weekly conversations in the beginning, then monthly ones.—O.M.

TYPICALLY MEN WANT TO MERGE ALL THE COUPLE'S MONEY WHILE WOMEN WANT TO KEEP AT LEAST SOME MONEY SEPARATE.

the path to respect. However, power and control are not compatible with intimacy. Relationships succeed only when both partners are willing to display their vulnerabilities to each other. It's important for men to know that failing to share power cheats them of the intimacy and love they want.

ANOTHER IMPORTANT difference between men and women concerns their interests in merging their money. Typically, men want to merge all the couple's money—while maintaining primary decision-making power. Women want to keep at least some money separate.

The fight goes like this:

HE: "Why do you want separate money? You must not trust me. Are you planning to file for a divorce?"

SHE: "Why do you want to merge all of our money? It must be that you want to control me."

There may be truth in both positions. Still, experience has led me to see a very positive, and probably unconscious, longing in both views, and it has to do with the challenge of intimacy. Merging, getting connected

and staying connected, is more difficult for men. At the first sign of conflict, it's easy for them to withdraw.

I believe that men's desire to merge the family money is a loving expression of the desire for intimacy and connection. Perhaps it is even a safeguard against their withdrawing. I have come to see that women want separate money as a loving expression of their need for healthy autonomy. Their biggest challenge in relationships is not losing themselves; it's holding on to their own sense of self.

Neither his demand for merged money nor her desire for separate funds is a position taken up against the spouse—although that is how partners tend to see it. When couples understand this, their new perspective has the power to transform their entire relationship.

American culture, I believe, makes a big mistake in pressuring married couples to merge all their money. It is in fact unwise for couples to merge money right away. Since couples don't talk about money before they marry, you don't know if you're tying yourself to an overspender in debt or a worrier who could drive you crazy.

Couples can merge some of their common assets for joint expenses, savings and investing and keep the rest separate. That definitely averts some kinds of conflicts. Your partner doesn't get to comment on how you spend your money. I've always kept a portion of money apart because I knew I was an overspender and I didn't want to mess up the family finances or credit rating.

Alternatively, couples could merge some money and only the woman could have separate funds. Solutions do not have to be symmetrical to work well. They just have to appeal

to the deeper needs of both partners. The difficulty is in making clear to the other what your own needs are.

MONEY ISSUES ARE different from other problems in relationships. They're harder to talk about and harder to resolve because of our extensive cultural conditioning. The most important thing in couples communication is empathy, or putting yourself in your partner's place. It is almost always more important to be heard and understood than to have a partner agree with what you say

Spouses who start talking genuinely about what they like about each other's money style create an atmosphere of safety and nondefensiveness. Once such a way of talking about money is established and once couples understand the positive intent of the partner, they can then work out a solution to almost any problem, a solution that best fits their own unique needs.

OLIVIA MELLAN, a therapist specializing in women's issues, found her true calling when a friend noted that money was the last taboo, discussed even less than sex and childhood trauma. "I felt like someone had hit me with a thunderbolt," she recalls. After giving a 1982 workshop on the topic with her perceptive pal, men, women and money "took over half my work and my life," she says. Mellan is in private practice with the Washington Therapy Guild and resides in Washington D.C. Her latest book, *Overcoming Overspending* (Walker) has just been released in paperback; her next, on women's myths about money, will be published next year.

PARENTAL RIGHTS

An Overview

Colby M. May

The issue of parental rights in the face of government intervention is not a new one in this country[1]; it has simply become a more burning issue as the intrusions have become more pronounced. As long ago as 1923, in a case called *Meyer v. Nebraska,*[2] the United States Supreme Court rejected the argument that the government's view of what led children to become patriotic and good citizens should prevail over the parents' view. The Court noted that in Plato's *Republic* the state was to rear children, and "no parent is to know his own child, nor any child his parent."[3] The Court concluded, however, that the U.S. Constitution was founded upon precisely the opposite principle—that parents and not the government should bear responsibility for raising children:

> Although such measures have been deliberately approved by men of great genius, their ideas touching the relation between individual and State were wholly different from those upon which our institutions rest; and it hardly will be affirmed that any legislature could impose such restrictions upon the people of a state without doing violence to both letter and spirit of the Constitution.4

Colby M. May is senior counsel, heading the Office of Government Affairs, American Center for Law and Justice, Washington, D.C.

1. As early as 1901, the Indiana State Supreme Court, in a ruling upholding the state's compulsory education law, stated, "[t]he natural rights of a parent to the custody and control of his children are subordinate to the power of the state." *State v. Indiana v. Bailey,* 157 Ind. 324 (1901).
2. *Meyer v. Nebraska,* 262 U.S. 390 (1923).
3. *Meyer,* 262 at 401–402.
4. *Meyer,* 262 at 402.

This article originally appeared in *The World & I,* May 1997, pp. 290–297. Reprinted by permission of *The World & I,* a publication of The Washington Times Corporation. © 1997.

Time and again, the Supreme Court has recognized the rights of parents to control the upbringing of their children—rights founded upon the First, Fifth, Ninth, and Fourteenth Amendments to the Constitution. As recently as 1990, the Supreme Court observed that, under the Fourteenth Amendment, the fundamental liberty interest of the parent to direct the education of the child is subject to strict scrutiny and cannot be overridden without showing a compelling state interest.[5]

On the local level, however, the culture wars are raging around the rights of parents in the health, education, and moral upbringing of their children. Local government encroachment into areas traditionally the province of parents has resulted in a populist outcry and possible congressional intervention. Some relatively recent examples of current case law serve to illustrate trends in the ongoing battle between parents and the government.

UPBRINGING

In the 1970s and early '80s the "children's rights" movement was in vogue. That line of sociological thinking led to the idea that children should have an equal say in their own upbringing. It was, perhaps, this underlying notion of childhood independence from parental authority and supervision that led the Washington State Supreme Court to find that parents could not punish a minor for involvement with sex and drugs.[6] Parents had grounded their eighth-grade daughter because she engaged in premarital sexual activity and smoked marijuana. When the parents continued to have difficulty getting their daughter to obey, they asked for state assistance. While recognizing that the parents had imposed "reasonable rules which were reasonably enforced" upon their daughter, the court nonetheless removed her from the home.

Social mores have guided much of the jurisprudence in the area of parental rights. In the 1960s the U.S. Supreme Court upheld a law banning the sale of pornographic magazines to children under seventeen years of age. In so doing the Court acknowledged that "[c]onstitutional interpretation has consistently recognized that the parents' claim to authority in their own household to direct the rearing of their children is basic in the structure of our society."[7]

Thirty years later, Texas parents were denied the opportunity to see a mandatory assessment test that asked students personal questions concerning their family life, moral values, and religious beliefs. The parents sued and won, alleging that their responsibility for the upbringing and education of their children had been infringed. The Texas Education Agency on appeal asserted that "the right to direct the education and upbringing of your child is *not* a fundamental right."[8] This position by the Texas Education Agency is not unique, but it is consistent with the view of many public educators that parental rights end at the schoolhouse gate.

EDUCATION

The battle concerning parental authority is most pronounced in the area of education. In the public school arena, recent state court rulings prevent parents from opting their children out of sexually explicit presentations that they find religiously or morally offensive. In a Massachusetts case, a presentation was given in which the instructor:

1) told the students that they were going to have a "group sexual experience with audience participation"; 2) used profane, lewd, and lascivious language to describe body parts and excretory functions; 3) advocated and approved oral sex, masturbation, homosexual sexual activity, and condom use during promiscuous premarital sex; 4) simulated masturbation; 5) characterized loose pants worn by one minor as "erection wear"; 6) referred to being in "deep sh__" after anal sex; 7) had a minor lick an oversized condom, after which the instructor had a female minor pull it over the male minor's entire head and blow it up; 8) encouraged a male minor to display his "orgasm face" for the camera; 9) informed a male minor that he was not having enough orgasms; 10) closely inspected a minor and told him he had a "nice butt"; and 11) made eighteen references to orgasms, six references to male genitals, and eight references to female genitals.[9]

The 1st U.S. Circuit Court of Appeals found that no conscience-shocking activity had occurred at the public school assembly, because no physical intrusive contact had transpired.[10] The court also found no constitutionally protected right for par-

5. *Employment Division v. Smith*, 110 S. Ct. 1595, 1617–18 (1990).
6. *In re Sumey*, 94 Wash. 2d 757, 621 P.2d 108 (1980).
7. *Ginsberg v. New York*, 390 U.S. 629, 639 (1968).

8. *Texas Education Agency v. Maxwell*, No. 14-95-00474-CV (5th Cir.), Appellants' Brief at 11.
9. *Brown v. Hot, Sexy and Safer Productions, Inc.*, 68 F.3d 525, 529 (1st Cir. 1995).
10. *Brown*, 68 F.3d at 531.

The Massachusetts State Supreme Court found no constitutionally protected right for parents to object to public school condom distribution to their children.

ents to opt their children out of the program.[11] In a similar decision, the Massachusetts State Supreme Court found no constitutionally protected right for parents to object to public school condom distribution to their children.[12] A contrary decision in New York found such a protected parental right.[13]

The issue of character development, which has come to the fore in recent years, has engendered community service requirements as an integral part of public school education. A North Carolina school board recently required community service for graduation and told parents which specific extracurricular activities their children could engage in to meet the requirement. An Eagle Scout, however, in pursuit of his scouting achievements was not considered to be fulfilling a "true and selfless" community service according to the school board.[14]

One of the most hotly contested areas of education is home schooling and the question of how much oversight public authorities can have over parents teaching their children. In 1993, the Supreme Court of Michigan considered two home-schooling cases that were consolidated for oral arguments. At issue in the case was Michigan's requirement that all teachers be certified to teach, thus including home-schooling parents. In both cases, the children tested well within the state-specified boundaries for their educational peer groups.

In the case involving a family that home-schooled because of religious convictions, the court found that the statute was unconstitutional because it violated the principles of religious freedom when combined with parental rights.[15] In the second case, involving a family home schooling for nonreligious reasons, the parents lost. The rationale of the court

was that the fundamental-rights analysis did not apply to a pure parental-rights claim without a religious component.[16]

MEDICAL

It is axiomatic that parents have a duty to their children for their health and medical upkeep. The government, acting in its *parens patriae* (the country as parent) authority, can override a parent's wishes concerning his child's medical treatment. Most notable are those situations where the government has prevailed over parents' religiously based objections to such treatment as blood transfusions.[17]

The issue of greatest concern for many parents has been their children's sexual education and involvement. A particularly contentious area has been parents' desire to intervene in a daughter's decision to have an abortion. The confluence of minors obtaining abortions and parental rights and responsibilities for medical care has led to a patchwork quilt of laws concerning medical procedures and parental authority. For example, in most states it is illegal for minors to get their ears pierced without parental consent. However, in many states government officials take the position that children's rights to serious medical procedures outweigh parental authority.

Beginning with *Carey v. Population Services,* 431 U.S. 678 (1977), the U.S. Supreme Court reviewed a New Jersey statute that made it a criminal offense to sell or distribute contraceptives to minors under the age of sixteen. The Court found this total prohibition to be in violation of the privacy right of minors who made the personal decision to use such devices. There was no majority opinion, however, on this particular issue. At that time, the justices declined to indicate a belief that parents have a con-

---

11. *Brown,* 68 F.3d at 532–533.
12. *Curtis v. Falmouth,* 420 Mass. 749, 652 N.E. 2d 580 (1995).
13. *Alfonso v. Fernandez,* 195 A.D. 2d 46, 606 N.Y.S.2d 259 (2 Dept. 1993).
14. *Herndon v. Chapel Hill—Carrboro City Board of Education,* No. 1:94-CV-00196.
15. *People of the State of Michigan v. Dejonge,* 501 N. W. 2d 127 (Mich. 1993).

---

16. *People of the State of Michigan v. Bennett,* 501 N. W. 2d 106 (Mich. 1993).
17. *People ex rel Wallace v. Labrenz,* 411 Ill. 618, 104 N. E. 2d 769, *cert. den.* 344 U.S. 824; *Custody of Minor,* 378 Mass. 732, 393 N. E. 2d 836; *Morrison v. State,* 252 S. W. 2d (Mo. app.); *Re Vasko,* 238 App. Div. 128, 263 N. Y. S. 552; *Mitchell v. Davis,* 205 S. W. 2d 812 (Tex. Civ. App.).

The World & I illustration by Marcia Klioze Hughes

upheld a statutory requirement of parental notification and/or consent prior to abortion if certain safeguards were met. The Court reiterated the basis for its transition on this issue in *Planned Parenthood v. Casey:*

We have been over most of this ground before. Our cases establish, and we reaffirm today, that a State may require a minor seeking an abortion to obtain the consent of a parent or guardian, provided there is an adequate judicial bypass procedure. . . .
Indeed, some of these provisions regarding informed consent have particular force with respect to minors: the waiting period for example may provide the parent or parents of a pregnant young woman the opportunity to consult with her in private, and to discuss the consequences of her decision in the context of the values and moral or religious principles of their family.[19]

This idea that parents have a right in counseling and being involved with their children's sexual decisions and upbringing has often not been embraced by government authorities. For example, some Georgia parents found condoms in their daughters' room and subsequently discovered that their two teenage daughters had been driven to a county health facility during school hours where they received Pap smears, AIDS tests, condoms, and birth control pills. The parents were not informed of these medical procedures and did not consent to these activities. Moreover, when contacted by the parents for the results of their daughters' Pap smears and AIDS tests, both the school district and the county health facility refused to release the information, claiming patient confidentiality.[20]

In 1944, the U.S. Supreme Court held that "[i]t is cardinal with us that the custody, care and nurture of the child reside first in the parents, whose primary function and freedom include preparation for obligations the state can neither supply nor hinder. And it is in recognition of this that

stitutional right to be notified by a public facility when it distributes contraceptives.

Later cases wrestled with the issue of a minor's right to receive contraceptives without parental notification or consent. Generally, courts applying *Carey* found that there was no independent fundamental "right of access to contraceptives," but access to contraceptives was essential to exercise the constitutional right of decision in matters of childbearing.[18] The underpinnings for the minor's right of private access to contraceptives remained grounded in the concept that the minor's right of privacy superseded the parents' right to direct their child's moral education.

In 1990, the Supreme Court began applying a different rationale to the issue of a minor's right to privacy in matters of childbearing, expressly overruling prior decisions on this point. In *Hodgson v. Minnesota,* 497 U.S. 417 (1990), the Court

---

18. *Roe v. Wade,* 410 U.S. 113 (1973); *Planned Parenthood of Central Missouri v. Danforth,* 428 U.S. 52, 74–75 (1976); *Bellotti v. Baird,* 443 U.S. 622 (1979).

19. *Planned Parenthood v. Casey,* 120 L. Ed. 2d 674, 729 (1992).
20. *Earls v. Stephens County School District,* No. 2:95-CV-0097 (N. D. Ga. Gainesville Division, 1995).

This idea that parents have a right in counseling and being involved with their children's sexual decisions and upbringing has often not been embraced by government authorities.

these decisions have respected the private realm of family life which the state cannot enter."[21] The Massachusetts Supreme Court recently disagreed with this standard, however, ruling that parents had no claim in regulating or prohibiting the distribution of condoms within the Falmouth County public schools. The court found that a parental rights claim could not be made unless the schools coerced students in the distribution of condoms.[22]

In the same vein, the 6th U.S. Circuit Court of Appeals affirmed a district court ruling that a Michigan couple did not have a fundamental parental right to prevent public school officials from forcing their third-grade son to undergo psychological counseling. The court held that the parents had no constitutionally protected right to object to the mental health treatments, or to even view the child's counseling records.[23] The parents' solution to this dilemma of unwanted public school psychological counseling was to remove their son from the public school system and place him in a private school.

CURRENT LEGISLATIVE TRENDS

In 1995 companion legislation was introduced by Sen. Charles Grassley (R-Iowa) and Rep. Steve Largent (R-Oklahoma) called the Parental Rights and Responsibilities Act (PRRA).[24] The purpose of the act was to place the burden upon government officials, rather than parents, to prove the necessity of a governmental intrusion upon parental rights. Largent testified before a Senate subcommittee that

[t]his protection is needed because the government is using its coercive force to dictate values, offend the religious and moral beliefs of families, and restrict the freedoms of families to live as they choose. State and lower Federal Court cases

across the country illustrate that often times courts are using an inappropriate and unconstitutional standard in their consideration of parental rights claims.[25]

The ACLU, the National Education Association, and a host of other groups opposed this legislation, which expired with the end of the 104th Congress. Generally, the argument in opposition to the PRRA (and similar state proposals) is that it would unduly burden state and local authorities by forcing them to prove the necessity of decisions that impact families. In addition, they argue that the legislation would limit literature choices for youth, as well as have a negative impact on state child-abuse laws.[26]

On the state level, efforts to strengthen parental rights have been made as proposals to amend state constitutions, as was the case in the November 1996 Colorado elections. While the measure was defeated, supporters have vowed to bring the measure up again, along with a more sophisticated "get out the message" effort to offset opposition by the large educational administrator and teacher unions. State laws codifying parental rights have also been proposed and are currently under consideration.

CONCLUSION

At a time when more and more Americans believe the family is under severe pressure from government activities— from court rulings in Hawaii that hold denial of a marriage license to members of the same sex to be illegal discrimination, to programs that distribute condoms to eleven-year-old students but forbid the teaching of abstinence—is it any wonder the issue of parental rights has

21. *Prince v. Massachusetts*, 321 U.S. 158, 166 (1944).
22. *Curtis v. Falmouth*, 420 Mass. 749, 652 N. E. 2d 580 (1995).
23. *Newkirk v. Fink*, 1995 WL 355664 (6th Cir. 1995) (unpublished decision).
24. *Parental Rights and Responsibilities Act of 1995*, S 984.
25. Testimony of Rep. Steve Largent before the Senate Subcommittee on the Courts, of the Judiciary Committee (December 5, 1995) at 1.
26. Daniel Katz, "Parental Rights without Responsibility," *Federal Lawyer* (September 1996), 39.

While the "Parents Movement" may be just beginning, parental rights, like all personal liberty issues, have been with us as a society from our country's founding.

become so serious? While the "Parents Movement" may be just beginning, parental rights, like all personal liberty issues, have been with us as a society from our country's founding. As James Madison so compellingly wrote in *Federalist* 51:

> What is government itself but the greatest reflections on human nature? If men were angeles, no government would be necessary. If angeles were to govern men, neither external nor internal government would be necessary. In framing a government which is to be administered by men, over men, the great difficulty lies in this: You must first enable the government to control the governed; and in the next place oblige it to control itself.

The right of parents to direct the upbringing and education of their children is a profound right indeed. In today's America, with its numbing array of challenges, it seems sure this issue will be forced evermore to the front.

Father Love and Child Development: History and Current Evidence

Abstract

Six types of studies show that father love sometimes explains as much or more of the variation in specific child and adult outcomes as does mother love. Sometimes, however, only father love is statistically associated with specific aspects of offsprings' development and adjustment, after controlling for the influence of mother love. Recognition of these facts was clouded historically by the cultural construction of fatherhood and fathering in America.

Keywords

father love; paternal acceptance; parental acceptance-rejection theory

Ronald P. Rohner[1]

Center for the Study of Parental Acceptance and Rejection, School of Family Studies, University of Connecticut, Storrs, Connecticut

Research in every major ethnic group of America (Rohner, 1998b), in dozens of nations internationally, and with several hundred societies in two major cross-cultural surveys (Rohner 1975, 1986, 1998c; Rohner & Chaki-Sircar, 1988) suggests that children and adults everywhere—regardless of differences in race, ethnicity, gender, or culture—tend to respond in essentially the same way when they experience themselves to be loved or unloved by their parents. The overwhelming bulk of research dealing with parental acceptance and rejection concentrates on mothers' behavior, however. Until recently, the possible influence of father love has been largely ignored. Here, I concentrate on evidence

showing the influence of fathers' love-related behaviors—or simply, *father love*—in relation to the social, emotional, and cognitive development and functioning of children, adolescents, and adult offspring. Moreover, I focus primarily, but not exclusively, on families for which information is available about both fathers and mothers—or about youths' perceptions of both their fathers' and mothers' parenting. My principal objective is to identify evidence about the relative contribution to offspring development of father love vis-à-vis mother love.

I define father love in terms of paternal acceptance and rejection as construed in parental acceptance-rejection theory (Rohner, 1986, in press). Paternal

acceptance includes such feelings and behaviors (or children's perceptions of such feelings and behaviors) as paternal nurturance, warmth, affection, support, comfort, and concern. Paternal rejection, on the other hand, is defined as the real or perceived absence or withdrawal of these feelings and behaviors. Rejection includes such feelings as coldness, indifference, and hostility toward the child. Paternal rejection may be expressed behaviorally as a lack of affection toward the child, as physical or verbal aggression, or as neglect. Paternal rejection may also be experienced in the form of undifferentiated rejection; that is, there may be situations in which individuals feel that their fathers (or significant male

From *Current Directions in Psychological Science*, October 1998, pp. 157-161. © 1998 by Ronald P. Rohner and the American Psychological Society. Reprinted by permission of Blackwell Publishers.

caregivers) do not really care about, want, or love them, even though there may not be observable behavioral indicators showing that the fathers are neglecting, unaffectionate, or aggressive toward them. Mother love (maternal acceptance-rejection) is defined in the same way.

FATHERHOOD AND MOTHERHOOD ARE CULTURAL CONSTRUCTIONS

The widely held cultural construction of fatherhood in America—especially prior to the 1970s—has two strands. Historically, the first strand asserted that fathers are ineffective, often incompetent, and maybe even biologically unsuited to the job of child-rearing. (The maternal counterpoint to this is that women are genetically endowed for child care.) The second strand asserted that fathers' influence on child development is unimportant, or at the very most peripheral or indirect. (The maternal counterpoint here is that mother love and competent maternal care provide everything that children need for normal, healthy development.) Because researchers internalized these cultural beliefs as their own personal beliefs, fathers were essentially ignored by mainstream behavioral science until late in the 20th century. The 1970s through the 1990s, however, have seen a revolution in recognizing fathers and the influence of their love on child development. Three interrelated lines of influence I have discussed elsewhere (Rohner, 1998a) seem to account for this revolution. The net effect of these influences has been to draw attention to the fact that father love sometimes explains a unique, independent portion of the variation in specific child outcomes, over and above the portion explained by mother love. In fact, a few recent studies suggest that father love is the sole significant predictor of specific outcomes, after removing the influence of mother love.

STUDIES SHOWING THE INFLUENCE OF FATHER LOVE

Six types of studies (discussed at greater length in Rohner, 1998a) demonstrate a strong association between father love and aspects of offspring development.

Studies Looking Exclusively at Variations in the Influence of Father Love

Many of the studies looking exclusively at the influence of variations in father love deal with one of two topics: gender role development, especially of sons, and father involvement. Studies of gender role development emerged prominently in the 1940s and continued through the 1970s. Commonly, researchers assessed the masculinity of fathers and of sons, and then correlated the two sets of scores. Many psychologists were surprised at first to discover that no consistent results emerged from this research. But when they examined the quality of the father-son relationship, they found that if the relationship between masculine fathers and their sons was warm and loving, the boys were indeed more masculine. Later, however, researchers found that the masculinity of fathers per se did not seem to make much difference because "boys seemed to conform to the sex-role standards of their culture when their relationships with their fathers were warm, regardless of how 'masculine' the fathers were" (Lamb, 1997, p. 9).

Paternal involvement is the second domain in which there has been a substantial amount of research on the influence of variations in father love. Many studies have concluded that children with highly involved fathers, in relation to children with less involved fathers, tend to be more cognitively and socially competent, less inclined toward gender stereotyping, more empathic, psychologically better adjusted, and the like. But "caring for" children is not necessarily the same thing as "caring about" them. And a closer examination of these studies suggests that it was not the simple fact of paternal engagement (i.e., direct interaction with the child), availability, or responsibility for child care that was associated with these positive outcomes. Rather, it appears that the quality of the father-child relationship—especially of father love—makes the greatest difference (Lamb, 1997; Veneziano & Rohner, 1998).

Father Love Is as Important as Mother Love

The great majority of studies in this category deal with one or a combination of the following four issues among children, adolescents, and young adults: (a) personality and psychological adjustment problems, including issues of self-concept and self-esteem, emotional

stability, and aggression; (b) conduct problems, especially in school; (c) cognitive and academic performance issues; and (d) psychopathology. Recent studies employing multivariate analyses have allowed researchers to conclude that fathers' and mothers' behaviors are sometimes each associated significantly and uniquely with these outcomes. The work of Young, Miller, Norton, and Hill (1995) is one of these studies. These authors employed a national sample of 640 12- to 16-year-olds living in two-parent families. They found that perceived paternal love and caring was as predictive of sons' and daughters' life satisfaction—including their sense of well-being—as was maternal love and caring.

Father Love Predicts Specific Outcomes Better Than Mother Love

As complex statistical procedures have become more commonplace in the 1980s and 1990s, it has also become more common to discover that the influence of father love explains a unique, independent portion of the variation in specific child and adult outcomes, over and above the portion of variation explained by mother love. Studies drawing this conclusion tend to deal with one or more of the following four issues among children, adolescents, and young adults: (a) personality and psychological adjustment problems, (b) conduct problems, (c) delinquency, and (d) psychopathology. For example, evidence is mounting that fathers may be especially salient in the development of such forms of psychopathology as substance abuse (drug and alcohol use and abuse), depression and depressed emotion, and behavior problems, including conduct disorder and externalizing behaviors (including aggression toward people and animals, property destruction, deceitfulness, and theft) (Rohner, 1998c). Fathers are also being increasingly implicated in the etiology of borderline personality disorder (a pervasive pattern of emotional and behavioral instability, especially in interpersonal relationships and in self-image) and borderline personality organization (a less severe form of borderline personality disorder) (Fowler, 1990; Rohner & Brothers, in press).

Father love appears to be uniquely associated not just with behavioral and psychological problems, however, but also with health and well-being. Amato (1994), for example, found in a national sample that perceived closeness to fathers made a significant contribution—over and above the contribution made by perceived closeness to mothers—to adult sons' and daughters' happiness, life satisfaction, and low psychological distress (i.e., to overall psychological well-being).

Father Love Is the Sole Significant Predictor of Specific Outcomes

In the 1990s, a handful of studies using a variety of multivariate statistics have concluded that father love is the sole significant predictor of specific child outcomes, after removing the influences of mother love. Most of these studies have dealt with psychological and behavioral problems of adolescents. For example, Cole and McPherson (1993) concluded that father-child conflict but not mother-child conflict (in each case, after the influence of the other was statistically controlled) was positively associated with depressive symptoms in adolescents. Moreover, father-adolescent cohesion was positively associated with the absence of depressive symptoms in adolescents. These results are consistent with Barrera and Garrison-Jones's (1992) conclusion that adolescents' satisfaction with fathers' support was related to a lowered incidence of depressive symptoms, whereas satisfaction with mothers' support was not. Barnett, Marshall, and Pleck (1992), too, found that when measures of the quality of both mother-son and father-son relationships were entered simultaneously into a regression equation, only the father-son relationship was related significantly to adult sons' psychological distress (a summed measure of anxiety and depression).

Father Love Moderates the Influence of Mother Love

A small but growing number of studies have concluded that fathers' behavior moderates and is moderated by (i.e., interacts with) other influences within the family. Apparently, however, only one study so far has addressed the issue of whether mother love has different effects on specific child outcomes depending on the level of father love. This study, by Forehand and Nousiainen (1993), found that when mothers were low in acceptance, fathers' acceptance scores had no significant impact on youths' cognitive competence. But when mothers were high in acceptance, fathers' acceptance scores made a dramatic difference: Fathers with low acceptance scores tended to have children with poorer cognitive competence, whereas highly accepting fathers tended to have children with substantially better cognitive competence.

Paternal Versus Maternal Parenting Is Sometimes Associated With Different Outcomes for Sons, Daughters, or Both

Many of the studies in this category were published in the 1950s and 1960s, and even earlier. Many of them may be criticized on methodological and conceptual grounds. Nonetheless, evidence suggests that serious research questions should be raised in the future about the possibility that associations between love-related parenting and child outcomes may depend on the gender of the parent and of the child. Three different kinds of studies tend to be found in this category.

First, some research shows that one pattern of paternal love-related behavior and a different pattern of maternal love-related behavior may be associated with a single outcome in sons, daughters, or both. For example, Barber and Thomas (1986) found that daughters' self-esteem was best predicted by their mothers' general support (e.g., praise and approval) but by their fathers' physical affection. Sons' self-esteem, however, was best predicted by their mothers' companionship (e.g., shared activities) and by their fathers' sustained contact (e.g., picking up the boys for safety or for fun).

Second, other research in this category shows that a single pattern of paternal love-related behavior may be associated with one outcome for sons and a different outcome for daughters. For example, Jordan, Radin, and Epstein (1975) found that paternal nurturance was positively associated with boys' but not girls' performance on an IQ test. Finally, the third type of research in this category shows that the influence of a single pattern of paternal love-related behaviors may be more strongly associated with a given outcome for one gender of offspring than for the other. For example, Eisman (1981) reported that fathers' love and acceptance correlated more highly with daughters' than with sons' self-concept.

DISCUSSION

The data reported here are but a minuscule part of a larger body of work showing that father love is heavily implicated not only in children's and adults' psychological well-being and health, but also in an array of psychological and behavioral problems. This evidence punctuates the need to include fathers (and other significant males, when appropriate) as well as mothers in future research, and then to analyze separately the data for possible father and mother

effects. It is only by separating data in this way that behavioral scientists can discern when and under what conditions paternal and maternal factors have similar or different effects on specific outcomes for children. This recommendation explicitly contradicts a call sometimes seen in published research to merge data about fathers' and mothers' parenting behaviors.

Finally, it is important to note several problems and limitations in the existing research on father love. For example, even though it seems unmistakably clear that father love makes an important contribution to offsprings' development and psychological functioning, it is not at all clear what generative mechanisms produce these contributions. In particular, it is unclear why father love is sometimes more strongly associated with specific offspring outcomes than is mother love. And it is unclear why patterns of paternal versus maternal parenting may be associated with different outcomes for sons, daughters, or children of both genders. It remains for future research to inquire directly about these issues. Until then, we can know only that father love is often as influential as mother love—and sometimes more so.

Note

1. Address correspondence to Ronald P. Rohner, Center for the Study of Parental Acceptance and Rejection, School of Family Studies, University of Connecticut, Storrs, CT 06269–2058; e-mail: rohner@uconnvm.uconn.edu or http://vm.uconn.edu/~rohner.

References

Amato, P. R. (1994). Father-child relations, mother-child relations and offspring psychological well-being in adulthood. *Journal of Marriage and the Family, 56,* 1031–1042.

Barber, B. & Thomas, D. (1986). Dimensions of fathers' and mothers' supportive behavior: A case for physical affection. *Journal of Marriage and the Family, 48,* 783–794.

Barnett, R. C., Marshall, N. L., & Pleck, J. H. (1992). Adult son-parent relationships and the associations with sons' psychological distress. *Journal of Family Issues, 13,* 505–525.

Barrera, M., Jr., & Garrison-Jones, C. (1992). Family and peer social support as specific correlates of adolescent depressive symptoms. *Journal of Abnormal Child Psychology, 20,* 1–16.

Cole, D., & McPherson, A. E. (1993). Relation of family subsystems to adolescent depression: Implementing a new family assessment strategy. *Journal of Family Psychology, 7,* 119–133.

Eisman, E. M. (1981). Sex-role characteristics of the parent, parental acceptance of the child and child self-concept. (Doctoral dissertation, California School of Professional Psychology at Los Angeles, 1981). *Dissertation Abstracts International, 24,* 2062.

Forehand, R., & Nousiainen, S. (1993). Maternal and paternal parenting: Critical dimensions in adolescent functioning. *Journal of Family Psychology, 7,* 213–221.

Fowler, S. D. (1990). *Paternal effects on severity of borderline psychopathology.* Unpublished doctoral dissertation, University of Texas, Austin.

Jordan, B., Radin, N., & Epstein, A. (1975). Paternal behavior and intellectual functioning in preschool boys and girls. *Developmental Psychology, 11,* 407–408.

Lamb, M. E. (1997). Fathers and child development: An introductory overview and guide. In M. E. Lamb (Ed.), *The role of the father in child development* (pp. 1–18). New York: John Wiley & Sons.

Rohner, R. P. (1975). *They love me, they love me not: A worldwide study of the effects of parental acceptance and rejection.* New Haven, CT: HRAF Press.

Rohner, R. P. (1986). *The warmth dimension: Foundations of parental acceptance-rejection theory.* Newbury Park, CA: SAGE.

Rohner, R. P. (1998a). *The importance of father love: History and contemporary evidence.* Manuscript submitted for publication.

Rohner, R. P. (1998b). *Parental acceptance-rejection bibliography* [On-line]. Available: http://vm.unconn.edu/~rohner

Rohner, R. P. (1998c). *Worldwide mental health correlates of parental acceptance-rejection: Review of cross-cultural and intracultural evidence.* Manuscript submitted for publication.

Rohner, R. P. (in press). Acceptance and rejection. In D. Levinson, J. Ponzetti, & P. Jorgensen (Eds.), *Encyclopedia of human emotions.* New York: MacMillan.

Rohner, R. P., & Brothers, S. A. (in press). Perceived parental rejection, psychological maladjustment, and borderline personality disorder. *Journal of Emotional Abuse.*

Rohner, R. P., & Chaki-Sircar, M. (1988). *Women and children in a Bengali village.* Hanover, NH: University Press of New England.

Veneziano, R. A., & Rohner, R. P. (1998). Perceived paternal warmth, paternal involvement, and youths' psychological adjustment in a rural, biracial southern community. *Journal of Marriage and the Family, 60,* 335–343.

Young, M. H., Miller, B. E., Norton, M. C., & Hill, J. E. (1995). The effect of parental supportive behaviors on life satisfaction of adolescent offspring. *Journal of Marriage and the Family, 57,* 813–822.

Recommended Reading

Biller, H. B. (1993). *Fathers and families: Paternal factors in child development.* Westport, CT: Auburn House.

Booth, A., & Crouter, A. C. (Eds.). (1998). *Men in families: When do they get involved? What difference does it make?* Mahwah, NJ: Erlbaum.

Lamb, M. E. (Ed.). (1997). *The role of the father in child development.* New York: John Wiley & Sons.

Rohner, R. P. (1986). (See References)

Parents Speak:

Zero to Three's Findings from Research on Parents' Views of Early Childhood Development

Matthew Melmed

How much do parents of babies and toddlers know about their children's intellectual, social, and emotional development at the earliest ages? What are parents doing to encourage healthy development of their babies in these interrelated domains? Zero to Three commissioned a study that included focus groups and a national poll to determine what parents know and believe about early childhood development, where they go for information and support, and how receptive they are to new information.

Both the focus groups and the poll revealed that parents have much less knowledge and information about their children's emotional, intellectual, and social development than they do about their physical development. Parents thirst for more information on how to promote their young children's healthy development.

As new findings in brain research emerge (see *Young Children*, May 1997, pp. 4–9), they should provide a major impetus for parents to understand their own ability to im-

prove their children's lives and indeed to show all of us—parents, grandparents, other relatives, educators, child care providers, employers, policy-makers, and others—how we can positively impact children's development. Crafting such messages effectively requires knowledge of what parents know and value about early childhood development. Following are the major conclusions of our research, designed to address these questions.

1. Although parents recognize the importance of early childhood, they do not see its full significance.

There is much progress to be made to convince parents of babies that the period from birth to age three is *particularly* significant and provides a unique opportunity for growth and learning. In our study, parents said they felt that all of childhood is important, but they saw birth to three as important years of child development only in general terms and within limits. These parents lack much of the new information that can help them as their child's first teacher. The focus group parents understood that babies need more than love—including stimulation, consistency, and sense of security—but they were mostly unaware of the depth of their influences on their babies' long-term development.

2. Parents feel most able to impact babies' emotional development.

Our inquiry looked at attitudes and knowledge in three developmental domains: intellectual, emotional, and social. Of the three, *emotional development may be the area in which parents believe they can have the most impact.* The parents in our research groups stressed the importance of making babies feel secure and loved from the very beginning. They said babies' feelings can be hurt and that babies read and interpret their parents' and other people's emotional cues.

The national poll found that 39% of parents felt they had the greatest influence over their child's emotional development as compared to the child's intellectual (19%) or social (16%) development. However, one out of every four parents report having the least information on how a child develops emotionally.

3. Laying down a foundation for social growth in the early years is not seen as critical.

When it comes to social development, the attitudes expressed by the parents in this study were quite different. Parents were often unsure that what happens to a child from

Matthew Melmed is executive director of ZERO TO THREE: National Center for Infants, Toddlers and Families (formerly the National Center for Clinical Infant Programs), a national organization dedicated to advancing the healthy development of babies and young children that is based in Washington, D.C.

birth to age three has long-term impact on social development. They see *social development as an area where a child can "catch up,"* and they feel that this area is less crucial than the other domains.

4. Parents may not recognize their power to shape their child's intellectual development.

The parents in this study said their young children are always learning. Yet the parents felt *less able to impact intellectual development than any other area of childhood development.* The parents described intellectual development as a process of absorption rather than as a process of *creation* of more capacity or development of cognitive abilities, as suggested by emerging brain research. Some said that an unstimulating environment does not deny a child intellectual development, because much of the intellectual self is "nature" not "nurture."

The poll revealed that only 44% of the parents felt totally sure that they could tell if their infant or toddler's intellectual development was on track. Parents (53%) were more certain about signs to watch for to see if their child's physical develop-

ment was on track; 37% felt this way about milestones of social development and 38% about emotional development.

5. Caregiver continuity and consistency is a hot-button issue for many parents.

According to research, the individuals with whom an infant or toddler spends the most time play a critical role in that child's emotional, social, and intellectual development, and limiting the number of caregivers is important for creating strong relationships that form the basis of learning. Yet the focus groups found limiting the number of caregivers is a hot-button issue with parents. The suggestion that either the consistency or a limited number of caregivers really matters made some parents—particularly those with multiple child care arrangements—feel uncomfortable, guilty, or nervous. These feelings unfortunately may lead to some of these parents rejecting the notion that caregivers have important relationships with babies. Some parents believe that if a child has a stable home life, whatever happens during child care may not be as important.

The poll found that caregivers other than these mothers or fathers played a major role in the lives of their young children. Only one in five babies or toddlers were cared for since birth exclusively by a parent; 60% of babies and toddlers are currently cared for on a regular basis by someone other than their parents. Half of all parents surveyed thought that the more caregivers a child has before age three, the better that child will be at adapting and coping with change.

6. Get parents the good news early on about the opportunity of children's first three years.

The parents in the focus groups made it clear that they learned about child development *on the job* as parents. It is important to raise the consciousness of parents *before* they have children or when their babies are very young. Reaching parents early may avoid having to battle guilt feelings of parents who feel they have failed if they took few steps to enhance their child's development before the age of two or three.

Parental guilt and denial could thwart efforts to increase parents' involvement in their children's early development. Learning that the period from birth to age three is extremely important in child development and that parents can actively influence it is not good news for those parents who feel they have missed the boat. It is motivating, on the other hand, to new and expectant parents.

7. Parents want specific information on what they can do with their child.

These results suggest that many parents of young children may need guidance if they are to maximize experiences in the early years. What

---

Sources of Data and Further Information

Zero to Three used two different research methodologies—focus groups and in-depth telephone surveys—to collect information from parents of very young children.

Focus groups— The public opinion research firm Belden and Russonello conducted eight focus groups with parents of children younger than age three and expectant parents, exploring their knowledge and perceptions of child development. Held between October 1996 and February 1997, the groups convened parents of varying levels of education and income, segmented by gender and race.

In-depth telephone survey— Between March 21 and April 1, 1997, Peter D. Hart Research Associates conducted an in-depth telephone survey among a representative sample of 1,022 mothers and fathers and legal guardians of children aged 36 months and younger.

More detailed information about the results of both studies is available at the ZERO TO THREE Website: **http://www.zerotothree.org;** see the "newsroom."

Parents' Perspectives on Their Children's Development: Selected Comments of Focus Group Participants

"If they get the emotional—the proper attachments, the love, the support that they need—they will feel confident to go out in the social situations . . . explore things and learn intellectually."— *a mother, Richmond*

"No matter what you do . . . not everything is programmable. . . . Whether a child's going to be intelligent or not is more or less something they're born with, the level of intelligence they can achieve. That is kind of hardwired."—*a father, Boston*

"Really [it] is your innate abilities which affect how you do in school, more so than your experiences. But the more experience you have, that's going to give you more curiosity and interest. But your performance is really based on your native intelligence."—*a mother, New York*

"I hope [having a limited number of caregivers is] not that important, because my child's on her third [caregiver]. Just don't tell me that I'm wrong."—*a mother, Boston*

"I feel that I'm getting better—that when she was born I was just so new at everything—and I'm hoping I get better and better day by day, month by month, and year by year. It scares me to death thinking [that in] a year—that's it—my time is up."—*a mother, Richmond*

"[The statement about child development before age three] makes me paranoid. . . . Even though I'm trying, I do the best I can, like if I do one thing wrong . . . I'm an idiot. . . . So, I think you always question yourself, even though you do the best that you can for them."—*a mother, New York*

"It is like you communicate with someone who speaks a foreign language—basically that's what you're doing."—*a mother, Richmond*

"[Babies] don't have instructions."—*a mother, Boston*

---

they lack is not just information on the importance of the earliest years but also specific steps, ideas, activities, and concepts for making the most of this time. For example, the parents in the focus group research said they believe babies communicate and are interpretable almost from birth; however, parents have difficulty understanding what their babies are communicating and what their behaviors mean. Many said it is hard to read a baby's cues and would appreciate help in learning how to do so.

The poll indicated that 60% of the parents of babies and toddlers were extremely or very interested in information about early brain development and how children learn, and an additional 21% said that they were somewhat interested. According to the poll, parents relied most on their informal networks—their parents or friends and neighbors—for information or advice. Only 2% mentioned their child's caregiver as someone to whom they usually turned for help.

8. Many parents do not recognize that they can create capacity by stimulating a child's brain in ways that match the child's level and interest.

According to the focus group research, many parents see their role largely as keeping their children from harm. The participating parents often stressed the negative impact of a poor emotional or social environment, situations they seek to avoid. Making a creative difference in the lives of children, through *improving the quality of their experiences and their relationships with the important people in their lives,* is a different way of thinking for many parents than what they have traditionally held to be their obligations to their children.

Nearly all the parents (95% of those polled) recognized that children learn from the moment they are born. Most parents (87%) assumed that the more stimulation a baby receives, the better. But, in fact,

parents and caregivers need to carefully match the amount and kind of stimulation to a child's development, interests, temperament, and mood at the moment.

9. Many parents see time as a major barrier to better parenting.

In the poll, more than one-third of parents (37%) indicated that one of the chief reasons they may need to improve as parents is because they don't spend as much quality time with their child as they would like. Half of all parents said that they ended most days feeling that they had spent less time with their young child than they wanted to—either a lot less time (20%) or a little less (27%).

What these results mean to early childhood professionals

In this study, parents seemed well aware of the general importance of the love and time they give their infants and toddlers, but they wanted more information about exactly *how* to influence their children's emotional and intellectual development in positive ways. These moms and dads feel good about many aspects of being parents to young children. Yet they recognize their ability to improve, and they display a genuine interest in doing so.

Indeed, the data reveal these parents' desire to play the most positive role they can in their children's development. They want to understand how to prepare in advance for parenthood; where to turn for day-to-day information, especially when their children are young; how to provide the best care for their children, even when they cannot provide it exclusively themselves; how to recognize signals and cues that inform them about their children's development; how they can affect most positively a young and growing brain; and what specific strategies and techniques they can use to help practice better parenting and give their young children the best possible start in life.

Early childhood professionals, especially those working in programs that serve infants and toddlers, are in an excellent position to respond to parents' desire for more information and support. New and creative ways of providing this type of assistance may be needed, however, as most of the parents surveyed do not automatically turn to their child's caregiver as an information source.

Finally, early childhood professionals should recognize what parents think would help them become better parents: (1) information to help them understand their child's feelings or needs and ways to handle difficult situations, and (2) more quality time with their child. Actions and strategies that especially support parents in these ways are likely to be the most helpful and the most welcome.

Do Parents Really Matter?

Once, parents were given all the credit—and all the blame—for how their children turned out. Then researchers told us that heredity determines who we are. The latest take: parents can work with their children's innate tendencies to rear happy, healthy kids. It's a message many parents will find reassuring—but it may make others very nervous.

By Annie Murphy Paul

David Reiss, M.D., didn't want to believe it. The George Washington University psychiatrist had worked for more than 12 years on a study of adolescent development—just completed—and its conclusions were a surprise, to say the least. "I'm talking to you seven or eight years after the initial results came out, so I can sound very calm and collected now," says Reiss. "But I was shocked." This, even though other scientists had previously reached similar conclusions in many smaller-scale studies. "We knew about those results, but we didn't believe it," says Reiss, speaking of himself and one of his collaborators, E. Mavis Heatherington, Ph.D. "Now we've done the research ourselves, so . . ." He sighs. "We're not ever going to believe it, but we're going to have to act as if we do."

What Reiss and his colleagues discovered, in one of the longest and most thorough studies of child development ever attempted, was that parents appear to have relatively little effect on how children turn out, once genetic influences are accounted for. "The original objective was to look for environmental differences," says Reiss. "We didn't find many." Instead, it seems that genetic influences are largely responsible for how "adjusted" kids are: how well they do in school, how they get along with their peers, whether they engage in dangerous or delinquent behavior. "If you follow the study's implications through to the end, it's a radical revision of contemporary theories of child development," says Reiss. "I can't even describe what a paradigm shift it is."

The way heredity shapes who we are is less like one-way dictation and more like spirited rounds of call and response.

The only member of the research team who wasn't surprised by the results, Reiss recalls, was Robert Plomin, Ph.D., a researcher at the Institute of Psychiatry in London. Plomin is a behavioral geneticist, and he and others in his field have been saying for years what Reiss has just begun to accept: genes have a much greater influence on our personalities than previously thought, and parenting much less. The work of behavioral geneticists has been the focus of considerable controversy among psychologists, but it has been mostly ignored by parents, despite ample attention from the media. That may be because such coverage has rarely described just how genes are thought to wield their purported influence. Behavioral geneticists don't claim that genes are blueprints that depict every detail of our personality and behavior; rather, they propose that heredity reveals itself through complex interactions with the environment. Their theories are far more subtle, and more persuasive, than the simple idea of heredity as destiny. It is by participating in these very interactions, some scientists now say, that parents exert their own considerable influence—and they can learn to exert even more.

Nature Meets Nurture

As behavioral geneticists understand it, the way heredity shapes who we are is less like one-way dictation and more like spirited rounds of call and response, with each phrase spoken by heredity summoning an answer from the environment. Scientists' unwieldy name for this exchange is "evocative gene-environment correlations," so called because people's genetic makeup is thought to bring forth particular reactions from others, which in turn influence their personalities. A baby with a sunny disposition will receive more affection than one who is difficult; an attractive child will be smiled at more often than a homely one. And the qualities that prompt such responses from parents are likely to elicit more of the same from others, so that over time a self-image is created and confirmed in others' eyes.

Even as genes are calling forth particular reactions, they're also reaching out for particular kinds of experience. That's because each person's DNA codes for a certain type of nervous system: one that feels alarm at new situations, one that craves strong sensations, or one that is sluggish and slow to react. Given an array of opportunities, some researchers say, children will pick the ones that are most suited to their "genotype," or genetic endowment. As they grow older, they have more chances to choose—friends, interests, jobs, spouses—decisions that both reflect and define personality.

In order for genes and environment to interact in this way, they need to be in constant conversation, back and forth. Since parents usually raise the children to whom they have passed on their genes, that's rarely a problem: they are likely to share and perhaps appreciate the qualities of their offspring. And the environment they provide their children with may further support their natural abilities: highly literate parents might give birth to an equally verbal child, then raise her in a house full of books. Developmental psychologists call this fortunate match "goodness of fit." But problems may arise if nurture and nature aren't on speaking terms—if a child's environment doesn't permit or encourage expression of his natural tendencies. That may happen when children's abilities don't match their parents' expectations; when their genetically-influenced temperament clashes with that of their parents; or when their environment offers them few opportunities to express themselves constructively, as is often the case with children who grow up in severe poverty. Research has shown that a poor person-to-environment match can lead to decreased motivation, diminished mental health, and rebellious or antisocial behavior.

The dialogue between genes and environment becomes more complicated when a sibling adds another voice. Although siblings share an average of 50 percent of their genes, the half that is different—and the kaleidoscopic ways that genes can combine—leads their genotypes to ask different questions and get different answers from what would seem to be the same environment. In fact, siblings create individual environments of their own by seeking out different experiences and by evoking different responses from parents, friends, and others. Like the proverbial blind men touching the leg, the trunk, or the tail of an elephant, they "see" different parts of the same animal. "Our studies show that parents do indeed treat their children differently, but that they are in large measure responding to differences that are already there," says Robert Plomin. "Family environment does have an effect on personality development, but not in the way we've always thought. It's the experiences that siblings *don't* share that matter, not the ones they do."

Kids In Charge?

One intriguing implication of behavioral genetic research is that children are in many ways driving their own development, through the choices they make, the reactions they elicit, even the friends they pick (see "The Power of Peers"). But parents are crucial collaborators in that process, and that means that their role in shaping their children may actually be larger than it first appears. *How* a parent responds to a child's genetically-influenced characteristics may make all the difference in how those traits are expressed, says David Reiss. In his formulation, the parent-child relationship acts as a sort of translator of genetic influence: the genotype provides the basic plot, but parenting gives it tone and inflection, accent and emphasis. He calls this conception of gene-environment correlation "the relationship code," and says that it returns to parents some of the influence his study would seem to give to genes. "Our data actually give the role of parents a real boost—but it's saying that the story doesn't necessarily start with the parent," says Reiss. "It starts with the kid, and then the parent picks up on it."

To Reiss, parents' role as interpreters of the language of heredity holds out an exciting possibility. "If you could intervene with parents and get them to respond differently to troublesome behavior, you might be able to offset much of the genetic influence" on those traits, he says. In other words, if genes become behavior by way of the environment, then changing the environment might change the expression of the genes. Although such intervention studies are years away from fruition, small-scale research and clinical experience are pointing the way toward working with children's hereditary strengths and weaknesses. Stanley Greenspan, M.D., a pediatric psychiatrist at George Washington Medical School and author of *The Growth*

THE POWER OF peers

IT'S A WORLD OUT OF A FANCIFUL children's book: a place where parents and teachers don't matter, where the company of other kids is most meaningful, where nothing much would change if we left children in their homes and schools "but switched all the parents around." That doesn't describe an imagined never-never land, however, but the environment that every one of us grows up in, contends Judith Rich Harris. The maverick writer and theoretician believes that peers, not parents, determine our personalities, and her unorthodox views have made the very real world of psychology sit up and take notice.

Harris, who is unaffiliated with any university or institution, laid out her radical theory in a 1995 *Psychological Review* paper, which was later cited as one of the year's outstanding articles by the American Psychological Association. Like behavioral geneticists, Harris believes that heredity is a force to be reckoned with. But she sees another powerful force at work: group socialization, or the shaping of one's character by one's peers.

Central to this theory is the idea that behavior is "context-specific": we act in specific ways in specific circumstances. "Children today live in two different worlds: home and the world outside the home," says Harris. "There is little overlap between these two worlds, and the rules for how to behave in them are quite different." Displays of emotion, for example, are often accepted by parents but discouraged by teachers or friends. Rewards and punishments are different too. At home, children may be scolded for their failures and praised for their successes; outside the home, they may be ridiculed when they make a mistake or ignored when they behave appropriately.

As children grow older and peer influence grows stronger, says Harris, they come to prefer the ways of peers over those of their parents. She like to use language as an example: the children of immigrants, she notes, will readily learn to speak the language of the new country without an accent.

They may continue to speak in their parents' tongue when at home, but over time the language of their peers will become their "native" language. Adopting the ways of their contemporaries makes sense, says Harris, because children will live among them, and not among older adults, for the greater part of their lives. "Parents are past, peers are future," she says.

It's evolutionarily adaptive, too. "Humans were designed to live not in nuclear families, but in larger groups," observes Harris. "The individuals who became our ancestors succeeded partly

of the Mind, is actively applying the discoveries of genetics to parenting. "Genes do create certain general tendencies, but parents can work with these by tailoring their actions to the nervous system of the child," says Greenspan. He believes that the responses children "naturally" elicit may not

----

The exact same temperament that might predispose a kid to become a criminal can also make for a hot test pilot.

----

be in their best interests—but that parents can consciously and deliberately give them the ones that are. "You have to pay attention to what you're doing intuitively, and make sure that is what the kids really need," he says.

A baby with a sluggish temperament, for example, won't respond as readily to his parents' advances as a child with a more active nervous system. Disappointed at their offsprings' lack of engagement, parents may respond with dwindling interest and attention. Left to his own devices, the baby may become even more withdrawn, failing to make crucial connections and to master developmental challenges. But if the parents resist their inclinations, and engage the baby with special enthusiasm, Greenspan has found that the child will change his own behavior in response. The same principle of working against the grain of a child's genotype applies to those who are especially active or oversensitive, suggests Greenspan, comparing the process to a right-handed baseball player who practices throwing with his left hand. "It feels funny at first, but gradually you build up strength in an area in which you would naturally be weak," he says.

Of course, honing a right-handed pitch is important, too. Parents can improve on their children's hereditary strengths by encouraging their tendency to seek out experiences in tune with their genes. "Parents should think of themselves as resource providers," says Plomin. "Expose the child to a lot of things, see what they like, what

they're good at, and go with that." By offering opportunities congenial to children's genetic constitutions, parents are in a sense improving their "goodness of fit" with the environment.

WILL YOUR KID GO TO YALE—OR TO JAIL?

For those traits that could easily become either assets or liabilities, parenting may be especially critical to the outcome. "The same temperament that can make for a criminal can also make for a hot test pilot or astronaut," says David Lykken, Ph.D., a behavioral geneticist at the University of Minnesota. "That kind of little boy—aggressive, fearless, impulsive—is hard to handle. It's easy for parents to give up and let him run wild, or turn up the heat and the punishment and thereby alienate him and lose all control. But properly handled, this can be the kid who grows up to break the sound barrier." Lykken believes that especially firm, conscientious, and responsive parents can make the difference—but not all behavioral geneticists agree. David Rowe, Ph.D., a University of Arizona psychologist and author of *The Limits of Family Influence,* claims that "much of the effort of 'superparents' may be wasted, if not because they had the ability to get along with the other members." The group continues to influence us in a number of ways: we identify ourselves with it, and change our behavior to conform to its norms. We define our group by contrasting it with other groups, and seek to distinguish our group by our actions and appearance. Within the group, we compare ourselves to others and jockey for higher status. We may receive labels from our peers, and strive to live up (or down) to them. Finally, we may be most lastingly affected by peers by being rejected by them. People who were rejected as children often report long-term self-esteem problems, poor social skills, and increased rates of psychopathology.

Our personalities become less flexible as we grow older, says Harris, so that "the language and personality acquired in childhood and adolescent peer groups persist, with little modification, for the remainder of the life span." It's a startling conclusion, but Harris claims that her greatest challenge lies not in persuading people that peers matter, but in convincing them that parents don't. She calls the belief in parents' enduring importance "the nurture assumption," and her forthcoming book by that title will argue that it's simply a myth of modern culture. She doesn't deny that children need the care and protection of parents, and acknowledges that mothers and fathers can influence things like religious affiliation and choice of career. But, she maintains, "parental behaviors have no effect on the psychological characteristics their children will have as adults."

In fact, she says, "probably the most important way that parents can influence their children is by determining who their peers are. The immigrants who move their children to another country have provided them with a completely different set of peers. But a less dramatic shift—simply deciding which neighborhood to live in—can also make a difference." From one area to another, she notes, there are substantial variations in the rates of delinquency, truancy, and teen pregnancy—problems parents can try to avoid by surrounding their offspring with suitable friends. Beyond that, however, children will make their own choices. "It's pretty easy to control the social life of a three-year-old," says Harris. "But once the kids are past age 10 or 12, all bets are off."

—A.M.P.

counter-productive." And as for exposing children to a variety of experiences, Rowe thinks that this can give genetically talented children the chance they need, "but not many children have that much potential. This may not be so in Lake Wobegon [where every child is "above average"], but it is true in the rest of the world."

But with an optimism worthy of Garrison Keillor, advocates of parental influence insist that genes aren't the end of the story "The old idea is that you tried to live up to a potential that was set by genes," says Greenspan. "The new idea is that environment helps create potential." His view is supported by recent research that suggests a baby is born with only basic neural "wir-ing" in place, wiring whose connections are then elaborated by experience. Both sides will have to await the next chapter of genetic research, which may reveal even more complicated interactions between the worlds within and without. In the long-running debate between genes and the environment, neither one has yet had the last word.

Unit Selections

Key Points to Consider

❖ How does an abusive relationship develop? What, if anything, can be done to prevent it? How can we help someone involved in such a relationship?

❖ If you felt your sexual relationship was troubled, how would you act?

❖ How would you react if you learned that your spouse or partner had been unfaithful? Under what circumstances would you consider extrarelational sex?

❖ What is the best way to work out the competing demands of work and family? What are your expectations regarding children's attitudes toward their parents' working?

❖ Discuss how the breakup of a relationship or a divorce affects the people involved. Should we have a goal of reducing the rate of divorce? If so, how? If not, why not? What about the children of divorcing/divorced parents? What should we be doing for them?

❖ What is your responsibility to the members of your family? What is their responsibility to you? What would you give up to care for your parents? What would you expect your children to give up for you?

❖ What makes the grief of children unique? What can be done to help them deal with loss?

 **Links**   ## www.dushkin.com/online/

These sites are annotated on pages 4 and 5.

Stress is life and life is stress. Sometimes stress in families gives new meaning to this statement. When a crisis occurs in families, many processes occur simultaneously as families and their members cope with the stressor and its effects. The experience of a crisis often leads to conflict and reduces the family members' ability to act as resources for each other. Indeed, a stressor can overwhelm the family system, and family members may be among the least effective people in coping with each other's responses to a crisis.

Family crisis comes in many forms; it can be drawn out or the crisis event can be clearly defined. The source of stress can be outside or inside the family, or it can be a combination of both. It can directly involve all family members or as few as one, but the effects will ripple through the family, affecting all of its members to one degree or another.

In this unit, we consider a wide variety of crises. Family violence and chaos are the initial focus. "Anatomy of a Violent Relationship" identifies patterns of abuse, two types of abusive men, and reasons why women stay in abusive relationships. The next two articles in this subsection specifically focus on children. "Helping Children Cope with Violence" shows how children growing up in violent surroundings can come away scarred for life, while "Resilience in Development" documents characteristics of children who show amazing ability to recover and adjust, even in highly dysfunctional families.

The next subsection deals with problems in sexuality and sexual relationships. A good sex life is important to the life of a relationship, yet the underlying meaning attributed to it makes it difficult to discuss. In "Sex & Marriage," ways in which a couple can improve their sex life are addressed. Taking another view of sexuality in a committed marriage, an interview with Hara Estroff Marano, in "Shattered Vows," presents what she has learned about infidelity via her therapy practice and research.

The subsection that follows looks at the work/family connection, with interesting results. "The Politics of Fatigue: The Gender War Has Been Replaced by the Exhaustion of Trying to Do It All" addresses gender differences in the workplace and the impact on family life as well as the overwhelming nature of the struggle to balance work and home. "A Progressive Approach to Caring for Children and Community" addresses a major concern of all working parents—the availability of high-quality day care for their children. The view of children of their working parents is presented in "Do Working Parents Make the Grade?" The changing role of fathers in the everyday life of the family is addressed in the final article, "Balancing Work and Family."

Divorce and remarriage are the subjects of the next subsection. In the first article in this subsection, Peter Kramer asks the question "Should You Leave?" or should you stay in a difficult relationship? Various

efforts to reduce the rate of divorce are detailed in "Divorce Reform: New Directions," along with a critique of the efforts. Then Benedict Carey, in "Is Divorce Too Easy?" says that women are especially paying the price of easy divorce, which has led a coalition of feminists and conservatives to want to change divorce laws in order to make breaking up more difficult to do. In the same vein, Aimee Howd in "Smart Plan to Save Marriages" describes a program that links church and community in an attempt to help more couples follow through on their marriage vows. Stresses faced by children of divorce are the focus of the final two articles in this subsection: "The Children of Divorce" and "After Divorce." These articles complement each other, with the second one chronicling Canadian efforts to help children deal with the long-term effects of their parents' divorce.

The nature of stress resulting from caring for others in the family is the subject of the final subsection. The first two articles address issues of providing care to a dying family member. "Hard Lessons" addresses issues of providing care for a family member with a debilitating, ultimately fatal condition. "A Harder Better Death" explores the choice of hospice care in the face of a painful, terminal condition. When these are read together, they present a picture of challenging, sometimes frustrating, work that also contains some reward. We often focus on the character of adult grief, forgetting that children also mourn, and do so in unique, developmentally specific ways. "How Kids Mourn" presents a picture of the special needs of children when they have experienced loss.

ANATOMY OF A
Violent
RELATIONSHIP

By Neil S. Jacobson, Ph.D., and John M. Gottman, Ph.D.

Each year at least 1.6 million
U.S. women are beaten by their husbands

Yet we know surprisingly little about why so many men erupt into violence, and why they feel such a need to control their women with brutal behavior.

Here, two leading marriage researchers plunge into the red-hot core of domestic abuse—observing violent couples in the heat of conflict—and surface with some startling answers.

Don was having a miserable day. There were rumors of layoffs at work, and his supervisor had been on his case for coming in late. Not only was he sick of not getting credit for doing his work well, he was sure he was about to get caught in some kind of vise he could not control. Now Don was test-driving the car he had asked his wife, Martha, to pick up from the garage. As he listened to his car's motor, he knew instantly that she had been hoodwinked. That damn rattle was still there when he drove up hills! By the time he pulled into their driveway, he was so mad that he almost hit Martha's car.

"What is it with you?" Don railed as he walked into the house. "Couldn't you tell that the damn car still wasn't running right?"

Martha, who was cooking dinner, responded calmly. "Is something wrong with the car? It sounded fine to me."

"Couldn't you tell you'd been had by the garage mechanics? Are you really that stupid?" he continued.

Martha started defending herself. "Wait a minute. I may know nothing about cars, but I resent being called 'stupid.' "

From *Psychology Today*, March/April 1998, pp. 60–65, 81, 84. Excerpted from *When Men Batter Women: New Insights into Ending Abusive Relationships*. Reprinted with the permission of Simon & Schuster. © 1998 by Neil Jacobson and John Gottman.

Don continued railing against the mechanics and against Martha for not standing up to them. He was beginning to see red, and he warned her to shut up.

But Martha didn't shut up. "If you're such a big man, why didn't you stand up to the mechanics the last time they gypped you?"

Don punched Martha in the face—hard. It was not the first punch of their marriage. But she deserved it, he told himself as he continued to hit her and yell at her. All he had wanted, he said, was a little empathy about his problems—and here she was siding with the enemy. Only a small part of him, a dim whisper in his brain, wanted to beg her forgiveness, and by the next day he would manage to squelch even that dim light of remorse.

How does a marital argument like this, one that seems to start out in near-ordinary frustration, escalate so quickly into violence? This question had come up time and again in our work as creators of couples-therapy techniques and in our two decades as social scientists studying marriage. We knew that the existing studies of the dynamics of battering didn't provide

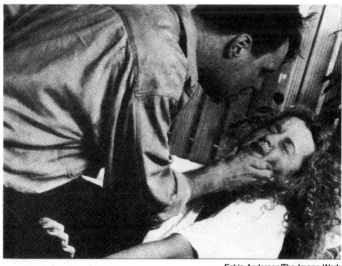

Esbin-Anderson/The Image Work

adequate answers, because they relied on after-the-fact reports by batterers and their victims, reports which are often biased and easily distorted. Particularly with battering, abundant psychological research shows that people are simply not reliable observers of their own or their intimate partner's behavior. So we decided to do something that no one had ever done before—directly observe the arguments of violent couples ourselves.

Using a simple public service announcement asking for couples experiencing marital conflict, we were able to obtain a sample of 63 battering couples, as well as a control group of couples who were equally dissatisfied with their marriage but had no history of violence. All these volunteers agreed to come into the laboratory, have electrodes hooked up to their bodies to record heart rate

and other vital signs, and be videotaped in the midst of arguments. (We also provided important safeguards, including exit interviews to ensure the woman's safety, and referrals to battered women's shelters.)

As you'll see, in the eight years of this study we made a number of myth-shattering discoveries:

- Batterers share a common profile: they are unpredictable, unable to be influenced by their wives, and impossible to prevent from battering once an argument has begun.
- Battered women are neither passive nor submissive; sometimes they are as angry as the batterers. But women almost never batter men.
- Batterers can be classified into two distinct types, men whose temper slowly simmers until it suddenly erupts into violence, and those who strike out immediately. This difference has important implications for women leaving abusive relationships.
- Emotional abuse plays a vital role in battering, undermining a woman's confidence.
- Domestic violence can decrease on its own—but it almost never stops.
- Battered women do leave at high rates, despite the increased danger they face when leaving the relationship.

Battering's Beginnings

Battering is physical aggression with a purpose: to control, intimidate, and subjugate another human being. It is always accompanied by emotional abuse, often involves injury, and virtually always causes fear in the battered woman. In our study, battering couples had at least two episodes of kicking or hitting with a fist, or at least one incident of potentially lethal violence, such as strangling.

Can women ever be batterers? In our study, we found that some battered women defend themselves, and hit or push as often as their husbands do. Some people claim that there is a huge underground movement of battered husbands. However, statistics on violent women do not take into account the impact and function of the violence. According to research conducted by Dina Vivian, Ph.D., at the State University of New York at Stonybrook, women are much more likely to be injured and in need of medical care than men, and much more likely to be killed by their husbands than the reverse. Women are the ones who are beaten up. These injuries help to sustain the fear, which is the force that provides battering with its power.

What about couples who periodically have arguments that escalate into pushing and shoving, but not beyond? We discovered large numbers of these couples, and we found that the husbands almost never become batterers.

While it is important to know about this low-level violence, we were concerned with the dynamics of severely violent couples.

Arguments under The Microscope

Through our research, we were able to reconstruct hundreds of violent arguments. Although we knew we would not directly observe violence between our subjects, we could observe their nonviolent arguments in the laboratory, ask them about these encounters, then judge their accounts of violent arguments by the accuracy of these reports.

When we put violent arguments under a microscope this way, we discovered a number of familiar themes. One of the most startling was our inability to predict when batterers would cross over into violence. While emotional abuse often preceded physical abuse, it was such a common occurrence in the relationship that it did not serve as an accurate warning sign. Further, there was no way for the battered woman to control when emotional abuse would turn into physical abuse. Martha could have shut up when Don told her to. But would this have stopped Don from hitting her? We have discovered that once an episode starts, there is nothing that the woman can do to affect its course.

Despite this inability, the women in our study did not become passive or submissive. Even when the batterers reacted to everyday requests with emotional abuse, the women typically responded calmly and assertively. We found that they wanted to inject as much normalcy into their lives as possible, and they didn't want to give up on their dream of the family life that they wanted.

However, in all the videotapes we made, never did we hear a batterer say anything like, "That's a good point," or "I never thought of that,"—comments that most married men (and women) say all the time during an argument. Instead, we observed that batterers became more aggressive when their wives asserted themselves. When Martha challenged him, we saw that Don responded violently in an attempt to maintain his dominance, no matter what the costs.

Another way that batterer's arguments diverged from those of nonviolent couples—perhaps the key difference—is that nonviolent couples have what we call "a withdrawal ritual," where at some point the escalation process stops or reverses itself. Some couples take breaks, other couples compromise, still others do both. In battering couples, the women are typically quite willing to stop at a point where they start to sense danger, but once the husbands are "activated," violence follows. Although the violence is unpredictable, we were able to identify certain warning signs. When belligerence and contempt during an argument were combined with attempts to squelch, control, or dominate a wife's behavior, that was

a sign that a batterer was close to crossing the line. Don's contemptuous way of asking Martha whether she was "really that stupid," and his attempt to dominate her by telling her to shut up, demonstrate a classic prelude to battering.

Surprisingly, both in the lab and at home, battered women expressed as much belligerence and contempt as their husbands did. Like most people, battered women get angry when they are insulted and degraded. We saw much effort on the part of the women to contain their anger, but it tended to leak out anyway. Nevertheless, their initial responses—like Martha's retort to Don about not standing up to the mechanics—could hardly be considered provocations to violence.

The Slow Burn: "Pit Bulls"

Men like Don metabolize anger in a kind of slow burn: it gradually increases but never lets up. We call them "Pit Bulls" because they grow more and more aggressive until they finally attack. These men, we have found, constitute about 80 percent of batterers.

Pit Bulls have unrelenting contempt for women, and yet are extremely dependent on them. This creates a unique dynamic in their behavior. In many unhappy marriages, when one partner (usually the woman) requests change, the other one (usually the man) resists change, and eventually the woman's requests become demands, and the man's avoidance becomes withdrawal. But Pit Bulls often both demand and withdraw. We can see this in the incessant demands that Don made of Martha. Everything she did (including getting the car fixed) was wrong because nothing she did was quite enough for Don. Martha had to watch every move she made, give up her friends and family, account for all of her time, avoid Don's jealousy, and try to satisfy what he called his "simple need for a little empathy." Yet even as she walked on eggshells, she was attacked for being a "stupid bitch." Don blamed Martha for his own neediness, and punished her for it almost every day they were together.

Through this scrutiny and these constant demands, Pit Bulls establish control. Control is important to these men because they genuinely feel that they will be abandoned if they do not maintain constant vigilance over their wives. One particularly sinister form of control they use is known as "gaslighting." This technique—which gets its name from the film *Gaslight*, in which Charles Boyer convinces Ingrid Bergman she is going insane—involves a systematic denial of the wife's experience of reality. For example, when one of our subjects slapped his wife in front of a neighbor, he denied that he had done it, telling her that this kind of behavior was inconsistent with his personality, and that her accusations of abuse came from

Can Batterers JUST STOP?

"Why do women stay?" That question haunts anybody who has observed domestic violence. But a far more practical question is, How can the men be stopped? Maryland psychologist Steven Stosny, Ph.D., has developed a remarkable and effective treatment program for battering men. Even a year after treatment, an astonishing 86 percent have ended the physical abuse, and 73 percent have stopped the verbal and emotional abuse. The national dropout rate for battering programs is one out of two; Stosny's is only one out of four.

Treating batterers is something that most therapists shy away from. How did you get into it?

I became interested in spouse and child abuse at the age of two. I grew up in a violent family, where we had police and ambulances coming to the door. It took a while for me to get up the courage to get into this field, and when I started a group with severe batterers, I wanted to learn how they got that way, to learn how to prevent abuse. I was surprised when they stopped being abusive.

So how do you approach batterers?

Our program is based on the idea that most batterers can't sustain attachment, and because of this, they become flooded with feelings of guilt, shame, and abandonment, which they regulate with aggression. We teach them a five-step technique called HEALS. First, we start with the concept of *Heal*. Our clients learn that blame is powerless, but compassion is true power, and has the ability to heal. Next, you *Explain* to yourself the core hurt that anger is masking: feeling unimportant, disregarded, guilty, devalued, rejected, powerless, and unlovable. All abusive behavior is motivated by these core hurts. Then you *Apply* self-compassion. Let's say your wife calls you a brainless twit, and you feel she doesn't love you. You want to punish her for reminding you that you're unlovable. We teach men to replace this core feeling with self-compassion. "She feels unloving, but she still loves me. My instinct might be to call her a filthy slut, but she said what she said because she's hurt and feeling bad." Then you move into a feeling of *Love*, for yourself and your wife. And finally, you solve the problem by presenting your true position without blaming or attacking the other person: you say, "I care about you, but I have a problem with your calling me a brainless twit." You are healing your core hurt through love rather than anger.

So you're saying the batterer is really trying to heal his hurt core, and he can do it with compassion instead of abuse. Still, how can someone used to physical aggression learn to be so rational?

We call it teaching Mr. Hyde to remember what Dr. Jekyll learned. These men have to learn emotional regulation and the rewards of change based on compassion. We ask them to remember an incident that made them angry, to feel the anger again, and follow the steps of HEALS 12 times a day for four weeks. It almost works like a vaccination. You feel the core hurt for five seconds at a time when you practice, and you develop an immunity to it.

Why is your dropout rate so low?

It's a 12-week program, and if they don't do their homework, they go to jail. We have surprisingly little resistance. I also say "If you don't feel much better about yourself, we'll give you your money back. You'll like yourself better when you're compassionate." I've treated over 1200 abusers in my career, and even the antisocial ones—no matter how justified they felt at the time—never felt proud of hurting someone they loved. Our group is about becoming proud.

Does this work even for the true sociopaths, the ones Jacobson and Gottman call Cobras?

These people are not afraid of the criminal justice system and they don't usually come to treatment. Most people in treatment are different. They're the dependent personalities who only hurt ones they love, and who get over-involved in the relationship. If sociopaths and people with antisocial personality disorders do come into treatment, they don't learn compassion. But they do learn to use emotional regulation techniques to keep from getting upset. Some of them use this as another form of superiority—you're going to get hysterical and I'm not—but it's better than beating up their wives in front of the children. It's a form of harm reduction.

Why does this work better than traditional treatment?

Most treatment programs focus on how men's domination causes domestic violence. We say that the real gender variable is that culture doesn't teach men to regulate their negative emotions, or sustain trust, compassion, and love. Numerous studies have shown that. We socialize girls and women to have an emotional vocabulary, and this has nothing to do with education level. We look into the eyes of little girls and reward them when they cry or express other emotions, but when a little boy expresses emotions, we call him a sissy. Boys are taught to keep vulnerable emotions submerged, and don't develop an emotional vocabulary.

And if you can't tell sadness from loneliness from disappointment from rejection from being devalued, the bad feelings get overloaded easily. The strongest emotion is anger.

What about the women? Do you counsel them at all?

We put the safety of the victim first. We say, "We're sure you're not going to be abused any more, but it's very unlikely you'll have a good relationship with your abuser." We tell the women that there's more to life than not being abused. And we have a higher separation rate than the average. While 75 percent of women and children in shelters go back to their husbands, out of 379 couples to go through our program so far, 46 percent of them have left their spouses.

How do you treat substance abusers?

We conduct our treatment simultaneously with substance abuse treatment. Even though this hurts our treatment outcomes—98 percent of our recidivism is from alcohol and drugs—it's important because the nervous system bounce makes a person more irritable when coming off a drug, and I prefer they have some skills first.

Roland Maiuro, Ph.D., of the University of Washington, has been conducting a controlled study using the antidepressant Paxil to treat abusers. Maiuro found that abusers has consistently low serotonin levels, which were perhaps rendered even lower by their negative patterns of behavior. Have you seen Prozac-like drugs work with batterers?

I always tell abusers to try antidepressants. Anything that increases serotonin will reduce shame. And shame causes anger and aggression. I'll bet money that when studies like Maiuro's come out, we will see a significant reduction in violence. The problem is getting them to take it.

They'll take any illicit drug, but they won't take Prozac. But Prozac and HEALS will work best. It may even get the sociopaths.

How can we prevent domestic violence from happening in the first place?

If you treat it in the early stages you can prevent murders from happening. But you can't do this with a gender war. Community meetings against domestic violence have one or two men, and few minorities. Saying you're against domestic violence scares off people, and attracts the ones who really believe in the battle of the sexes. By demonizing the batterer, it makes him more isolated.

But if we make community organization about being for the creation of safe and secure families, they will have a much broader appeal.

her own disturbed mind. Although her face still hurt from the slap, she thought to herself that maybe she had made it all up. The neighbor, a friend of the husband's, went along and said he didn't see anything.

This technique of denying the woman's reality can be so effective that, when used in combination with methods to isolate the woman from other people, it causes battered women to doubt their own sanity. This is the ultimate form of abuse: to gain control of the victim's mind.

Lightning Strikes: "Cobras"

When Don and Martha started arguing, Don's heart rate would go up, he would sweat, and he'd exhibit other signs of emotional arousal. Most people show this response. However, we were astonished to find that as some batterers become more verbally aggressive, there is a decrease in heart rate. Like the cobra who becomes still and focused before striking its victim at over 100 miles an hour, these men calm themselves internally and focus their attention while striking swiftly at their wives with vicious verbal aggression.

When we separated these calm batterers from those who became internally aroused, we found other profound differences between the two groups. These "Cobras"—who constituted about 20 percent of our sample—were more likely to have used or threatened to use a knife or a gun on their wives, and were more severely violent than the other batterers. Only three percent of Pit Bulls had a history of extramarital violence, while 44 percent of Cobras did. And while about 33 percent of Pit Bills qualified for a diagnosis of "antisocial personality disorder"—which includes a long history of impulsive criminal behavior, childhood episodes of lying, stealing, fire setting, and cruelty to animals—fully 90 percent of the Cobras met the criteria. Finally, even though both groups abused alcohol at high rates, Cobras were more likely to be dependent on illegal drugs, such as cocaine and heroin, and were much less emotionally attached to their wives.

George was a typical Cobra. In the year prior to entering our research project, George had threatened to kill Vicky numerous times. One night several weeks before coming to see us, George came home late after he'd been out drinking and found Vicky and their two year-old daughter Christi sharing a pizza. Vicky was angry with him for missing dinner, and ignored him when he arrived. Her silence angered him, and he shouted, "You got a problem?" When she remained silent, he slammed his fist into the pizza, knocked her off the chair, dragged her across the room by her hair, held her down, and spat pizza in her face. He then beat her up, yelling, "You've ruined my life!"

The contrast between this incident and the altercation between Don and Martha over the car shows how Cobras are far more emotionally aggressive towards their wives at the start of their arguments than Pit Bulls. While Don became increasingly heated and less controlled over the course of the argument, George escalated the situation extremely rapidly, using both physical and verbal abuse in the service of control, intimidation, and subjugation. He was in Vicky's face twice as fast as she ever expected. This quick response is typical of the way Cobras control their wives—a tactic which they use because it often quiets the partner quickly and with minimal effort.

Another main difference between Cobras and Pit Bulls is that Cobras come from more chaotic family backgrounds. In our study, 78 percent of the Cobras came from violent families, compared to 51 percent of Pit Bulls. (In the population at large, 20 to 25 percent of children grow up in violent homes.) George's childhood was a classic example. He was beaten and neglected by both parents, and sexually abused by his prostitute mother's male customers. Like other Cobras, he came from a background that seriously crushed the implicit trust that every child has in his or her parents. This horrible childhood background, we believe, had somehow led the Cobras to vow to themselves that no one would ever control them again.

MEN CAN CHANGE

An astonishing 54 percent of our male volunteers showed decreases in violence during the second of two follow-up years. In fact, some men no longer met our standards for being included in our violent group. But

> **Batterers subscribe to an "honor code" that makes them unable to accept any influence—no matter how gentle—from women.**

this decrease in violence may be misleading. Once control is established over a woman through battering, perhaps it can be maintained by continued emotional abuse with intermittent battering used as a terrifying reminder of what is possible in the marriage. Cobras' violence was so severe that it may have been easier for them than for the Pit Bulls to maintain control through emotional abuse alone. Still, only seven percent of batterers in our study stopped their violence altogether in the two-year follow-up period.

We did observe several examples of husbands stopping the violence when it was unsuccessful in controlling their wives. George stopped beating Vicky as soon as she responded to his bullying with anger of her own.

WHEN WOMEN WON'T LEAVE

Three years after our two-year follow-up, we recontacted many of the battered women and their husbands. Despite the greater incidence of mental illness, drug addiction, emotional abuse, and severe violence in Cobra relationships, the typical pattern among the Cobra couples was for the wives to be committed to the marriages. While almost half of Pit Bull marriages dissolved within two years, by the five-year follow-up point, only 25 percent of women married to Cobras had left them; these women not only recognized the danger of trying to leave them, but often were quite attached to them.

Why would a woman be attached to a man as dangerous as George? Surprisingly, Vicky—like 80 percent of women married to Cobras—tested normal on our personality scales. However, she described her childhood as a "war zone" where her father would one day be absent and disengaged, and then suddenly become physically abusive toward Vicky's mother and all of the kids. She ran away from home to find a better life. And when she became pregnant by George, she tried to build her dream life. With her dashing new husband, she would finally have the home she had always wanted.

But when Vicky realized her dream of a normal, nonabusive relationship would never come to pass with George, she made the decision to leave. With Vicky and other battered women, "giving up the dream" was a pivotal step in shifting from fear to contempt and a determination to leave. Battered women need to be helped to "give up the dream" sooner, and this process should occur in conjunction with a careful safety plan and the support of an experienced helper.

Once Vicky implemented her safety plan, which included restraining orders against George and notifying his employer, the Navy, she found that George lost interest in her and went on to new pursuits. We found that Cobras will not pursue women who leave them unless it is easy and causes them little hassle to do so. But there are exceptions, and this is where help from an expert is essential.

Pit Bulls are the opposite of Cobras: easier to leave in the short run, but harder to leave in the long run. When Martha left Don and called it a trial separation, Don had little problem with it. But when she continued the separation for more than a month, he began to abuse and stalk her.

After three years of this, Martha consistently and forcefully asserted her rights. She divorced him. She hung up on him. She ended a definitive conversation with a "F___ you!" and refused to talk to him. Don might have killed her at this time. Pit Bulls have a great capacity to minimize, deny, or distort reality, and they can often justify to themselves stalking, continued abuse, and at times even murder. But Martha got lucky. Don began to leave her alone when it was clear that she would no longer be responsive to his threats. By that time, she had decided that even death was preferable to being under Don's spell.

EMERGING FROM HELL

We began this study with the goal of learning about the relationship between batterers and battered women, and we learned a great deal. We expected to focus on the men, especially when we came upon the distinction between Pit Bulls and Cobras. But during our exit interviews, we found the women in our study to be resourceful and courageous, and over time we began to realize that our work was also about the heroic struggle of battered women. These women start with a dream and truly descend into hell, and for a period of time seem stuck there. But they do not give up. They continue to struggle. Our main cause for optimism is that many of them emerge from hell and live to love again.

Helping Children Cope With Violence

Lorraine B. Wallach

Lorraine B. Wallach, M.A., is one of the founders of the Erikson Institute in Chicago and is presently a faculty member there. Her recent work includes staff training around issues of children and violence.

Children who grow up in violent communities are at risk for pathological development because growing up in a constant state of apprehension makes it difficult to establish trust, autonomy, and social competence.

Violence is epidemic in the United States today. The murder rate in this country is the fifth highest in the world. It is 10 times higher than England's and 25 times that of Spain. For many inner-city children, violence has become a way of life. In a study of more than 1,000 children in Chicago, 74% of them had witnessed a murder, shooting, stabbing, or robbery (Kotulak, 1990; Bell, 1991). Almost half (47%) of these incidents involved friends, family members, classmates, or neighbors. Forty-six percent of the children interviewed reported that they had personally experienced at least one violent crime. These figures are similar to those found in other U.S. urban areas, such as Baltimore (Zinsmeister, 1990), Los Angeles County (Pynoos & Eth, 1985), and New Orleans (Osofsky, Wewers, Hann, Fick, & Richters, 1991).

Children are exposed to several kinds of violence, including child abuse and domestic violence. And there are communities where violence is endemic, where gang bangers, drug dealers, petty criminals, and not-so-petty criminals rule the streets. For children living in these conditions, feelings of being safe and secure do not exist.

Children who are not designated victims of assault can be unintended victims. Shoot-outs between gangs and drive-by shootings result in the wounding, and often killing, of innocent bystanders. In addition, the psychological toll of living under these conditions is immeasurable. The children in these neighborhoods see violence and hear it discussed. They are surrounded by danger and brutality.

Child abuse, other domestic violence, and neighborhood violence can harm development

The effects of this kind of violence on children are widespread and can permeate all areas of development, beginning in infancy and continuing through childhood. The first task a baby faces is the development of trust—trust in the caregiving environment and eventually in himself. Achieving a sense of trust is com-promised by growing up in a violent community. Many families find it difficult to provide infants with support, love, and affection in a consistent and predictable manner when they live in a constant state of apprehension—not knowing when they are going to be victims of violence. Toddlers have difficulty developing a sense of autonomy when their families cannot help them explore their environments because their surroundings are filled with danger. Preschoolers, too, are inhibited from going out into the world. Just at the age when they should be expanding their social contacts and finding out about people beyond the family, they are restricted by the dangers lurking outside. Many children living in high-rise housing projects and other dangerous neighborhoods are cooped up inside all day because it is unsafe to go out-of-doors. The situation is even more tragic when children experience violence within the family. Where can a child find protection when she is victimized within her own home? Although domestic violence occurs in *every* kind of neighborhood, the effects may be even more damaging when compounded by the harmful effects of growing up in *violent* neighborhoods.

Children who grow up under conditions that do not allow them to develop trust in people and in themselves or learn to handle day-to-day problems in socially acceptable ways are at risk for pathological development; they are at risk for resorting to violent behaviors themselves. The anger that is instilled in children when they are mistreated or when they see their mothers or siblings mistreated is likely to be incorporated into their personality structures. Children learn by identifying with the people they love. They also identify with the people who have power and control. When children see and experience abuse and violence as a way of life, when the people who are responsible for them behave without restraint, the children often learn to behave in the same manner.

Another serious problem for children living in chaotic communities is that the protectors and the dangerous people may be one and the same. The police, who are supposed to be protectors, are often seen as dangerous by community members. In his book *There Are No Children Here*, Alex Kotlowitz (1991) describes how a young man who is idolized by his housing project community because he is successful, has graduated from high school, is not caught

Julia Andrews

It is particularly important for children who come from chaotic environments to have firm but appropriate limits, even though children who feel powerless may try to provoke adults into a battle of wills in an effort to make themselves feel important.

The young child's protectors and the dangerous people in her life may be one and the same.

up in gangs, and is still his own person is mistakenly killed by the police. What do children think when their idol is gunned down by the people who are supposed to protect them?

Children are confused when they cannot tell the good guys from the bad guys. Their teachers and the media tell them that drug dealers are bad and are the cause of the problems in the community, but the children may know that cousins or friends or even older brothers are dealing. Some people have likened the inner city, especially housing projects, to war zones; but in a war the enemy is more often than not on the outside, and usually everyone knows who he is.

Children growing up with violence face risks other than becoming violent themselves. Children who live with danger develop defenses against their fears, and these defenses can interfere with their development. When children have to defend themselves constantly from outside or inside dangers, their energies are not available for other, less immediately urgent tasks, such as learning to read and write and do arithmetic and learning about geography and history and science. In addition to not having enough energy to devote to schoolwork, there is evidence that specific cognitive functions such as memory and a sense of time can be affected by experiencing trauma (Terr, 1981).

Boys and girls who are victims of abuse and who see abusive behavior in their families can grow up feeling as if they are responsible for what is happening. Young children cannot always differentiate between what is real and what is part of their inner lives. The literature on divorce has made clear that many children believe that they have caused the breakup of the family, even though it had nothing to do with them (Wallerstein & Kelly, 1980; Hetherton, Cox, & Cox, 1982). Children who feel guilty about the violence in their families often perceive themselves as being bad and worthless. Feelings of worthlessness can lead children to the idea that they are not capable of learning, which leads, in turn, to a lack of motivation to achieve in school.

Children who experience trauma may have difficulty seeing themselves in future roles that are meaningful. Lenore Terr (1983), in her study of the schoolchildren of Chowchilla who were kidnapped in their school bus, found that the views of their future lives were limited and often filled with anticipation of disaster. Children who cannot see a decent future for themselves cannot give their all to the present task of learning and becoming socialized.

Living in unpredictably frightening situations makes children feel as if they have no control over their lives. We know that young children

> # When children have to defend themselves constantly from inside and outside dangers, there is little energy for schoolwork. There is also evidence that specific cognitive functions such as memory and a sense of time can be affected.

need to feel as if they can direct some parts of their lives, but children who are victims of violence learn that they have no say in what happens to them. This sense of helplessness interferes with the development of autonomy.

It is difficult for children to keep on growing and maturing when they have been traumatized because an almost universal reaction of children to traumatic occurrences is regression. Children slip back to stages at which they felt more secure. This is particularly true when they have only a tenuous hold on their current status.

What makes some children more resilient than others, and what can we do?

As depressing as all this sounds, however, it does not mean that all children who experience violence are doomed. It is known that some children are more resilient and withstand trauma and stress better than others. If a child has an easy temperament and makes a good fit with

his primary caregiver, he or she is more likely to be off to a good start. Some lucky children are born to strong parents who can withstand the ravages of poverty and community violence and still provide some security and hope for their children. Children are shaped not only by their parents' behavior but also by their parents' hopes, expectations, motivations, and view of the future —including their children's future.

It is important to remember that children are malleable, that what happens in the early years is important, but that many children can overcome the hurts and fears of earlier times. Many can make use of positive experiences that occur both inside and outside their families. Child care centers, recreation programs, and schools can be resources for children and offer them alternative perceptions of themselves, as well as teaching them skills. One of the things that help determine the resiliency of children is the ability to make relationships and to make use of the people in their environments, people who provide to children what they do not get in their families or who supplement what their families cannot offer.

Child care professionals can help offset the negative effects of violence in the lives of young children by providing that supplement. Although teachers, social workers, and human service personnel cannot cure all of the hurts experienced by children today, they can make a difference.

1. The first thing they need to do is to make sure that their programs provide opportunities for children to develop meaningful rela-

> A kindergarten teacher in a Chicago public school was discussing her dilemma concerning two boys in her classroom. All of the children were at their tables, engaged in drawing, when the teacher noticed these boys crawling under the tables, pretending to have guns. When one of the boys saw the teacher watching them, he reassured her, "Don't worry, we're just playing breaking into an apartment." The teacher questioned whether she should let the play continue or offer a more socially acceptable view of behavior. How should she react? A Head Start teacher in the group said that the boy who was taking the lead in this game had been in her class the year before, and that his family's apartment had been burglarized. The boy had been very frightened and, after that experience, had changed from a confident, outgoing youngster to a quiet and withdrawn child. Here it was a year later, and he was just beginning to play out his experience. He was becoming the aggressor in the play instead of the helpless victim. And he was regaining some of his old confidence.

tionships with caring and knowledgeable adults. Teachers and other staff members can offer each child a chance to form an important relationship with one of them, a relationship within which the child can learn that there are people in the world who can be of help. The best thing to offer children at risk is caring people, people who are available both physically and emotionally.

Some years ago the famous Chicago analyst Franz Alexander (1948) coined the term *corrective emotional experience* to explain the curative power of therapy, and that term best describes what child care professionals can do for children at risk. A corrective emotional experience means having a relationship with another person that touches one's deepest core—not a relationship that is superficial or intellectual, but one that engages the emotions. It means having a relationship within which a person can redo old patterns and ties. It means feeling safe enough within a relationship to risk making basic changes in one's psychic structure. Children cannot be forced into these kinds of relationships; they can only be offered the opportunities with the hope that they take advantage of them.

Some children attach easily, and it does not take much effort on the part of the adults for these children to form attachments; these are usually the children who have had a good relationship in their past. Other children have not been lucky enough to have had the kind of relationship that makes them want to seek out others and repeat this satisfying experience; these children need more help in forming ties and trusting alliances.

What can adults do to stimulate relationships with children who do not come easily to this task? They can look into themselves and see if they are ready for this kind of relationship—a relationship that makes demands on their emotions, their energies, and their time. Relationships with children who have inordinate needs and who do not have

past experiences in give-and-take partnerships are not 50–50 propositions; adults must meet these children more than halfway.

2. Child care professionals can organize their schedules and their time with the children so that they provide as much consistency as possible. Attachment can be encouraged by reducing the number of people a child encounters during the day and by maximizing the amount of meaningful time and activity the child has with one adult. In this way each child is allowed to form an attachment to one person. There are several models—including therapeutic centers, child-life programs, and primary-care nursing—that use relationship as the principal tool in their interventions. Establishing significant relationships with the children who have suffered from trauma is the most important thing that can be done, and it is the basis for all of the work that follows. What is this other work?

3. Child care professionals must provide structure and very clear expectations and limits. All children, especially young children, need to know where they stand, but it is particularly important for children who come from chaotic environments to have firm but appropriate limits. It should be noted that they do not take to this kind of structure easily.

It is not something they have experienced before, and the newness of it may cause anxiety and tension, just as any new situation does.

Some children see the structure of a new setting as an opportunity to assert themselves and force the adults into power struggles. Children who feel powerless may try to provoke adults into a battle of wills in an effort to make themselves feel important. But even though some of the neediest children may rebel against structure, no matter how benign, it is important to provide it so that the boundaries are clear.

4. Early childhood professionals should offer children opportunities to express themselves within the confines of a comfortable and consistent schedule, with clear expectations about behavior. Children need to air their emotions; they need to tell their stories. They can do this in several activities that can be a part of any good program for children.

Except for life-sustaining activities, play is, of course, the most universal activity of children

Through play, children learn about the physical and social world. As they play, children develop a map of the world, a map that helps them make sense of the complexities that

---

A nine-year-old boy in a shelter for battered women told a story about his recurring dream. This is what he said: "I dreamed of someone taking me away. He was dressed like a lady, but he had a moustache. I went inside the house. It was dark. The lights were out, and there were people inside having a party. It was ugly. They were eating worms and they asked me to try one. I took one and threw it away. Then I opened the door, and the light came on in there, and I saw there were no more ghosts, and I saw I was sleeping. When I dream like that, I become afraid."

It was obvious that the boy was expressing his fears, but the exact meaning of the details was not evident—not until one of the child care workers who knew the mother reported that the abusive father was bisexual and brought his male sexual partners to the family's apartment. It then became clear that in addition to struggling with feelings about an abusive father, the boy was also frightened and confused about the meaning of his father's behavior and probably about his own sexual identification. In this case the child was able to tell about a disturbing dream through the telling of a story, and the adults were able to understand it with additional information about his family.

define the world today. Play, in the context of a corrective experience, offers children who live with chaos and violence a chance to redraw their world map.

Play provides an avenue for children to express their feelings. Children who are angry or hurt can take their anger out on toys, dolls, and stuffed animals. Children who feel isolated or lonely can find solace in pretending to live in a world with lots of friends. Children who are frightened can seek safety within a game by pretending to be big and strong. In other words, children can play out their own scenarios, changing their real life situations to their own design. They can invent happy endings. They can reverse roles and become the big—instead of the small—people. They can become the aggressors rather than the victims.

Play also allows children to repeat some of the bad things in their lives. Some people think that children want to forget the frightening or horrible things that they have experienced and try to put these events out of their minds. Some people think that children's play reflects only happy experiences; and many times it does. But some children gain strength from repeating situations that were overwhelming to them, as a way of trying to come to terms with the experiences.

Traumatic events have a way of staying with us. Sometimes they are repeated in dreams. Adults may review these events by talking about them with their friends and even with strangers. Adults, through discussion—and children, through play—gain control over trauma by repeating it again and again. Repetition allows the trauma victim to absorb the experience little by little, come to grips with what happened, and learn to accept it or live with it.

Expressive art is very therapeutic

In addition to being given many opportunities for dramatic play, chil-

Josephine, the child of an abused mother, told a story about a girl with red eyes who bit and scratched her mother because she was angry at her and the devil got into her body. The child care worker listened and accepted her story, thereby accepting the child's feelings. In subsequent sessions, after establishing a more trusting relationship with the child, the worker told her a story about the same little girl who told the devil not to bother her and who talked to her mother and how she was going to try harder to be nicer. By using the same characters and theme, she offered the little girl another way of relating to her mother. At the same time, the mother's worker helped her understand her own anger and supported her in trying to alter her behavior toward her daughter.

dren can benefit from a chance to paint and draw. Just as some children make sad or frightening events into happy occasions in their play, others may draw pictures of happy times, even when they are living in far-from-happy circumstances. They draw pictures of nice houses with flowers and trees and sunshine. Others draw pictures that are, or that represent, disturbing things in their lives. They draw angry or violent pictures and find solace in expressing their feelings through art and conquering their fears by putting them on paper.

Storytelling can bridge to valuable conversation

Storytelling is another way in which children can handle difficult situations and express their inner thoughts. Sharing the telling of stories can be an excellent way to open up communication between adults and children. It can establish rapport between the two and lay the basis for further discussions of a child's difficulties. It is easier for the adult to understand stories than to interpret drawings or play, and the adult is able to engage a child in a conversation about her or his story.

This does not mean that the stories children tell can be accepted verbatim. Just as play and drawing allow children to express themselves symbolically, so do stories offer them a chance to communicate an idea or feeling without acknowledging its closeness to reality. Adults often cannot understand a child's story without having some outside information about the child's life.

If we understand what children are telling us through their stories, we can help them by participating with them in storytelling. Gardner (1971) used this method in his therapy with children. After the child told a story, Gardner told the same story but with a different, healthier ending. Although teachers are not therapists, they can engage children in joint storytelling sessions and offer alternative endings to the stories told by the children.

Collaboration with families is critically important

Direct work with children is invaluable, but if it can be combined with help for parents, its effectiveness can be increased. Young children are best understood in the context of their families and communities. Professionals need to know the facts about a child's life situation, and that information can be gained from the adults who know the child well.

In addition to obtaining information from parents, the most effective help for a child is in collaboration with help for the family. Because the child is entwined with his family for many years, it is important to make changes in his familial relationships, if possible; even small changes can be important.

It is not possible for teachers and other child specialists to also be social workers and parent therapists. The person who makes contact with a child, however, is often in a good position to establish a working alliance with the child's parents. This alliance can then be used to refer parents to community agencies, clinics, churches, or self-help groups for the support, guidance, or therapy that they need. Making a good referral takes skill and patience. It cannot be done quickly, which means that teachers and child care workers must have the time to talk to parents and to make home visits if necessary. They must have time to establish contact with families as an essential part of their work with children who suffer the consequences of violence.

The problems spelled out here are formidable. They will not be easy to solve, but professionals who see children on a daily basis can be an important part of the solution. They cannot cure all of the ills and solve all of the problems that confront children today, but they can offer these children a chance to face and accept their feelings and to see alternative ways of relating to others. If child care professionals can help some—not all, but some—children find alternatives to destructive behavior, be it toward themselves or others, they have helped break the cycle of violence.

References

Alexander, F. (1948). *Fundamentals of psychoanalysis.* New York: W.W. Norton.

Bell, C. (1991). Traumatic stress and children in danger. *Journal of Health Care for the Poor and Underserved, 2*(1), 175–188.

Gardner, R. (1971). *Therapeutic communication with children: The mutual storytelling technique.* New York: Science House.

Hetherton, E.M., Cox, M., & Cox, R. (1982). Effects of divorce on parents and children. In M. Lamb (Ed.), *Non-traditional families.* Hillsdale, NJ: Lawrence Erlbaum.

Kotlowitz, A. (1991). *There are no children here.* New York: Doubleday.

Kotulak, R. (1990, September 28). Study finds inner-city kids live with violence. *Chicago Tribune,* pp. 1, 16.

Osofsky, J., Wewers, S., Hann, D., Fick, A., & Richters, J. (1991). *Chronic community violence: What is happening to our children?* Manuscript submitted for publication.

Pynoos, R., & Eth, S. (1985). Children traumatized by witnessing personal violence: Homicide, rape or suicide behavior. In S. Eth & R. Pynoos (Eds.), *Posttraumatic stress disorder in children* (pp. 19–43). Washington, DC: American Psychiatric Press.

Terr, L. (1981). Forbidden games: Posttraumatic child's play. *Journal of American Academy of Child Psychiatry, 20,* 741–760.

Terr, L. (1983). Chowchilla revisited: The effects of psychic trauma four years after a schoolbus kidnapping. *American Journal of Psychiatry, 140,* 1543–1550.

Wallerstein, J.S., & Kelley, J.B. (1980). *Surviving the breakup: How children and parents cope with divorce.* New York: Basic Books.

Zinsmeister, K. (1990, June). Growing up scared. *The Atlantic Monthly,* pp. 49–66.

Resilience in Development

Emmy E. Werner

Emmy E. Werner is Professor of Human Development at the University of California, Davis. Address correspondence to Emmy E. Werner, Department of Applied Behavioral Sciences, University of California, Davis, 2321 Hart Hall, Davis, CA 95616.

During the past decade, a number of investigators from different disciplines—child development, psychology, psychiatry, and sociology—have focused on the study of children and youths who overcame great odds. These researchers have used the term resilience to describe three kinds of phenomena: good developmental outcomes despite high-risk status, sustained competence under stress, and recovery from trauma. Under each of these conditions, behavioral scientists have focused their attention on protective factors, or mechanisms that moderate (ameliorate) a person's reaction to a stressful situation or chronic adversity so that his or her adaptation is more successful than would be the case if the protective factors were not present.[1]

So far, only a relatively small number of studies have focused on children who were exposed to biological insults. More numerous in the current research literature are studies of resilient children who grew up in chronic poverty, were exposed to parental psychopathology, or experienced the breakup of their family or serious caregiving deficits. There has also been a growing body of literature on resilience in children who have endured the horrors of contemporary wars.

Despite the heterogeneity of all these studies, one can begin to discern a common core of individual dispositions and sources of support that contribute to resilience in development. These protective buffers appear to transcend ethnic, social-class, and geographic boundaries. They also appear to make a more profound impact on the life course of individuals who grow up in adversity than do specific risk factors or stressful life events.

Most studies of individual resilience and protective factors in children have been short-term, focusing on middle childhood and adolescence. An exception is the Kauai Longitudinal Study, with which I have been associated during the past three decades.[2] This study has involved a team of pediatricians, psychologists, and public-health and social workers who have monitored the impact of a variety of biological and psychosocial risk factors, stressful life events, and protective factors on the development of a multiethnic cohort of 698 children born in 1955 on the "Garden Island" in the Hawaiian chain. These individuals were followed, with relatively little attrition, from the prenatal period through birth to ages 1, 2, 10, 18, and 32.

Some 30% of the survivors in this study population were considered high-risk children because they were born in chronic poverty, had experienced perinatal stress, and lived in family environments troubled by chronic discord, divorce, or parental psychopathology. Two thirds of the children who had experienced four or more such risk factors by age 2 developed serious learning or behavior problems by age 10 or had delinquency records, mental health problems, or pregnancies by age 18. But one third of the children who had experienced four or more such risk factors developed instead into competent, confident, and caring adults.

PROTECTIVE FACTORS WITHIN THE INDIVIDUAL

Infancy and Early Childhood

Our findings with these resilient children are consistent with the results of several other longitudinal studies which have reported that young children with good coping abilities under adverse conditions have temperamental characteristics that elicit positive responses from a wide range of caregivers. The resilient boys and girls in the Kauai study were consistently characterized by their mothers as active, affectionate, cuddly, good-natured, and easy to deal with. Egeland and his associates observed similar dispositions among securely attached infants of abusing mothers in the Minnesota Mother-Child Interaction Project,[3] and Moriarty found the same qualities among infants with congenital defects at the Menninger Foundation.[4] Such infants were alert, easy to soothe, and able to elicit support from a nurturant family member. An "easy" temperament and the ability to actively recruit competent adult caregivers were also observed by Elder and his associates[5] in the resourceful children of the Great Depression.

By the time they reach preschool age, resilient children appear to have developed a coping pattern that combines autonomy with an ability to ask for help when needed. These characteristics are also predictive of resilience in later years.

Middle Childhood and Adolescence

When the resilient children in the Kauai Longitudinal Study were in elementary school, their teachers were favorably impressed by their communication and problem-solving skills. Although these children were not particularly gifted, they used whatever talents they had effectively. Usually they had a special interest or a hobby they could share with a friend, and that gave them a sense of pride. These interests and activities were not narrowly sex typed. But the boys and the girls grew into adolescents who were outgoing and autonomous, but also nurturant and emotionally sensitive.

Similar findings have been reported by Anthony, who studied the resilient offspring of mentally ill parents in St. Louis;[6] by Felsman and Vaillant, who followed successful boys from a high-crime neighborhood in Boston into adulthood;[7] and by Rutter and Quinton, who studied the lives of British girls who had been institutionalized in childhood, but managed to become well-functioning adults and caring mothers.[8]

Most studies of resilient children and youths report that intelligence and scholastic competence are positively associated with the ability to overcome great odds. It stands to reason that youngsters who are better able to appraise stressful life events correctly are also better able to figure out strategies for coping with adversity, either through their own efforts or by actively reaching out to other people for help. This finding has been replicated in studies of Asian-American,

Caucasian, and African-American children.[2,9,10]

Other salient protective factors that operated in the lives of the resilient youths on Kauai were a belief in their own effectiveness (an internal locus of control) and a positive self-concept. Such characteristics were also found by Farrington among successful and law-abiding British youngsters who grew up in high-crime neighborhoods in London,[11] and by Wallerstein and her associates among American children who coped effectively with the breakup of their parents' marriages.[12]

PROTECTIVE FACTORS WITHIN THE FAMILY

Despite the burden of chronic poverty, family discord, or parental psychopathology, a child identified as resilient usually has had the opportunity to establish a close bond with at least one competent and emotionally stable person who is attuned to his or her needs. The stress-resistant children in the Kauai Longitudinal Study, the well-functioning offspring of child abusers in the Minnesota Mother-Child Interaction Project, the resilient children of psychotic parents studied by Anthony in St. Louis, and the youngsters who coped effectively with the breakup of their parents' marriages in Wallerstein's studies of divorce all had received enough good nurturing to establish a basic sense of trust.[2,3,6,12]

Much of this nurturing came from substitute caregivers within the extended family, such as grandparents and older siblings. Resilient children seem to be especially adept at recruiting such surrogate parents. In turn, they themselves are often called upon to take care of younger siblings and to practice acts of "required helpfulness" for members of their family who are ill or incapacitated.[2]

Both the Kauai Longitudinal Study and Block and Gjerde's studies of ego-resilient children[9] found characteristic child-rearing orientations that appear to promote resiliency differentially in boys and girls. Resilient boys tend to come from households with structure and rules, where a male serves as a model of identification (father, grandfather, or older brother), and where there is some encouragement of emotional expressiveness. Resilient girls, in contrast, tend to come from households that combine an emphasis on risk taking and independence with reliable support from a female caregiver, whether mother, grandmother, or older sister. The example of a mother who is gainfully and steadily employed appears to be an especially powerful model of identification for resilient girls.[2] A number of studies of resilient children from a wide variety of socioeconomic and ethnic backgrounds have also noted that the families of these children held religious beliefs that provided stability and meaning in times of hardship and adversity.[2,6,10]

PROTECTIVE FACTORS IN THE COMMUNITY

The Kauai Longitudinal Study and a number of other prospective studies in the United States have shown that resilient youngsters tend to rely on peers and elders in the community as sources of emotional support and seek them out for counsel and comfort in times of crisis.[2,6]

Favorite teachers are often positive role models. All of the resilient high-risk children in the Kauai study could point to at least one teacher who was an important source of support. These teachers listened to the children, challenged them, and rooted for them—whether in grade school, high school, or community college. Similar findings have been reported by Wallerstein and her associates from their long-term observations of youngsters who coped effectively with their parents' divorces[12] and by Rutter and his associates from their studies of inner-city schools in London.[13]

Finally, in the Kauai study, we found that the opening of opportunities at major life transitions enabled the majority of the high-risk children who had a troubled adolescence to rebound in their 20s and early 30s. Among the most potent second chances for such youths were adult education programs in community colleges, voluntary military service, active participation in a church community, and a supportive friend or marital partner. These protective buffers were also observed by Elder in the adult lives of the children of the Great Depression,[14] by Furstenberg and his associates in the later lives of black teenage mothers,[15] and by Farrington[11] and Felsman and Vaillant[7] in the adult lives of young men who had grown up in high-crime neighborhoods in London and Boston.

PROTECTIVE FACTORS: A SUMMARY

Several clusters of protective factors have emerged as recurrent themes in the lives of children who overcome great odds. Some protective factors are characteristics of the individual: Resilient children are engaging to other people, adults and peers alike; they have good communication and problem-solving skills, including the ability to recruit substitute caregivers; they have a talent or hobby that is valued by their elders or peers; and they have faith that their own actions can make a positive difference in their lives.

Another factor that enhances resilience in development is having affectional ties that encourage trust, autonomy, and initiative. These ties are often provided by members of the extended family. There are also support systems in the community that reinforce and reward the competencies of resilient children and provide them with positive role models: caring neighbors, teachers, elder mentors, youth workers, and peers.

LINKS BETWEEN PROTECTIVE FACTORS AND SUCCESSFUL ADAPTATION IN HIGH-RISK CHILDREN AND YOUTHS

In the Kauai study, when we examined the links between protective factors within the individual and outside sources of support, we noted a certain continuity in the life course of the high-risk individuals who successfully overcame a variety of childhood adversities. Their individual dispositions led them to select or construct environments that, in turn, reinforced and sustained their active approach to life and rewarded their special competencies.

Although the sources of support available to the individuals in their childhood homes were modestly linked to the quality of the individuals' adaptation as adults, their competencies, temperament, and self-esteem had a greater impact. Many resilient high-risk youths on Kauai left the adverse conditions of their childhood homes after high school and sought environments they found more compatible. In short, they picked their own niches.

Our findings lend some empirical support to Scarr and McCartney's theory[16] about how people make their own environment. Scarr and McCartney proposed three types of effects of people's genes on their environment: passive, evocative, and active. Because parents provide both children's genes and their rearing environments, children's genes are necessarily correlated with their own environments. This is the passive type of genotype-environment effect. The evocative type refers to the fact that a person's partially heritable characteristics, such as intelligence, personality, and physical attractiveness, evoke certain responses from other people. Finally, a person's interests, talents, and personality (genetically variable traits) may lead him or her to select or create particular environments;

this is called an active genotype-environment effect. In line with this theory, there was a shift from passive to active effects as the youths and young adults in the Kauai study left stressful home environments and sought extrafamilial environments (at school, at work, in the military) that they found more compatible and stimulating. Genotype-environment effects of the evocative sort tended to persist throughout the different life stages we studied, as individuals' physical characteristics, temperament, and intelligence elicited differential responses from other people (parents, teachers, peers).

IMPLICATIONS

So far, most studies of resilience have focused on children and youths who have "pulled themselves up by their bootstraps," with informal support by kith and kin, not on recipients of intervention services. Yet there are some lessons such children can teach society about effective intervention: If we want to help vulnerable youngsters become more resilient, we need to decrease their exposure to potent risk factors and increase their competencies and self-esteem, as well as the sources of support they can draw upon.

In *Within Our Reach,* Schorr has isolated a set of common characteristics of social programs that have successfully prevented poor outcomes for children who grew up in high-risk families.[17] Such programs typically offer a broad spectrum of health, education, and family support services, cross professional boundaries, and view the child in the context of the family, and the family in the context of the community. They provide children with sustained access to competent and caring adults, both professionals and volunteers, who teach them problem-solving skills, enhance their communication skills and self-esteem, and provide positive role models for them.

There is an urgent need for more systematic evaluations of such programs to illuminate the process by which we can forge a chain of protective factors that enables vulnerable children to become competent, confident, and caring individuals, despite the odds of chronic poverty or a medical or social disability. Future research on risk and resiliency needs to acquire a cross-cultural perspective as well. We need to know more about individual dispositions and sources of support that transcend cultural boundaries and operate effectively in a variety of high-risk contexts.

Notes

1. A. S. Masten, K. M. Best, and N. Garmezy, Resilience and development: Contributions from the study of children who overcame adversity, *Development and Psychopathology, 2,* 425–444 (1991).
2. All results from this study that are discussed in this review were reported in E. E. Werner, Risk resilience, and recovery: Perspectives from the Kauai Longitudinal Study, *Development and Psychopathology, 5,* 503–515 (1993).
3. B. Egeland, D. Jacobvitz, and L. A. Sroufe, Breaking the cycle of child abuse, *Child Development, 59,* 1080–1088 (1988).
4. A Moriarty, John, a boy who acquired resilience, in *The Invulnerable Child,* E. J. Anthony and B. J. Cohler, Eds. (Guilford Press, New York, 1987).
5. G. H. Elder, K. Liker, and C. E. Cross, Parent-child behavior in the Great Depression, in *Life Span Development and Behavior,* Vol. 6, T. B. Baltes and O. G. Brim, Jr., Eds. (Academic Press, New York, 1984).
6. E. J. Anthony, Children at risk for psychosis growing up successfully, in *The Invulnerable Child,* E. J. Anthony and B. J. Cohler, Eds. (Guilford Press, New York, 1987).
7. J. K. Felsman and G. E. Vaillant, Resilient children as adults: A 40 year study in *The Invulnerable Child,* E. J. Cohler, Eds. (Guilford Press, New York, 1987).
8. M. Rutter and D. Quinton, Long term follow-up of women institutionalized in childhood: Factors promoting good functioning in adult life, *British Journal of Developmental Psychology, 18,* 225–234 (1984).
9. J. Block and P. F. Gjerde, *Early antecedents of ego resiliency in late adolescence,* paper presented at the annual meeting of the American Psychological Association, Washington, DC (August 1986).
10. R. M. Clark, *Family Life and School Achievement: Why Poor Black Children Succeed or Fail* (University of Chicago Press, Chicago, 1983).
11. D. P. Farrington, *Protective Factors in the Development of Juvenile Delinquency and Adult Crime* (Institute of Criminology, Cambridge University, Cambridge, England, 1993).
12. J. S. Wallerstein and S. Blakeslee, *Second Chances: Men, Women and Children a Decade After Divorce* (Ticknor and Fields, New York, 1989).
13. M. Rutter, B. Maughan, P. Mortimore, and J. Ousten, *Fifteen Thousand Hours: Secondary Schools and Their Effects on Children* (Harvard University Press, Cambridge, MA, 1979).
14. G. H. Elder, Military times and turning points in men's lives, *Developmental Psychology, 22,* 233–245 (1986).
15. F. F. Furstenberg, J. Brooks-Gunn, and S. P. Morgan, *Adolescent Mothers in Later Life* (Cambridge University Press, New York, 1987).
16. S. Scarr and K. McCartney, How people make their own environments: A theory of genotype-environment effects, *Child Development, 54,* 424–435 (1983).
17. L. Schorr, *Within Our Reach: Breaking the Cycle of Disadvantage* (Anchor Press, New York, 1988).

Recommended Reading

Haggerty, R., Garmezy, N., Rutter, M., and Sherrod, L., Eds. (1994). *Stress, Risk, and Resilience in Childhood and Adolescence* (Cambridge University Press, New York).

Luthar, S., and Zigler, E. (1991). Vulnerability and competence: A review of research on resilience in childhood. *American Journal of Orthopsychiatry, 61,* 6–22.

Werner, E. E., and Smith, R. S. (1992). *Overcoming the Odds: High Risk Children From Birth to Adulthood* (Cornell University Press, Ithaca, NY).

SEX
& Marriage

Experts say sex is vital to healthy relationships. Why is it so difficult for couples to do what's good for them?

By Patricia Chisholm

Max is recalling what sex was like before the big job, kids and mortgage. "I was a walking hormone," he says, laughing a little with his wife, Julie, in the basement of their comfortable Montreal home. The thirtysomething parents of two young children, who asked that their real names be withheld, used to fool around at least five times a week. Now, they say, they are lucky to make love that many times a month because they are either physically exhausted or mentally distracted by their demanding daytime roles—his as a boss, hers as a stay-at-home mom. Unlike many couples, though, Max and Julie haven't lost their sense of humour about what they view as a temporary decline in their physical intimacy. "It's a little sad—sex is such an enjoyable, amazing experience, " Max says. "We still really enjoy it. But now I find I'm often just too tired at night. I can get it up, but I just can't get up off the couch." Ah, sex. It's one of the few pleasures left that doesn't bloat the waistline, cause cancer or break the family budget. Researchers claim it even helps prevent wrinkles, and psychologists say it can rejuvenate the most tired relationship. According to a 1998 *Maclean's*/CBC poll, 78 per cent of married Canadians (as opposed to 61 per cent of single respondents) said they were sexually active, and 87 per cent of married Canadians said they were "satisfied" with their sex lives. Sexual monogamy has never been easy, though, and that fact has become depressingly clear to the great glut of baby boomers who grew up with the pill and unprecedented sexual freedom but now are struggling with aging bodies, sexual boredom, marital

spats and plain old exhaustion. So much for the Summer of Love.

There is no easy way out, either. The divorce rate is falling as concerns about splintered families and AIDS prompt more people to recognize that breaking up really is hard to do. Statistics Canada reported this year that the number of divorces has fallen for four years in a row, from 78,880 in 1994 to 67,408 in 1997—a 14.5-per-cent drop. Edward Laumann, a University of Chicago sociologist who studies sexual dysfunction, says people appear to be staying together longer, despite lots of problems with sex, because they are realizing that changing partners costs huge amounts of time, money and energy, with no guarantees. "They are aware that divorce is not a one-year experience," he says.

Of course, some passions cannot be revived, and some couples find it's easier to stay put and just be celibate. But in general, therapists say good sex is a hallmark of solid, long-term relationships. It's an opportunity to relax, to put everyday pressures aside and, especially, to reinforce emotional intimacy and physical closeness. More couples are turning to sex aids like toys and videos to ignite passions, while others are exploring unconventional options like long-term affairs and group sex. The permutations may be endless, but one thing is clear: sex, or the lack of it, still speaks volumes. "If you want to look at what is going on in your relationship, look at your sex life—it won't lie to you," advises Sig Taylor, a Calgary marriage counsellor. "It's a barometer, and it's usually the last thing to go. If couples get to the point

From *Maclean's*, August 9, 1999, pp. 22-26. © 1999 by Maclean Hunter Publishing Ltd. Reprinted by permission.

129

The elation people experience at the beginning of a relationship is really more akin to a drug-induced high

where there is no sexuality anymore, the relationship is pretty much dead."

Most people are reluctant to talk about an unconventional or problematic sex life, making it one of the last real taboos. But in fact, problems of one kind or another are strikingly common. One of Laumann's recent studies found that, over a one-year period, 43 per cent of women and 31 per cent of men between the ages of 18 and 59 experienced some kind of sexual impediment, including lack of desire, erectile dysfunction and pain during intercourse. "These are huge numbers," he said, "and it's probably an underestimate—people don't like to admit they have problems with sex."

No wonder people don't want to talk about their troubles—the message in the media is that only losers are sitting it out. Explicit, even kinky sex now permeates movies, magazines and the Internet. *Eyes Wide Shut*, the late Stanley Kubrick's heavily hyped film, features the unlikely scenario of a married couple descending into the depths of their own, profoundly disturbing sexual fantasies. Against that backdrop, simple sex with a partner who never changes—except to acquire a few more sags and bags every year—can start to seem, well, ordinary.

What's to be done? Experts say the vast majority of aging-related sexual ailments—erectile dysfunction, pain during intercourse and lack of lubrication—can be cured medically. But lasting solutions have to start with talk. "If couples pretend nothing is wrong, it only prolongs the problem," says Laumann. "Discussing it takes the edge off." The consequences of not talking can blight a life. "At the beginning of our marriage, things were great," says Frank, a 68-year-old retired Ontario businessman who asked for anonymity. "We had sex a couple of times a week and we were great friends." But their sex life declined sharply after they started having kids—he and his wife now have three grown children. "I felt I was inadequate," he says. "There were so many times I quietly hid my face under the sheets and cried."

He and his wife separated, but they have since struck an uneasy truce and now live together, although their sex life never resumed. Recently, he learned from a TV talk show that it is common for sexual appetites to fluctuate widely from year to year, and that the combination of life pressures and hormones is usually to blame. "I think we need to talk more about sex," he says now. "If I had known this was her body and not me, I would have done everything to fight for her."

Hormones can be responsible for the ups as well as the downs. The elation people feel early in a relationship is akin to a drug-induced high and is just about as sustainable, experts say. "The amount of adrenaline in the body is so great, you can get by with almost no sleep," says Richard Dearing, director of the Marriage Therapy Program at the University of Winnipeg. "You just don't have the energy to keep that going for more than a few months."

As passions abate, couples stand back and take a hard look at one another. Details of character and temperament kick in, and partners begin to make decisions based on compatibility. They may also notice that sex plays different roles in their respective lives. Libidos can differ wildly, partly because of natural hormonal levels—testosterone in men, androgen in women—and partly because of the approach that individuals take to sex. Dearing, like many therapists, has found that, typically, men use sex to feel good, while women need to feel good before they get into bed. The result when life gets stressful? He wants to, she doesn't.

Of course, there are no rigid categories when it comes to sex drive, and for many couples the roles are reversed. In either case, a mismatch can create big problems. Sipping a glass of white wine on a restaurant patio in Vancouver, a 38-year-old woman reflects on the recent breakup of her four-year, live-in relationship. "I realize that sex can't always be the priority," she says. "But for me, it's a way to let go of the day's hassles. You can get into it, just for the sake of pure, physical pleasure." She stayed with her partner for two years after their sex life ended, a phase that began when he was laid off. Despite her repeated efforts, it never resumed. "There was nothing I could do to reach him, and after a while I stopped trying because the rejection was too hard to take. It was horrible," she recalls. "A relationship to me is a partnership—you play as a team. When something as basic as your physical intimacy breaks down, it's impossible to think of yourself that way anymore. One of you has broken the contract."

Even when two people agree on what they want out of life, and seem to be getting it, sex can suffer. Phil Bentley, 44, and John Doleman, 37, have lived together in Toronto for more than a decade. Unlike many couples, gay or straight, their early years together were tough because they decided to put all their efforts into paying off a large mortgage. They took in boarders and each worked at two jobs. "The house was always full of people so we didn't have many opportunities to be alone," says Bentley. Now, they have more time for one another, and that has translated into better sex. "After this amount of time being together, we are more honest with each other about our sexual needs," says Doleman.

National TV sex-show host Sue Johanson bursts into laughter when the subject of sex and marriage is raised. "The two are not simpatico, " she chortles, only half in

The payoff for couples who remain intimate through a marriage's stress-plagued middle years can be extraordinary

jest. But this grandmother has listened to thousands of tales of woe, and she believes there are many ways to revive flagging sexual appetites. As a first step, she says, couples should set aside time for the occasional date. She counsels couples to play games, such as hide-and-seek—in the nude and in the dark. Sex toys can rev things up as well, she contends, although she has found that men are often threatened if a woman buys a vibrator. "They say, 'What do you need that thing for, you've got Mr. Ever Ready here.' But once men use it to stimulate their partner, they're home free—they think it's great."

In fact, there is something of a revolution under way in the area of sex aids, especially for women. Shops like Womyns' Ware in Vancouver and Good For Her in Toronto coax women inside with tasteful decor and shelves free of hard-core videos and magazines, or cheap, crudely made products. At Womyns' Ware, for instance, a sound system plays warm jazz in a light-filled room where merchandise is arranged so that those browsing for lubricants can avoid coming face-to-face with customers sampling handcuffs and leather floggers.

There is also a relatively new line of erotic videos aimed at women, called Femme. Developed by retired porn star Candida Royalle, 48, the videos feature complex story lines and shun sex scenes that degrade women. "There's a lot more out there that is couple-oriented," notes Montrealer Josey Vogels, who writes a syndicated weekly column called *My Messy Bedroom*. "Women want to explore their sexuality more, but they don't want to go to some sleazy hole in the wall—they don't want to feel creepy."

But bedroom toys cannot save a sex life that is undercut by marital conflict or fatigue. "Women are angry because they are aware that they are doing much more of the housework than men are," Johanson says. "A couple gets into bed and he has this copulatory gaze and she just looks at him and thinks, 'This is just one more person to service.' " If they want more sex, she says, men will "have to pick up more of the slack around the house—enough of this nonsense."

Leslie, a mid-40s Victoria-area mother of two young boys, can relate. With a demanding managerial job, and jammed off-hours—daily commutes to two schools, plus appointments for tutoring, soccer, sailing—Leslie says she retreats to the bedroom with one thing in mind. "By the time my head hits the pillow, I'm ready to pass out," she says. Her husband helps a lot with the kids, she says, but she is still the one who knows if it's pizza day at school or whether the dog needs a rabies shot. Too often, sex simply falls to the bottom of her "to-do" list. "Making a date with your mate is good advice, but I also know I should be doing two miles a day on the

treadmill," she says wryly. "Trying to recapture the fun you had when you were young is like trying to remember Grade 9 chemistry—you know what apparatus to use, but you're not sure which chemicals you need to get a reaction."

Experts say there are peaks and valleys in everyone's sex life. Claude Guldner, professor emeritus at the University of Guelph and one of Canada's leading sex therapists, says desire tends to follow a U-shaped pattern in most marriages: it is intense during the courtship phase, dips down with the arrival of children and—if couples are lucky—swings strongly upward again when children are older. Often, those at the bottom of the U fail to realize that they may be devoting too much energy to parenting at the expense of their marriage. "We need to educate people that 'husbanding and wifing' continues, even though you are now fathering and mothering," he says.

Some people understand that lesson without being taught. Cheryl, a 40-year-old Halifax hairdresser, and Bob, 43, who works in the offshore gas industry, have been married for 10 years. When their now-five-year-old son was born, the first three months were "challenging," recalls Cheryl, who with her husband requested anonymity. "We just realized that every time we would get intimate, our son would start crying. That was a given and we would just laugh." She says grabbing a few moments here and there is enough to keep sex alive. "Even if it's five minutes in the shower in the morning, when junior is having his catnap, it's better than nothing," she says.

Cheryl says she and her husband have ups and downs, and that things can be especially difficult when her husband arrives home after a month offshore. "I always think of my relationship as the hardest thing I will do in my life, as well as the best thing," she muses. "It's hard to keep yourself present with somebody, to keep yourself vulnerable and open. It's hard to be intimate."

Mutual neglect can do much more than lead to bad sex—it can torpedo a marriage if it spawns infidelity. Guldner, who specializes in counselling couples grappling with the fallout from cheating, says that except for chronic philanderers, affairs are rarely about sex. Usually, the cheater is avoiding another issue: they are turned off by a partner' s weight gain, for instance, or they are too often left alone by a spouse obsessed with work. "Many, many people say that sex in the affair isn't nearly as good as it was with their partner," Guldner says. But if couples are willing to confront one another with their problems, they often survive an event that, in the past, was widely viewed as unforgivable. That is partly because cultural shifts have weakened old notions of sexual possessiveness. "There is less exclusivity to the sexual act now because so many people have had premarital sex," Guldner points out.

Some see a discreet affair as a viable alternative. Susan, a Toronto manager in her late 30s who requested anonymity, is deeply committed to her family, even though she has carried on a secret affair for nine years. What she gets from her lover is not better sex, she explains, but intellectual companionship and support in her professional life. Despite that, she has no intention of leaving her husband, with whom she has three school-age children. "Marriage is such a difficult, complex relationship," she says. "I would just be exchanging one set of problems for another if I left. And I think that children have the right to grow up in a home with both parents."

The payoff for couples who remain intimate through a marriage's stressful middle years can be extraordinary. Dartmouth, N.S., residents Les and Joan Halsey have treated sex as a precious, fragile wonder that is integral to the success of their 44-year marriage. "We realized early that it was very important," says Les, 65. "Once a month, we would go out for a candlelight dinner. Taking the time is so important—it's not just going to the bedroom and saying, 'OK, let's have sex now.' "

Joan, 64, recalls times when life got in the way of their physical intimacy—job changes, caring for their three children, periods of depressed libido. And she candidly admits that it was sometimes work for a couple married at 21 to keep themselves from straying. "The seven-year itch, living in suburbia, wild parties—it's only by the grace of God we didn't go that route," she says. And she has some advice for those still battling it out in the trenches. "Don't just have a home, children, work," she advises. "Do things that interested you before you were married. We always had a little bit of something just to ourselves—it keeps us healthy. And now that our family has left the nest, we have this whole new journey together." The motto for marriage, then, is "better sex than sorry."

With Ruth Atherley and Chris Wood in Vancouver, and Susan McCelland in Toronto

Shattered Vows

Hold on to your wedding ring. It's difficult, but possible, to repair the damage caused by infidelity. Increasingly, that's what couples want. But let go of assumptions. In an interview with Editor at Large Hara Estroff Marano, a leading expert challenges everything you think you know about the most explosive subject of the year. By Shirley Glass, Ph.D.

Infidelity appears to be the topic of the year. What has struck you most about the reaction to what may or may not be some kind of infidelity in high places?

Whatever horror or dismay people have about it, they're able to separate the way the President is performing in office and the way he appears to be performing in his marriage. That's especially interesting because it seems to reflect the split in his life. We don't know for sure, but he apparently is very much involved in his family life. He's not an absentee father or husband. Whatever it is that they share—and they share a lot, publicly and privately—he has a compartment in which he is attracted to young women, and it is separate from his primary relationships.

Is this compartmentalizing characteristic of people who get into affairs?

It's much more characteristic of men. Most women believe that if you love your partner, you wouldn't even be interested in an affair; therefore, if someone has an affair, it means that they don't love their partner and they do love the person they had the affair with. But my research shows there are many men who do love their partners, who enjoy good sex at home, who nevertheless never turn down an opportunity for extramarital sex. In fact, 56% of the men I sampled who had extramarital intercourse said that their marriages were happy, versus 34% of the women.

That's how I got into this.

Because?

Being a woman, I believed that if a man had an affair, it meant that he had a terrible marriage, and that he probably wasn't getting it at home—the old keep-your-husband-happy-so-he-won't-stray idea. That puts too much of the burden on the woman. I found that she could be everything wonderful, and he might still stray, if that's in his value system, his family background, or his psychodynamic structure.

I was in graduate school when I heard that a man I knew, married for over 40 years, had recently died and his wife was so bereaved because they had had the most wonderful marriage. He had been her lover, her friend, her support system. She missed him immensely. I thought that was a beautiful story. When I told my husband about it, he got a funny look that made me ask, What do you know? He proceeded to tell me that one night when he took the kids out for dinner to an out-of-the-way restaurant, that very man walked in with a young blonde woman. When he saw my husband, he walked out.

How did that influence you?

I wondered what that meant. Did he fool his wife all those years and really not love her? How is it possible to be married for over 40 years and think you have a good marriage? It occurred to me that an affair could mean something different than I believed.

Another belief that was an early casualty was the hydraulic pump theory—that you only have so much energy for something. By this belief, if your partner is getting sex outside, you would know it, because your partner wouldn't be wanting sex at home. However, some people are even more passionate at home when they are having extramarital sex. I was stunned to hear a man tell me that when he left his affair partner and came home he found himself desiring his wife more than he had in a long time, because he was so sexually aroused by his affair. That made me question the pump theory.

Many of our beliefs about the behavior of others come from how we see things for ourselves. A man who associates sneaking around with having sex will, if his wife is sneaking around, find it very hard to believe that she could be emotionally involved without being sexually involved. On the other hand, a woman usually cannot believe that her husband could be sexually involved and not be emotionally involved. We put the same meaning on it for our partner that it would have for us. I call that the error of assumed similarity.

What infidelity research have you done?

My first research study was actually based on a sex questionnaire in *Psychology Today* in the '70s. I analyzed the data, looking at the effect of extramarital sex, length of marriage, and gender difference on marital satisfaction and romanticism. I found enormous gender differences.

Men in long-term marriages who had affairs had very high marital satisfaction—and women in long-term marriages having affairs had the lowest satisfaction of all. Everybody's marital satisfaction went down the longer they were married, except the men who had affairs. But in early marriages, men who had affairs were significantly less happy. An affair is more serious if it happens earlier in the marriage.

Explaining these gender differences was the basis of my dissertation. I theorized that men were having sexual affairs and women emotional affairs.

Are affairs about sex?

Sometimes infidelity is just about sex. That is often more true for men. In my research, 44% of men who said they had extramarital sex said they had slight or no emotional involvement; only 11% of women said that. Oral sex is certainly about sex. Some spouses are more upset if the partner had oral sex than if they had intercourse; it just seems so much more intimate.

What is the infidelity in infidelity?

The infidelity is that you took something that was supposed to be mine, which is sexual or emotional intimacy, and you gave it to somebody else. I thought that we had a special relationship, and now you have contaminated it; it doesn't feel special any more, because you shared something very precious to us with someone else.

There are gender differences. Men feel more betrayed by their wives having sex with someone else; women feel more betrayed by their husbands being emotionally involved with someone else. What really tears men apart is to visualize their partner being sexual with somebody else.

Women certainly don't want their husbands having sex with somebody else, but they may be able to deal with an impersonal one-night fling better than a long-term relationship in which their husband was sharing all kinds of loving ways with somebody else.

Why are affairs so deeply wounding?

Because you have certain assumptions about your marriage. That I chose someone, and the other person chose me; we have the same values; we have both decided to have an exclusive relationship, even though we may have some problems. We love each other—and therefore I am safe.

Voices of *Infidelity*

I was working full-time, as was my wife; I was going to school and we were caring for our son. Little time was left for each other. The night I received my acceptance to medical school, in April, she told me she was unhappy and was attracted to someone else.

We began counseling. A month later, she told me she was in love with him and was very confused. I was feeling insecure in the relationship; it was coming out as anger.

In June, the wife of the guy called and told me that Lori was having an affair with her husband. The heat in my chest began to slowly grow. Lori beeped in on the line; I told her, "I know and I'm on my way" to her office; he worked with her. Now in a full rage, I stalked through the office looking for him, but she had told him I was coming and he'd left the building. I announced that "[He] is screwing my wife!" Then I verbally vented all my anger in front of the building, where Lori was waiting before leaving to get my son from daycare.

When you find out your partner has been unfaithful, then everything you believe is totally shattered. And you have to rebuild the world. The fact that you weren't expecting it, that it wasn't part of your assumption about how a relationship operates, causes traumatic reactions.

And it is deeply traumatic.

It's terrible. The wounding results because—and I've heard this so many times—I finally thought I met somebody I could trust.

It violates that hope or expectation that you can be who you really are with another person?

Yes. Affairs really aren't about sex; they're about betrayal. Imagine you are married to somebody very patriotic and then find out your partner is a Russian spy. Someone having a long-term affair is leading a double life. Then you find out all that was going on in your partner's life that you knew nothing about: gifts that were exchanged, poems and letters that were written, trips that you thought were taken for a specific reason were actually taken to meet the affair partner.

To find out about all the intrigue and deception that occurred while you were operating under a different assumption is totally shattering and disorienting. That's why people then have to get out their calendars and go back over the dates to put all the missing pieces together: "When you went to the drugstore that night and said your car broke down and didn't come home for three hours, what was really happening?"

This is necessary?

In order to heal. Because any time somebody suffers from a trauma, part of the recovery is telling the story. The tornado victim will go over and over the story—"when the storm came I was in my room . . ."—trying to understand what happened, and how it happened. "Didn't we see the black clouds? How come we didn't know?"

And so they repeat the story until it no longer creates unmanageable arousal?

Yes. In fact, sometimes people are more devastated if everything was wonderful before they found out. When a betrayed spouse who suspected something says, "I don't know if I can ever trust my partner again," it is reassuring to tell them that they can trust their own instincts the next time they have those storm warnings. But if somebody thought everything was wonderful, how would they ever know if it happened again? It's frightening.

One question people these days are asking you is, Is oral sex really infidelity?

The question they ask is, Is oral sex really adultery? And that's a different question, because adultery is a legal term. It is also a biblical term. The real issue is, Is

---

ADVICE TO *Hillary*, ALL DEARLY *betrayed*, AND *nearly* BETRAYED

• Yes, oral sex really is infidelity.

• It's a boundary problem, not a love problem.

• Some woman or other is going to give him a second chance to prove that he can be faithful. Decide if that woman can be you.

• Faithfulness is not a virtue that falls out of the heavens—it's a skill. And it can be learned. . . . [see] (www.smartmarriages.com).

• Disregard what other people say. All that matters is your ability to rebuild trust.

• Recognize your power and use it to renegotiate your relationship from the bottom up.

• Despite the hurt and anger, love can still survive.

• You may want to consider your shared history, shared goals, and shared commitment to important causes.

• Affairs are less a reflection of the partner and the marriage than of broader forces in the culture that undermine monogamy.

• You may look realistically at your partner's other qualities and decide that on balance you prefer your spouse to other potential partners.

—*The Editors, with Peggy Vaughan, author of* The Monogamy Myth.

oral sex infidelity? You don't need to ask a psychologist that—just ask any spouse: "Would you feel that it was an infidelity for your partner to engage in that type of behavior?"

Would women answer that differently from men?

It is not necessarily a function of gender. People might answer it differently for themselves than for their partners. Some people maintain a kind of technical virginity by not having intercourse. However, even kissing in a romantic, passionate way is an infidelity. People know when they cross that line from friendship to affair.

So you don't have to have intercourse to have an affair?

Absolutely. There can be an affair without any kind of touching at all. People have affairs on the Internet.

What is the *sine qua non* of an affair?

Three elements determine whether a relationship is an affair.

One is secrecy. Suppose two people meet every morning at seven o'clock for coffee before work, and they never tell their partners. Even though it might be in a public place, their partner is not going to be happy about it. It is going to feel like a betrayal, a terrible deception.

Emotional intimacy is the second element. When someone starts confiding things to another person that they are reluctant to confide to their partner, and the emotional intimacy is greater in the friendship than in the marriage, that's very threatening. One common pathway to affairs occurs when somebody starts confiding negative things about their marriage. What they're doing is signaling: "I'm vulnerable; I may even be available."

The third element is sexual chemistry. That can occur even if two people don't touch. If one says, "I'm really attracted to you," or "I had a dream about you last night, but, of course, I'm married, so we won't do anything about that," that tremendously increases the sexual tension by creating forbidden fruit in the relationship.

Another question you told me people now ask is, "Are you a liar if you lie about an affair?" How do you answer?

Lying goes with the territory. If you're not lying, you have an open marriage. There may be lies of omission or lies of commission. The lie of omission is, "I had to stop at the gym on my way home." There is the element of truth, but the omission of what was really happening: "I left after 15 minutes and spent the next 45 minutes at someone's apartment."

The lies of commission are the elaborate deceptions people create. The more deception

Lori had asked me not to tell my family we were having problems; thus, I was cut off from my major support system. I wanted to punish her by holding her up to public scrutiny. I gathered everyone from both families and proceeded to tell them the whole story.

After I cooled down, we spent a month "working" on the relationship. Then she filed for divorce. I am left with a huge amount of anger at him and at her even though it is so many months later. I've never had the opportunity to vent my anger at him and still fantasize about tracking him down and beating him senseless. After all the time and emotional investment I'd put into this relationship, they intentionally damaged it until it was unsalvageable.

I am now beginning med school, and we are sharing physical and legal custody of our son. Oh, and her love was fired from his job as a result of this indiscretion.—*BH*

❧

I had an affair with my neighbor. I was friends with his wife. We spent a

and the longer it goes on, the more difficult it is to rebuild trust in the wake of an affair.

The deception makes a tremendous psychological difference to the betrayed spouse. What about to the person who constructed the deception?

Once the affair's been discovered, the involved partner could have a sense of relief, if they hate lying and don't see themselves as having that kind of moral character. They'll say, "I can't understand how I could have done a thing like this, this is not the kind of person I am."

Some people thrive on the game. For them, part of the passion and excitement of an affair is the lying and getting away with something forbidden.

There are some people who have characterological problems, and the affair may be a symptom of that. Such people lie about their accomplishments; they are fraudulent in business. When it's characterological, I don't know any way to rebuild trust; no one can ever be on sure footing with that person.

So there is always moral compromise just by being in an affair?

Which is why some people, no matter how unhappy they are in their marriage, don't have affairs. They can't make the compromise. Or they feel they have such an open relationship with the spouse that they just could not do something like that without telling their partner about it.

Do affairs ever serve a positive function—not to excuse any of the damage they do?

Affairs are often a chance for people to try out new behaviors, to dress in a different costume, to stretch and grow and assume a different role. In a long-term relationship, we often get frozen in our roles. When young couples begin at one level of success and go on to many achievements, the new person sees them as they've become, while the old person sees them as they were.

The unfortunate thing is that the way a person is different in the affair would, if incorporated into the marriage, probably make their spouse ecstatic. But they believe they're stuck; they don't know how to create opportunity for change within the marriage. A woman who was sexually inhibited in marriage—perhaps she married young and had no prior partners—may find her sexuality in an affair, but her husband would probably be thrilled to encounter that new self.

How do you handle this?

After an affair, I do not ask the question you would expect. The spouse always wants to know about "him" or "her": "What did you see in her that you didn't see in me?" Or, "What did you like about him better?" I always ask about "you": "What did you like about yourself in that other relationship?" "How were you different?" and "Of the way that you were in that other relationship, what would you like to bring back so that you can be the person you want to be in your primary relationship?" "How can we foster that part of you in this relationship?"

That's a surprise. How did you come to know that's the question to ask?

There is an attraction in the affair, and I try to understand what it is. Part of it is the romantic projection: I like the way I look when I see myself in the other person's eyes. There is positive mirroring. An affair holds up a vanity mirror, the kind with all the little bulbs around it; it gives a rosy glow to the way you see yourself. By contrast, the marriage offers a makeup mirror; it magnifies every little flaw. When someone loves you despite seeing all your flaws, that is a reality-based love.

In the stories of what happened during the affair, people seem to take on a different persona, and one of the things they liked best about being in that relationship was the person they had become. The man who wasn't sensitive or expressive is now in a relationship where he is expressing his feelings and is supportive.

Can those things be duplicated in the marriage?

That's one of the goals—not to turn the betrayed spouse into the affair partner, but to free the unfaithful spouse to express all the parts of himself he was able to experience in the affair.

I see a lot of men who are married to very competent women and having affairs with very weak women. They feel: "This person needs me." They put on their red cape and do a lot of rescuing. They feel very good about themselves. That makes me sad, because I know that even though their partner may be extremely competent, she wants to be stroked too. She wants a knight in shining armor. Perhaps she hasn't known how to ask.

Do people push partners into affairs?

No. People can create a pattern in the marriage that is not enhancing, and the partner, instead of dealing with the dissatisfaction and trying to work on the relationship, escapes it and goes someplace else.

That is the wrong way to solve the problem?

Yes. Generally when a woman is unhappy, she lets her partner know. She feels better because she's gotten it off her chest. It doesn't interfere with her love. She's trying to improve the relationship: "If I tell him what makes me unhappy, then he will know how to please me; I am giving him a gift by telling him."

Unfortunately, many men don't see it as a gift. They feel criticized and put down. Instead of thinking, "She feels lonely; I will move toward her and make her feel secure," they think, "What is wrong with her? Didn't I just do that?" They pull away. If they come in contact with somebody else who says to them, "Oh, you're wonderful," then they move toward that person. They aren't engaged enough in the marriage to work things out. The partner keeps trying and becomes more unpleasant because he's not responding.

She becomes a pursuer, and he becomes the distancer.

When she withdraws, the marriage is much further down the road to dissolution, because she's given up. Her husband, unfortunately, thinks things are so much better because she's no longer complaining. He doesn't recognize that she has detached and become emotionally available for an affair. The husband first notices it when she becomes disinterested in sex—or after she's left! Then he'll do anything to keep her. That is often too little too late.

By then she is often committed to someone on the outside?

Yes, which is why when women have affairs, it's much more often a result of long-term marital dissatisfaction.

Can you predict which couples will get involved in affairs?

Social context is a predictor. If you're in an occupational or social group where many people have affairs, and there's a sexually per-

lot of time together. (My husband works long hours and all weekend.) I started to work for my neighbor part-time and started to feel excitement build.

The affair lasted five months. We stopped many times but would find ourselves back in each other's arms. The sex was O.K.; I felt that was what I had to give him to get what I wanted—the words about how sexy I was, something I never heard from my husband.

His wife found out and told my husband last year; he left for three months. He would show up nightly after the kids were asleep, call me a whore, and scream at me. I'd be sobbing on the floor. I never wanted to end my marriage.

My husband finally started counseling with me and moved back in. The neighbors moved away three months ago.

My husband told me last week he wants a divorce. After a week of begging him to stay, I found love letters and hotel reservations from a girl in Houston. He said it's his second chance for love. I am devastated. My kids will suffer the rest of their lives for my mistakes.—*NC*

missive attitude, you're more likely. Also if you come from a family where there's a history of affairs—the most notorious are the Kennedys, where the men have a certain entitlement. Coming from one of the Mediterranean cultures, like the Greek, where the double standard is alive and well, is another predictor.

You're saying that an affair is not always about the marriage. There are often cultural or contextual pulls into affairs. This is important information for women, because women blame themselves.

And society blames women.

So affairs can happen in good marriages. Is the marriage really good?

Sometimes one person thinks the marriage is fine and the other doesn't. That may be because the more dissatisfied person hasn't communicated their dissatisfaction. Or they've communicated it and the partner has discounted it. But after an affair, people often try to justify it by rewriting unhappiness into the marital history. They say, "I never really loved you," or "You never really acted like you loved me." That is just a way to make themselves feel that they didn't do such a terrible thing.

Why do some people in unhappy marriages have affairs and others do not?

Number one is opportunity. Number two is values. Some people do not think an affair is justified for any reason. Others think it's okay if you're not getting it at home or if you "fall in love" with another person.

Surveys show that for women, the highest justification is for love; emotional intimacy is next. Sex is last on their list of justifications. It's the opposite for men; sex scores the highest.

Is infidelity in a long-standing marriage the same as in one of shorter duration?

It is potentially more threatening to the marriage when it happens earlier, and the chances of the marriage surviving are less, particularly where the woman is having an affair.

Did she choose the wrong mate?

She thinks so, especially if her affair partner is the opposite of her husband.

From your perspective, what's going on?

She's growing and changing, and she chooses somebody she sees as more similar to herself. Usually it's someone at work. Her husband may be working very hard in his profession or going to school and not paying much attention to her. She feels a little lonely, and then she gets involved. Or maybe her husband is very caring, and the relationship is so supportive and stable that it doesn't have a challenge for her.

The opportunities for affairs have changed radically in the past 20 years. Men and women are together all the time in the workplace, and workplaces are sexy places. You dress up, you're trying your best, there's energy in the air.

And you're not cleaning up vomit or the hot water heater that just flooded the basement. And it's not at the end of the day when you're exhausted. Also, you're working together on something that has excitement and meaning.

One of the major shifts is that more married women are having affairs than in the past. There are several reasons. Today's woman has usually had more experience with premarital sex, so she's not as inhibited about getting involved sexually with another man. She has more financial independence, so she's not taking as great a risk. And she is working with men on a more equal level, so the men are very attractive to her.

What do people seek in an affair partner?

Either we choose somebody very different from our partner, or we choose somebody like our partner used to be, but a younger version. A woman married to a really sweet guy who helps with the dishes, who is very nurturing and very secure, may at some point see him as boring and get interested in the high-achieving, high-energy man who may even be a bit chauvinistic. But if she's married to the man with the power and the status, then she's interested in the guy who is sensitive and touchy-feely, who may not be as ambitious.

Is this just the nature of attraction?

It has to do with the fact that people really want it all. Probably the only way to get it all is to be in more than one relationship at the same time. We have different parts of ourselves.

The other flip-flop in choice of affair partner reflects the fact that the marriage often represents a healing of our family wounds. Somebody who lacked a secure attachment figure in their family of origin chooses a mate who provides security and stability. It's healthy to seek that balancing.

But after we've mastered that, we often want to go back and find somebody like that difficult parent and make that person love us. There is a correlation between the nature of the attachment figure and the affair partner; the person is trying to master incomplete business from childhood. As a result, some people will choose an affair partner who is difficult, temperamental, or unpredictable. Under those circumstances, the unfaithful partner is often caught in a triangle.

What do you mean?

The person maintains the marriage, and can't leave it, and maintains the affair, and can't leave that either. Tension arises when either the affair partner or spouse applies pressure on them to get off the fence. The spouse provides security and a sense of family, the affair partner excitement and passion. When the involved spouse says, "I don't know which person to be with," what they really want is to keep both.

The challenge is, how do people satisfy all of their needs within the marriage?

It is a false belief that if I'm incomplete, I have to be completed by another person. You have to do it through your own life, your own work, for your own pleasure,

through individual growth. The more fulfilled you are, in terms of things that you do separately that please you, the more individuated and more whole you are—and the more intimate you can be. Then you're not expecting the other person to make you happy. You're expecting the other person to join you in your happiness.

> When women have affairs, it's much more often a result of long-term marital dissatisfaction.

Are more couples trying to survive affairs these days?

People are more willing to work through them. People are saying, I'm willing to work this through, but we have to solve whatever problems we have; we have to get something out of this; our marriage has to be even better than it was before.

More men are calling to come in for therapy. That's a very positive sign. The downside is, it's often too late. By the time men are alarmed, the woman is too distanced from the marriage.

What other changes do you see in affairs these days?

Cyber affairs are new. For some people the computer is very addictive. They get very caught up in it. It's hiding out, escaping. And an affair is an escape—from the

realities of everyday life. These two escapes are now paired.

The other danger on-line is that people can disguise who they are. Think of the roles you can take on if you hide behind a screen. More so than in workplace affairs, you can project anything onto the other person.

You can act out any fantasy you want. You can make this other person become anybody you want them to be. There's a loosening up, because you're not face-to-face with the person.

This attracts only a certain kind of person, doesn't it?

We don't know yet. I always get e-mail questions from people who are concerned because their partner is having an on-line relationship with somebody. Or their partner had an affair with somebody they met on-line. It's very prevalent, and it's very dangerous.

If you're talking to somebody on the computer, and you begin to talk about your sexual fantasies, and you're not talking to your partner about your sexual fantasies, which relationship now has more sexual chemistry? Which has more emotional intimacy? Then your partner walks in the room, and you switch screens. Now you've got a wall of secrecy. It has all the components of an affair. And it's easy.

Technology has impacted affairs in another way, too. Many people have discovered a partner's affair by getting the cellular phone bill, or by getting in the car and pushing redial on the car phone, or by taking their partner's beeper and seeing who's been calling. We're leaving a whole new electronic trail.

Has that changed the dynamics or the psychology of affairs in any way?

In the past, when someone was suspicious they could ask their partner: "What's going on? You seem distant lately." If the

'HOW DO I *Know* YOU WON'T *Betray* ME *Again*'

The following are signs of recovery, healing, and hope for a committed future together.

The unfaithful partner:
• recognizes and understands the individual vulnerabilities that contributed to the affair—curiosity, depression, need for excitement, and rescue fantasies are common ones—and views them as danger signals.
• shows empathy for the pain caused by the infidelity.
• assumes responsibility for the betrayal, regardless of any problems that existed in the marriage.

The betrayed partner:
• is able to recognize when his/her partner might be lying again.
• refuses to put his/her head in the sand.
• refuses to give without getting anything back.

Together you develop a united front:
• You can refer to affair-related events with calmness, perhaps humor.
• You can make united decisions concerning fallout from the affair, such as intrusive phone calls or a request for AIDS testing, and jointly manage present and future encounters with the affair partner.
• Your marriage is stronger; there's more reciprocity, more caring and communication, and better conflict management.
• You see eye to eye on the value of exclusivity and monogamy because of the pain the infidelity caused.
• You share responsibility for changing the relationship.
• You make more time for yourselves as a couple, apart from your children's needs, as a way to strengthen the friendship and erotic bond between you.—SG

partner denied anything was wrong, there wasn't a whole lot a person could do. Now there's tangible evidence people can utilize to find out if their hunches are indeed true.

There is a public conception of affairs as glamorous, but the aftermath is pretty messy. How do we square these views?

They're both true. In those captured moments, there is passion and romance. We're in Stage One of relationship formation—idealizing the partner. This Stage One can go on for years, as long as there's a forbidden aspect.

The admiration and positive mirroring can go on for a long time—until you get to a reality-based relationship. And this is why so many affairs end after the person leaves the marriage.

How many affairs survive as enduring relationships?

Only 10% of people who leave their relationship for affairs end up with the affair partner. Once you can be with the person every day and deal with all the little irritations in a relationship, you're into Stage Two—disillusionment.

How do most affairs get exposed?

Sometimes the betrayed partner will just ask, "Are you involved with somebody else?" Sometimes the affair partner, when it's a woman, does something to inform the wife—she sends a letter or even shows up on the doorstep. She asks, "Do you know where your husband's been?" Her motivation is not to be helpful but to break up the marriage. But often she's the one who then gets left out.

Sometimes people find out in horrible ways. They read about it in the newspaper, or they get a sexually transmitted disease. Or the cell phone bill arrives. Or their partner gets arrested—if there is a sexual addiction, the partner may be caught with prostitutes. Sometimes, somebody is suspicious and checks it out by going to the hotel room to see whether their partner's alone, or by hiring detectives.

Can all relationships be fixed?

No. What I look for is how the unfaithful partner shows empathy for the pain that they have caused when the betrayed spouse starts acting crazy.

In what way do they act crazy?

They're very emotional. They cry easily, their emotions flip-flop. They are hypervigilant. They want to look at the beeper. They have flashbacks. In the car, they hear a country-western song and start crying or accusing. They obsess over the details of the affair. Although these are common post-traumatic reactions to infidelity, their behavior is very erratic and upsetting to them and their partner. How

much compassion the partner has for that is one hallmark.

Another sign of salvageability lies in how much responsibility the unfaithful partner takes for the choice they made, regardless of problems that pre-existed in the marriage. (We definitely need to work on the weaknesses of the marriage, but not to justify the affair.)

If the unfaithful partner says, "You made me do it," that's not as predictive of a good outcome as when the partner says, "We should have gone to counseling to deal with the problems before this happened." Sometimes the unfaithful partner doesn't regret the affair because it was very exciting.

One of the big strains between the partners in the primary relationship is the way they perceive the affair partner.

> ## People often try to justify an affair by rewriting the marital history. They'll say, 'I never really loved you.'

How so?

A lot of the anger and the rage the betrayed spouse feels is directed toward the affair partner rather than the marital partner: "That person doesn't have any morals"; "That person's a home wrecker." To believe that of the marital partner would make it difficult to stay in the relationship.

At the same time, the person who had the affair may still be idealizing the affair partner. The unfaithful spouse perceives the affair partner as an angel, whereas the betrayed person perceives them as an evil person.

It's important at some point in the healing process for the involved person to see some flaws in the affair partner, so that they can partly see what their partner, the betrayed spouse, is telling them. It's also important for the betrayed spouse to see the affair partner not as a cardboard character but as a human being who did some caring things.

Is there anything else that helps you gauge the salvageability of a relationship after an affair?

Empathy, responsibility—and the degree of understanding of the vulnerabilities that made an affair possible.

What vulnerabilities?

There are individual vulnerabilities, such as curiosity. Somebody gets invited for lunch, and they go to the house because they're curious. They must learn that getting curious is a danger sign. Or if some damsel or guy in distress comes with a sad story, they learn to give out the name of a great therapist instead of becoming their confessor and confidante. Knowing what the vulnerabilities are helps you avoid them.

And relationship vulnerabilities?

The biggest one I see today is the child-centered marriage. I tell couples, If you really love your kids, the best gift you can give them is your own happy marriage. You can't have a happy marriage if you never spend time alone. Your children need to see you closing the bedroom door or going out together without them. That gives a sense of security greater than what they get by just by being loved.

Today's parents feel guilty because they don't have enough time with their kids. They think they're making it up to them by spending with them whatever leisure time they do have. They have *family* activities and *family* vacations. To help them rebuild the marriage, I help them become more couple-centered.

There has to be a separate layer of adult relationship?

The affair represents a man and a woman getting together in a dyad and just devoting themselves to each other. Very busy couples sometimes have to actually look at their calendars and find when they can spend time together.

Are there other vulnerabilities?

One is: getting too intimate with co-workers. One way to guard against danger is, if there's somebody you really like at work, then include them as a couple; invite that person and their partner to come over so that there isn't a separate relationship with that person. That's not a guarantee; people do have affairs with their best friend's spouse.

Can you tell whether someone is secretly continuing the affair?

A sign that the affair is continuing is when the unfaithful partner isn't doing anything caring and keeps making excuses—"I don't feel it yet," or "It would be false if I did it now." Sometimes it feels disloyal to the affair partner to be too caring.

Is it hard to get over an affair without a therapist?

It's hard to do *with* a therapist. People can get over it, but I don't know that they resolve the issues. Usually the unfaithful person wants to let it rest at "Hi hon, I'm back. Let's get on with our lives. Why do we have to keep going back over the past?" The betrayed person wants to know the story with all the gory details. They may begin to feel *they're* wrong to keep asking and may suppress their need to know because their partner doesn't want to talk about it. They may stay together, but they really don't learn anything or heal.

Can it ever be the same as it was before?

The affair creates a loss of innocence and some scar tissue. I tell couples things will never be the same. But the relationship may be stronger.

How do you rebuild trust?

Through honesty. First, I have to build safety. It comes about by stopping all contact with the affair partner and sharing your whereabouts, by being willing to answer the questions from your partner, by handing over the beeper, even by creating a fund to hire a detective to check up at random.

It also requires sharing information about encounters with the affair partner before being asked; when you come home, you say, "I saw him today, and he asked me how we're doing; I said, I really don't want to discuss it with you."

That's counterintuitive. People think that talking about it with the spouse will create an upset, and they'll have to go through the whole thing again. But it doesn't. Instead of trying to put the affair in a vault and lock it up, if they're willing to take it out and look at it, then the trust is rebuilt through that intimacy. The betrayed spouse may say, "I remember when such-and-such happened." If the unfaithful spouse can say, "Yeah, I just recalled such-and-such," and they bring up things or ask their partner, "How are you feeling? I see you're looking down today, is that because you're remembering?," trust can be rebuilt.

Eventually, the questioning and revealing assume a more normal level?

Yes, but things will often pop up. Someone or something will prompt them to remember something that was said. "What did you mean when you said that?" Or, "What were you doing when that happened?"

In the beginning, the betrayed partner wants details. Where, what, when. Did you tell them you love them? Did you give them gifts? Did they give you gifts? How often did you see them? How many times did you have sex? Did you have oral sex? Where did you have sex, was it in our house? How much money did you spend? Those kinds of factual questions need to be answered.

> Unless the unfaithful partner shows empathy for the pain they have caused, the marriage can't be helped.

Eventually the questions develop more complexity. How did it go on so long if you knew that it was wrong? After that first time, did you feel guilty? At that point they're in the final stages of trauma recovery, which is the search for meaning.

And they have come to a joint understanding about what the affair meant?

By combining their stories and their perceptions. A couple builds trust by rewriting their history and including the story of the affair. Some couples do a beautiful job in trying to understand the affair together, and they co-create the story of what they've been through together. When couples really are healed, they may even tease each other with private little jokes about something that they know about the affair partner or about something that happened during the affair. You can see that they finally have some comfort with it.

One of the signs that they are working in a much more united way is that their perception of the affair partner becomes more integrated—not all evil or all angel, but a human being who perhaps did manipulate but also was caring.

Some people, particularly men, are philanderers; they have repeated affairs. What's going on?

First of all, there are different kinds of philanderers. Sometimes it's easier to deal with this kind of infidelity, because there isn't the emotional involvement; sometimes it's harder, because it's such an established pattern.

One question I explore with somebody who has had lots of sexual relationships is whether it's an addiction or, in the case of men particularly, a sense of entitlement. There are some women now in positions of power who also seem to be treating sex in the same casual way and exploiting power in the same way as male philanderers. Nevertheless, in our culture, there is a sense of male privilege that condones and even encourages affairs.

How does entitlement affect matters?

If a man feels entitled, he experiences little guilt. Also, it is not necessarily a compulsive behavior; he has the ability to choose to stop it—if he changes his attitudes, if he sees what the consequences are, if he comes to believe that marriage means more than being a provider but being a loving father or caring husband. Even if he doesn't see anything wrong with philandering, if he can see the pain it causes someone he loves, he may really make the vow not only to his partner but to himself.

A sexually addicted person usually uses sex the way others use drugs: they get anxious, they say they're not going to do it, but then they're driven toward it. They get a momentary gratification followed by remorse. They decide they're not going to do it again, then they do.

There's a compulsive quality.

There is also often remorse and guilt. If they get into therapy, they may learn what addiction means in their life. Often, there's an emptiness that's linked to a need for excitement. There may be an underlying depression. They then begin to deal with the underlying source of that compulsive behavior.

What is the single most important thing you want people to know about infidelity?

BOUNDARIES. That it is possible to love somebody else, to be attracted to somebody else, even if you have a good marriage. In this collegial world where we work together, you have to conduct yourself by being aware of appropriate boundaries, by not creating opportunities, particularly at a time when you might be vulnerable.

That means that if you travel together, you never invite someone for a drink in the room; if you just had a fight with your spouse, you don't discuss it with a potential partner.

You can have a friendship, but you have to be careful who you share your deepest feelings with. Although women share their deep feelings with lots of people, particularly other women, men are usually most comfortable sharing their feelings in a love relationship. As a result, when a relationship becomes intimate and emotional, men tend to sexualize it.

There may be a history of incest or sexual abuse. Some woman may be turning the tables by using their sexuality to control men rather than be controlled by them, or they may be using sex as a way to get affection, because they don't believe that they can get it any other way. Some people may be acting out like rebellious adolescents against a spouse who is too parental.

What is happening in relationships that are parental or otherwise unequal?

Sometimes there is an over-functioning spouse and an under-functioning spouse. One partner takes on a lot of responsibility—and then resents it. The more a person puts energy into something and tries to work on it, the more committed to the relationship that person is. The other partner, who is only semi-involved in the relationship, is freer to get involved in an affair; they're not as connected to the marriage.

This is interesting because the popular notion is that the person who has the affair wasn't getting enough at home. The reality is that they weren't giving enough at home.

How do you handle that?

In rebuilding that relationship, more equity has to be created. The issue isn't what can the betrayed spouse do to make the partner happy—it's what can the unfaithful spouse do to make their partner happy. In research and in practice, my colleague Tom Wright, Ph.D., and I have observed that when you compare who does more—who is more understanding, who is more romantic, who enjoys sex more—the affair is almost always more equitable than the marriage. Usually, the person was giving more—more time, more attention, more compliments—in the affair than in the marriage. If they can invest in the marriage what they were doing in the affair, they'll feel more.

There is some research showing that people are more satisfied in equitable relationships. When relationships are not equitable, even the over-benefited partners are not as satisfied as those in equitable relationships.

You seem to be constantly reversing the conventional wisdom about affairs.

I've noticed that when younger women get involved in affairs early in the marriage and then leave, often they have not been invested in the marriage. They're working hard, climbing a ladder; the husband is the one making dinner while she's working late. He is the devastated one, because he is really committed and has given a lot. But he is peripheral in her life.

I've seen several couples who had a plan they agreed on, to build a house, or for one partner to go back to school. The person who had the responsibility for carrying out the plan was totally engrossed in it, while the other person felt so neglected that they then had an affair. The betrayed person felt terribly betrayed, because he or she thought he was working for their future. But he didn't necessarily listen to distress signs.

A relationship is like a fire. You can let it go down, but you can't let it go out. Even though you're in another part of the house, you have to go back every once in a while to stoke the coals.

> People think a person having an affair isn't getting enough at home. The truth is, the person isn't giving enough.

Do you ever counsel people directly to leave a relationship?

I would support a betrayed spouse ending the relationship if a period of time has gone by in which they have tried to work on the relationship but the affair continues secretly.

Leaving a bad marriage without trying to repair it first is like buying high and selling low. Better to see how good you can make it, then look at it and ask: Is this good enough?

What percentage of couples make it?

Those who stay in therapy and have stopped the affair have a real good chance. After an affair is first uncovered and the involved person vows to stop it, it usually doesn't stop right away. That would be coitus interruptus; there has to be some kind of closure. There will be secret meetings to say good bye or to make sure that you can really let go. But that should happen in the first few weeks or months.

Are some occupations or settings particularly conducive to affairs?

I don't know any place where the risk is low. When I was doing research for my dissertation, I went to the Baltimore-Washington airport and to an office park and gave out questionnaires. I'd go up to the men, quite imposing in their pinstripe suits and starched collars, and ask if they'd complete an anonymous research questionnaire on marriage.

I was stunned when the forms came back; so many of the men who had looked so conservative had engaged in extramarital sex. It is now known that, while we suspect the liberals, conservative men are actually more likely to be having extramarital affairs—because they split sex and affection. There are the nice girls you marry and the wild girls you have sex with.

The double standard is alive and well.

Men who score high on traits of authoritarianism are more likely to separate sex and affection than men who are low in authoritarianism. Military officers fall into this category.

People in high-drama professions—among doctors, those in the ER, trauma surgeons, cardiologists—engage in a certain amount of living on the edge that is associated with affairs. Certainly, being in the entertainment business is a risk; there's a lot of glamor, and people are away from home a lot. Often you're in a make-believe world with another person.

To hear that a person can be happily married and having an affair is surprising.

I often get asked, "How can women stay with men who have repeated affairs?" Many people believe the Clintons have some kind of an arrangement.

I don't know anything about their marriage, but I do know that it's more comfortable for people to believe they have an arrangement. When something bad happens to others, we distance ourselves from it, try to find an explanation that couldn't possibly apply to us.

You use the metaphor of walls and windows in talking about affairs.

There is almost always a wall of secrecy around the affair; the primary partner does not know what's happening on the other side of that wall. In the affair, there is often a window into the marriage, like a one-way mirror.

To reconstruct the marriage, you have to reverse the walls and windows—put up a wall with the affair partner and put up a window inside the marriage. Answering a spouse's questions about what happened in the affair is a way to reverse the process. It's a matter of who's on the inside and who's on the outside. Sometimes people will open windows but not put up walls. Sometimes they put up walls but don't open the windows. Unless you do both, you cannot rebuild safety and trust in the marriage.

The Politics of Fatigue

The gender war has been replaced by the exhaustion of trying to do it all

By Richard Morin and Megan Rosenfeld

Washington Post Staff Writers

Men and women have declared a cease-fire in the war that raged between the sexes through much of the last half of this century. In its place, they face common new enemies—the stress, lack of time and financial pressure of modern life.

A new national survey has found that after nearly a generation of sharing the workplace and renegotiating domestic duties, most men and women agree that increased gender equity has enriched both sexes. But both also believe that the strains of this relatively new world have made building successful marriages, raising children and leading satisfying lives ever more difficult.

The problem that now unites them, as warehouse operations manager James Lindow, 35, of Green Bay, Wis., puts it, is "the lack of time you spend with your life."

Large majorities of more than 4,000 men and women questioned in a series of surveys last fall placed high importance on having a successful marriage and family. At the same time, equally large majorities of working men and women said they felt bad about leaving their children in the care of others, and wished they could devote more time to their families and themselves.

Surprisingly, although men and women agreed they should have equal work opportunities, and men said they approved of women working outside the home, large majorities of both said it would be better if women could instead stay home and just take care of the house and children.

Majorities of men and women believe there still are more advantages to being a man rather than a woman, and that most men don't understand the problems women face. And the survey shows that in some areas, the reality of daily existence for two-career families still has not caught up with changed attitudes.

Most men in the polls said they were happy to share child care and domestic chores with wives who work outside the home. Yet household duties remain sharply divided along gender lines. Working mothers still do twice as much housework as their husbands, and more than half of all women questioned expressed at least some dissatisfaction with the amount of help their husbands provide around the house.

"I think men are beginning to get it, at least some are, some of the time," says survey respondent Traci Hughes-Velez, 34, of Brooklyn, N.Y., director of compensation for a major corporation. "But there are times they don't. My husband just doesn't seem to get it when I tell him that I feel I'm always on duty. When we're at home, I'm the one who always has an eye out for our son, making sure he's eating on time, things like that."

The survey shows that real differences in perspective and perception remain between the sexes. Men are more likely to support increases in defense spending; women more favorably disposed toward health care for uninsured children. Women are more likely than men to be religious and to value close friendships; men are more likely than women to want successful careers and wealth, and more likely to value an "active sex life."

But rather than emphasizing their differences and blaming many of life's problems on each other, men and women share a sense of conflict and confusion about how to make it all work under today's pressures. To a large extent, the politics of resentment have become the politics of fatigue.

The Washington Post is examining how men and women are managing in this transformed world based on a series of five nationwide surveys sponsored by The Washington Post in collaboration with researchers from Harvard University and the Henry J. Kaiser Family Foundation.

The people surveyed came from all walks of life and all parts of the country. They included people like B. J. Sande, a 32-year-old mechanical engineer from Chattaroy, Wash., and Phyllis Wilkes, a 68-year-old San Franciscan retired from waitressing in a restaurant called Clown Alley. A sewing machine operator, a preschool teacher, a woman on welfare, a man looking for a job—they all spoke with conviction about how their lives are mostly better but definitely harder.

This story describes some of the consequences of the gender revolution, as revealed in survey data, in conversations with men and women, and in interviews with social scientists.

◘

IN JUST THE PAST THREE DECADES, MOST AMERICANS agree that changing gender roles have dramatically altered their lives at work and at home.

Government statistics confirm what they see every day: The world of work is increasingly a man's and a woman's world. Between 1970 and 1995, the percentage of women ages 25 to 54 who worked outside the home climbed from 50 percent to 76 percent, sociologists Suzanne Bianchi and Daphne Spain reported in their recent book "Balancing Act."

Changes in Gender Roles

Men and women agree that the changes in gender roles in recent years have been both good and bad, and nostalgia for the lifestyle of the 1950s lingers, according to a new series of national surveys by The Washington Post/Henry J. Kaiser Family Foundation/ Harvard University.

Q: How much change do you think there has been in recent years in the relationship between men and women in their roles in families, the workplace and society?

	Men	Women
A great deal	36%	33%
Quite a lot	**40**	**43**
Only some	20	21
None at all	4	3

Q: Do you think these changes have been mainly good for the country, mainly bad, or have they been both good and bad?

	Men	Women
Mainly good	23%	13%
Mainly bad	14	12
Both good and bad	**62**	**72**
No difference	1	1

Q: Considering everything, do you think it would be better or worse for the country if men and women went back to the traditional roles they had in the 1950s, or don't you think it would make a difference?

	Men	Women
Better	35%	42%
Worse	35	33
No difference	29	21

Changed Roles Make Things Harder

For each of the following aspects of life, please tell me whether you think this change [in the relationship between men and women in their roles in families, the workplace and society] has made things easier or harder for people in this country, or whether it hasn't made much difference:

	Men	Women
For parents to raise children		
Easier	12%	14%
Harder	**80**	**80**
Not much difference	6	5
For marriages to be successful		
Easier	12%	15%
Harder	**70**	**72**
Not much difference	13	11
For families to earn enough money to live comfortably		
Easier	31%	22%
Harder	**60**	**69**
Not much difference	7	8
For men to lead satisfying lives		
Easier	22%	30%
Harder	**53**	**44**
Not much difference	22	21
For women to lead satisfying lives		
Easier	42%	34%
Harder	**44**	**50**
Not much difference	10	14

Other numbers tell a richer story. The percentage of lawyers and judges who are women doubled to 29 percent between 1983 and 1996, while the percentage of female physicians increased from 16 to 26 percent. Today, nearly a third of all professional athletes are women—almost double the proportion in 1983.

Women currently make up nearly half of all entry- and mid-level managers in American corporations, up from 17 percent in 1972. But the executive suite remains disproportionately male: A 1995 survey of Fortune 500 corporations found that only 1 in 10 corporate officers and fewer than 3 percent of all chief executive officers are women.

In higher education, gender equity is a reality. Slightly more than half of all bachelor's degrees were awarded to women last year, and the percentage of doctoral degrees granted to white women has increased from 25 percent in 1977 to 44 percent in 1993. Among African Americans, women receive more of the doctorates.

At home, men do more around the house than their fathers ever did. But the burden still falls on women: On average, working mothers do about 20 hours of housework a week, down from 30 hours two decades ago, while their husbands are doing 10 hours a week, up from five hours, Bianchi said in the book. And it's still women who say they're responsible for the way the house looks, according to the Post-Kaiser-Harvard polls.

The survey of couples with children found that women still do most of the food shopping, laundry, cooking, cleaning, arranging for child care and babysitters, and taking children to appointments or after-school activities—even when both parents work full time. Men tend to mow the lawn, shovel the snow and take out the trash, the survey found.

IN IMPORTANT WAYS, THE SURVEY SUGGESTS THAT WE have yet to find new patterns of living that recognize the real workloads of two-career couples with children, and some resentment, nostalgia and fatigue are reflected in the survey results.

"I work, my husband works, I come home and I work. I clean the house and I do my laundry," says Susan Gehrke, 44, a tenant assistant for the elderly in La Crosse, Wis. "Someone comes over and the house is a mess, they don't look at the man and think, 'What a slob,' they look at her and say, 'What a slob.' "

Says Lindow, 35, the Green Bay warehouse operations manager, whose wife also works full time: "Your kids are going to the day care, or wherever they are taken care of by somebody else. By the time you get done with your job, you've got to rush home and make supper, do whatever, and then you have to run your kids somewhere else. You don't get enough time to spend with your wife anymore, either, because you are both working. You're lucky if you get to see your wife one or two hours a day. What kind of quality time is that?"

Age, more than sex, shapes attitudes toward the changing roles of men and women, the survey suggests. Younger men and women were far more likely than their elders to say the change in gender roles has made their lives better.

"These changes have made a lot of people's lives better and it's made some people's lives worse," says the 32-year-old Sande, who is single. He adds: "Any time there is a change like there has been in my generation, there is always going to be some growing pains. But as a whole I think it's moving toward the direction of making things easier, better."

Powerful social and economic forces nourish and sustain the trends that create these tensions. Two out of three men and women surveyed agreed that it takes two incomes to get by these days; about half the respondents—men and women—said they work mostly because they must.

ONE OUT OF EVERY FIVE WORKING WOMEN SAID she would cheerfully quit her job if only she could afford to—but so did 1 in 5 men surveyed. Today, even mid-career crises are gender-neutral.

"I did stay home with my daughter the first couple years, but financially you just can't make it on one salary anymore," says Kelly Lynn Cruz, 22, of Henderson, Md., who is between jobs and has one child and another on the way. "It's hard on my family, anyway. I don't get to spend as much time with my child. The housework isn't always done, which makes me feel like I'm not always doing my job."

Why is the housework her work? "It just is," she says with a laugh, adding that "he helps. But it's mainly my job. I take care of the inside, he takes care of the outside."

Perhaps not even the '50s housewife worked this hard at home: "I've had grandmothers tell me their daughters work far harder and spend more time with their children than they did" in the 1950s, says Sharon Hays, a sociologist at the University of Virginia who studies family structure.

Many Americans say that mounting pressures to be it all and to have it all put many relationships on the rocks. In the survey, 7 in 10 said there's too much pressure on both men and women today to realize the American ideal: marriage, family and a successful career. Many survey respondents in subsequent interviews said they put the pressure on themselves. Not surprisingly, those who felt this tension most acutely also were more likely to say it's harder to make marriages and families work.

"There's too much pressure on everyone, period, whether they're men or women," says Karen Mapp, a 42-year-old PhD candidate and researcher in Boston.

In response to these pressures, 4 in 10 of those surveyed said, it would be better to return to the gender roles of the 1950s, a dimly remembered world of television's Ozzie and Harriet and their blithe suburban existence.

"I definitely think it would be good to go back," says Rose Pierre-Louis, 40, a social worker in Brooklyn, N.Y., who was among those interviewed in the poll. "Kids aren't being raised, they're just growing up. Nobody's getting married anymore. There's no respect between men and women, [or from] children for their parents."

BUT JUST AS MANY AMERICANS SAY THEY AREN'T eager to go back—particularly young people, who do not bear the burden of their parents' nostalgia.

"I've never been under the impression that I couldn't do something because I was a woman," says Jennifer Wedberg, 25, a graphics designer who lives in Lisle, Ill. "It would be a shame if things went back to the way they were in the '50s. ... It's easier to grow up knowing that some day you're just going to get married and be a mom or a wife, and now it's more complex, you have to figure out what you want to do with your life. ... But I think more choices is always a good thing."

Young women like Wedberg have many of the same conflicts—over whether to stay home or take an outside job after having children—that their mothers might have had. But they also believe they are entitled to be full participants in areas of life their mothers had to fight to enter, and they assume their personal identity includes a job or a career.

Similarly, young men generally accept that their lives at work and in the home have changed, and with these transformations have come new duties, responsibilities and rewards. "I'd just as soon stay home with the kids," says Lindow, who adds that it doesn't bother him that his wife has a better job than he does.

"I think a lot of the problems we hear of now are because we have raised our standards," says Christopher M. Moeller, 22, a radio reporter in Des Moines. "We're more involved in each other's lives. ... We value equality, we value everybody wanting to have self-esteem, to get everything they want, and I don't see where imposing a limit on more than half of our population accomplishes that."

Washington Post assistant director of polling Claudia Deane and staff researcher Robert Thomason contributed to this report.

A Progressive Approach to Caring for Children and Community

Is more institutionalized day care the answer?

By Cynthia Peters

Feminists—particularly white liberal feminists—have long considered quality day care to be a key factor in our ability to balance work and family life. Now, suddenly, day care is getting some mainstream support; legislators of all stripes, the President and Hillary Clinton, as well as some major corporations are behind it. What happened? What changed? Is it a progressive victory?

Although mostly middle and upper class women still face pressure to stay home with their children, there has been a decided shift toward day care from both conservative and liberal elements in government and from the corporate world. Needless to say, the change is not motivated by concern for gender equality. It is not even really about what is best for children, though it is framed that way. It is about a growing awareness that working parents are more productive when they have fewer childcare worries and that children—the next generation of workers—will be more productive if they have received their training from an early age. These are the reasons clearly articulated by the heads of government and corporations. Trotting out studies that prove a mere truism, i.e., the first months and years of a child's life are key to their development, they offer a feel-good backdrop for what is actually a productivity squeeze. The ideas that are left unarticulated but are a powerful motivator in day care policy changes are: (1) that it can help justify welfare reform which is sending thousands of poor women into menial jobs and their children into substandard care; (2) that to produce not only better workers, but better consumers, day care with no place for the community and for familial ties outside the marketplace can be a powerful tool for profits.

Granted the burden of raising children and nurturing family and community ties has fallen unfairly on women. Gender in-

equality has left women dependent on men and the State, and/or doubly burdened by the need to provide an income as well as nurture the family. Feminists are correct to identify childcare help—both from men and from society in general—as a key factor in the breakdown of patriarchy. Granted also that there is nothing sacred about community and family life. They are social constructs and can reinforce repressive roles just as the marketplace can. Still, there needs to be more democratic debate about what happens to children. We need to hear from diverse communities about their childcare needs. At present, Clinton is consulting the Secretary of Defense about how the military runs its very "successful" day care operation (*Boston Globe,* 10/2/97), and the Child Care Action Campaign, a national non-profit organization, is encouraging businesses to partner with agencies in their area to invest in childcare. (*Parade Magazine,* September 21, 1997.) Those in power should not be allowed to determine what happens to children. Their policies and proposals will reflect their needs and the concerns and logic of their institutions. The outcome may have short-term benefits for some women and children, but feminists and progressives at a grassroots level and from diverse communities should be debating and strategizing better ways to take care of children.

Day Care As Wal-Martification

Being a mom in late 20th century America is hard work. Not only do many of us have to produce an income to make ends meet—or, just as importantly, desire to work to have a balanced life—we are also held responsible for every twist and turn of our children's psyches and behavior.

Originally published in *Z Magazine*, January 1998, pp. 37-43. © 1998 by Cynthia Peters. Reprinted by permission.

Between the combined efforts of Sigmund Freud and Benjamin Spock, most people seem to believe that mothers are at fault for just about all of society's ills, quite a feat given that we have had close to zero access to power, privilege, and resources. Meanwhile, the job description is close to impossible. As Mary Kay Blakely says, "Mothers are somehow expected to exceed all human limits... You go to work when you're sick, maybe even clinically depressed, because motherhood is perhaps the only unpaid position where failure to show up can result in arrest" (*American Mom, Motherhood, Politics, and Humble Pie*).

As difficult as it may be to be a full-time mother, imagine that after doing your unpaid work in the home, you then take your children to a day care center and go out and do your underpaid work in the labor force—often in the dirtiest, most dangerous, least acknowledged jobs. Then, immediately after finishing your underpaid job you pick up your children from day care and resume your unpaid job, all the while keeping the following statistics in mind: 15 percent of children cared for by people other than their parents are in "childcare centers of such poor quality that their health or development is threatened." Infants are more likely to get poor care than older children; a 1993 study of childcare centers found that 40 percent of facilities serving infants were of such poor quality as to be possibly injurious. "The CFC [Center for the Future of Children] concludes that 70 percent of childcare is mediocre" (*The Nation*, "Childcare brain drain?" Ann Barnet and Richard Barnet, May 12, 1997).

If you are a welfare mother now required to work for your benefits, you may have had to leave your child with a "provisional" child care provider whose only qualification is that s/he has no criminal record. Or perhaps you have used your child care voucher to leave your child in a family day care that once had a six-child maximum but now, due to "relaxed standards," has "taken in thirty-four" (as happened recently in Wisconsin, according to the *Progressive*, October 1997).

Of course women should not be held responsible for every minute of our children's care. Nor should we, for any reason, feel compelled to put them in substandard care. Nor should we be limited to these two choices: 24 hours of Mom-duty vs. 10 hours of who knows what. Leaving children in a place where the care is "possibly injurious" or even "mediocre" is nothing less than violence against families and children. But calling for more day care slots—even the high quality variety—is not the ultimate progressive answer to childraising. While it may alleviate a short-term burden for families, day care that is mandated by the needs of the marketplace is damaging to small children and weakens community ties. Many day care centers disconnect children from daily family and community life and train small children in the ideologies and regimens of schools, factories, and offices.

What's Wrong With Day Care?

Those of you who have visited a quality day care center are probably wondering what I'm talking about. In fact, you may know a child who finds it a wonderfully enticing place—everything is scaled to her height; there are different play "stations" where she can entertain herself; she can curl up on the rug in the reading corner; she can open the trunk full of dress-up clothes; play pretend; or pull out any number of games and toys that are placed on shelves at the appropriate height. She has a hook for her coat and a cubby for her lunch box—both brightly labeled with her name. The room is decorated with educational colorful images, perhaps the letters of the alphabet, pictures of other children, and barnyard animals. She has the opportunity to listen to music, sing and dance, and play outside. Perhaps there is attention to diversity. They celebrate Hanukkah and Kwanzaa as well as Christmas. This particular child is lucky; she has teachers who, although woefully underpaid, sincerely like their work and care about the child.

There is no one particular feature of this package that makes day care centers problematic, nor is the whole package necessarily a problem in every instance. But in the context of late 20th century America, given the needs of our economy, the socializing force of educational institutions, and the pressures on families and communities, we should seriously evaluate the role of day care centers in shaping daily life as part of a progressive agenda.

Here is another take on the lessons our day care center child may absorb: Her learning and play, her growth and development, need to be structured and facilitated by professionals. There are no mentors for her, nor are there any young ones that she can in turn help usher through the months and years. She will not get a sense of her intrinsic worth as a member of a community that has a reason for being and a set of daily tasks that have varying degrees of meaningfulness, and that incorporates her at whatever developmental stage she might be, provides a variety of models for her, and invests her with a sense of the rhythms of everyday life. Instead, she gets the rather profound message that her role is to be entertained (educated, enriched, etc.) until someone picks her up and takes her home for some quality time. The lesson is an early one in consumption: She may be missing out on finding meaning in organic relationships but she can always come into the day care to consume some stimulation and entertainment instead.

Furthermore, she learns about class position and hierarchy. Rather than absorb the needs and values and cultural norms of her community, she integrates herself into an institution—learning to please the caregivers, compete with her peers for attention, divvy her day into structured activities, accept the rules and guidance of the authority figures, and mark time by her movement from the infant room to the toddler room and on to the pre-school room. Just as the U.S. educational system produces young adults schooled to take their place among the powerful or in the office, the factory, the service sector, or the permanent underclass, so early childhood education will help produce the workers we need. Yes, some day cares promote cognitive development, teach positive social skills, and empower young minds, but you can be sure that class position is a key determinant of who learns what.

Does this mean good day care is impossible? No. Even mediocre day care can offer a respite to young children who come from dysfunctional or oppressive families. Some of the social skills kids learn in day care might balance the authoritarian, mostly patriarchal, nature of the family. There are studies that show children in day care have more tolerance and understanding of diversity and a less rigid sense of gender roles. Under certain conditions, a high quality pre-school experience has been shown to truly make the difference in an underprivileged child's educational experience. And for parents, particularly mothers, dependable affordable day care can facilitate an improved quality of life—one that allows women pursuits outside the home and that gives children a more active female role model. For some, day care can literally mean a step out of poverty.

Many toddlers and pre-schoolers who are thriving in their family and community lives might enjoy and benefit from a few hours a week in something like a day care center. We've all seen children's faces light up when they enter a child-friendly room. They rush from toy to toy and delight in the plastic food that they can cook in the child-sized oven. But do they want to do this all day every day? Not necessarily. I see kids who are motivated to do what the grown-ups or older kids are doing. They observe us, model themselves after us, and join in the best they can. They want to get their hands in the soapy dishwater, follow the big kids around the neighborhood, and pound their hands on the computer keyboard.

Even if kids appeared to truly enjoy being in day care, is that the model of human activity and relationships we would want for them?

In a typical day care center, kids do not have the opportunity to join in any adult activities. Any onsite adults have nothing to do but care for them, observe them, direct their play, break up squabbles, etc. Suddenly, unself-conscious play and experimentation is managed and scheduled by childcare experts who, for the sake of their own sanity and the smooth functioning of the day care center, need the children to meet fairly rigid expectations. I agree with John Holt (in *Freedom and Beyond*) when he bemoans the trendy thinking that says children lack the "careful and loving attention of people who have been specially trained to attend to them and have nothing to do but attend to them." It's as if "growing up were a process that could not happen unless we made it happen. Not so. What children need and want are more chances to see us adults when we are about our adult business, whatever that may be, and more time in which we leave them strictly alone."

Of course, integrating kids into family and community life has quite a few expectations as well. In the course of observing us adults going about our business, kids will be schlepped around on errands, taken to job sites, asked to play quietly at the office, expected to get along in different homes where there are different values and activities, and required to chart their own course when it comes to playing, creating friendships, and just passing the time. In a home- or community-based setting, there are lots of expectations, just as in a day care. But there are some key differences. One is, kids who spend less time in day care are, from the beginning, integrated into our lives, participating in the culture we are part of and thus preserving it, and perceiving that they are a meaningful part of everyday life. This is important in a society that wants to protect cultural diversity, and give children and families some-

thing to identify with besides the acts of making money and then spending it. Two, some activities are proscribed, but not much is prescribed. John Holt argues that a child experiences much more freedom and self-direction when she is told what she can't do as opposed to what she can do. Thus, saying to a child, "You can't play with the knives, the Drano, or yesterday's compost" but leaving her the rest of the kitchen means she's been given a wide berth. In a day care center setting, the play is much more prescribed. It's time to jump on the trampoline, take a nap, stand in line, read a book, etc. Three, in a home-based setting, kids and parents or caregivers are more likely to participate in community.

Four, lest anyone think I have painted too rosy a picture, it's hard work. The tedium is sometimes intolerable. Chattering with a toddler for too many hours in a row can be unfulfilling and truly draining. We need breaks from our children and vice-versa. We (and our children) need multiple opportunities throughout the day to bond with and relate to others, and adults need time to work. Furthermore, being part of community life can be fraught with difficulty. Child-rearing and community building are undervalued invisible jobs that women do. Society needs to recognize and value women's work and men need to share the load.

Building an extended web of family, household members, friends and babysitters is not necessarily easy, possible, or even desirable for everyone. But I believe it is something progressives should support at least as much as day care. By working the care of our children into our daily lives, we build and strengthen networks that otherwise would not have been there. As a social change activist, I think it is important to bring children into strong, diverse, democratic communities that are a form of resistance to bureaucratic service providers and market values.

In an Australian pre-school study called The Mt. Druitt Project, families participated in either center-based or home-based care for their pre-school age children. The latter experienced an unexpected benefit: "the parents who participated in the home-based program established a network to organize other social, educational, and welfare activities independent of the project." By keeping their children in a home-based environment, parents and siblings presumably interacted much more around the care of the pre-schoolers. They forged bonds—and built community—in their effort to educate their children, and these bonds flowed into other aspects of their lives. The families whose children were sent off to center-based care did not develop these networks.

Some day care—particularly when it is locally owned, operated out of the home, and/or collectively constructed by adults and children—can foster community, build networks among children and relatives, and offer a safe space that more or less leaves the kids "strictly alone." Many day care providers, whether they are running their business out of their home or working for a national day care chain, care deeply about their work. But even the most dedicated day care worker cannot replace social responsibility for children. When progressives lobby for childcare, we should conceive of ways that government and workplace policy can be changed to foster networks and communities that will provide continuity and support to children and families.

Looking to History

Once upon a time feminists made the jump from abortion rights—the limited ability to terminate a pregnancy—to reproductive freedom—the broader ability to have children if you want them, health care when you need it, and control over your body vis-a-vis the medical establishment and reproduction. By taking into account the needs, desires, and problems facing women of color, poor women, and lesbians, feminism moved from protecting the legal right to an abortion to a much more pro-active visionary agenda that gave women a chance to articulate how they wanted to be in the world as sexual subjects and mothers. Now, another leap is in order. We need to define how we want to raise our children. We need to say what we mean by good day care, and then we need to make sure it is available to those who want it. We also need safe nurturing communities that help us raise our children. This is not a call for women to become full-time homemakers. Men need to play an equal role in the lives of their children and communities. No one should be confined to an isolated home. Nor should anyone suffer the straitjacket of menial work that consumes all our energies. Reproductive freedom is about producing and reproducing ourselves, our children, our families and our communities outside the market sphere. It is about really being able to choose how we want to raise our children. It is about having healthy functional families and communities that are meaningful because all participate in nurturing, mentoring, learning, producing, working and playing, and that welcome children into this process.

In their book, *A Tradition That Has No Name*, Mary Field Belenky, et al., investigate how unempowered people "help each other move out of the silence, claim the power of their minds, exercise their leadership, and come to have a real say in the way their lives, families, and communities are being run." The authors look to the African American tradition of developing leadership from grassroots sources and nurturing community and "homeplaces" outside the reach of the white status quo. In her book, *Yearning*, African American cultural critic bell hooks says: "Historically, African-American people believed that the construction of a homeplace, however fragile and tenuous (the slave hut, the wooden shack), had a radical political dimension. Despite the brutal reality of racial apartheid, of domination, one's homeplace was the one site where one could freely confront the issue of humanization, where one could resist. Black women resisted by making homes where all black people could strive to be subjects, not objects, where we could be affirmed in our minds and hearts despite poverty, hardship, and deprivation, where we could restore to ourselves the dignity denied us on the outside in the public world."

In *Black Feminist Thought*, Patricia Hill Collins calls these women "community othermothers," and Charles Payne, in I've Got the Light of Freedom, calls those who nurture community "leaders in the developmental tradition." In *Double Stitch: Black Women Write About Mothers and Daughters*, Collins

suggests that black women's role as community othermothers encouraged black women's social activism. Their feelings of responsibility toward all their community's children gave rise to a "more generalized ethic of care." Without romanticizing the hardship that gave rise to the need to create private safe space, we can draw lessons from a tradition that nurtured community and valued it as a site of resistance, a place that could preserve values not found in the mainstream.

Parade Magazine recently reported that "48% of the 9.9 million children under age 5 who need day care are looked after by relatives . . . Preschoolers from poor families are 50% more likely to be cared for by relatives than those whose families live above the poverty line." The article implies that the situation is obviously in need of repair. But can we be certain of that? Is the child posted in front of the TV all day? Is he ignored by a depressed exploited mother? Is he forging bonds with grandparents, relatives, siblings, and neighbors who care about him and are invested in his well-being for no other reason than that he is one of them? We should look at what's really going on in those families, and we should be open to hearing what those families want. We should look at how diverse communities reinforce ties and we should consider the possibility that the care of children is an important community builder, one that roots children and families in traditions outside consumer-driven, white middle-class America.

In his acceptance speech of the 1991 New York State Teacher of the Year Award, John Taylor Gatto lists the seven most important lessons of schoolteaching: confusion, class position, indifference, emotional and intellectual dependency, conditional self-esteem, and surveillance. After 26 years of teaching, Gatto has come to believe that "institutional schoolteaching is destructive to children" and that the seven lessons he is entrusted with passing along are "prime training for permanent underclasses, people deprived forever of finding their own special genius."

Ira Shor, Henry Giroux, Paulo Freire, John Holt, and many others have contributed to a rich progressive critique of educational systems, the relationship between the development of capitalism and public education, the ways that schools train our young people in the whys and wherefores of a consumer culture and workaday world that requires an uncritical respect for authority, ability to tolerate boredom, and acquiescence to fragmented uncreative work. Now that pre-school age children are being ushered into educational institutions at an earlier age and faster rate than ever before, it's time for progressives to take notice. What do we want for our small children? How do we want to care for them? What sorts of families and communities do we hope they will have access to?

What We Should Be Working For

• *True choices about how to be in a family.*

We need a system of social supports and benefits that would allow parents to take paid leave from their jobs to be with their small children if they wanted.

Work schedules should be flexible and should allow parents to take care of family needs. Rather than provide emergency nanny services and birthday cakes on short notice, work culture should support parents' efforts to parent their children. To fully achieve this, we have to remind ourselves that a big part of parenting is simply being around. Moms and Dads are not service delivery systems, easily replaced by emergency nannies, cake-makers, and other stand-ins. We cannot meet children's needs by purchasing services for them. Although many services are helpful and necessary and should be affordable to all, they are a far cry from the radical restructuring of work and community life that we really need to support families and children, and to allow communities to reproduce themselves outside the corporate sphere.

Community life needs to be structured in such a way that values all community members, fosters networks of support and care, and welcomes children as part of the pleasure and responsibility of the entire community.

• *Make a range of quality day care options available.*

What makes a "quality" day care should be widely debated by different communities—not the government, not corporate America, and not just the white middle class. We need to hear from all the families and communities that have been raising children for centuries using extended family networks and community resources. Rather than disrupt those organic networks, we should support them. A range of good choices should be available.

We need to critically evaluate the way that a corporate bureaucratic mentality has seeped into not only the educational system, but also the day care system, and we need to propose alternative structures and institutions for families and children.

• *We need a reinvigorated feminist agenda that continues to expose and amend gender inequality in families.*

Men still only do a fraction of the total household chores. In two-parent heterosexual families, forget the emergency nanny service, get Dad to stay home with the sick kid.

Let's continue to raise consciousness about the way men's public lives are valued more than women's. Let's demand that social policy and work rules see men as active parents and incorporate their needs.

We need parental leave, not maternity leave. We need extra days off for Moms and Dads to stay home because the children are sick or just to spend time in the community.

We need comparable worth so that families do not have to decide it is more economical to send Dad into the work force and leave Mom at home.

We need social benefits that make it possible for single parents to raise their children outside of poverty.

We need to abolish the tax breaks and other institutional supports for straight marriage and nuclear families.

Cynthia Peters, formerly a member of the South End Press collective, is a freelance writer.

Book Excerpt: In the debates over quality time and how to balance work and family, kids are rarely heard. A new 'Ask the Children' study reveals how kids rate their moms and dads—and what children really want. BY ELLEN GALINSKY

Do Working Parents Make The Grade?

WHENEVER I MENTION THAT I AM STUDYing how kids see their working parents, the response is electric. People are fascinated. Parents want to know what I have found, but inevitably they are nervous, too. Sometimes they say, "I wonder what other people's children would say. I'm not sure that I'm ready to hear what mine have to say!"

Why has a comprehensive, in-depth study of this question never been conducted? Because we have been afraid to ask, afraid to know. But now I feel the time is right. The answers of children are illuminating, not frightening. They help us see that our assumptions about children's ideas are often at odds with reality. Ultimately, this information will help us be better parents— and better employees, too. In fact, adding children's voices to our national conversation about work and family life will change the way we think about them forever.

Many of the debates we've been having about work and family miss the mark. For example, we have been locked in a longstanding argument about whether it is "good or bad" for children if their mothers work. Numerous observational studies have found that having a working mother doesn't harm children, yet the debate still rages. Another way to assess this issue is to see whether children of

mothers who are not employed and children of working mothers differ in the way they feel they are being parented. In our "Ask the Children" study, we had a representative group of more than 1,000 children in grades three through 12 to evaluate their parents in 12 areas strongly linked to children's healthy development, school readiness and school success. In their responses—rendered in actual letter grades—having a mother who worked was never once predictive of how children assess their mothers' parenting skills. We also found that while the amount of time children and parents spend together is very important, most children don't want more time with their parents. Instead, they give their mothers and fathers higher grades if the time they do spend together is not rushed but focused and rich in shared activities.

It may seem surprising that children whose mothers are at home caring for them full time fail to see them as more supportive. But a mother who is employed can be there for her child or not, just as mothers who are not employed can be. Indeed, children of nonworking fathers see their dads less positively when it comes to making them feel important and loved and to participating in important events in the children's lives. Fathers who work part time are less likely to be seen as encouraging their children's learning. Perhaps fathers who work less than

Family Values

56% of parents think their kids want more time together; only 10% of kids want more time with Mom, 15.5% with Dad. Most kids, however, feel they have enough time.

62.5% of parents say they like their work a lot. Only 41% of children say Dad enjoys his job, and 42% says the same about Mom.

44.5% of kids say time with Mom is rushed, 37% say so with Dad. Only 33% of parents think time with their kids is rushed.

23% of kids want their parents to earn more; 14% of parents think kids want this.

From *Newsweek*, August 30, 1999, pp. 52-56. Excerpted from *Ask the Children* by Ellen Galinsky (Morrow, 1999). © 1999 by Ellen Galinsky. : Reprinted by permission of William Morrow and Company, Inc.

Grading
Dad

He instills good values, but doesn't always know what 'really' goes on

SUBJECT	A	B	C	D	F
Raising me with good values	69%	18%	8%	4%	2%
Appreciating me for who I am	58	21	11	8	2
Encouraging me to enjoy learning	57.5	24	12	4	2
Making me feel important and loved	57	22	13	6	2
Being able to go to important events	55	22	13	5	5.5
Being there for me when I am sick	51.5	20	16	8	4
Spending time talking with me	43	24	19	10	4
Establishing traditions with me	41	26	15	11	7
Being involved in school life	38	24	19	12	7
Being someone to go to when upset	38	22	15	12	13
Controlling his temper	31	27	20	10	12
Knowing what goes on with me	31	30	17	12.5	10

NOTE: GRADES GIVEN BY CHILDREN IN SEVENTH THROUGH 12TH GRADES

employed mothers and those with mothers at home do not differ on whether they feel they have too little time with Mom.

What the largest proportion of children (23 percent) say that they want is for their mothers and their fathers to make more money. I suspect that money is seen as a stress-reducer, given children's other answers. The total number of children who wish that their parents would be less stressed or less tired by work is even larger: 34 percent make this wish for their mothers and 27.5 percent for their fathers. Sympathy for working parents comes through loud and clear: "I would like to thank the parents of America for working so hard to earn money," says one 15-year-old girl. "I know that a working parent goes through so much for their children."

The study also reveals what children learn from their parents about the world of work. Only about two in five children think their parents like their work a lot, compared with 62.5 percent of parents who say they do. That's probably because many of us have said to our kids, "I have to go to work." Or "I wish I didn't have to leave." We seem to talk around children rather than with them about our jobs. And our reluctance to talk to our children about our work has meant that young people are getting haphazard rather than intentional information, sometimes blaming themselves for distress we pick up on the job, and not fully appreciating the potential of their own future careers.

As a result, many children play detective to figure out what is going on in our jobs that upsets or elates us. They study our moods at the end of the workday. One of our young subjects says you can tell if your parents are in a bad mood "because you get a short and simple answer. If they had a bad day, they won't talk. Or they will just go off by themselves."

What makes a good parent? Through our interviews with parents and children, eight critical parenting skills emerged. We then asked the children in our national survey to grade their own mothers and dads on those criteria. They are:

1. Making the child feel important and loved
2. Responding to the child's cues and clues
3. Accepting the child for who he or she is, but expecting success
4. Promoting strong values
5. Using constructive discipline
6. Providing routines and rituals to make life predictable and create positive neural patterns in developing brains
7. Being involved in the child's education
8. Being there for the child

Which of these skills earned parents the highest—and lowest—grades? Among children in the seventh through the 12th grades, mothers are given the highest grades for being there when the child is sick (81 percent gave their mothers an A) and for raising their children with good values (75 percent). They receive the lowest grades for controlling their tempers

full time or who are unemployed are feeling financial and role strain, which could affect how they interact with their children.

That children can appreciate the efforts of working parents is clear. Said one 12-year-old son of working parents: "If parents wish to provide some of the better things in life, both parents need to work and share the home and children responsibilities." A 15-year-old girl whose father works full time and whose mother does not said: "Your children may not like you working now, but it will pay off later on."

The problem isn't that mothers (and fathers) work: it is how we work and how work affects our parenting. For example, we asked the children in this study, "If you were granted one wish to change the way that your mother's or your father's work affects your life, what would that wish be?" We also asked more than 600 parents to guess what their child's response would be. Taken together, 56 percent of parents assume that their children would wish for more time together and less parental time at work. And 50 percent of parents with children up to 18 years old say they feel that they have too little time with their child—fathers (56 percent) even more so than mothers (44 percent).

But only 10 percent of children wish that their mothers would spend more time with them, and 15.5 percent say the same thing about their fathers. And surprisingly, children with

Time spent in shared activities wins parents high marks—
but not if it feels hurried or rushed

when their children make them angry (only 29 percent gave their mothers an A) and for knowing what is really going on in their children's lives (35 percent). The age of the child makes a difference. Younger children consistently rate their parents more favorably than older ones, which no doubt reflects the way teenagers separate emotionally from their parents.

Money also matters. In analysis after analysis, the children's perception of their families' economic health is strongly linked to how they rate their moms' and dads' parenting skills. Although the public often views the problems of children as primarily moral in nature, our analyses show that families that do not have to worry about putting bread on the table may have more to give to their children emotionally. They also may be able to raise their children in more positive, cohesive communities.

These findings illustrate why it is so important to ask the children rather than to rely on our own assumptions. The issue of time with children has typically been framed in the public debate as a mothers' issue. But when we ask the children, we see that fathers need to be front and center in this discussion, as well.

Children in the seventh through the 12th grades judge their fathers less favorably than their mothers in some important respects, such as making their child feel important and loved and being someone whom the child can go to if upset. Teenagers are more likely than their younger counterparts to want more time with their fathers. Thirty-nine percent of children 13 through 18 years old feel they have too little time with their fathers, compared with 29 percent of children 8 through 12 years old.

We found that the quantity of time with mothers and fathers does matter a great deal. Children who spend more time with their mothers and fathers on workdays and nonworkdays see their parents more positively, feel that their parents are more successful at managing work and family responsibilities, and see their parents as putting their families first. "I think that if the parents spend more time with their children, they will become better people in life," says a 12-year-old boy whose father works part time while his mom stays home.

But to move beyond simply cataloging the number of hours children and parents spend together, we looked at what parents and children do while they are together, such as eating a meal, playing a game or sport or exercising, doing homework (together) and watching TV. For all these activities, the same pattern holds: the more frequently parents and children engaged in them together, the more positive the assessment parents got from their children.

But spending time together isn't enough. Many children said their interactions with parents feel rushed and hurried, and they gave their mothers and fathers lower marks as a result. More than two in five (44.5 percent) children feel that their time with their mother is rushed, while 37 percent feel their time with their father is rushed. Some mentioned mornings as

Grading Mom

She's there during illness, but sometimes loses her temper

SUBJECT	A	B	C	D	F
Being there for me when I am sick	81%	11%	5%	2%	1%
Raising me with good values	75	15	6	3	2
Making me feel important and loved	64	20	10	5	1
Being able to go to important events	64	20	10	3	3.5
Appreciating me for who I am	64	18	8	6	5
Encouraging me to enjoy learning	59	23	11.5	3	3
Being involved in school life	46	25	14	10	6
Being someone to go to when upset	46	22	14	8	9
Spending time talking with me	43	33	14	6	4
Establishing traditions with me	38	29	17	10	6
Knowing what goes on with me	35	31	15	10	9
Controlling her temper	29	27.5	20.5	12	11

particularly hectic times for their families. One 12-year-old girl said of her mother: "She's rushing and telling me to rush … And my backpack weighs a ton, so if she walks me to school, it's like running down the street. I'm like, 'wait up …'"

Predictably, children are more likely to see their parents positively if their time together is calmer. For example: of children 8 through 18 years of age who rate their time with their mothers as very calm, 86 percent give their mothers an A for making them feel important and loved, compared with 63 percent of those who rate their time with their mothers as very rushed. And 80 percent of children who feel their time with their fathers is very calm give them an A for "appreciating me for who I am," compared with only 50.5 percent of those who rate their time with their fathers as very rushed.

The flip side of feeling rushed and distracted with children is concentration and focus. In one-on-one interviews, we asked parents to describe moments when they felt particularly successful at home. Over and over, we heard the word "focus." The mother of a 12-year-old says: "It's the time you spend with your children [when] you are really focused on them that's good; not a distracted time."

Of children in the seventh through 12th grades, 62 percent say that mothers find it "very easy" and 52 percent say that fathers find it very easy to focus on them when they are to-

Kids who think their families are financially secure feel more positive about Mom and Dad

gether. And children are very attuned to the times when their parents are truly focused on them: "They're not just saying normal things like 'uh huh . . . uh hmmm.' They seem to be very intent on what I'm saying, they're not just looking away," said a 10-year-old boy. Some children even have "tests" of whether their parent is focusing on them. For example, one 13-year-old boy throws nonsense statements — like "a goldfish on the grass"—into the middle of a sentence to check out whether his parents are really listening to him.

Every analysis we conducted revealed that when children feel that their mothers and fathers can focus on them, they are much more likely to feel that their parents manage their work and family responsibilities more successfully and put their families before their work. And they give their parents much higher marks for all of the parenting skills we examined.

So, is it quantity time or quality time? Clearly, the words we're using to describe time within the family are wrong. To change the debate, we need new words. Since "focus" is the word that parents use to describe the quality of time they treasure most, I suggest we use it. And since parents and children highly value the quantity of time they spend being together, whether sharing a meal or just being around each other in a nonrushed way, we need a phrase for that, too. Children need focused times and hang-around times.

I hope that, as a result of this book, the conversations around work and family will change. When parents and children talk together about these issues, reasonable changes can be made. Children will tell us how some things could be better. Yes, they will still try to push our guilt buttons. Yes, they will still read our moods and plead their case for what they want because kids will be kids. But we are the adults, and we set the tone for our relationships with our children.

I repeat the wisdom of a 12-year-old child: "Listen. Listen to what your kids say, because you know, sometimes it's very important. And sometimes a kid can have a great idea and it could even affect you." So let's ask the children.

Balancing
Work and
Family

by Joseph H. Pleck

*Fathers who live with their families are spending
more time with their children. At the same time,
more fathers are not living with their families*

Stories in the media often portray contemporary
men balancing an active family role with the
breadwinning responsibilities of a career. At the
same time, commonly held wisdom suggests that yesterday's men—even those from just a few decades
ago—often failed at that juggling act, serving primarily as full-time workers and participating in few, if
any, family activities. These images of present and
past men, however, might arise more from folklore
than fact. By studying exactly what activities American men do now, and have done in the past, social scientists find an interrelated web of trends that are
changing men's roles.

In 1956 Swedish sociologist Alva Myrdal and British historian Viola Klein published *Women's Two Roles:
Home and Work*. Their title introduced what became
the leading understanding of the change in adult
women's lives in industrial societies over the first half
of the 20th century. In addition to their traditional
child-rearing and homemaking role within the family,
women were increasingly engaging in a second role:
paid employment outside the family. In the decades
subsequent to *Women's Two Roles*, Myrdal and other sociologists have tentatively suggested that in the long
run, women could not succeed at both roles unless
men also took on more family responsibilities. Our society is still just beginning to recognize that men, too,
face the challenge of dual roles.

Are Men Doing More in the Family?

Since the mid-1970s other social scientists and I have
systematically studied the changing ways in which
contemporary American men combine and prioritize
their work and family responsibilities. In attempting
to analyze these changes, many people—especially students, journalists and scholars—often ask: Are men doing more in the family now than they did in the past?
That question can be examined on many levels. For example, beyond simply knowing how much time men
spend with their families, one might examine what
men do during their family time and what it means
to them. This changing role for men also leads to
larger social implications.

Although men still perform less child care than women, good evidence indicates that the participation of men in family activities is increasing.

Today's American men spend less of their lives working than their predecessors did. In comparison to men of the early 20th century, they now enter the labor force later and retire earlier. In addition, the average number of hours that men work each week also decreased substantially during the first half of this century, but there is some controversy about whether such decreases have continued. Even more interest—and controversy—surrounds a related question: Do today's men spend more time taking care of children and doing housework?

One long-term comparison came from the so-called Middletown project, in which sociologists Robert and Helen Merrill Lynd studied Muncie, Inc., in the 1920s. In 1924 about 10 percent of Muncie's working-class wives reported that their husbands spent no time with their children, and 68 percent said that their husbands spent more than an hour a day. In 1978 Theodore Caplow of the University of Virginia and Bruce A. Chadwick of Brigham Young University repeated most of the Lynds' interview procedures with a similar sample in Muncie. In their study, only 2 percent of working-class wives reported that their husbands spent no time with their children, and 77 percent reported that their husbands spent more than an hour a day. In both studies, the figures were similar for what the Lynds called "business-class" families, in which the husbands held white-collar jobs.

Many more comparisons can be made with data collected since 1965. Some of the most important of these studies have used so-called time diaries. Home economists developed this technique in the 1920s, but it fell into disuse until its reinvention in the 1960s. With this method, respondents report—in their own words—what they were doing at each moment of the previous day, starting at 12 A.M. The respondents list each activity, when that activity stopped, what they did next, when that stopped, what they did after that and so on, until reaching the following midnight. They might also be asked other questions about each activity, such as whether a television was on or who was with them. Responses are then coded into specific categories, such as baby care and indoor playing, which can be combined into broader categories, such as child care.

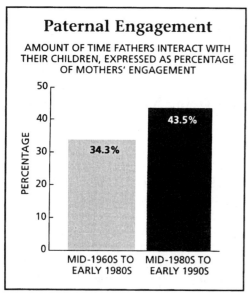

Paternal Engagement

AMOUNT OF TIME FATHERS INTERACT WITH THEIR CHILDREN, EXPRESSED AS PERCENTAGE OF MOTHERS' ENGAGEMENT

- MID-1960S TO EARLY 1980S: 34.3%
- MID-1980S TO EARLY 1990S: 43.5%

LAURIE GRACE

PATERNAL ENGAGEMENT is the category of activities in which fathers interact with their children. Examples include playing with children (right), reading to them and helping with their homework. Paternal engagement is increasing, but mothers still spend more than twice as much time interacting with their children (above).

BERND AUERS

In the studies that do not use time diaries, fathers are often asked to simply estimate how much time they spend with their children each day. To make sense of the more recent data collected with time diaries as well as with other methods for estimating time-use patterns, Michael Lamb of the National Institute of Child Health and Human Development, James Levine of the Families and Work Institute and I proposed two categories: paternal engagement and paternal availability. Paternal engagement consists of direct interaction with a child, which is described by the father in language indicating that he thought of the activity as taking care of the child. Paternal availability adds to this the amount of time the father and child are in the same vicinity but engaging in different activities.

Lamb, Levine and I discovered that different time-diary studies often interpret the same behavior differently. For example, "talking with children" might be considered part of child care in some studies but not in others. To identify trends across studies, we converted the data about fathers' time with children in each study from an absolute amount, such as 76 minutes a day, to a percentage of the mothers' interactions, such as 32 percent. Consequently, results of the different studies could be converted to a common standard of measurement—fathers' time as a proportion of mothers.

Using this approach to review 11 national or local studies that collected data between the mid-1960s and the early 1980s, Lamb, Levine and I found that fathers' engagement was on average about one third of mothers' and their availability was about half of mothers'. When I recently examined 13 similar studies that reported data collected between the mid-1980s and the early 1990s, fathers' engagement had risen to 43.5 percent of mothers', and paternal availability had risen to 65.6 percent. In addition, many studies have shown that when fathers are more involved with their children because they want to be, the fathers' involve-

BERND AUERS

PATERNAL AVAILABILITY is a measurement of the amount of time fathers spend in the vicinity of their children, either interacting with them or not. The category covers activities such as working on the computer while the children play video games (above). In recent years, paternal availability has risen to nearly two thirds of maternal availability (bottom).

ment benefits the children's cognitive and social development.

Although men still perform less child care than women, good evidence indicates that the participation of men in family activities is increasing. Nevertheless, most of the data come from studies of married fathers, which overlook a substantial part of the adult male population.

More Diverse Family Roles

Even though some data show that U.S. men's involvement with the family has risen, other indicators suggest the contrary. For example, the increase in divorce rates since the 1950s has weakened many men's family ties. Most divorced fathers' contact with their children drops off rapidly after divorce. Almost half of all divorced fathers have not seen their children in the past year, and high proportions of them do not

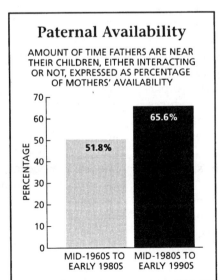

Paternal Availability

AMOUNT OF TIME FATHERS ARE NEAR THEIR CHILDREN, EITHER INTERACTING OR NOT, EXPRESSED AS PERCENTAGE OF MOTHERS' AVAILABILITY

51.8% — MID-1960S TO EARLY 1980S
65.6% — MID-1980S TO EARLY 1990S

LAURIE GRACE

pay child support. (More than 80 percent of court-ordered child-support money is never actually paid.) What is more, the recent increase in the proportion of men who never marry also indicates decreasing family involvement. Most unmarried fathers—teen and adult—refuse to accept any responsibility for their children.

These phenomena, however, are more complex than they first appear. For example, although the increase in divorce during the 1960s and 1970s appeared dramatic compared with the unusually stable divorce rate during the 1950s, rates of divorce have actually been relatively stable at about 50 percent for nearly two decades. In addition, divorced fathers' loss of interest in their children is not the only possible source of the rapid decrease in contact. For instance, many divorced mothers do not want continuing contact between their ex-spouses and their children.

In their 1991 book *New Families, No Families?*, Frances K. Goldscheider of Brown University and Linda J. Waite of the University of Chicago perceptively argue that American family life is not changing in two contradictory directions. In two-parent families, fathers' involvement with children and overall gender equality are increasing; however, two-parent families have become a smaller proportion of all families. Families headed by single mothers are becoming more common, and thus, more children overall do not have a resident father.

Goldscheider and Waite's analysis helps to make sense of the perhaps surprising finding that ethnicity and socioeconomic status show little if any consistent association with the amount of child care performed by married fathers. These variables primarily influence fathers' behavior by determining whether fathers get and remain married, not by affecting how fathers act when they are married.

How might these demographic and behavioral trends play out in the future? The downside trend—more children in single-parent families—has leveled off, because the divorce rate has been stable for nearly two decades and the out-of-wedlock birth rate has also leveled off in recent years. The upside trend—greater father involvement in married two-parent families—appears to be continuing. This produces a positive overall trend toward greater paternal involvement. Nevertheless, the disparity between the experiences of children growing up in married two-parent families and those of children in single-parent families will continue to grow.

This discussion usually contrasts two groups—resident, married fathers versus nonresident, never-married or divorced fathers—but my research suggests that there is a surprisingly large and unrecognized third group: resident, unmarried fathers. Jeffrey L. Stueve of the University of Illinois and I analyzed a nationally representative sample of fathers between

the ages of 22 and 26 who live with their children. Nearly 60 percent were the children's biological father, residing with and married to the children's biological mother, but more than 40 percent were not. Resident, unmarried fathers have several subtypes: cohabiting biological fathers (13 percent of the total number of resident fathers), cohabiting stepfathers (8 percent) and fathers raising biological and unrelated children alone (6 percent). Married stepfathers have been studied more than any of these subgroups but are less frequent (5 percent). Fathers in "blended" families—in which they are living with children *and* stepchildren—make up 8 percent of the total. Men were defined as "cohabiting" if they were living with a female partner at the time of the study; there was no minimum length of time for the relationship. This wide variety of family types suggests that researchers need to broaden their studies to include all kinds of fathers.

For a long time, social scientists assumed that men's and women's experiences must be opposite in all respects. For example, past researchers often thought that if family is more central than work for women's identities, work must be more central than family for men's identities. Nevertheless, research has never borne out this expectation. My research in the 1970s, using self-report questionnaires, showed that family is far more psychologically central to men than work, just as is true for women. Other recent studies concur.

Someone might say that men merely report the socially desirable response. To sidestep that potential criticism, one could compare how strongly men's overall psychological well-being is linked to their satisfaction with either family life or work life. Using two mid-1970s surveys, I found the men's levels of family satisfaction explained twice as much variance in their psychological well-being as their levels of work satisfaction did—just like women. Rosalind C. Barnett of Brandeis University replicated my findings with more recent samples.

Of course, more subtle differences might exist between the family identities of men and women. In studies of so-called emotional transmission from work to family, for example, Reed W. Larson of the University of Illinois showed that a father's mood at the end of a workday influences a mother's mood when they're together at home far more than her prior mood affects him. In fact, a father's mood at work more strongly influences a mother's mood at home than her own mood at work affects her mood at home. Larson's findings suggest an important difference in the place of work and family in fathers' and mothers' personalities: fathers carry their workplace emotions home with them, but mothers keep their family experience insulated from workplace pressures.

Other research, however, suggests unexpected similarities. For example, Ellen Hock and Wilma Lutz of Ohio State University found that fathers and mothers experienced similar levels of anxiety over separation from their children during the first two years of parenthood. Research today is just beginning to flesh out a full understanding of the differences and similarities in men's and women's family identities.

Actions and Expectations

Less evidence exists about how the character of men's behavior in the family has changed. What is available continues to find gross differences between fathers' and mothers' behavior with children. With infants, mothers' behavior is more smoothing and predictable, and fathers' is more stimulating and unpredictable. With older children, mothers provide more caregiving, and fathers engage in more play.

Some conservatives suggest that a new social pressure encourages fathers to "act like mother." For instance, David Blankenhorn of the Institute for American Values says that a new cultural "script" pushes dad toward androgyny under the label of "Mr. Mom." I see little evidence, though, of this alleged new ideal. Other researchers and I recognize the importance of fathers' providing children with financial support and developmental guidance as well as supporting the mother in her relationship with the children. Moreover, we have not claimed that greater paternal involvement necessarily has positive effects, and we have not recommended that fathers should act like mothers. Indeed, several of my colleagues and I contend that fathers' play with children might have more positive consequences for their children's development than fathers' caretaking time, because play interaction is more socially and cognitively stimulating. In any event, no recent evidence finds fathers actually acting more like mothers in terms of their specific activities or behavioral style, so conservatives need not be so concerned.

I also question whether the current cultural script about fathering really has shifted in favor of greater involvement with children. Within the general belief that it is desirable for fathers to be more involved lurks a hidden qualification: not if it negatively impacts their jobs. For example, a recent survey of large companies showed that fathers are usually entitled to parental leave on the same basis as mothers—but when company employees were asked how many days a father should be entitled to take, 90 percent said none.

Social Implications

Although men's changing work-family balance affects their children, their spouses and the men themselves, we must also consider broader effects: the consequences of these changes on social institutions. The two different directions in which men's work-family patterns have changed—an increase in paternal involvement among married men and a simultaneous increase in divorce and fatherhood outside marriage—must be considered separately.

Men's decreasing tendency to be married fathers forces more children to face significant risks in their development. In recent years, our society has developed better strategies to increase the number of child-support court orders directed at absent fathers and to encourage their compliance with the orders. Nevertheless, even with the highest feasible child-support payments and maximum paternal compliance, many children in these families will live in poverty, and most of them will need some form of public assistance.

Robert E. Emery of the University of Virginia found that court data over the past two decades indicate a large rise in the proportion of fathers who share legal custody but only a small increase in the proportion sharing physical custody—in other words, actually living with their children. Emery's studies, however, point to a possible intervention effort: divorce mediation, in which the couple negotiates a settlement instead of fighting it out in court. Emery found that divorce mediation leads to more contact between fathers and children 12 years after divorce than the standard divorce process does.

Other intervention efforts can effectively promote parental responsibility among teenage fathers and reduce the incidence of out-of-wedlock births, especially

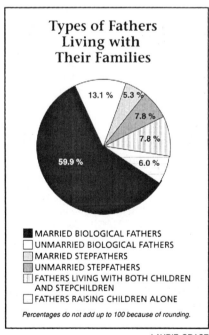

Types of Fathers Living with Their Families

13.1 %   5.3 %
7.8 %
7.8 %
59.9 %   6.0 %

■ MARRIED BIOLOGICAL FATHERS
□ UNMARRIED BIOLOGICAL FATHERS
▨ MARRIED STEPFATHERS
▨ UNMARRIED STEPFATHERS
□ FATHERS LIVING WITH BOTH CHILDREN AND STEPCHILDREN
□ FATHERS RAISING CHILDREN ALONE

Percentages do not add up to 100 because of rounding.

LAURIE GRACE

***UNCONVENTIONAL FATHERS** make up about 40 percent of all fathers who live with their children. Studies show that cohabiting fathers and stepfathers are particularly common, at 13.1 and 7.8 percent, respectively.*

among teenage women. Unfortunately, our government's recent approach—eliminating increases in benefits to mothers who have additional children while on welfare—is not one of them. This approach has not resulted in lower rates of out-of-wedlock births in the states that have passed such laws. Recently attention has turned to possible ways of reducing the incidence of divorce by making it more difficult to obtain or by creating a class of marriage in which divorce is not permitted. These latter efforts are, at best, controversial in their feasibility and desirability.

Married fathers' increasing involvement with their children also has social ramifications for the workplace. In a 1977 national survey that I co-directed for the U.S. Department of Labor, I developed the first measures of the extent to which employed married men and women experience conflict between their work and family roles. In that survey, and in much of the research conducted subsequently by other investigators, the married mothers and fathers reported similar levels of conflict. Other studies show that parenthood is associated with increased absences or lateness at work to a similar degree for men and women and that work-family disruptions, such as a breakdown in child-care arrangements, affect men's well-being at least as much as women's.

Impetus for Change

Men's conflicts between their work and family responsibilities create pressure to change the workplace, which adds to the impetus for change already created by the rising numbers of employed mothers. Over the past two decades, for examples, enough men fought for parental leave on the same basis as women—generally unpaid—to generate a well-established body of case and administrative law affirming this right. In fact, fathers initiate a significant proportion of the grievances regarding denial of parental leave filed with the U.S. Department of Labor under the 1993 Family and Medical Leave Act. In January 1999 one father—Kevin Knussman, a helicopter paramedic with the Maryland State Police—received a $375,000 jury award for denial of leave. Knussman's award was the largest ever granted to a father in a parental leave case.

Although men's changing work-family patterns are triggering demands for more flexible workplace poli-

cies, the changes are sure to be contested. In fact, considerable resistance to greater workplace flexibility exists today, despite the social attitudes favoring more involvement of fathers in family life. The resistance stems from the hidden qualification mentioned earlier: the belief that fathers' family involvement should not affect their job performance in any way.

As a result, the shifting pattern of work-family commitments for men will most likely mirror the pattern experienced by women. Policy changes in the workplace have been important, but we should remember that employed mothers have nonetheless needed to work out accommodations between their work and family lives largely on an individual basis, relatively invisible from public view. And the widespread resistance to paternity leave suggests that companies are even less sympathetic to their male employees' work-family problems. So it is likely that the accommodations that most employed fathers create to balance their work and family responsibilities will, to an even greater degree, be largely private and thereby socially unrecognized and unsupported.

The Author

JOSEPH H. PLECK has studied the changing roles of men and women for more than 25 years. He earned a Ph.D. in clinical psychology from Harvard University in 1973 and is now professor of human development and family studies at the University of Illinois. In 1997 he received the Distinguished Contribution to Family Psychology Award from the American Psychological Association. He serves on the editorial boards of *Sex Roles: A Journal of Research*, the *Journal of Gender, Cultural Diversity and Health*, and *Men and Masculinities*; he is also an associated editor of the *Journal of Men's Studies*.

Further Reading

BETWEEN FATHER AND CHILD: HOW TO BECOME THE KIND OF FATHER YOU WANT TO BE. Ronald Levant and John Kelly. Penguin Books, 1991.

FATHERHOOD: CONTEMPORARY THEORY, RESEARCH, AND SOCIAL POLICY. Edited by William Marsiglio. Sage Publications (Thousand Oaks, Calif.), 1995.

THE ROLE OF THE FATHER IN CHILD DEVELOPMENT. Third edition. Edited by Michael E. Lamb. John Wiley & Sons, 1997.

WORKING FATHERS: NEW STRATEGIES FOR BALANCING WORK AND FAMILY. James A. Levine and Todd L. Pittinsky. Harvest Books, 1998.

Should *You* Leave?

HERE THE AUTHOR OF **LISTENING** TO **PROZAC** TURNS HIS EAR TO **PEOPLE** ON THE THRESHOLD OF LEAVING A **ROMANTIC** RELATIONSHIP. BUT GIVING **ADVICE** TO SUCH FOLK, HE FINDS, ISN'T AS STRAIGHT-FORWARD AS YOU **MIGHT** THINK.

BY PETER D. KRAMER, M.D.

"How do you expect mankind to be happy in pairs when it is so miserable separately?"
—Peter De Vries

YOU ARE IN A DIFFICULT RELATIONSHIP, ONE THAT FEELS painful to stick with or to leave. You imagine there is something particular a psychiatrist can offer—perhaps the fresh perspective of a neutral observer. You want to know how your relationship looks from the outside. Is your partner impossible, or do you bring out the worst in others? Are you too tolerant, or too demanding? If you could decide which view to accept, you would know just how to behave. You have had it with the slow, self-directed process of psychotherapy; you want a frank and immediate response, an expert opinion.

I am sympathetic toward your wish for immediacy and plain talk. But often people who ask for advice in such matters are really looking for someone to blow up at when the rules indicate they should leave, but they dearly want to stay. Or perhaps you want permission. Sometimes a child can skate only when a parent is on the ice right beside; the parent becomes the child's nerve or guts, even the stiffness in the child's ankles. You may need what the child skater needs: additional self. If this is what you require of me, you will tell me what you already know you should do, and I will confirm your conclusions. But if you have a good supply of self, then the choice you are confronting must be a difficult one, or else you would have already made a decision.

I take it that you are in love, or have been, or think you might be in time. Love, not operatic passion: Those who are swept off their feet rarely ask questions. And since you go to the trouble to seek an expert opinion, you must value the investment of emotion and the crea-

tive effort you have put into your relationship. Intimacy matters to you, shared experiences, time together. And you imagine that people should and can exercise control in affairs of the heart.

To this picture I might add that you already know the conventional wisdom. Television, romance novels, late-night radio call-in shows, and self-help books all provide exposure to the tenets of psychotherapy. Characters advise one another continually: Walk away from abuse. Don't bet on actively reforming an alcoholic. Communicate. Compromise on practical matters. Hold fast to your sense of self. Take emotional crises to be opportunities for growth. Expect and accept imperfection. No one is a stranger to these commonplaces.

But you hope to be an exception. You feel different enough to ask whether the conventional bromides illuminate your special predicament. Perhaps you fear that you are inept at judging partners, so that when it is time for others to leave, you should stay, because you will do no better next time. Or you are more vulnerable than others, less able to bear transitions. You have been telling yourself as much, and you hope that a neutral observer will agree.

IRIS'S STORY

HERE IS HOW I IMAGINE WE COME TO MEET. THE BELL RINGS, and you are at my office door. "Iris," I say, not concealing my surprise. My daughter used to play on the same soccer team as your nephew, and I remember admiring your spirit while your marriage and publishing career were unraveling. You assure me that you are not here for psychotherapy. You want help with a predicament.

You have not done well with men, you say. Your large-boned and angular stature, and what they call your fierceness, scares them off. Those few who are attracted to tough women don't give support when you need it,

*HOW CAN YOU **STAY** WITH A **MAN** WHO SEES **YOU** THIS **WAY?** AND YET YOU ARE **TEMPTED** TO.*

hate any sign of vulnerability—or are outright sadists. Randall seemed the sole exception. He is a man with enough confidence to enjoy forthright women and enough awareness of his own wounds to allow for frailty.

Randall courted you vigorously, tried to sweep you off your feet. He has given you the happiest two years of your life. He is sweetly handsome, separated, en route to divorce. Having grown up in a difficult family in a neighborhood that chews up its children, he now works with wayward youth. Best of all, unlike your ex-husband, who publicly humiliated you with a younger woman, Randall loves you alone.

At least that's what you thought until two weeks ago, when you went to download your e-mail. You received an extraordinary bundle of messages, all forwarded from bunny@univ.edu. You knew who this Bunny was: a touchy-feely social worker who runs a clinic Randall consults to. She had sent you the modern equivalent of the stack of letters, tied in a ribbon, deposited on the wife's dressing table. Although there was no evidence in the e-mail that Randall had slept with Bunny, he had revealed a few of your intimate secrets—enough to make you physically sick. And in his postings, Randall kept referring to you as Prickly Pear—barbed on the outside, tender within—the same term he had once used for an ex-girlfriend. You suddenly understood his m.o.: commit to one woman, then denigrate her to another.

When you felt able to stand, you left work, stopped for a moment at a florist, and drove to Randall's condo. Once there you shoved your purchase, a small cactus, into the open lips of the disk drive on his PC. For good measure, you erased his hard drive and threw his modem in the oven and set it to self-clean. You packed your clothes and bathroom

paraphernalia. Then you pulled a jar of gravy from the fridge. You spread the contents onto Randall's favorite rug and left his dog Shatzi to do her worst.

As you drove home, you were overcome with the awareness that you love Randall as you have never loved another person. And indeed, since then Randall has done all of the right things. He's broken off contact with Bunny, plied you with flowers, called the lawyer and directed that his divorce be set in motion, resumed treatment with his therapist and invited you in for joint sessions. But you realize that you are in one of the classic bad arrangements between lovers. Ran-

HEADS **I STAY,** *TAILS* **I LEAVE . . .**

For most of human history, the question of whether to leave a long-term relationship was almost irrelevant. Marriage was seen as an unbreakable contract, and the economic perils of a solo existence made abandoning one's partner difficult, particularly for women. Throw in legal and religious restrictions against divorce and leaving simply wasn't an option. As late as 1930 famed psychiatrist Karl Menninger refused to advise women to leave their husbands—even in cases of repeated philandering or abuse.

Today, most of the social and practical impediments to leaving have fallen, but the decision to do so remains psychologically daunting. "There's no litmus test you can give a partner that determines whether you should leave, or whether this person is good partner material," notes family therapist Diane Sollee, M.S.W. So figuring out whether to leave remains a complex and intensely personal calculation incorporating issues ranging from the philosophical—How happy am I?—to the profoundly practical: Can I find somebody better?

The upshot: Nobody can give you a definitive formula for when to try to salvage a relationship and when to move on. But here are some issues to keep in mind:

THAT'S MY STORY AND I'M STICKING TO IT

When pondering whether to leave, most people retrace the history of their relationship, taking a mental inventory of the good times and the bad. But there's a hidden pitfall in this technique, notes University of Minnesota psychologist William J. Doherty, Ph.D., author of *Soul Searching: Why Psychotherapy Must Promote Moral Responsibility*. The problem: Our memories tend to be biased by how we're feeling at the moment. So when people are feeling pessimistic about their relationship, says Doherty, they "unconsciously put a negative spin on everything—how they met, why they got married." And they're more likely to overlook happier times.

Let's say you and your spouse eloped right after high school. If you're feeling hopeless about the relationship at the moment, you're especially likely to describe the elopement as the act of two impulsive, foolish kids. "But two years earlier, when you were feeling better about the relationship, you would have told the story in a whole different way," says Doherty. Instead of viewing your teenage marriage as impulsive, you might have fondly remembered it as an exceedingly romantic act by two people passionately in love.

This memory bias colors the relationship history you present to friends, family, counselors, and other confidants. So these individuals may wind up advising you to pull the plug on a relationship that isn't as bad as you've portrayed. (The same bias, of course, gives you an unrealistically rosy view of your relationship during good times.) And even if you don't consult others, your own ruminations on whether to leave will be similarly slanted. None of this means that your relationship history is irrelevant to the decision to leave—only that the evidence may not be as clear-cut as you initially think.

dall is behaving like a naughty boy who buries himself in the skirts of the mother he has injured and sobs apologies. Looking back, you see that even your tornado-like attack on his apartment was only an enactment of his basic fantasy: woman as avenger. How can you stay with a man who sees you this way?

And yet you are tempted to. That there is something flawed about Randall makes him seem more accessible, less puzzling. Now that his flaws are laid out, you feel pecu-liarly well-matched with him. After the fall, he seems more truly yours. You feel alive when you are with Randall. You still trust and admire him. Besides, you want to sustain this complex, intimate liaison you have done so much to nurture. Are you mad? Do these things ever work?

To say the obvious—that you must leave a man who has been dishonest, contemptuous, and incapable of commitment—doesn't seem to suffice. I know too little about you to answer the question you are asking, which is not whether most people should leave in these circumstances (they should) but whether you and Randall form an exception. I am taken with the odd detail that you feel more comfortable with Randall after the fall; to you, it is a relief to know that for all his kindness he is as crazy as you. I like your argument that even after the betrayal, there remains in your ledger a balance of trust in Randall's column. And since you are indicating that you have every intention of letting the relationship proceed, I feel un-motivated to throw myself in your path. You're making a bad bet, but I have seen worse bets succeed.

"To go ahead with the relationship will require all of your skills," I say. Business skills, people management skills, negotiation skills, every skill you possess. But you can risk continuing the relationship if you make that risk an occasion for your own maturation, for attaining something you can bring with you if the relationship fails, as it likely will. If you can be single-minded about what you need, and if you can let him be who he is—in that delicate combination of self-assertion and caring and disengagement, there will be hope that you will grow and that he will then grow to meet you.

WHY STAY?

AS A THERAPIST, I LEAN IN THE DIRECTION of reconciliation. I lean that way in part because of my experience that simple interventions sometimes suffice to hold together couples who seem on the verge of separation, and that those repaired relationships proceed ordinarily well. Moreover, second marriages do not seem gloriously better than first marriages, or if they do, it is

---

HOW MOTIVATED IS YOUR PARTNER?

"Assessing whether you should leave may require assessing whether you have tried to stay," notes psychiatrist Peter Kramer, M.D., What he means is that relationships take work, and that couples often abandon relationships that would be successful with a little more effort. Indeed, adds Sollee, it's ironic that couples who are expecting a baby "will take months of classes to get ready for that one hour in which the mother pushes out the baby, but they don't take the time to [get counseling] on how to keep the marriage alive."

Given that every relationship requires effort, the fact that a relationship is somewhat rocky is not in itself a sign that a couple should split. What's more important, says Peter Frankl, M.D., a psychiatrist at New York University School of Medicine, is how motivated the partners are to give each other a chance to work out viable solutions to their particular problems. This motivation, says Frankl, is the best predictor of whether a troubled relationship will succeed. "I've turned around some marriages that were on the brink of divorce," he says. But if your partner isn't motivated to put some work into the relationship, the odds of success fall—and leaving may make more sense.

ADVICE DEPENDS ON THE ADVISOR

Visit three different doctors for your sore throat and you're likely to get similar diagnoses and treatments. Ask three different therapists whether you should leave your ailing relationship, however, and the advice you get may differ dramatically. The reason: a therapist's speciality—marriage counseling, individual therapy, groups—is linked to his or her feelings about commitment.

Marriage and family therapists are, by nature, inclined to keep people together. "I would never advise a couple to divorce," says Atlanta psychiatrist Frank Pittman, M.D., who feels that telling people to end a marriage is akin to advising a parent to put a child up for adoption. "You don't do it, especially when there are kids involved." (Pittman did feel comfortable, however, advising a pair of newlyweds to break up when he learned that the wife had cheated on her husband during the honeymoon.)

On the other hand, individual therapists, whose training in treating troubled relationships may range from extensive experience to a single seminar in graduate school, are more likely to see a relationship as something that should be sacrificed if it interferes with a client's happiness. "I read a case study of a woman who stayed with the same analyst through five marriages," says Sollee. "And that analyst helped end all five marriages." Minnesota's Bill Doherty calls such cases "therapist-assisted marital suicide," noting that by repeatedly asking their clients whether they are happy, "the therapist is basically saying, 'Why do you stay?'"

Because therapists typically maintain a neutral stance with regard to what a client does—the better to appear objective—these philosophical differences on the importance of saving relationships may not be immediately apparent. But they're always present, warns Doherty. The lesson for those who seek counsel from therapists: Keep in mind that the advice you get may be more of a reflection of your therapist's personal values than a scientifically valid assessment of the "correct" thing to do.—P.D.

I **LIKE** *YOUR* **ARGUMENT** *THAT EVEN* **AFTER** *THE* **BETRAYAL** *THERE REMAINS A BALANCE OF* **TRUST.**

often because the second marriage benefits from efforts or compromises that might as readily have been applied to the first.

People tend to choose partners who operate at an emotional level similar to their own. To stay with a flawed relationship thus may entail tacit acknowledgment of your own limitations. And coming to grips with your limitations, and those of your relationships, is an important form of personal development. If you are loyal and slow to say goodbye, I might say leave, because leaving would represent facing your fears. But if your tendency is to cut and run, I lean towards staying and altering perspective. If you leave, will you find greater satisfaction elsewhere? Most relationships, after all, are practice. That's why, in a culture that allows dating, people have more relationships than they have marriages. Not only because they're finding the right person, but because they're learning how to do it.

SANDY AND MARK

PERHAPS YOU HAVE LITTLE IN COMMON WITH IRIS. YOUR STORY is simpler, quieter. As you enter my office, I am aware of a critical sensibility. You approve, I think, of the framed photographs of the walls, though you squint at one and judge it prosaic.

In your soft voice, you say that you have known almost from the start that there were problems in your marriage. Now that you have the chance, you are determined to get a little help about whether to stay on.

You and Mark married just after high school and then moved from your hometown. It has always been Mark-and-Sandy: People run the words together, like warm and sunny or, lately, cool and cloudy. You shared fine taste, an appreciation of the arts and of the art in daily life. Having seen enough fighting and drinking in your own families as you grew up, you promised implicitly to protect each other from any more indignities.

Then you panicked when Mark leaned on you in his childish way. He resented the stress of competition on the job and the pressures associated with being a bread-winner, and would come home feeling unappreciated. In childhood, you had the responsibility for the care of your brothers, and you never felt you could do right by them. You lacked confidence that you could make another person feel better. So merely to think of Mark heading home worn out and hungry for affection made your day seem black. When he walked through the door and saw you

already drained, he would shrink away. You felt his withdrawal as another sign of your inability to give or elicit nurturance. You became hopeless and more needy than Mark could bear. I hope you will not feel diminished when I say yours has been a marriage between melancholics.

But you maintained the marriage in its early years by carrying on affairs with married men. To you, an adoring man is solace from the isolation Mark imposes. Although you felt dirty, in your bluest states you were buoyed by these dalliances. You felt that you had no choice, that life is too bleak without at least the pretense of admiration. As a result of these affairs, you were more emotionally available for Mark, and your support allowed Mark to do better at the office. And what surprised you through the course of these events is how much tenderness you continued to feel for Mark. He tries hard in a world he is not made for, and sometimes he succeeds.

Over the past couple of years, your odd jobs—making up gift packages in pharmacies and florist shops, designing window displays for boutiques—have turned into a career. Your work in a fabric shop led to requests that you consult on interior design. A former lover has begun small-scale commercial production of your decorated mirrors, boxes, and picture frames. This good luck has allowed you to feel secure month in, month out. There are no more lovers, though with your patron the door is open, especially now that his own marriage is headed for divorce.

For a while Mark seemed to disapprove of your commercial success, as if you had gone over to the enemy, the movers and shakers, in a way that were disloyal to your joint view of the world. Now Mark has told you he has a platonic girlfriend. He needed you to know of his near-peccadillo, because for him it throws the marriage into question. You know he does not really want a lover. He is asking for reassurance that you, despite your success, still want him. Lately, however, you have found yourself thinking that here is an opportune moment for you to leave.

I recognize this crisis—change in a member of a depressive couple. Marriages between emotionally sensitive people can be models of the best human beings are capable of. But the result can also be a stifling sort of peas-in-a-pod marriage such as yours, one made overtly stable by an implicit promise never to change, never to move toward the wider world. Although the stalemate

IF YOU ARE **LOYAL,** *I MIGHT SAY* **LEAVE,** *BECAUSE LEAVING* **REPRESENTS** *FACING YOUR* **FEARS.**

is often broken when a patient is "transformed" by medication, career success such as yours can have this function too. Now you are over your depression, and the question is whether you should stay.

This is a moment for remarriage or separation. Since you care so deeply for Mark and admire so many of his qualities, and since you have come so far with him, you may choose to let the marriage play itself out further. You could suggest to Mark that he seek treatment for depression, although what seems to be at issue is personality style rather than illness. If you stay put, you may next find Mark turning angry, which I would consider progress. Or you may find instead that he will move forward to join you, and you will be able to judge, after these many years together, whether a period of real marriage is possible.

Are you thinking of divorce and marriage to your patron entrepreneur? How could you not be? This is a frequent response to recovery from prolonged depression—entry into a highly "normal" marriage, one focused on pleasure rather than ideals, on the future rather than the past. This solution has its dangers. The patron may be someone who enjoys and demands dependency in a wife, while you take pride in your hard-earned autonomy, your quiet toughness and firm balance. And yet I have seen such relationships work. Perhaps your entrepreneur will treasure you and challenge you and rejoice with you in the bounty of life, and you will hold on to what is precious in your sadness without having sadness possess you.

The only apt advice is to say that you will need to fiddle with this problem as you have with others, quietly, from around the edges, at your own pace. You will need to be an artisan, here as elsewhere, and to rely on your unerring sense of the fitting. You seem someone who would prefer to find just the right time for leaving and to craft your exit in a way that pleases you—if you are to leave at all.

MATTER OF TRUST

HOW DOES A PERSON WHOSE FAITH IN HIS OR HER PARTNER HAS been breached decide whether to stay? Hungarian psychiatrist Ivan Boszormenyi-Nagy refers to what he calls "residual trust." Loss of trustworthiness, he observes, is rarely absolute. Each relationship contains an invisible slate or ledger of give and take, what I might call a "trust fund." Partners deposit trustworthy acts, earn merited entitlement, and owe due obligations. Strong balance sheets make stable marriages. But if one partner continually overdraws the account, the other will feel justified in retaliating or leaving—though other factors, such as good sex, excessive guilt, or power arrangements, might complicate the decision.

An additional complication is that people are poor bookkeepers. They attribute credits and debts to the wrong accounts. In Nagy's view, ethical relations are in-

tergenerational. A child is due reliable care by his parents and is owed restitution if he doesn't get it, but once he reaches adulthood there is no one appropriate from whom to seek it. So the deprived child will enter adulthood with a destructive sense of entitlement. In marriage, this creates further injustice, since it is not the spouse who created the imbalance in the books. Perhaps you demand excessive loyalty because you have been treated disloyally elsewhere, just as your wife demands support that she has been denied elsewhere. If you treat the other unjustly, however, the relationship will be further depleted of resources of trust.

NORA

What made you ask for a consultation is something that will sound trivial. Philip gave you a public tongue-lashing at a recent party, and the hostess took you aside. Nora, she said, if you will not stay here with me tonight and tell Philip goodbye, you must at least promise that you will see someone else.

You want me to understand how decent Philip can be. Often you wonder what's wrong with you that you cannot bring that Philip back. What you loved was his self-assurance, his calm in the face of turmoil. Back then, you were attractive, and—you wonder whether I can believe this—accustomed to avid responses from men. In Philip, you met a man who made you want to earn his

"The only distinctive thing I know about ending enslavement in a relationship is that sometimes you get a gift—an act by your partner that crystalizes what you should do."

admiration. You gladly merged your consulting business into his, and moved from a business relationship to courtship.

When you discovered you were pregnant by Philip, you were secretly thrilled. You had believed you were infertile, because in years of unprotected sex with an old boyfriend, you had never conceived. But Philip turned icy cold—how could you do this to him? He would marry you, but on the condition that you abort the pregnancy. You aborted, which was more horrible for you than Philip could know, or that you would let him know, since you wanted to enter the marriage as the sort of woman he demanded, a happy one. What was funny was that you loved him all the more, loved his little boy squeamishness about intimacy.

After the marriage you started falling apart, failing him in small but important ways. At the office, you might fail to pass on a phone message, or in the middle of a meeting make a comment that infuriated him. He began to demand—with every reason—that you stay in the office and do grunt work.

When Philip was finally ready to have children, you failed to give him any. There has been unspoken resentment about that, you suspect. And now you sometimes wonder if he is turning his attention elsewhere. You came across a document that seems to show he co-owns a condominium with a woman. He yells at you so much over little things, you can't image what would happen if you asked him about the condo.

What put you up to asking for advice was a word in Philip's diatribe at the party—he called you a dried-up prune. You know what he meant: infertile. That one epithet seemed to step over the line. You realized, in a confused moment, that some of what has kept you in the marriage is loyalty to your lost pregnancy—your lost unborn child. After what you sacrificed, the marriage *has* to work. You feel foolish asking whether you should leave a man you love and who has put up with so much from you.

If I thought I could get away with it, if you were not too skittish, I would advise you to leave. But I am afraid that if I give you advice in full measure you will bolt. My first goal is not to lose you; my second is to make you less isolated within your fearful perspective. The only rhetoric at my service is the look on my face when you say "prune." Not horror or astonishment, just your expression plus a little extra. I want to underline what you have said.

Sometimes I think of enslavement in relationships as a hypnotic phenomenon: The enslavers induce a substitution of their will for the subject's. They are vampires, gaining strength as their victim wastes away; the commanding and decisive executive by day flourishes on the blood of the wife he drains by night. Lesser degrees of possession are the root of many ordinary relationship troubles. The demanding impose expectations, while the loyal are exploited for their loyalty.

After 20-odd years in the field, the only distinctive thing I know about ending enslavement is that sometimes you get a gift—an act by your partner that crystalizes what you should do—and if you receive such a gift you had better recognize and accept it. Usually I hear about these gifts in retrospect. A woman who is now doing well tells me about an incredible act of overstepping by her former possessor: He knocked up a single mother with four kids and wanted to move them in. Or the act may seem indistinguishable from the person's habitual behavior, as with Philip's shockingly unreasonable diatribe at the party.

I take your response to the gift Philip offers as an important part of our transaction because it is your own. If you have filled your life with authoritative others who tell you what to do, I will not want to validate that behavior. In highlighting this gift, I hope to instead validate what remains of your perspective. I offer the self-help bromide "listen to your own voice," with this difference: I point to one of your voices and say this one, and not the others. The voice that says: No human being should be asked to give what that man demands nor accept what he imposes.

MY MISGIVINGS ABOUT GIVING ADVICE

Despite the psych jockeys on the radio, despite the widespread acceptance under managed care of therapies that entail little more than the quick proffering of an opinion, despite my own enduring curiosity about advice, I find the prospect of advising slightly illicit. I am suspicious of books of advice: When I read a self-help precept, I think that the opposite advice might be equally apt, for someone. The advice that I have valued in my own life has never turned on fixed maxims or canned metaphors. More crucially, lists of precepts don't work like targeted advice because lists contain inherently constraining messages. They seem to say that complex matters are knowable, that a given process leads to

> *"I am suspicious of advice books: When I read a self-help precept, I think that the opposite advice might be equally apt. The advice I have valued has never turned on fixed maxims."*

foreseeable results. It implies a thin and predictable world, whereas the sort of advice that has mattered to me bespeaks a quite tentative optimism, the optimism of the quest of whose outcome is finally unknowable.

Thus, even after an extended interview, as we have had, you might remain unknown to me in important ways. This, then, is the advisor's dilemma: Like a partner in a troubled relationship, an advisor faces an other who is at once transparent and opaque. I will offer a perspective, you will add it to those you already entertain, and you will stay, or leave, or remain in limbo.

DIVORCE REFORM
NEW DIRECTIONS

DAVID M. WAGNER

There is a new issue coming down the pike in the state legislatures. It is not yet a speeding train, but its headlights are visible. It is being talked about not only in the house publications of the pro-family movement but also in mainstream magazines and in books from prestigious publishers. One state has already passed a law embodying this emerging issue; others have at least held hearings on it.

The issue is: bringing down our out-of-control divorce rate by repealing, or at least modifying, no-fault divorce.

No-fault divorce—which swept through the states from the late 1960s through the early '80s, pushed by elites with virtually no public airing of the issues—is a proven failure, albeit one that is deeply entrenched in state law and in the American psyche. Today the no-fault revolution is over, and the counter-revolution is beginning, offering more security to spouses and children and restoring to marrying couples the precious freedom that the no-fault revolution took away: the freedom to make a binding commitment.

Marriages, like business partnerships, don't work out automatically. They require heavy investments, by both parties, of time, effort, and otherwise permissible enjoyments forgone. No one should take offense at the comparison between marriage and a business partnership: Of course, marriage is much more than a business partnership; the problem with modern no-fault law is that it treats marriage as much less than a business partnership. To give marriage contracts the same level of enforcement that we give business contracts, though perhaps still not adequate,

would nonetheless be a considerable improvement over the status quo. That is what all the reformers whose efforts we are examining are trying to do.

DIVORCE AND FAMILY LAW

Divorce law, and family law is general, are located at the state level in our federal system. Therefore, experiments in repairing the ravages of the divorce revolution are going forward in several state legislatures. This multipronged progress allows for different experiments to be tried. Defenders of states' rights have often referred to the states as the "laboratories of democracy."

Given the ravages of the no-fault revolution, it is not surprising that at least a few state legislators are interested in repealing it outright. In the 1996–97 legislative year, two divorce reform bills were put forward in Pennsylvania. One was a straightforward repeal of no-fault—simply stripping Pennsylvania's no-fault clauses right out of the statute book, leaving fault grounds as the only avenues to divorce. This bill was inspired by one legislator's reading of a report on no-fault produced by the Pennsylvania Family Institute.

Unfortunately, the only legislator to sponsor this bill was the one who authored it.

The other bill would have retained a person's unilateral right to seek a no-fault divorce but would have given the spouse—the one not seeking the divorce, and presumably resisting it—the right to a judicial hearing before the no-fault divorce could be granted.

About ten years ago, says Phyllis Witcher, president of Protecting Marriage and an activist on behalf of this bill, "the Pennsylvania legislature eliminated the possibility that one spouse could get a hearing on fault issues, by

Mr. Wagner is a lawyer and a senior writer at Insight *magazine.*

From *Current,* February 1998, pp. 7–11. This article originally appeared in *The World & I,* January 1998, pp. 289–301. Reprinted by permission of *The World & I,* a publication of The Washington Times Corporation. © 1998.

adding a new clause specifying that no hearing was required when one spouse sought a no-fault divorce. My bill would have simply repeated that 'no hearing required' clause. Judges might still have refused to grant fault hearings, as they did before the clause was added, but that's OK—I appreciate the need for incrementalism."

This is an interesting example of a bill that would do more than it seems to do. It could actually be a powerful protector for the nonfaulty, nondivorce-seeking spouse, when faced with a spouse whose conduct during the marriage has been bad and who is now seeking a divorce. It would give a little extra leverage to the nonfaulty party. In the best case, the possibility of a hearing on fault might deter the divorce altogether. If not, then it might at least inspire the at-fault party to be more generous when it comes to division of property.

If the fault hearing is granted, the nonfaulty party's position is greatly improved. For example, the judge might reason: "I can't deny Mr. Jones the no-fault divorce he is asking for. But my gosh, I've just heard evidence of how he maltreated Mrs. Jones, dallied with floozies, bought a Porsche while telling his kids to work their way through college, and so forth. I can't deny him the divorce—but I can sure take it out of his hide when it comes to dividing up the property!" Or, "I can at least make sure he only sees the kids during solar eclipses." (Though I use male pronouns throughout, it should be noted for the record that the at-fault party could well be the wife.)

And that's not all. The badly behaving, divorce-seeking spouse would know in advance that the other spouse is entitled to the hearing and that the judge might reason as described above. That in itself would give him an incentive to refrain from the divorce. Even better, the incentives created by the hearing entitlement might inspire at-fault spouses to get their act together and cease their faulty behavior, thus saving the marriage.

That last-mentioned possibility is the real aim of this approach to reform. It provides the answer to the natural question: Why would the non-divorce-seeking spouse want to prevent a divorce from a spouse like that? The answer is that we are trying here to reform the structure of legal incentives under which marital relationships develop. As advocates of this approach argue, a system that keeps fault evidence out of the divorce process is in effect a subsidy for marriage-destroying behavior. To borrow a term from pop psychology, it makes the law an enabler of marital fault. It says to potentially malfeasant spouses: You can do anything you want, and it won't impair either your right to a divorce or your chances of a favorable economic settlement. Change that, say advocates of this bill. Make fault cost! That way, there will be less of it, and more marriages will survive.

These two bills failed to make serious legislative progress, and the Pennsylvania Family Institute is far from certain that they will be reintroduced in 1998. However, they provoked the formation of a divorce reform task force and the holding of hearings. Pennsylvania reformers have gotten their legislature's attention.

THE LOUISIANA EXPERIMENT

Meanwhile, Louisiana did something in 1997 that forces divorce reformers to take notice: It actually passed a bill.

This bill in effect creates two types of marriages: one that can be dissolved through the all-too-familiar no-fault process, and one that has somewhat tighter requirements for divorce. Couples elect one form or the other at the time they get married. This is sometimes called a two-tier or multitier approach; sometimes a gasoline analogy is used, the two types of marriage being referred to as "premium" or high-test" versus "regular." But Louisiana prefers to call its new "premium" marriage option by a nobler name: covenant marriage.

The new Louisiana statute begins with an explicit reenactment of the state's no-fault law, but this time with an important qualifying preface: "Except in the case of a covenant marriage. . . ."

The meat of the law begins under the heading "Covenant Marriage." Section A of this part of the statute is worth quoting in full:

> A. A covenant marriage is a marriage entered into by one male and one female who understand and agree that the marriage between them is a lifelong relationship. Parties to a covenant marriage have received counseling emphasizing the nature and purposes of marriage and the responsibilities thereto. Only when there has been a complete and total breach of the covenant commitment may the non-breaching party seek a declaration that the marriage is no longer legally recognized.

As enacted, the Louisiana law allows either spouse in a covenant marriage to seek a divorce on the following grounds, similar to old-time fault grounds: adultery by the other spouse (*other* here will mean the spouse not seeking the divorce); felony by, and imprisonment or execution of, the other spouse; abandonment by the other spouse for a year, with refusal to return; spousal or child abuse by the other spouse; living separate and apart for two years.

The two-year separation clause was added during the legislative process to meet the demands of reluctant legislators. The bill's sponsors regarded it as a costly concession but worthwhile to get the bill through.

Pennsylvania reformers say that their state's no-fault statute already requires two years of separation; so arguably, Pennsylvania's no-fault regime is already the equivalent of Louisiana's new "covenant" regime. But differences between a state's "premium" marriage and the same state's "regular" marriage matter more than any similarities between that state's laws and those of some other state. States have limited but meaningful sovereignty in family law. If one state offers its marrying couples a choice between a form of marriage in which divorce is easy and a form of marriage in which divorce is (somewhat) more difficult, it has contributed to the marital well-being of its own citizens. The Louisiana legislature is not responsible for Pennsylvania's divorce rate.

Clearly, however, Louisiana has not abolished divorce, even for covenant marriages. What it has done is to offer a legal harbor for a choice that many marrying couples actually want to make. One of the problems with protecting a law that allows people to make and break all important personal commitments is that it actually eliminates a right that many people want: the right to make a permanent commitment that the law will respect. If we imposed "unilateral no-fault breach of contract" on business law, allowing people to reject their commercial contracts because they no longer felt like being bound by them, commerce would collapse. No one would regard such a "right" as enhancing their freedom: On the contrary, they would realize that they had been much more free when they still had the freedom to make contracts that their commercial colleagues could take seriously. It's no different with marriage.

COVENANT

A "covenant" is essentially a contract that is also more than a contract. While there are many cases and treatises that use the terms *contract* and *covenant* interchangeably, there are also noticeable differences. For example, an enforceable restriction on the use to which land may be put is called a "covenant running with the land." It is not a mere contract: It binds subsequent purchasers of the land regardless of whether those purchasers would have arrived at the same contract with their neighbors had it been up to them.

A business contract, by contrast, is an agreement reached at arm's length between equals. The parties to it do not give of themselves as person: They interact only at the economic level. True, economic activity is an important part of human personhood, but it is far from the whole of it. We recognize this in ordinary speech. If we say about a man and a woman in a workplace that their relationship is "strictly business," we probably mean that their relationship is both nonromantic and nonsexual. Or, if we are using the phrase with bitter irony, then we are probably saying that the relationship is sexual but not romantic; either way, we are saying that they are holding something back, not giving of their full selves. Marriage, by contrast, does involve a complete, mutual self-giving. At least, it did back when our marital law was still shaped by Judeo-Christian notions about marriage.

Marriage in Louisiana now has two "tiers," and there is no reason in principle why more "tiers" may not be added, if not in Louisiana then perhaps elsewhere. The Louisiana model has paved the way for multitier marriage. It forces us to think about what it would be like if the most apt analogy ceased to be the gas station, with its "regular," "plus," and "premium," and were to become instead the ice cream store—Baskin-Robbins with its "31 flavors!"

Would this mean the complete privatization of marriage? Marriage sits at the junction of the public and private. The marital home is a zone of privacy, but marriage as a legal institution constitutes a public manifestation of will to enter into the privileges and obligations of this state in life. There is an irreducibly public aspect to the act of contracting a marriage: It is a declaration before the community, and the community is a stakeholder, even if it is not the primary one.

One possible criticism of any multitiered approach is that it undervalues the public aspect of the marital declaration. Traditionally, a marrying couple said in effect to the community: We want to enter into what you recognize as marriage. Allowing couples to choose their own marital law regime moves toward a state in which they will say: We want to enter into only what we call marriage.

One cartoon generated during the debate in Louisiana illustrates the problem of privatized marital law. In it, a pastor about to perform a wedding ceremony asks the bride and groom to consult the "menu" of marriage options. A printed placard carries a whole range of them, from lifelong commitment to drunken fling.

PROBLEMS OF COVENANT MARRIAGE

Unfortunately, the flip side of extending a legal option to those who believe marriage is a lifelong, binding relationship between a man and a woman, as Louisiana has now done, is that other constituencies may become interested in getting a slice of the pie. A legal system that recognizes both "standard marriage" and "covenant marriage," with no basis in principle for preferring one over the other, may likewise have no basis in principle for refusing to create such categories as "trial marriage," "plural marriage," or "same-sex marriage." The rationale for each one would be the same as for covenant marriage: Make it available for those who want it.

Another aspect of the Louisiana law with which some divorce reform advocates are not entirely comfortable is its counseling requirement. As we have seen, applicants for a covenant marriage must show the they have received "couseling emphasizing the nature and purposes of marriage and the responsibilities thereto." Furthermore, for couples married under covenant marriage, counseling is also required as a precondition for a decree of legal separation, a first step toward divorce.

This raises the question of what kind of counseling will be considered legally adequate. At one extreme, the state could be so narrow in its definitions and directive in its approach that it would encroach on the professional freedom of counselors, and also on constitutionally protected religious freedom in the case of clergy and religiously based counselors. The new Louisiana statute goes to the other extreme by allowing any counseling that "emphasiz[es] the nature and purposes of marriage and the responsibilities thereto" for purposes of premarital counseling, and any counseling at all for purposes of fulfilling the counseling requirement prior to obtaining a separation decree. This approach raises the possibility that counseling quite adverse to the state's goal of protecting marriage could be received in fulfillment of a state's legal requirement.

Beyond the difficulties of monitoring the content of counseling without being too directive, counseling requirements of all sorts strike some observers as an unnecessary strengthening of government's increasingly therapeutic role in American life. Counseling is already being offered as a sort of cure-all for all kinds of social ills, as though the human tendency to commit evil were the result of a deficit of good advice.

CHILDREN

Still another problem sometimes comes up in the discussion of multitiered marriage law (albeit not in the case of the Louisiana act). Some would-be divorce reformers have proposed that the upper tier—with decreased access to divorce—would be defined by the presence of children in the marriage. This proposal draws its strength from the fact that when a couple has children, those children are obvious stakeholders in the marriage who would probably be hurt by the divorce. Many from the liberal side of the asile, who are reluctant to endorse preservation of marriage as a social goal in its own right, are willing to do so when their "child-saver" instinct has been activated.

The problem with this approach is that it turns the having of children into the real solemnization of the marriage, and that is very problematic, especially for married couples who suffer the grief of involuntary childlessness.

You can break off a dating relationship with no legal formalities at all. To break off an engagement, you may have to soothe family members and friends, and perhaps return some presents, but you still don't have to go to a judge. Under no-fault, you can break off a marriage by going through some legal proceedings that, while tiresome, nonetheless do not require you to give any reason beyond no longer wishing to be married to your spouse. Under some reform proposals, the bond takes on a permanent or quasi-permanent character only when the first child comes along. Turning "standard" marriages into covenant marriages when the couple has children, but only then, would turn the having of children into the fourth step of a chain that runs from dating to engagement to marriage to marriage plus children.

The bad effects of this would be seen, not in the couples that have children, but in the couples who don't. The law would be telling them that they are somehow "less married" than their procreating peers. Without downplaying the personal satisfaction and the social utility of child-bearing, and without endorsing childlessness as a choice (a choice sometimes made for selfish reasons, or for reasons that mask selfishness under a gloss of "responsibility"), couples who happen to be childless are nonetheless entitled to equal respect for their marriages.

Childlessness is often an unchosen state, and married couples involuntarily afflicted with it often make great contributions to society through their charitable and cultural works, by helping to "parent" their nieces and nephews and their friends' children, by serving as foster parents, and through the witness of fidelity and hope that they give to their friends, family, and neighbors. It is needlessly cruel to tell them that society values their marriages less than others. Doing so could even marginally increase the divorce rate among such couples, depriving many spouses of the lifetime companionship on which they should be able to depend, and depriving society of the benefits that married couples with more time and resources on their hands can offer.

Society's interest in strengthening the institution of marriage is not advanced by anything that would diminish the importance of what takes place at the wedding ceremony.

PRIVATIZATION OF MARRIAGE LAW?

Undoubtedly, the offering of more legal options increases private discretion. But as long as the list of options is relatively short—and, more importantly, as long as all the options have a legal definition in the codebook—it seems premature at best to say that the field in question has been privatized.

True privatization of marriage law would occur if marriage law were abolished alto-gether, leaving churches and private parties to develop any kind of informal marital law they might like but with no support from the state. This has been proposed by radical feminist theorists such as Martha Albertson Fineman of the Columbia University Law School. Underneath a libertarian gloss, the goal of such proposals is to abolish marriage.

But a multiplicity of legally recognized forms of marriage stops far short of this. Theoretically, as long as all the marital options have been defined in the public law, marital law has not been privatized. But one would have to concede that marriage law had been privatized in effect, if not in theory, if the law were to offer a large number of options covering a wide range of degrees of commitment, as in the cartoon referred to earlier. But Louisiana has not merely added a tier to its marriage law: It has added *this* tier, namely, covenant marriage. More tiers could theoretically be added, but the introduction of each new one would raise particular issues that would then be debated on their merits.

Advocates of "same-sex" marriage" did not get their idea from the Louisiana covenent marriage movement. To the extent that covenant marriage advocates rested their case on pure choice, arguing that their bill merely facilitates the choices of some Louisianans, they may have to face later on the argument that other Louisianans want to make other choices. But they are free to reply that not all choices are equal. Not all human choices are good just because they are choices. That's why we have criminal laws.

Proposals for further expansion of marital options can and will be debated on their individual merits. Adding covenant marriage to the code did not predecide any of these debates.

WILL IT WORK?

The debate over the merits of Louisiana's two-tier/covenant marriage law is dominated by one intransigent fact: The bill passed. The reforms proposed in Pennsylvania might have done much more good, but they have yet to get out of the legislative starting gate. Could Louisiana's solution perhaps be an example of what computer programmers twenty years ago used to call a "cluge," meaning a quasi-solution that eliminates the symptoms of a problem while leaving the underlying problem unsolved?

Under its new law, Louisiana continues to say that marriage with a no-fault divorce option is a perfectly fine form of marriage. Furthermore, because its political appeal is based on the concept of choice, it arguably endorses the notion that choice is everything, and personal and societal expectations nothing, where marriage law is concerned. Thus, it leaves some of the fundamental problems of the divorce problem unsolved. Does it at least remedy the effects of the problem?

To be considered effective, a reform proposal first has to get enacted, and then, once it is part of the law, it has to contribute to the fading of the divorce culture and the restoration or creation of a marriage culture. That the Louisiana proposal passes the first test is simply a matter of record. Will it pass the second?

Backers expect that covenant marriage will prove more popular than "regular" marriage with new couples. The promises contained in the covenant option may be more in line with what most young people getting married really want. And anyway, say backers, what kind of suitor is going to say, "Will you be my wife, with a no-fault divorce option?"

If covenant marriages prove popular, and show a significantly lower divorce rate, then the divorce culture itself will lose popularity and the way may open up for more extensive reforms later on. Even if this does not happen, a lower divorce rate is a worthy goal in itself.

Nonetheless, the divorce reform community should not put all its eggs in that basket. Because a reform such as Louisiana's tends to excite less opposition and to be more politically sellable than other approaches, divorce reformers may be tempted to make it the flagship proposal on their movement, or even its only proposal. This might cause the movement to fall short of its goal, which is to get rid of the family-destroying divorce culture and its prime legal tool, unilateral no-fault divorce. Louisiana's approach is an excellent way to allow couples to contract away from the no-fault regime, and to showcase a better view of marriage. But the movement will probably find it wise to keep other legislative options on the table as well.

is divorce too easy?

By Benedict Carey

We have stopped taking marriage seriously, say the experts and women are paying the price. That's why a surprising coalition of conservatives and feminists want to make breaking up harder to do.

HE MUST HAVE BEEN RELIEVED to get out of the house and into the open. He'd tried to be casual, waiting until breakfast was over, when the kids were preparing for school, waiting until his wife, almost ready for work herself, came to the door to see him off. What was it he had said? "We're getting a divorce. Give me a call later." The basics, anyway. Then he was gone.

"It was an announcement, not a conversation," Susan Blumstein, now remarried, says of the day her first husband left, in 1990. "We talked that day, and then that same week we went to see his brother the lawyer, who had already prepared papers. It was a done deal."

From *Health*, September 1999, pp. 122-124, 138-141. © 1999 by Time Health Media Inc. Reprinted by permission.

Susan had assumed all along that their marriage was the done deal–an assumption, she now concedes, that may have blinded her to her husband's discontent. After 18 years of partnership, after raising two children to adolescence, after all the diapers and dishes and damp dental floss, one does indulge a few simple faiths. "You don't just *think* of yourself as a married person," she says, "you *are* a married person. It's part of what you are, everything you do." But the family's life together vaporized in less time than it takes to put out the recycling bins, and there was nothing she could do about it.

She had no idea what might be next, no notion of what slights the world reserves for a divorced, middle-aged mother of two. She had to break the news to everyone: her friends, her coworkers, her boss. She lost her place in her social group. Many mornings she woke up afraid, profoundly unsure of who she was. "I have heard divorce described as a kind of death," Blumstein says. "That sounds right to me."

She kept the Birmingham, Alabama, house and got custody of their two children, a girl, then age 17, and a boy, 11. She dropped several rungs on the economic ladder. (Divorce on average leaves ex-wives 20 to 30 percent poorer than ex-husbands, mainly because child support doesn't cover all of a child's living expenses.) Once comfortable, the family was suddenly strapped. And she had scant expectation of starting a new relationship; divorced mothers who retain custody don't get bachelor pads and long nights out in the bargain.

It would have come as no surprise to Susan to hear that, compared to married people, divorced individuals are three times as prone to depression, twice as likely to drink heavily, and three times more liable to commit suicide. She might have been too overwhelmed to care that they're also at higher risk of developing cancer or heart disease. "We have been studying this subject for a long time now," says Linda Waite, a University of Chicago sociologist whose book, *The Case for Marriage,* is due out next year. "Being married changes people's behavior in ways that make them better off."

Susan did gain one thing from her divorce: a set of previously undreamed-of anxieties about her children's future. The kids were suddenly subdued, spending more time at friends' houses. "They just didn't want to be here," she says. But they were old enough, fortunately, to understand what was happening; kids under the age of ten don't fare as well. Sociologists have found that children who grow up in split families are twice as likely to eventually divorce, twice as likely to drop out of school earlier, and much slower to support themselves.

Americans sometimes toast their own divorces, but few would celebrate their country's distinction as the world's divorce leader. Between 40 and 50 percent of first-

"I have heard divorce described as a kind of death," says Susan Blumstein. "That sounds right to me."

time marriages break up in the United States. Perhaps a third of divorces end poisonous unions to the benefit of everyone involved, say researchers. In the other two-thirds, the vital security of family life is evident only after it has been irrevocably lost. Women in particular pay the price, financially and emotionally.

For decades now, legislators, religious leaders, and social reformers have debated how to lower the divorce rate. It is a very tall order. No policy can re-create the society of the 1950s that supported traditional households. No one is going to abolish the economic sovereignty and independence women have earned in the past few decades, which has given them the freedom to leave an unbearable marriage. And no advertising campaign can convince a nation of divorced people to seriously stigmatize divorce.

But legislators can change laws, and they are beginning to do just that. In August 1997 the state of Louisiana started allowing people to choose a marriage option more binding than the standard no-fault contracts that have governed marriage and divorce in most states since the 1970s. Called covenant marriage, the new statute is a favorite among religious conservatives. What's surprising is that some feminists and many progressives have allowed themselves to be counted among the faithful–especially those who, like Waite, have studied the consequences of divorce for women.

Diane Sollee is founder and director of the Coalition for Marriage, Family, and Couples Education, a group of professional counselors, researchers, educators, and policy-makers. "No-fault laws were originally meant to give people an easy way out of a bad marriage," she says, "but we've been using the statutes to make a quick exit from any marriage."

Covenant marriage is sometimes called "I do, and I really mean it" marriage. It differs from the conventional contract in two important ways. First, it requires that couples receive professional marital counseling–before

the wedding and, if it comes to it, prior to filing for divorce. Second, the law prohibits a mutually agreed-upon, nofault split until husband and wife have lived apart for two years. Currently, in most states, the waiting period for a divorce can range from six to 18 months and can be waived altogether. The only way to dissolve a covenant marriage in less than two years is by going to court and proving that your spouse committed adultery, a felony, or physical or sexual abuse, or has moved out for a year and won't return.

The agreement gives leverage to spouses who want to preserve their marriage, says the statute's composer, Katherine Spaht, a law professor at Louisiana State University in Baton Rouge. "What we have now amounts to legalized abandonment," she says. "This law says, 'You leave me, I set the terms.'"

Spaht's zeal derives from what she has witnessed among Louisiana's modern professional class of lawyers, doctors, and academics. "I was seeing friends of mine, women in their forties and fifties, being left behind when their husbands decided they were tired of them. A man I know, a surgeon, just left his wife of 23 years for a younger woman. He was just up and gone. I believe that is simply not right. It shouldn't be that easy," she says. "Many of these women chose to raise their children. Even if they kept working, they made significant sacrifices to put their families first. What's a woman supposed to think when half of all marriages fail and here's a man proposing to her, asking her to give up a career? It's crazy.'

In 1996 Spaht met a state representative named Tony Perkins who shared her view. Together they drew up the covenant bill, which passed by a vote of 99 to 1. "We had liberal Democrats with us from very early on," says Perkins, a Republican. "Here was a bill that commits people to at least try to make their marriages work, and it's voluntary. It was hard to vote against."

NOT LONG AGO, voting against marriage counseling would have been easy. New York State had laws on the books in the 1960s and early 1970s that required couples to get therapy, yet the effect on the divorce rate was negligible. If anything rates increased, helping to expose marriage counseling for what it then was: a profession as starved for answers and direction as its clients.

"The professional stance of the American Association for Marriage and Family Therapy was neutrality," says Sollee, a past associate director. "That meant we were neither pro-marriage nor pro-divorce. We thought we should be working for what was best for each spouse. Often the so-called marriage therapist would be advising couples to divorce."

Nine years ago when Susan met Chris Blumstein, the man who would become her second husband, one of the things they talked about, besides the surreal suddenness of being abandoned (Chris had been, too), was the absence of effective counseling. Susan doubts it would have saved her first marriage, but she still feels cheated that they couldn't at least have given it a chance.

Chris and his first wife *did* seek advice—in vain. "We went to a professional counselor who said, 'Come back with a list of what you want most out of marriage.' Well, I came back with a list of 26 things, and she just had one: 'I want him to spend more time with the kids.' She was right. But our problems went deeper than that, and we refused to deal with them. So did our counselor. What kind of counseling is that?"

It's the traditional kind, Sollee says, and it's on the way out, thanks to groundbreaking marriage research done in the 1980s. Psychologists interested in relationship dynamics began using videotape to observe how couples spar over the small, I-thought-you-were-going-to-pack-that nuisances that often escalate into scalding arguments. The scientists also started using blood pressure monitors, stress hormone tests, and urinalysis to provide a record of physiological stress during these spats.

"The new technology allowed you to see what was going on inside," says Sollee, "even if you had stoic New Englanders there holding everything in."

These experiments demonstrated something astonishing: Couples who stayed to-

> Our laws tell a story, and for 30 years now they've been telling us that committed marriage isn't important.

gether fought as frequently, and over precisely the same things, as did couples who split up. "Experiment after experiment showed this, until we couldn't avoid it," says Sollee. "We *all* have irreconcilable differences. Every couple has them. Those who have successful marriages simply have learned ways of talking about their problems. They may never solve them. But they know how to talk about them."

The importance of this discovery to the field of marriage counseling cannot be overstated. Most marriage advisers are neutral no

longer. Barring extreme circumstances, they don't put personal needs before the relationship. Most have abandoned the traditional emphasis on solving each spouse's individual problems in favor of what Sollee calls marriage education—a relationship course, in effect, that teaches skills and strategies for disarming emotional grenades.

The model is called PREP, for Prevention and Relationship Enhancement Program, developed in 1980 by clinical psychologist Howard Markman. Markman's methods are straightforward. For example, he coaches couples to discuss problems in what he calls speaker-listener technique, in which one person gripes, then the listener paraphrases the complaint, and vice versa.

In practice, this technique is not all that unnatural; it simply provides a framework for the sort of empathetic conversations most couples have had. Other tactics include taking time-outs when tempers flare, and spending an hour weekly to discuss your relationship.

In an ongoing Denver-area study, Markman found that 8 percent of couples who took his course broke up, separated, or divorced within five years. But that number rose to 16 percent of the couples in the control group. A similar trial in Germany reported that only 4 percent of a PREP group divorced after three years, compared to 24 percent of those who got no counseling. On every measure of marital stability—number of fights, amount of affection, level of trust—the

Making Divorce Work

My husband and I divorced when our son Patrick was four and our daughter Morgan was six. Patrick cried and asked for cookies, then couldn't eat them. "I told you not to do this," said Morgan.

"I know, baby," I said, tears sliding down my face. This was my first taste of that curious callousness of a mother. I would have died for them, but I would not, for their sake, go on living with a good man I no longer loved.

Jim was 21 years my senior—he had been my college English professor—and we had begun to grow apart. He once snapped off a radio I was listening to, saying he had only a finite number of hours left on earth, and did not want to spend any of them listening to rock music. I snapped it back on.

One day while sitting at a red light, I realized I was no longer in love, and hadn't been for some time. It seemed to me then reason enough to leave. It still

does. But I went home and cried, desperately afraid of what I was about to do—to him, to the kids, to myself, condemning us all to the bitterness and the pain of divorce.

Shortly after I made my decision, a comment from an acquaintance took me by surprise. "I think it's terrible when people give up like that," she said. "I can't respect that at all." Her parents had been married for 45 years, she said, through some very hard times. She respected that kind of commitment. Anything short of it was giving up.

I respected it, too; it seemed to me an immense achievement. But what my husband and I were doing also struck me as immense. We were attempting to divorce without destroying the family.

"You should know joint custody works in only 10 percent of cases," said the first lawyer I spoke to. I found another lawyer.

Jim kept the kids Sunday through Wednesday night, and they were mine the

rest of the week. By the time the divorce papers came thumping through the mail slot, several years after we had separated, Jim and I were neighbors. I had moved into the flat below his so we could raise the kids together more easily. It took civility, effort, and luck, but we made it work.

Would my kids have been happier had we stayed together? Of course. But they're doing fine. Over the years, we've developed an odd kind of extended family. The other night we had our usual Sunday dinner together: My husband of seven years, Bill, grilled steaks, Jim brought down fresh strawberries, Morgan had a tofu burger, and Patrick, now 19 and 6 foot 3, ate an entire T-bone before heading out to his summer restaurant job. Afterward, as I was getting ready to go to the movies, I heard Morgan tell a friend on the phone, "All of my parents are going out. Want to come over?"
—ADAIR LARA

couples who had taken the course were better off.

"I don't give people wedding presents anymore," says Sollee. "I give a weekend of marriage education. It's far more valuable than a table setting or a salad bowl."

The covenant statute doesn't specify any particular type of counseling; lawmakers decided against that. It is the binding promise to do *something,* however, that sells covenant marriage to people who otherwise wouldn't buy it.

Bob Downing, a Louisiana District Court judge, and his wife, Pamela, decided last year to renew their vows under the covenant license. "It was his idea," says Pamela, "and I asked myself, Why? I mean, my first vows were my vows, and this wasn't going to make them any more sacred. But I eventually decided that the counseling was a good safety valve, and I like the agreement up front to do it. If you can't agree to that, what kind of commitment do you have?"

NOT MUCH OF ONE, most married people would agree. But behind the commonsense appeal of the law, some see a dark trend: covenant marriage as a step back to the more acrimonious days of fault-based divorce. Back in the sixties, divorce laws were relaxed in the United States because they were out of step with people's behavior. Throughout this century, Americans who wanted out have found a way to make it happen–by heading off to Reno, by leaving the country, most of all by fabricating evidence of infidelity or abuse. No-fault laws made the system a more honest one.

They've also made the process more humane. "The most offensive thing to me is the suggestion that somehow no-fault divorces are easy," says Terry O'Neill, a law professor at Tulane University in New Orleans and past president of the Louisiana chapter of the National Organization for Women. "Just think of the divorced people you know. They all got divorces for reasons that were very important, very real for them. This covenant law is really all about punishment. It punishes people for wanting to get out of a marriage, even a bad marriage. As if it weren't already difficult enough to go through a divorce."

Linda Waite doesn't deny the real pain of no-fault divorce; she's been through one herself. She's nonetheless concerned by a telling statistic: Thirty years ago, just 40 percent of Americans believed ending a troubled marriage could benefit a husband or a wife. These days, 80 percent share that belief, according to the General Social Survey, a government poll of social attitudes. "This amounts to a very large and very real change in attitudes toward committed marriage," she says.

Most Americans still want to be married; surveys are clear about that. The romantic ideal is intact. It is the reality of marriage, the thing itself, that has lost its place in the public imagination. All the mundane give-and-take that is part of a normal relationship can disappoint sentimental couples, Waite says. And the ease of walking out makes the union that much more fragile.

"When people are in more binding contracts they tend to invest more in the kids, and become more emotionally dependent on each other in the best ways," Waite says. "They put their well-being in a partnership, in a trust. They become part of a larger network of people, including spouses' parents, siblings, and friends. All of this helps enormously."

Katherine Spaht puts it more simply. "I believe our laws tell a story," she says. "And for 30 years now they've been telling us that committed marriage isn't that important."

Spaht's legislation tells an imperfect story, to be sure; experience suggests that many of these Louisiana covenants will blow up for perfectly valid reasons. But the law does provide for a different narrative than the one we've been hearing for decades. It challenges couples to honor their promises and marriage counselors to do their job, and has prompted lawmakers around the country to think seriously about the benefits of marriage preparation and rehabilitation. Deeper than that, the law says that there is more to marriage than romantic love.

ON VALENTINE'S DAY LAST YEAR, dozens of churches in Louisiana held collective ceremonies in which married parishioners renewed their vows. In Baker, near Baton Rouge, the Bethany World Prayer Center had 500 couples in attendance. Another 100 convened in the venerable First Presbyterian Church downtown. "I think we were all surprised at how emotional the ceremonies were," says Russ Stevenson, senior pastor at First Presbyterian. "One fellow came up to me and said, 'Reverend that was more beautiful than the first time.'"

The ceremonies had the feel of a mass public demonstration–a March for Marriage, so to speak–and the sensation persists in the humid delta air around the city. Says Pamela Downing: "Our own kids have so many friends whose parents are divorced that I felt this was a way to let them know we are in this for keeps."

She and husband Bob joined the Valentine's Day ceremonies, affirming 18 years of marriage. Katherine and Paul Spaht (28 years) also participated, along with Russ and Sherrill Stevenson (38 years). And at the Baton Rouge Christian Center Church, after seven years together, stood Susan and Chris Blumstein, ready to make the long walk down the aisle for the last time.

Benedict Carey is a contributing editor.

Smart Plan to Save Marriages

By Aimee Howd

Gloomy divorce rates are the norm in the United States, but a program linking church and community could help more couples follow through with their wedding vows.

Pragmatic, booming America has become a cold place for romance. Today's staggering divorce statistics suggest six in 10 marriages in the United States will fail, most within the first few years.

The rate of cohabitation is up 700 percent since 1970, as a divorce-shy generation looks unsuccessfully for the way back to the stability their grandparents enjoyed but their parents left behind. More than half of all marriages in the United States are preceded by cohabitation, as couples "try to get to know each other first." Yet those who live together before marriage increase their odds of divorce by 50 percent. In fact, fewer people than ever bother to marry today and three-fifths of America's children will grow up in single-parent homes. The price of disintegrating family ties may be seen in social ills ranging from increased alcoholism to doubled school dropout rates for single-parent families to higher mortality rates for divorced men and women.

"All of this in a nation where 74 percent of marriages still occur in church," pondered syndicated *New York Times* ethics and religion columnist Mike McManus. The gloomier the figures for the institutions of marriage and family, the more desperately McManus looked for answers. In 1995, he wrote a book, *Marriage Savers: Helping Your Friends and Family Avoid Divorce,* proposing a private-sector program to tap church and community resources to strengthen existing marriages and provide "marriage insurance" for engaged couples. His ideas are catching on.

"The core reform is a simple idea," says McManus. "In every congregation there are couples with solid, vibrant marriages who could be of help to other couples but have never been asked, trained or inspired to do so." After all, according to George Gallup, 69 percent of Americans are members of a church or synagogue, and 43 percent attend services each week. If people lived the faith they professed, reasoned McManus, the United States no longer would host one of the world's highest divorce rates. Churches should encourage rigorous premarital counseling, teaching the skills necessary for a healthy marriage instead of just serving as "blessing machines." Marriage Savers engages the churches and the community, says Harriet McManus, who cochairs the small nonprofit with her husband, rendering it more effective than pro-marriage legislation. "A law can only work at the margins in helping people love each other," she says. "Churches can help couples bond."

And its broad community appeal makes Marriage Savers more than just another well-meaning church program. In February 1999, 20 local clergy made Culpeper, Va., the 100th community to hammer out a marriage preparation and enrichment document—dubbed by McManus a "community marriage policy." He explains: "Specifically, congregations across denominational lines are agreeing to require couples to undergo a rigorous four months of marriage preparation that includes taking a premarital inventory, meeting with a mentoring couple and attending classes on 'the Biblical foundations of

marriages, management of finances, conflict resolution and the influence of intergenerational family history and dynamics,' as the Culpeper clergy put it. It communicates the conviction by pastors that what God has joined together the church should hold together."

Less than 10 months had passed between the day Chris, 32, and Sarah, 25, met in their work at a local hospital and the November day they said "I do." Their church held a hush as bridesmaids in dark green gathered at the altar of Christ Lutheran Church, crimson flowers in hand. Pachelbel's Canon was played and 150 heads turned to follow Sarah's progression down the aisle toward a new life as the wife of Chris Arnold.

While many churches invest far more in helping an engaged couple prepare for the day of the wedding than for a lifetime union, Christ Lutheran's director of pastoral care and family life, the Rev. Jeffrey Meyers, had led 40 other suburban Kansas City, Kan., clergy in signing a Community Marriage Covenant and was committed to doing whatever he could to strengthen the marriages of couples who came to him.

"He told us there would be some guidelines: They request that couples promise not to live together and that they commit to chastity. And he said we would be matched up with a mentor couple," says Sarah. She and Chris admit that they hesitated a bit before discussing intimate matters with a mentor couple they never had met. But the Weisses had been trained in administering a premarital inventory called PREPARE, which gave both couples a starting point for discussion. Although the inventory showed that Chris and Sarah matched fairly closely on most issues, "there were some areas where we had been wearing rose-colored glasses," Sarah says.

Both strength and growth areas were probed. After watching marriages around them founder, they welcomed the help and motivation to work through their expectations and their plans for their family. Most importantly, says Sarah, the mentors "made us responsible to God."

Already convinced by McManus' book that building strong couples is the first step toward stronger families and communities, Meyers in 1996 had accepted McManus' challenge to pool his resources with others in his community. He began calling other pastors. By May 1997, the community agreement was signed among the city's clergy. Inquiries about their policy keep coming in from surrounding communities. At the grass-roots level, "Mike's movement is starting to take on a life of its own," Meyers says.

Citing a Harvard University Press study which claims that 70 percent of divorces occur needlessly, Meyers says a church's commitment to responsible marriage creates the opportunity to reach 40 percent of those who walk away from a marriage for no good reason. "It challenges them to stick with it for their own well-being, the well-being of their community, their church and their children."

Marriage Savers literature says divorces have plummeted 35 percent in Kansas City and its suburbs in the two years since the Community Marriage Policy was implemented. (Across the river, in Kansas City, Mo., there was no Community Marriage Policy and divorces increased during the same period.) In Modesto, Calif., the divorce rate also fell 35 percent over a decade, following the implementation of a Community Marriage Policy; in only one year there was a 7 percent decrease in Eau Claire, Wis., and a 14 percent decrease in Chattanooga, Tenn. In 18 cities with a marriage policy, Marriage

> 'Any effort to link people in marriage is praiseworthy. Marriage is not this magic thing that just happens. Couples need a level of competence going into it.'

Savers reports, there are decreasing divorce rates at 10 times the national average.

Demographer Robert Rector of the Heritage Foundation in Washington says the data are difficult to contradict. "The burden of proof lies with anyone else who would try to figure out what [else would be] going on here. There is a fire behind the smoke. This is the most optimistic and effective program that we have in the United States today."

Meyers is careful. "Who knows? Let's look at it 10 years from now and see if we can sustain those rates."

But Larry Bumpass of the University of Wisconsin's Center for Democracy tells **Insight** it is too early for family-values advocates to feel secure. He believes data from his heavily cited National Survey of Families and Households suggest that any stabilization or decrease in divorce may be attributed to increasing rates of cohabitation among the undecided. "I would be very skeptical—based on what I know—of their ability to evaluate how divorce had changed in these communities," he says of the figures cited by Marriage Savers.

But if all the statisticians in the world were laid end to end, it is pos-

sible they still wouldn't reach a conclusion. Regardless of whether the hopeful statistics pan out, say those who have seen this program in action, Marriage Savers makes sense. In February the McManuses spoke to the Wisconsin Assembly at the invitation of House Speaker Scott Jansen. On Jan. 15, Florida's newly elected governor, Jeb Bush, signed onto Tallahassee's new Community Marriage Policy along with 64 clergy, saying he hoped it would be a "model for the rest of the state."

Glenn Stanton, director of the conservative Palmetto Family Council and author of *Why Marriage Matters,* puts it this way: "Although more research is needed to document results, any effort to link people in marriage and link them well is praiseworthy. Marriage is not this magic thing that just happens. It is work. Couples need a level of competence going into it."

Stanton says that competence is most effectively taught not by marriage authorities, but at the community level. "If the couple next door has been married 40 years, they are obviously doing something right." As for the future, he is optimistic: "Generation X is the first generation of Americans coming of age under their parents' divorces. This has affected them deeply and significantly. They are not necessarily traditionalists or conservatives, but they do know what they want—family stability."

For the Arnolds, unlike many of their generation, the transition from single to married life has been relatively easy with few surprises, thanks to a continued relationship with their mentor couple. "Our vows weren't the traditional ones," says Sarah. "We added, 'Depending upon God for strength and wisdom, we pledge ourselves to the establishment of a Christian home. Together we will constantly seek God's will and honor Christ in our marriage.' It kind of wrapped up all the planning we had done. We wanted to say with all of those witnesses there that this was how our marriage was going to be."

The Children of Divorce

by Glenn T. Stanton

Nineteen seventy-four was the first year that more marriages in America were ended by divorce than by death.

This made it a watershed year, for at that point the majority of family change became something we chose to do to ourselves rather than something that happened to us.

Today, approximately 45 percent of children born to married parents are likely to see their parents divorce before they reach the age of 18.

Prior to the late 1960s, it was generally believed that a child's need for family security was greater than a parent's need for marital happiness. It was thought, therefore, that significant effort should be invested in keeping rocky marriages together "for the sake of the children."

But then a psychological revolution emerged that focused on the well-being of the individual rather than the larger social fabric. This spawned a new and influential profession of family therapists and child-welfare advocates who believed that a child's greatest need was not stability but parents happy in their relationships. This would be guaranteed, the therapists said, if parents could move freely out of bad relationships into "better," more fulfilling ones. Only then could children have the loving, nurturing parents their fragile development required.

This thinking is seen in psychologist Fritz Perls' mantra of individualism, which became the tacit wedding vow of many couples marrying in the early '70s:

> I do my thing, and you do your thing.
> I am not in this world to live up to your expectations
> And you are not in this world to live up to mine.
> You are you and I am I,
>   And if by chance we find each other, it's beautiful.
> If not, it can't be helped.

Therefore, divorce shifted from constituting a social ill to virtually being a personal good, a liberating and enriching event for parent and child. The country plunged into a new age of family formation, exhibiting near-absolute confidence that family health and child welfare would blossom.

In the intervening quarter century, social scientists have observed, collected data, and reported on the outcome of this experiment with the American family. What have the researchers found?

WALLERSTEIN'S PIONEERING WORK

One of the first scholars to undertake a long-term study of divorce's impact on children was Judith Wallerstein, a psychologist who founded the Center for the Family in Transition in Corte Madera, California. When she started her work in 1971 at the University of California at Berkeley, little was known about how people coped with the death of marriage, and she wanted to conduct a serious and thorough analysis.

The conventional wisdom at the time was that divorce was a brief crisis that soon resolved itself, leaving life better for all concerned. But very little serious work had been done in this area.

Based on this early understanding of divorce, Wallerstein sought enough grant money to observe 60 just-divorced families over a period of 12 to 18 months. She assumed the families would resolve their problems and move on with their lives. She wanted to learn the processes by which families coped with and overcame divorce.

But what she found stunned her. At the one-year mark, most of her subject families had not resolved their problems.

"Their wounds were wide open," she explained. "An unexpected number of children were on a downward course. Their symptoms were worse than before. Their behavior at school was worse. Our findings

COREL

■ *Permanent pain:* Research shows that, no matter how old the child, the impact of the parents' divorce increases rather than subsides over time.

were absolutely contradictory to our expectations."

Realizing she needed a longer observation period with her subject families, Wallerstein presented another grant proposal to extend her follow-up to five years. Those results are presented in her first book, *Surviving the Breakup: How Children and Parents Cope with Divorce,* in which she explains that while some of their children were doing better at the five-year mark, "we were deeply concerned about a large number of youngsters–well over a third of the group–who were significantly worse off than before."

Many of these children were clinically depressed, were doing poorly in school, and had difficulty with peer relationships. Some early disturbances, such as sleep, education, and behavior problems, had become persistent. Wallerstein also found that the divorce was not welcome news to the children.

"Many of the children, despite the unhappiness of their parents," she wrote, "were relatively happy and considered their situation neither better nor worse than that of other families around them. . . . The lightning that struck them was the divorce, and they had not even been aware of the existence of a storm."

A BROODING, BUILDING SADNESS

Wallerstein extended her observation of these families for five more years, and these findings are found in her highly acclaimed book *Second Chances.* The children's experiences she relates are, for the most part, very sad.

But data from her 25-year follow-up, which she presented this summer at a professional meeting, reveal the greatest cause for alarm.

As adults, these children speak with great sadness of their "lost" childhood, which vanished at the news of their parents' divorce, and their constant fear of total abandonment. The pain stemming from their parents' breakup increased rather than subsided over time.

"Unlike the adult experiment," Wallerstein explains,

the child's suffering does not reach its peak at the breakup and then level off. On the contrary. Divorce is a cumulative experience for the child. Its impact increases over time. . . . The effect of the parents' divorce is played and replayed throughout the first three decades of the children's lives.

Specifically, half the children in this group developed severe drug and alcohol problems in their early teens. Only two of the families made a serious effort to interrupt these substance-abuse problems.

Divorce's Ripple Effect

Some 45 percent of children born to married parents today are likely to see their parents divorce before they reach the age of 18. A 25-year study of the children of divorced families found that divorces often caused children:

◆ to become clinically depressed,

◆ to do poorly in school,

◆ to struggle with peer relationships.

This and other scientific studies showed that children of divorce exhibited:

◆ a surge in alcohol and drug problems,

◆ more negative self-concepts,

◆ greater conflict with parents,

◆ a lower standard of living,

◆ a greater risk of being a single parent,

◆ poorer physical health.

dren, they question Wallerstein's findings on the severity of those effects.

Wallerstein responds that she never claimed her work was broadly representational but rather was a unique, long-term observation of how one group of adults and children fared in the shadow of divorce. Rather than collecting impersonal, quantitative data on the families, she pursued a qualitative and subjective approach, sitting down and talking with them, drawing from their personal stories and experiences.

Most important, her conclusions have largely been vindicated by a significant and growing scientific literature.

THE LARGER BODY OF DATA

E. Mavis Hetherington, a psychologist from the University of Virginia, is another early pioneer in the study of divorce and its impact on adults and children. She conducted a six-year follow-up in the early 1970s on 180 families, comparing divorced *and* intact families.

Like Wallerstein, Hetherington found that young children of divorce grossly distorted fears of total abandonment, reasoning that if one parent could just leave, so could the other. They were also unrealistically optimistic about their parents reconciling and bringing the family back together.

Hetherington discovered that divorced parents monitor the activities and whereabouts of their children less than do parents who are together. Divorced parents, she found, "know less about where their children are, who they are with, and what they are doing than do mothers in two-parent households."

In fact, boys from divorced homes reported being involved in more antisocial behavior without their parents' knowledge than children in any other type of family group. Girls from broken homes are more likely to become involved in sexual activity and at a younger age than children from intact homes.

Although all of their parents had college educations and professional careers, the great majority of the children were unable to attain the same level of success their parents had. Most of the adult children expressed anxiety about romantic relationships and the prospect of marriage. They bitterly regretted the fact they had not grown up embraced by a healthy marital relationship.

One of the study subjects said, "Sometimes I think I was raised on a desert island. Love with sexual intimacy is a strange idea to me." Another lamented her predicament as follows: "I don't ever want to get divorced. So, I can't marry."

WALLERSTEIN'S CRITICS

Wallerstein's research is not without its critics. Two of the most notable are Frank Furstenberg of the University of Pennsylvania and Andrew Cherlin of Johns Hopkins University.

In their book, *Divided Families: What Happens When Parents Part,* they claim it is "highly likely" that Wallerstein's data exaggerate the prevalence of long-term problems of divorce. This exaggeration, they explain, is attributable to methodological problems in her sample selection. Her study population was relatively small, they note, and the families came to Wallerstein voluntarily for short-term therapy, indicating there were preexisting problems.

Defending herself, Wallerstein says the children were prescreened and accepted into the study only if they proved to be "developmentally on target" (normal) prior to the divorce.

But Furstenberg and Cherlin note that Wallerstein had no control group of children from intact families. They charge that this makes it impossible to attribute the children's problems solely to divorce with any scientific certainty. While the two critics do not disagree that divorce can have deleterious effects on chil-

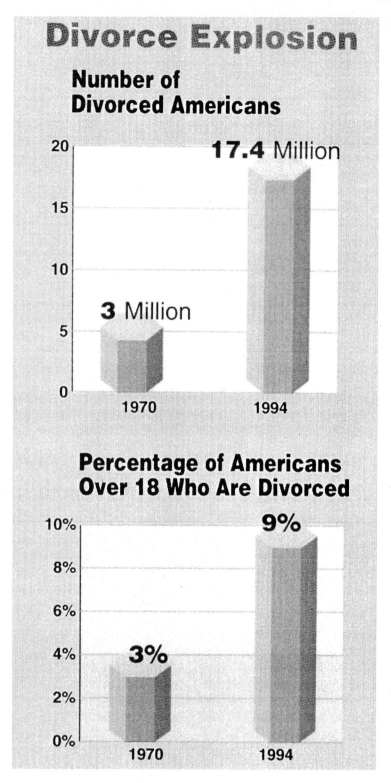

Divorce Explosion

Number of Divorced Americans

17.4 Million

3 Million

1970   1994

Percentage of Americans Over 18 Who Are Divorced

9%

3%

1970   1994

intact families reported positive relationships with both parents, compared with only 26 percent in situations of divorce.

Conversely, in intact families, only 18 percent of children reported having negative relationships with both parents, while 30 percent of kids from broken homes reported the same.

Zill, like Wallerstein, found the "effects of marital discord and family disruption were visible for 12 to 22 years later in poor relationships with parents, and [there is] an increased likelihood of dropping out of high school and receiving psychological help."

'METAANALYSES' OF PUBLISHED STUDIES

Paul Amato, a sociologist from the University of Nebraska, has done some interesting studies on how divorce affects children. Rather than observing children and analyzing their experiences as Wallerstein and Hetherington did, or looking at nationally representative statistics as Zill did, Amato examined the substantial body of published data on how divorce touches children.

In this process, called *metaanalysis*, a researcher examines a whole body of data, considering all its disagreements and inconsistencies, and attempts to come to an informed, balanced conclusion.

One of Amato's metaanalyses, looking at how divorce affects young children, draws from 92 published studies and a collective sample of more than 13,000 children. Another piece of research, involving 37 separate studies and a collective population sample of over 80,000 children, examined how divorce affects children as they enter their adult years. He required that each of the studies examined in both analyses contain a sample of children living in both broken and intact homes.

Amato found that, compared with kids in intact families, young children of divorce had lower aca-

Another leader in this field of research is Nicholas Zill. Working with data from the National Survey of Children, he discovered that the tide of divorce not only negatively affects the children of broken families but even youngsters in intact families. He found that more than half of all

elementary-school children, based on the knowledge that friends' parents have split, become afraid for the future of their family when their parents argue.

Regarding the health of parent-child relationships after divorce, Zill found that 55 percent of children in

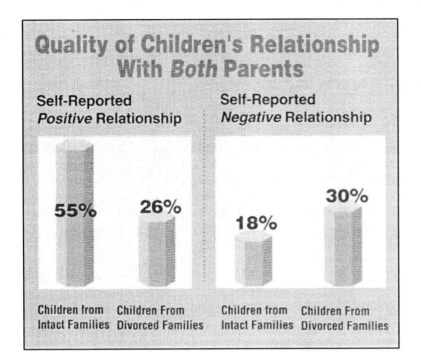

Quality of Children's Relationship With *Both* Parents

Self-Reported *Positive* Relationship

55% — Children from Intact Families

26% — Children From Divorced Families

Self-Reported *Negative* Relationship

18% — Children from Intact Families

30% — Children From Divorced Families

demic achievement, more behavioral problems, poorer psychological adjustments, more negative self-concepts, greater social difficulties, and more problematic relationships with both mothers and fathers.

This led him to conclude that "the view that children of divorce adapt readily and reveal no lasting negative consequences is simply not supported by the cumulative data in this area."

Amato's examination of how divorce affects children in their adult years confirms Wallerstein's findings: The pain does not subside but in many areas becomes more intense.

Amato found that, compared with adults from intact homes, people who grew up in broken homes had lower job status, poorer psychological well-being, a lower standard of living, less marital satisfaction, a heightened risk of divorce, a greater risk of being a single parent, and poorer physical health.

Based on his research, Amato concludes that "the long-term consequences of parental divorce for adult attainment and quality of life may prove to be more serious than the short-term emotional and social problems in children that are more frequently studied."

In general, then, although all the facts may not yet be in, the picture that is emerging of the new "divorce culture" from the available research is one of troubling grimness, the effects of which may hit America with waves of social and economic problems for generations to come.

Glenn T. Stanton is director of public policy research at Focus on the Family in Colorado Springs, Colorado. He is also the author of **Why Marriage Matters: Reasons to Believe in Marriage in Postmodern Society** *(Piñon Press, 1997).*

COREL

■ *Drag on education:* Divorce has been shown to impair children's performance in the classroom and to promote dropping out. Here youngsters wait for a school bus.

AFTER DIVORCE

BY SHARON DOYLE DRIEDGER

PARENTS ARE STRUGGLING TO PUT KIDS FIRST

Marjorie leans against the window sill in an Edmonton courthouse, rolling her eyes with impatience. "It's Saturday, for Christ's sake," the mother of three grumbles. "I'll skip out if I can." Marjorie, who refuses to give her last name, is a reluctant participant in a workshop on divorce. So is Jerry Miller: the solemn-faced father of two teenagers complains that he is "upset by this outside interference on a family matter." But since last October, when Alberta introduced Canada's first compulsory divorce education program, anyone who wants to go to court with a dispute about child support, custody or access must first attend a six-hour course called Parenting After Separation. The irreverent call it "Splitsville High." Here, learning how to negotiate with a hostile spouse is lesson number 1. "On a scale of one to 10, how would you rate your ability to communicate with your ex?" asks instructor Stephen Andrew. Hands fly up for the lowest score: about a third, it seems, can barely speak to their former partners without a fight. Only two claim a civil relationship. The rest fall into an uneasy middle ground. "Oh," says Andrew, "we've got our work cut out for us today."

Welcome to divorce 101, a modern attempt to solve an all-too-modern problem. Alberta's program teaching parents how to handle marital breakup is part of a divorce reform movement now sweeping North America. Nova Scotia, British Columbia, Ontario and several other provinces are planning to introduce similar courses. Meanwhile, divorce schools are now available in 40 American states and mandatory in three. Often, the initiative comes from judges tired of playing King Solomon to vindictive parents. Courtrooms are jammed with thousands of parents fighting over child support, custody

and access. Aggravating the problem are recent massive cuts in legal aid, forcing many parents to represent themselves. Meanwhile, a small but vocal fathers' rights movement is playing gender politics, claiming that a biased legal system is routinely leaving them with hefty support payments and little in the way of access.

Late last month, those fathers got a chance to air their controversial views in the political arena, along with grandmothers, women's groups and representatives of children's rights organizations. In the first of a series of cross-country hearings, a special joint committee of the Senate and the House of Commons explored the emotional, psychological and legal aspects of custody and access. The atmosphere in both Toronto and Montreal was poisonous: men sneered and heckled so viciously when women talked about wife battering that Conservative Senator Ermine Cohen began to cry, fearing that the hearings had become a "war zone." The committee travels to Vancouver, Calgary, Regina and Winnipeg later this month, then continues to the Atlantic provinces in May. "Everybody has a brother or sister, parent or neighbor involved in a divorce," says Liberal Senator Anne Cools, one of the most outspoken members of the committee. "It's now time to look at the plight of the children. The problems are enormous."

Divorce, once meant to liberate families from unnecessary misery, appears to have caught many children in its crossfire. In the 1970s, the traditional wisdom that children might be harmed by divorce came to be viewed as quaint—as hopelessly outdated as *Father Knows Best. The Creative Divorce,* a 1970s best-seller and *The Brady Bunch,* a popular sitcom about a sprawling blended family, signaled a shift to a positive new attitude. "If di-

vorce could make one or both parents happier, then it was likely to improve the well-being of children as well," explains American social historian Barbara Dafoe Whitehead in her controversial 1997 book, *The Divorce Culture.* Now, she says, "we are sadder but wiser."

And angrier. Anti-divorce sentiment is leading the push for tougher divorce laws. The backlash is particularly strong in the United States, where close to half of all marriages break down. Last year, Louisiana introduced "covenant" marriages, in which couples opt for a contract, making it more difficult to divorce. In Canada, the numbers are stark: before the introduction of the Divorce Act in 1968, the divorce rate sat at eight per cent. By 1987, a year after the institution of no-fault divorce, that figure had skyrocketed to 44 per cent; last year, it had fallen to 40 percent. "The levels have come down, and are relatively stable," says Robert Glossop, director of the Vanier Institute of the Family in Ottawa. "But they are stable at a historically unprecedented high rate." Last year, he notes, about 60,000 children were involved in a custody dispute.

There is no doubt that some children are better off after their parents divorce. "Many are relieved that they no longer live in abusive families, with fear and violence and squabbling," says University of Alberta sociologist Susan McDaniel. But there is growing evidence that many children suffer long-term damage. Judith Wallerstein, a renowned California psychologist, was the first to announce the bad news in the early 1980s, when she began to publish reports of a study on children from divorced families. Her findings were ominous: they warned of long-term psychological, emotional and social problems, including high rates of suicide. Experts debate how many chil-

 From *Maclean's,* April 20, 1998, pp. 39–43. © 1998 by Maclean Hunter Publishing Ltd. Reprinted by permission.

dren are affected and to what extent. "But it doesn't matter whether it's 20 percent or 50," says Rhonda Freeman, head of the Toronto divorce support service Families in Transition. "In 25 years, I have yet to meet a child who has no effects."

In the cramped waiting room of Freeman's downtown centre, children have left stark testimony to their feelings. A bulletin board, divided down the middle, offers kids a chance to express both the good and the bad things about divorce. Most important, Freeman told the children to place the board where their parents would have no way of avoiding it. On the "bad" side is scribbled: "You don't do anything with both parents together any more." As well: "I am still sad. They are still fighting." On the "good" side? "I got two cats." "They stopped fighting." In between are crayoned pictures of parents and children, some together, some apart, plus houses and a radiant sun.

Freeman, a pioneer in helping families cope, is convinced that three primary factors lead to severe psychological difficulties: parental conflict, poverty and parental abandonment. In turn, those psychological problems are increasingly linked to teen pregnancy, drug abuse and other social problems. And policy-makers are starting to add up the costs. Paul Szabo, federal MP for Mississauga South, who last year introduced legislation to make divorce counselling mandatory across Canada, has produced two booklets about the public burden of divorce. Szabo writes: "The consequences of family breakdown are greater demands on our health and social programs and more crime."

Should parents stay together for the sake of the children? A recent Statistics Canada poll shows that those under 30 are more inclined than baby boomers to believe they should. Still, few would advocate a return to the punitive pre-Divorce Act days when it took an Act of Parliament to end a marriage, and even then, only on grounds of adultery, often using pre-arranged photos taken by private eyes. "Divorce is necessary," says York University sociologist Anne-Marie Ambert. "It is a safety valve for serious cases of abuse, overt hostility and an absolutely miserable marriage." At the same time, Ambert's extensive research for her book *Ex-Spouses and New Spouses* shows that a large proportion of divorced couples come to regret their decision. "In one third of the cases, there were no serious grounds for divorce and they themselves would

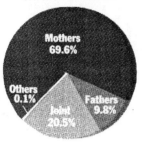

WHO GETS THE KIDS?
Custody outcomes in 1994
SOURCE: STATISTICS CANADA

Mothers 69.6%
Others 0.1%
Joint 20.5%
Fathers 9.8%

say things like, 'If I had to do it over again, I wouldn't do it.'"

Intriguingly, secular voices are joining the typically faith-based chorus against divorce. "I think people often give up too easily," says best-selling author and psychologist Peter Kramer (*Should You Leave?*). "People are more energetic and zestful and satisfied when they fulfill their obligations than when they forsake them. And our greatest obligation is probably to children." Still, Kramer concedes, "for all that this has been studied, nobody knows whether staying in a bad relationship is worse for children. I think the quality of divorce has probably improved somewhat. People have to start looking at divorce as a stable social institution, at making it more child-friendly."

In fact, while some couples end their marriages *War of the Roses*-style, others are forging responsible, civilized reconfigurations, often with two active households. "Couples part without destroying the lives of those they love," writes California sociologist Constance Ahrons in *The Good Divorce*. "These divorces don't make headlines—what they do is model the beginnings of a quiet social revolution." Such parents are helping to ease the transition by reducing the acrimony, and remaining active in their children's lives. There is a burgeoning market for storybooks about blended families, with such titles as *We're Doing It* and *Being a Family*. Since its introduction in Canada in 1987, Rainbows, an international support group for children, has attracted thousands to weekly peer-support sessions held in schools, churches and community centres across the country. There is also a growing acceptance of a new cultural norm: the multi-parent families that span two or more households.

Tommy Cloherty is part of that quiet revolution. When the Montreal production clerk's marriage ended

eight years ago, he had no intention of losing touch with his daughter and son, now 15 and 13. At the time of their breakup, he and his spouse, Mary Ann Cloherty, put aside their ill feelings. "We avoided courts," says Cloherty, who is legally separated. Now, the children alternate, in three-week stints, with each parent. Friends and acquaintances, he reports, find it unusual that he and his new partner, Diane Paquette—also divorced with two children—are on such good terms with his ex-wife. "Mary Ann has been over here for dinner," says Cloherty. "It's weird but it works. The kids are happy, so we're happy."

Fathers' rights advocates argue that such arrangements should be accepted as the norm. Department of Justice statistics show that in 1994, only 20.5 per cent of the 78,800 divorce cases where a custody decision was made resulted in a shared parenting arrangement. Of the remaining cases, only 9.8 per cent granted custody to fathers. "You cannot have an effective role when you see your children for 48 hours every second weekend," says Sean Cummings, a Halifax divorce counsellor. "In many cases, fatherhood is happening between the hours of 4:30 and 6 p.m. at McDonald's every second Friday." The National Shared Parenting Association—an organization led largely by fathers that has joined ranks with grandparents—is lobbying for a change in the Divorce Act, making shared custody automatic in every divorce, except in cases involving abuse. And activists want the courts to stop using the words "custody" and "access"— with their implications of ownership. "If I am married, I am a parent," says Cummings. "But if I get divorced, I have access. Well, access is something we have to refrigerators and cars. It should be referred to as 'parenting time.'"

✳ ✳ ✳

"I remember Daddy used to tuck me in at night and I remember I was still waiting and he didn't because that was when he first divorced," says six-year-old Kimberley Gauthier.

"Now we are living far from Daddy and we only get to see him a little bit of time," says her eight-year-old sister, Anne-Marie.

"The divorce is bad because I don't always like to go from one to the other and back again," says 11-year-old Philippe Gauthier. "I like being with both at the same time. It gets complicated."

Every second weekend, Montreal businessman Gerald Gauthier, 49, drives six hours down the 401 so he can spend time with his three children in Toronto. "They live with their mother and I have what is known as visitation rights," says Gauthier, who has been separated since 1995. Gauthier is appealing the decision that allowed his wife to move to Toronto last year. "It is very difficult to accept that a court can take your children away from you and call you just a paying visitor," says Gauthier. "I really haven't accepted that yet and I don't know if I ever will."

Many angry fathers insist that the legal system is stacked against them. "Pick a courtroom—any courtroom," says Stacy Robb, a 42-year-old former truck driver and president of D.A.D.S. Canada, one of several fathers' rights groups. "Time and again, mom is getting custody and dad is paying support." Robb and other fathers' rights advocates claim that women "routinely" make false allegations of abuse to win custody of their children. And Katherine McNeil, a Vancouver child custody consultant, backs up fathers' claims that women make false accusations to win custody. "It happens regularly," says McNeil. She tells of a recent case in which a father was jailed and lost custody of his children after he was charged with assaulting his wife. "He was a stay-at-home dad, bonded with the kids, and the mother's conduct was abhorrent," she says. "But the judge was a traditionalist who favored custody to the mother."

York's Ambert says that, while some fathers have legitimate grounds for complaint, "the simple fact is that, on average, mothers have the raw end of the deal." Mothers, especially in the first few years after divorce, often bear the financial responsibility. In Canada, non-custodial parents—mostly fathers—owe a total of $1 billion in support payments to ex-spouses. "A lot of fathers who see their children regularly and think they are good fathers are actually what you call Sunday daddies," says Ambert "They are simply having a good time with their kids, whereas mothers are responsible for school schedules, homework, doctors appointments, babysitters."

Women's advocates, and many men, are appalled at the guerrilla-like tactics of such radical fathers rights' groups as D.A.D.S. Canada and FACT, who have jammed the telephone lines of child support enforcement agencies, picketed "deadbeat moms" and "deadbeat judges," and posted vitriolic messages on the Internet. Robb defends his organization's activities: "They call us fanatics because we've got the moxie to get up and say, 'Hey, something's wrong with the system.'"

FOR THE SAKE OF THE CHILDREN?

Percentage who would stay in a marriage for their children

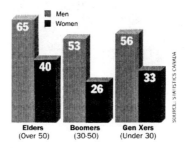

SOURCE: STATISTICS CANADA

But women's groups say that FACT and other men's groups—most of them formed within the past two years—are reacting to recent government initiatives to crack down on parents who owe child support, as well as to new federal guidelines that generally increase payments to custodial mothers. "It's a backlash," says Toronto lawyer Carole Curtis. "Men are against women's demands for better treatment after separation."

Women's advocates believe that there are good reasons why mothers are granted access in the majority of cases. "Mothers are the primary care-takers," says Vancouver lawyer Laura Spitz. "It is not biased to recognize that and give them custody." Lawyers representing women say that fathers' demands for custody are often just bargaining chips. "Mothers are so frightened of losing custody that they will give up money at the drop of a hat," says Curtis. "And fathers are willing to let them do that." Family law specialists say that many divorced women are open to co-parenting arrangements, but find that fathers drop out of children's lives. Even when parents are granted joint custody, many children eventually gravitate to the mother's home. "The majority of my clients want fathers to have more access," says Spitz, "and can't get them interested."

✳ ✳ ✳

Mothers have rights. Fathers have rights. But what's best for the children? "The whole debate should come back to a child focus," says Freeman, "to what a child needs." Experts say it would be a mistake to legally impose shared parenting on every divorced family. "Growing up is much bigger than being with your daddy or your mommy," says Wallerstein. "A lot of it takes place on the playgrounds, with friends, listening to music by yourself."

Nor can every divorced couple manage to reach the post-divorce ideal of shared parenting. "It requires phenomenal co-operation and a certain level of income," Curtis observes. "To have two houses, or even two apartments, is very expensive."

Not all divorced parents have the level of trust, respect and ability to communicate required for shared parenting to work. "You have to value each other and respect each other," says Wallerstein. "You have to be able to say, 'Jimmy is sick today,' without the other parent saying, 'I've heard that excuse before.'" Shared parenting, she points out, means a closer emotional proximity. "You have to have parents who can stand living close without going to pieces when they learn every detail of the other's life. The child is going to come back and say, 'Oh, Daddy has a new girlfriend.' What are you going to do? Muzzle the child?"

At the same time, the current legal presumption that the primary care-taker should win custody may not adequately recognize the critical role of both mothers and fathers. "It is sensible to maintain a collaborative situation where both parents are available to the child psychologically, financially and socially," says Adam Horvath, a professor of psychology at Simon Fraser University in Burnaby, B. C. Edward Kruk, a professor of social work at the University of British Columbia, believes it is crucial to distinguish between a father's involvement in child care and actual attachment. "Fathers form very close bonds with their children," says Kruk. "In the vast majority of families, both are primary parents in the sense of children's attachment." But Kruk cautions against what he calls a "one-shoe-fits-all approach" to divorce. He believes in preserving the relationship that children had with their parents before the breakup. "When fathers are very involved in all aspects of child rearing," says Kruk, "they can continue to do that."

The emotional pain of divorce is often accompanied by a harsh economic sting. "A decline in the standard of living is inevitable because you have two households to support," says Queen's University political scientist and child support expert Ross Finnie. Carl, a Mississauga, Ont., airline employee, and his wife, a flight attendant, tried to avoid the financial crunch by continuing to live in the family home. "I am a mole," says the father of two children, aged 12 and 14. "I live in the basement." Although shift work helps keep them apart, they often end up in arguments, sometimes in front of the children. Still, he adds, "the children

COPING WITH PAIN

The sunflower room at St. Bernadette School in Edmonton is a small, cheerful space, with vivid pictures of trees and blossoming flowers on the walls. It is the reassuring space where a small group of children gather weekly to share their emotions in a support group called Rainbows. A few are dealing with the grief caused by a death in the family. But most are coping with the loneliness, anger and even hatred they feel after their parents have divorced. They share experiences with others their age, under the supervision of an adult facilitator. "It really is a good idea," said on 11-year-old participant in the program at St. Bernadette last winter. "It helps you understand that your parents love you even though they are breaking up."

For many children, the emotional upheaval from a divorce results in behavioral problems, failing grades or sleepless nights. Concerned parents often turn to child psychologists for help. But over the past 11 years, thousands have tried Rainbows, a program for elementary schoolchildren created in 1983 by Suzy Yehl Marta, a nurse whose three young sons struggled after her divorce. The Schaumburg, Ill, resident brought the program to Ottawa in 1987. Now, Rainbows, as well as the adolescent and adult versions, are offered at more than 870 schools, churches and community centres in every province but Saskatchewan. "You never see it advertised," said Rainbows Canada national director Thelma Cockburn, 62, a retired teacher from Barrie, Ont. "It has grown because parents find it helps their children's self-esteem, their behavior and their grades at school."

Offered free of charge—operating costs are covered through fund-raising—the Rainbows program is designed to teach children to cope with their emotions by talking about them. Trained volunteers guide children through 14 sessions dealing with many of the repercussions of divorce: the desire to blame one parent, hopes for parental reconciliation, absentee fathers and the changes that occur when one parent remarries. According to Lonny Jeffrey, who teaches Rainbows at St. Bernadette and two other schools, a parent's dating often triggers the most serious emotional upheaval. "A lot of kids hate the new person," says Jeffrey. "They'll do whatever they can to break up the relationship."

Marion Oudman, a 41-year-old nursing aide from Edmonton, turned to Rainbows last June because her daughters, now 15 and 13, became deeply resentful when she remarried—five years after separating from their father. "The program helped in a way I never could," says Oudman. "Some of the kids had stepparents who weren't so nice, and they would tell my daughters, 'Hey, you've got it good.'" For other children, the emotional crisis begins as soon as their parents' marriage breaks down. Lee Hagen, a 42-year-old Edmonton lawyer, separated in August, 1994, when her daughter was 6 and her son was 4. Both children became angry and defiant. Hagen tried Rainbows, and signed them up for the program twice. "I wouldn't say they're back to where they were when we were together," says Hagen, "but they're much better."

Child psychologists and others who have studied the impact of divorce on children generally agree that programs like Rainbows are effective. What most parents want to know is: how effective? Rhonda Freeman, director of the Toronto support service Families in Transition, concluded in 1995 after a three-year study of 82 children that the best results occur when a child and the custodial parent participate in concurrent programs. California-based researcher Judith Wallerstein, one of North America's leading experts on divorce, believes that peer-group discussions can reduce the intense loneliness that many children feel after divorce. But she dismisses the notion that it is a substitute for psychotherapy. "Making connections with other children is terribly important for these youngsters because half the class can be divorced and every child feels, 'Why me?'" says Wallerstein. "But if the child needs treatment, the child needs treatment."

Whatever its limitations, Rainbows and its companion programs have attracted enthusiastic supporters across the country. Heather Dubois, a 17-year-old Grade 12 student from Barrie, has gone through several years of counselling since her parents separated a decade ago. Last fall, she decided to try Spectrum, the adolescent version of Rainbows. "I loved it," she says. "You notice that other people actually think and feel the way you do. You hear someone say they're mad at their father, and blame him for not making their life easy, and you say, 'Wow, I'm not the only one.'"

Peer-group talks help to air anger and grief

D'ARCY JENISH *with SHARON DOYLE DRIEDGER in Edmonton*

---

have a home, whether it's stable or unstable."

* * *

Last June, the federal government introduced new child support guidelines, hoping to eliminate some of the friction over child support. The mandatory guidelines link the size of the payments to the salary of the non-custodial parent. A parent with two children earning $50,000 pays $700 a month, for instance, and one earning $20,000, $285. It has eliminated disputes in certain cases and helped lift women and children out of poverty. But critics say the guidelines, which the court is required to apply in almost every case, in fact, are creating more fights over custody. According to the guidelines, a parent must pay the amount specified in the tables if they have custody less than 40 per cent of the time.

But many fathers claim the law is unfair. Alar Soever, a Toronto geologist, has custody of his two children, aged 10 and 7, five nights out of every 14 during the school year, with holiday time shared equally with his wife. Based on that custody agreement, the judge calculated that he spends 38 per cent of his time with his children and ordered him to pay $1,200 per month. "I end up with a lower standard of living than my wife, even though my expenses are fairly similar to hers," says Soever, who is challenging the order in court. "The issue is whether I get credit for my parenting."

Critics argue that Canada's family law system pits parents against each other in a win or lose situation that is damaging to children. "The notion that litigation solves custody or parenting problems is ludicrous," says University of Ottawa family law professor Julian Payne. "It may even make them a lot worse." Do lawyers promote hostility? "It is an adversarial system and some lawyers take the position that their job is to put their client's best interests first," says Halifax lawyer Philip Mix. A lawyer, he says, might inform a client, "if your spouse sees the children any more than 40 per cent of the time, then there is a possibility that your support will be reduced." That, adds Mix, "is not illegal, or immoral—it's a statement of the law. But it creates another area whereby the parties will war." But Payne argues that it is unfair to blame lawyers for the hostility parents—and children—feel when a family comes apart. "The battle is not created by the legal system," he says. "These people are in conflict, and human nature is often at its worse in the divorce process."

Cathy Simons, an Ottawa legal secretary, used the mediation process to help hammer out a parenting agreement with her ex-husband after they separated seven years ago. She and her ex met in their mediator's living room and painstakingly went through all their conflicting issues. "He would give on a point, and I would give on a point," says Simons. The result was a detailed document that specified how much time their two children would spend in each household and how decisions would be made on medical and education issues. "The idea was to reinforce that we were joint parenting," explains Simons. In practice, she says, "it is parallel parenting—he deals with issues his way and I deal with issues my way."

Rarely do the two even speak. Instead, the children, Abigail, 8, and Roy, 10, carry a lined black notebook back and forth between their two homes. Each parent writes in times and dates for the children's appointments, birthday invitations and other reminders. So strained is their relationship that they also rely on the black book to settle disputes about discipline or school problems. Now the former spouses are renegotiating their agreement in a new round of mediation—one that is proving even more difficult than the last. "Each parent wants to maintain the time they had," says Simons. "But the children want to make sure they get to go to their sports or dance activities. They start saying, 'It doesn't really matter which parent we are with—we have a life here.'"

For Simons, and thousands of other Canadian parents, life after divorce is a series of compromises and negotiations. "When you have children, you really cannot get rid of your ex," notes Ambert, "not if you care about the well-being of your children." Many cannot—or will not—cope with that reality. Some parents become disheartened and fade out of their children's lives. Others remain in a perpetual postmarital war zone. "Let's not be sanctimonious," says Ambert. "Sometimes people are so humiliated and betrayed that even good parents can't put kids first." And some critics believe that legislators should stay out of the divorce process altogether. Curtis estimates that about 10 per cent of her clients are "hostility junkies" who never stop fighting. She tells of parents needing an immediate court order: "She's in a shelter because he beat her up or he's at the airport, on his way to Saudi Arabia with the kids. We have to let go of the notion that we can solve all these cases."

The divorce workshop in Edmonton wraps up on time, at 4 p.m. Participants—including Marjorie—line up to receive the blue certificate that will prove to the court that they attended the Parenting After Separation course. Blane Collison, a 28-year-old photographer, sporting a broad smile and a gold ring in his right ear, says the course has already made a difference in his life. For a time, his former wife, Shelley Collison, had refused to allow him to see their two-year-old daughter, Blaire. But she changed her mind after attending the workshop a month earlier. "It made me focus on Blaire, not on my problems with Blane," the 28-year-old administrative assistant explains. "He is her father and you can't deny the child. If you do, they end up resenting you as they get older."

Wallerstein applauds the Alberta initiative. "They must have some very enlightened judges," she says. "There is a need to help families deal with their issues, and a need to teach them how to do so." In the end, does a child of divorce have any hope for a happy future? "You can't tell the next day," she cautions. "But are some children able to have good lives and good marriages and good careers? Yes of course. The issue is better parenting."

EMBRACING OUR MORTALITY

♦ ♦ ♦ ♦ ♦ ♦ ♦

HARD LESSONS

Learning to let go of the uncontrollable

ELLEN PULLEYBLANK

Ellen Pulleyblank, Ph.D., is a psychologist in private practice. Address: 230 California Avenue, Suite 200, Palo Alto, CA 94301.

HANGING ON THE WALL OF OUR LIVING ROOM in Palo Alto was a photograph of my 3-year-old daughter, Sarah, hands on her hips, her name emblazoned on her sweatshirt. She was formidable even at that age, taking on her six-foot father, never flinching as he towered above here, challenging her typical response of "No." She would build a fort in her room and decide who could enter and who would be barred. No easy child to live with, but how I admired her will. When she was a teenager, Sarah looked at that photograph on the wall, and then at her father, inert in his wheelchair, hooked up to a ventilator. The now 14-year-old Sarah asked me where I thought that feisty little girl had gone. I imagined that, like me, she had been slammed so hard by circumstance that she had simply disappeared.

In the summer of 1985, during a sabbatical year in Europe, my husband, Ron, began having trouble tying knots. Then came difficulty with riding a bicycle and undoing buttons. In October, at a hospital in the Netherlands, he was diagnosed with Amyotrophic Lateral Sclerosis, or Lou Gehrig's Disease. By the end of the year, he could not dress himself and fell frequently. Just before Christmas, a year later, he could no longer breathe on his own and was put on a ventilator. He came home from the hospital—via ambulance—to round-the-clock nursing care.

He could not feed himself, and it became progressively harder for him to swallow and speak. His body, below the neck, became utterly still. And that is how we lived—Ron and I and our daughters Caitlin and Sarah—for seven years.

During those years, part of me vanished. I am embarrassed when I remember how strong and certain I used to be. Until Ron was diagnosed, I believed unquestioningly in personal responsibility and free will. I had faith in human beings' capacity for change, and I took that faith forward into my life, into my work as a therapist, and into my relationships.

Such beliefs had shaped my life since the time in my early twenties when I was hospitalized with what was then called a nervous breakdown. Ron and I were newly married, and he was in graduate school, studying electrical engineering. I had no idea what I was going to do with my life and I couldn't stop crying. One day a young woman, also a patient at the hospital, jumped off the roof. At that moment, I realized that I was the only one who could keep myself safe and alive.

I went to graduate school, began to work as a family therapist, got my Ph.D., and took care of my growing family. In the 1970s and early 1980s, when we lived in Stockton, California, I was part of a group of women who raised $1 million dollars to start a multi-service womens' center. I was often admired for my guts, my energy and my willingness to help—qualities that I took for granted, without even noticing the personal and so-

cietal supports that held me up and made it possible for me to be so confident.

That is the part of me that vanished after Ron got sick. At first, I tried to take charge, make do, run the show, but I couldn't keep it up. I began to see the world as a place containing tragic forces beyond our understanding, beyond our ability to adapt. I was humbled by now little I knew about myself, others and the universe.

Now, after Ron's illness and death, my psychology practice is less about relieving suffering or changing experience or circumstances and more about learning how to bear suffering and stay alive. Before, I believed that right thinking, feeling and acting led to relief, and that I could help show the way. But tragedy showed me that sometimes there can be no relief, at least not at first. There was nothing I could do that even touched the depth of my family's pain and difficulties.

Watching Ron become more and more disabled and ultimately choose to die changed what I now pay attention to and how I respond. My work with my clients now is built on what I learned:

To bear pain by paying attention to it;

To witness the suffering of others by staying present and doing only what is possible;

To stop expecting rational explanations for the unexplainable;

To ask the community for help;

To let go of control of the uncontrollable; and

To focus less on our responsibility to ourselves, and more on what we have to offer each other.

I remember sitting on the deck one afternoon with Ron. He was cold. I massaged his arms and hands, got him more warm clothing, and moved his chair into the sun. He was still cold and he was crying. I realized that all I could do was sit next to him and bear the pain with him. It was so little, but it was all I could do and I couldn't do it for long.

FOR MONTHS AFTER RON CAME home from the hospital and was on the ventilator, I would sometimes sit bolt upright in the middle of the night, thinking that something horrible was about to happen, and then realize that it already had. I would try to figure out what to do, try to distract myself, and then give up and lie awake. One night, in desperation, I went toward my fear instead of moving away from it—I gave it all my attention, feeling the physical sensation in the pit of my stomach, and watching: I didn't fight my sensations; I let go of control. I stopped trying to protect myself from the stark terror of the unknown. I was swept up and knocked out by my fear.

By then, Ron was sleeping alone in a hospital bed, his ventilator beeping regularly through the night. For months I could not decide where to sleep. Sometimes I spent the night on the living room couch or in a spare upstairs bedroom. Wherever I lay, I began to follow the nightly ritual of going toward my pain. When I couldn't stand it, I would count backwards for relief, follow my breath, and then go toward my fear again. One night, I had the unmistakable feeling that I was being held in loving arms. This feeling came back from time to time, giving me comfort and a sense of well-being. After a while, I learned how to summon it at will, by breathing, staying with my pain and remembering and thinking of loving arms.

SIMON, A SHORT, PUDGY, BEARDED man, wearing a yarmulke, his clothes in disarray, asked for a session alone. Usually I see him with his wife or with other family members. He tells me that he has brought a list of reasons why he's having such a hard time looking for a job.

"I am too old. I am too fat," he reads. "The market is very bad right now. If I move to where the children are, they might move away and then where would I be? I am depressed and have little enthusiasm."

I fidget, wondering if I remembered to turn off the oven. I ask questions designed to show him how he is giving up his power and refusing to take responsibility for himself. He goes along with me for a while and then says, with surprising clarity, "You just don't get what is happening to me."

Three years earlier, his father, aged 86, had died suddenly. Simon had called on Sunday, as he usually did, and his mother had told him his father was out for a walk. Later that night, Simon's father had a heart attack, but his mother didn't let Simon know, because she didn't want to upset him. The following Thursday, his father was dead.

Simon dissolves into tears. "I miss my father," he wails.

"I am sorry," I say, " and I am sorry I didn't understand what a hard time you are having and how hard it must have been to write that list. Please read it to me again."

"I am too old. I am too fat. The market is very bad right now. If I move to where the children are, they might move away and then were would I be? I am depressed."

I listen intently, my own tears flowing as he focuses on his losses, finally offering him the attention he needs to stay with the pain.

◆ ◆ ◆ ◆

I remember sitting on the deck one afternoon with Ron, trying to help him. He was having a bad day. He was cold. I massaged his arms and hands, got him more warm clothes, and moved his chair into the sun. He was still cold and he was crying. I realized that all I could do was sit next to him and bear the pain with him. It was so little, but it was all I could do and I couldn't do it for long. My pain walled up, threatening to overwhelm me. I got up and went inside, leaving Ron on the deck, retreating from his suffering into my own.

Sometimes, now, I can bear incredible pain, and sometimes I can help my clients bear it too. Sometimes all we can do for one another is witness suffering by staying present.

SUSAN, WHOSE FATHER HAS COMmitted suicide, complains of confusion, exhaustion and feelings of anxiety when she is with her mother. She tells me all she is doing to try and help, while her mother stays mired in grief.

I suggest we sit together and just watch our breathing. It is a miracle: we don't have

to do anything, the breath just comes. I ask her to imagine her mind as a sky and let thoughts, feelings and images fly by, in and out, not minding what flies through. Then I ask her to direct her attention to her body and suggest she locate where the strongest sensations are. I tell her to focus her attention on these sensations, to go toward them rather than move away from them.

Susan says it is unbearable knowing how sad her mother feels. She desperately wants to help. Obviously, we could work on boundary issues (and no doubt we will in other family sessions) but now I find myself working with Susan's desire to help. I ask her if she is willing to learn to witness her mother's pain and not try to change it. She struggles with this idea for a while and then I ask her to close her eyes again and practice watching her mother in pain. Silently she weeps as she watches her mother grieve, but her own breathing slows and deepens. She leaves the session later with a sense of relief.

◆ ◆ ◆ ◆

Before Ron was diagnosed, I thought that I could make sense of almost anything. I had lived in other cultures and worked with families from different ethnic backgrounds. I knew how to step aside and hear and appreciate different versions of reality and other experiences of suffering. Ron and I had always tried to understand each other and to communicate, and by and large we'd succeeded. Nothing, I felt, was insurmountable. But that began to change on the day in the Netherlands that I went to Ron's hospital room and met the doctor in the corridor. He was grave. Without looking me in the eye, he told me that Ron would die within the year. He said it would be better if I did not tell him.

I immediately went into Ron's room and told him what the doctor had said. I was determined that whatever happened, we would face it together and talk about it. He looked at me without saying very much, and then we cried. We cried, along with our two daughters, for about two weeks.

Afterward, Ron decided he would go on with his life, as much as he could, as though nothing had changed. He continued his sabbatical, and when the year was over, he went back to work as an electrical engineer at Hewlett Packard in Palo Alto. I helped him dress in the morning, and his colleagues gave him rides to work and carried his lunch tray for him. In December, after he woke up unable to breathe, the doctor in the emergency room told me that if we didn't put him on a ventilator, he would die. We didn't understand then that if you choose to turn a ventilator on, you will someday have to choose to turn it off.

Ron came home and worked half-time, using a special computer. He focused on staying alive, on keeping things the same. He continued to enjoy life and to value every

Therapy is more than helping clients to take appropriate and responsible action to achieve their goals. I meet regularly with a group of therapists and physicians to explore what might be called "the work of the soul"—learning how to face the broad questions of human existence and to tolerate the realization that much of life is beyond our control.

day. Although his determination to go on was inspiring, he found it hard to understand why the children and I were grieving and why we felt so overwhelmed. His unspoken demand to us was that everything be as normal as possible, and that we not be too sad. As he struggled to stay alive, his world narrowed and he became oblivious to us. He stopped thinking about money and didn't notice when things were broken in the house. His most significant relationships were often with the nurses who cared for him 24-hours-a-day and who saw his illness from his perspective.

We lived parallel lives. I needed Ron to understand my fear and grief. He needed me to be unemotional and accept him as he was. He was angry with me for grieving, for trying to separate, although we never gave up the effort to understand each other. I was appalled at my inability to accept our circumstances. Nothing made sense.

Only in the last months of his life could Ron acknowledge the effects his illness had on him and on us. Just before Ron died, when even I could barely understand his labored speech, we talked about what had happened to us. It was beyond understanding. Only at the end could we look at each other with kindness and forgiveness, realizing that we both had tried our best, but for the most part, we had failed. Things sometimes just don't make sense, and no amount of understanding and empathy or talk will explain them.

GABRIELLE, AGED 12, CAME IN with her father, George, and her new stepmother, Joan. Her parents divorced three years ago, after her mother fell in love with a neighbor and asked her father to leave. Her father has since remarried, and Joan has two children of her own. For months, Gabrielle has been raging and throwing tantrums, both at her own mother's house and with Joan.

She has decided not to speak to Joan either in my office or at home. Her rage has turned into a silent protest. Her father cares for her deeply and is worried about her. Joan is angry and disappointed because no matter what she does, Gabrielle does not like her and will not cooperate.

Gabrielle's father patiently describes his daughter's feelings to me. He tries to coax here to talk. She won't. I become interested in her silence and wonder out loud if, with her silence, Gabrielle has found a way to express her anger without hurting herself or others. I ask George and Joan to talk about what it will take to allow her silence, to respect it and to admire her honestly. Gabrielle looks out from behind the pillows she is hiding under. I ask them if we might sit together in silence and acknowledge with Gabrielle how difficult things have been, and how, from her point of view, none of it makes any sense. At the end of the session, Gabrielle cautiously begins to speak.

◆ ◆ ◆ ◆

About two years after Ron went on the ventilator, we started to run out of money. I couldn't think straight and I wasn't sleeping. One day I had lunch with my friends from the Stockton women's center. I had always been seen as the strong one, and they still saw me that way. They marveled at how I could do it.

Finally, I looked at them and said, "Help me. I can't do it. I can't." I felt such shame. How often I had offered to help others, feeling so magnanimous, blithely unaware of how hard it is to turn to others, to say you cannot manage your life on your own.

Of course they helped me. A community formed around us. People raised money—about $300,000 over the next few years. Others visited or gave me respite time or helped us take Ron on extravagant outings to the symphony and even on vacations to a cabin near the sea. Near the end of Ron's life, a group of friends began meditating at our house weekly.

I had never thought of myself as the kind of person who would need help. Without the help that I asked for and received, we would have become destitute in every way.

NAOMI CAME TO SEE ME WITH her parents, deeply confused about the source of her sadness. She is 14, very depressed, and refuses to go to school. She says she feels like an outsider and is treated like one. She tells me she lives in a community where everyone looks and tries to act the same. Her father, whose parents were Holocaust survivors, remembers going through much the same thing when he was younger. Her mother thinks Naomi has always been very sensitive, and mentions her own family's history of depression.

But when I meet with Naomi alone, she tells me more about the tangled communal and familial roots of her sorrow. Once, she tells me, her father came to her school and talked about what had happened to his parents in Auschwitz, and the kids snickered. None of their families had known similar experience. Since then, she has told other kids very little about her background. How is she to feel part of her community when her experience is so different, and she has shared so little of it? As she talks, I am reminded of how I felt walking around the streets of Palo Alto when Ron was disabled, looking at all the perfect houses and wondering what I was doing there with my disheveled life.

In family sessions, Naomi's father talks more about his own feelings of isolation when he was growing up. He tells Noami how identifying with his history and with other Holocaust survivors had helped him. He realizes he hadn't told her this before because he hoped that she could be unaffected by the tragedy, but now he helps her become part of a community stretching through space and time.

The more Naomi acknowledges, to herself and to others, how the Holocaust has influenced her, the easier her life becomes. She makes a new friend at Wednesday-night school at Temple. At school, she begins to build community not by trying to fit in, but by identifying with her history and asking her friends to listen to her experiences. She is surprised to find out that most of the time, they are interested and friendly.

IN THE SPRING OF 1993, RON WROTE a letter to our families, telling them that he had begun to think about dying. It had become almost impossible for him to use the computer. He was losing all speech. When I asked him whether we should sell the house, he finally realized that we were $150,000 in debt. I was exhausted; both of our daughters had stayed close to home, their lives on hold. For eight years, he had been determined to stay alive and keep things the same, and now he began to let go. Month by month, conversation by conversation, Ron got clearer and clearer. One day he decided to die, just as he decided so many other things in his life. He would think and think, and suddenly he would know.

Once he made the decision, he began to say goodbye in one halting conversation after another. By then, very few of us could understand him. I could do so only by focusing all my attention on each word. If I got a word wrong, even if it was close in meaning, Ron would ignore my attempt and repeat his word again and again, until I got it right. He said all of his goodbyes in his own way.

Then it was time. We sat in the living room—Ron, our daughters, Caitlin and Sarah, me, the doctor and a woman friend. The doctor gave Ron a small dose of morphine so he could relax.

Ron wanted to die naturally, without tubes or drugs. The doctor first removed the gastrostomy tube and then the ventilator. As soon as the tubes were gone, Ron's face changed. The strained, frozen look on his face melted, and my handsome husband returned. I found myself breathing more deeply, letting go deeper and deeper, as if my life depended on it. I was as if I was birthing Ron's death. My daughters, our friend and I held onto each other. Ron's body did not move as he died, and yet we all felt him leap out of that chair. Sarah later said she had literally held us down, because the energy was so strong that she was afraid it would lift us all away. She had held onto me especially, because she thought I might want to leave with him, and she was right.

It is only recently that I feel glad that I am still here and not with Ron. Death seems so close. Life paled in the face of death. Only time, tears and loving arms made it possible for me to return to what I think of as "normal."

What I learned in all this is that birth and death are somehow the same, but each has its time and place. Ron's choice to go on the ventilator extended his life until the time when he was ready, after exploring all the possibilities he could see, to die.

In my work with clients, I find that quite often they, too, are talking about either their fear of death or their fear of life. I find myself asking them more about their views of life and death, and more about their spiritual beliefs and the practice of prayer. Over the past year, I have contemplated suicide, not knowing how to reattach myself to the earth. I wanted to die, partly out of curiosity, partly to follow Ron. Mostly I was caught in a flood of pain that did not let me see anything beyond my own suffering. But I chose to live: my suicide would have disrupted my possibilities here on earth. I once heard Carl Whitaker speak about all the forms of suicide he had considered, and how he ultimately chose life as the best form, since it, too, leads to death. I see the choices that Ron and I made in that same light: Though they may both sound like acts of will—choosing life, choosing death—I see them both as a letting go of control, as reentering a stream that is hurtling us to who knows where.

ASSISTED SUICIDE: DO WE REALLY KNOW WHAT WE WANT?

A Harder Better Death

My father and I would have helped my mother end her life if she'd asked. Instead she wanted to die naturally, at home. As difficult as that became, **hospice made it the right choice.**

BY PETER FISH

I UNDERSTOOD THINGS WERE NOT GOING TO BE ALL right the moment the plane landed. It was a small commuter airport in Southern California. We'd made our descent over lemon orchards and a bright bend of the Pacific, touched down, taxied to a stop in front of the terminal.

I saw my father leaning against a chain-link fence. For the first time in my life I was watching him cry. § WE WERE A FAMILY WHO JOGGED, watched our cholesterol, and scheduled annual checkups. Dying took us by surprise. A few weeks before, my mother had complained of a pain in her ribs. She was a three-times-a-week golfer, a yoga enthusiast, an ocean swimmer, a woman who at 72 looked easily ten years younger. She assumed she had merely pulled a muscle. But the pain refused to disappear. She scheduled an appointment with the family doctor. "I can't see what could be wrong with someone as healthy as you," he said. § BUT THE DOCTOR ORDERED AN MRI, and then a CAT scan and a biopsy. What they revealed was the reason my father stood among strangers crying. An aggressive adenocarcinoma of unknown origin— perhaps breast, perhaps lung, we never found out—had metastasized throughout my mother's ribs and spine. § "I THINK

From *Health*, November/December 1997, pp. 108–114. © 1997 by Time Publishing Ventures, Inc. Reprinted by permission.

Until that moment *hospice* was a word I associated with made-for-TV MOVIES IN WHICH GUEST STARS DIED UPLIFTING DEATHS IN GARDEN SETTINGS.

YOUR MOTHER is going to have a lot of trouble with this cancer," said the oncologist when we got to the hospital.

A lot of trouble. That wasn't the half of it.

Sitting in a quilted nightgown in her hospital bed, my mother was tanned, cheerful, and stunned. A few weeks earlier she and my father had been planning summer cruises. Now they were planning the remaining months of her life.

I asked her how she felt. "Mad," she said. That was it. We would always have a hard time discussing her illness. Optimism was such a family creed we lacked the vocabulary for crisis. But my mother did make it clear that she did not want to remain in the hospital. She wanted to go home.

Until that moment *hospice* was a word I associated with made-for-TV movies in which guest stars died uplifting deaths in garden settings. Now, we were told, hospice could help us care for my mother at home. Suddenly, and for the next few months, hospice became the center of our lives.

Our house acquired the grim energy of a military headquarters. We accumulated bedpans, walkers, safety railings. We installed a buzzer my mother could press when she required pain medications; its alarm sawed the air like the horn on a navy submarine. Chilling in the refrigerator was an array of narcotics. I had not realized private citizens could legally possess. We had a new bed: a heavy electric device designed to lift my mother's frail body on a cushion of air, with coils and baffles that hissed as malevolently as Darth Vader. Most important, we had the hospice staff—doctors, nurses, social worker—making sure my father and I could handle the bed and bedpans, the narcotics and buzzers, the reality of my mother's dying.

March, April, May. The cancer was, as the oncologist promised, aggressive. Each month, each week, each day was a diminishment. My mother was confined to downstairs, then to her bedroom and bathroom, then to her bed. My father brushed her hair and massaged her legs and feet. The hair turned brittle and fell out; she lost all feeling in her legs. I read to her. We examined family photo albums. Shots from the fifties and sixties: my parents glamorous at the Coconut Grove, laughing with golf buddies during some Sweethearts' Tournament. In later snapshots I was present: cradled by my mother at Bryce Canyon in Utah, capped and gowned beside her at college graduation.

Sometimes as my mother and I flipped through these Kodak moments of a life now drawing to a close, I would reassure myself: At least we are home. Home was nothing fancy, just a Southern California beach house, the kind of place where you stowed your surfboard in the carport and then tracked sand into the living room, and when you opened any window you heard the sound of the sea. But my mother loved it here. How well we were doing, I told myself, that she could remain.

Or I thought we were doing well, until one night I was driving up the Pacific Coast Highway. It had been a lousy week. My mother was paralyzed now, and drifting in and out of consciousness. My father and I had argued. It was suddenly clear that despite everyone's hard work and good intentions she was going to die, and sooner than we had thought possible. Each half mile I stopped the car and threw up at the side of the road. By the time I reached Mugu Rock, a plug of granite jammed into the Pacific, I was propped against the car thinking, She can't go on, I can't go on, none of us can go on. For the first time in my life I considered the act usually referred to as euthanasia. No details entered my mind, just the simple fact: My father and I could end this.

I expected a thunderclap. I possessed—still possess—a strong if untutored religious faith and a clear sense that ending someone's life was sin. Yet there I stood thinking any sin would be preferable to continuing this nightmare.

The moment passed. I did nothing. The ending came on its own, soon enough. My mother grew weaker, aging with the withering that cancer brings. She drifted away. It was as terrible and powerful a thing to witness as seeing someone pulled from you by the tide. She died on Father's Day. I had brought my father a card and a bottle of cognac that we were drinking when we heard her breathing stop.

This was a death whose particulars were orchestrated by a hospice program. For two decades

If hospice promises comfort and growth at the end of life, why don't we embrace it? WHAT'S STANDING BETWEEN US AND THE GOOD DEATH WE WANT?

the hospice movement has been aiding families like mine. Hospice offers the hope that death need not be painful, impersonal, or entangled in technology. It offers the hope that death, while inevitable, need not be unendurable.

"What do Americans say they most want to avoid?" asks Ira Byock, a Missoula, Montana, physician who is president of the American Academy of Hospice and Palliative Medicine. "They don't want to die in pain. They don't want to die isolated and abandoned. They don't want to be a burden—particularly a financial burden—on their families." Hospice, Byock and his allies maintain, can ease all these fears.

Given our current frustration with the American way of death, hospice should be enjoying a moment in the sun. Instead the movement finds itself out in the cold—not under direct attack so much as threatened with irrelevance. As I did, a lot of Americans are standing by a dark highway and saying, This can't go on. They're wondering if the best death isn't the quickest death. And unless they have a change of heart, the hope that hospice holds out may simply be . . . beside the point.

RIGHT NOW IT APPEARS the country is intent on living out that Woody Allen joke: "It's not that I'm afraid to die. I just don't want to be there when it happens." Organizations such as the Hemlock Society and Compassion in Dying lobby for physician-assisted suicide with the kind of can-do grassroots enthusiasm we expect from the Sierra Club or Mothers Against Drunk Driving. In Oregon they passed the Death With Dignity Act, legalizing physician-assisted suicide. They have pushed their arguments up to the U.S. Supreme Court. In the meantime pathologist Jack Kevorkian has helped more than two dozen people end their lives, some by injection, others by inhaling carbon monoxide in the back of his van. One poll showed that 90 percent of American believe they should have some control over the place and even the time of their deaths.

To be sure, many physicians and ethicists count the current debate on the right to die as long overdue. At least we are finally acknow-

ledging that American medicine, so good at so many things, does a poor job of helping people who are dying.

"We're doing terribly badly," says geriatrician Joanne Lynn, director of George Washington University's Center to Improve Care of the Dying. In a recent study on the last days of the hospitalized terminally ill, Lynn and fellow researchers tracked 2,500 patients. They found that four out of ten suffered from severe pain and eight out of ten from severe fatigue. Of dying in America, Lynn says, "It is reasonable to be afraid."

"I have a terrible time with Jack Kevorkian," says Connie Holden, executive director of Hospice of Boulder County in Colorado and one of the nation's most articulate advocates of improving end-of-life care. "I find his methods repugnant. But he turned the light on a topic that needed to have attention paid to it." Likewise, the suicide-minded Hemlock Society may seem morbid and extreme. But, Holden says, "They are just regular folks who have had a bad experience in dying."

Avoiding a bad experience in dying. That is what hospice is all about.

One way of understanding hospice is that it is the only medical institution designed solely for the dying. When a patient is given a terminal diagnosis of six months or less and agrees to hospice care, he or she abandons aggressive treatment of the disease. Generally patients will not receive chemotherapy or blood transfusions nor be connected to respirators or feeding tubes. Typically, they will not be cared for in a hospital or nursing home but in their own homes.

In giving up a hospital's aura of stainless steel crisis, patients and their families put their faith in the ministrations of the hospice team—physicians, nurses, nurse's aides, and social workers, all trained in end-of-life care. The team makes sure that symptoms are managed, pain is controlled, and family members are not shattering under the pressure of illness. Medicare and private insurance plans normally cover the visits.

My father and I knew nothing of hospice before we scanned the local program's tasteful pastel brochures. We knew nothing about anything. To imagine how ill-suited we were to tending a ter-

WHEN IT'S TIME for HOSPICE

THE DECISION TO ENTER A HOSPICE PROGRAM is never easy. Doctors, patients, and family members must all admit a life is ending, stop trying to cure the disease, and shift their goal to helping the patient die at home surrounded by the people and things he or she most loves. If you find yourself facing the death of someone close to you, here's what you might want to know.

WHEN HOSPICE SHOULD START As difficult as it is, families ought to turn to hospice months rather than days or weeks before death seems imminent, experts advise. This gives caregivers time to adjust to the stresses of their role, and increases the likelihood of a rewarding close to the loved one's life. Medicare and most other insurers will pay for hospice as long as a physician certifies that the patient appears to have less than six months to live.

WHERE HOSPICE TAKES PLACE Nearly always in the patient's home, with the bulk of care provided by family and friends. Residential hospices are rare, and much of their cost isn't covered by Medicare.

WHAT HOME HOSPICE PROVIDES A variety of assistance to caregivers: training in attending to a dying patient; a nurse available by phone 24 hours a day; several weekly visits by professionals who might include a doctor, a nurse, health aides, or a social worker; medication for pain and symptom control; supplies; durable medical equipment; chaplain services; and bereavement counseling.

HOW TO CHOOSE A PROGRAM Ask if it is certified by Medicare, which ensures that physicians, nurses, social workers, health aides, volunteers, and chaplain are on staff. To select among certified hospices, ask the patient's doctor, nurse, hospital social worker, or discharge planner for advice. Also, pay attention to your impressions. "The first contact with a hospice program is important," says Connie Borden of Hospice by the Bay in San Francisco. "Does someone come out to the home and take the time to listen to your concerns and answer your questions?"

WHEN IT'S COVERED Medicare and many private plans will pay for the program. "Even if hospice isn't covered, be persistent," says Borden. "Talk with the insurer's case manager. There may be a pot of money for care."

FOR MORE INFORMATION Call or write the National Hospice Organization, 1901 N. Moore St., Suite 901, Arlington, VA 22209; 800/658–8898. Find the NHO's home page at www.nho.org. *A Consumer Guide to Hospice Care*, a 32-page booklet published by the National Consumers League, includes a helpful checklist for evaluating programs. Send a check or money order for $4 to 1701 K St. NW, Suite 1200, Washington, DC 20006; or call 202/835–3323.

—*P.F. and Anne Johnson*

minally ill patient full-time, you would have to imagine Abbott and Costello starring in "ER."

But we managed. We got better at it. A few times a week (more often as my mother neared death) someone from hospice would visit to check that my mother was reasonably comfortable, to monitor the cancer, to see whether my father and I were beginning to crack. Our favorite was the social worker: a dark-haired, athletic woman not unlike my mother in her youth. She radiated the kind of good health you think will rub off on you, and she did not seem bothered that when my father and I spoke with her we often began to cry.

Nurses and nurse's aides were more problematic. We were hard on them. One nurse arrived a half hour late. We demanded a replacement. Another was brusque. We replaced her, too. Later I understood that we'd been focusing our anger at the cancer on these people. But eventually we found the perfect nurse, who bustled pleasantly and told my mother how pretty she looked. She knew what her patient needed to hear.

Our biggest fear was that my mother would experience intolerable pain. But my mother did not suffer horribly. That, say hospice experts, is usually the case. "Pain management has gotten much better," says Laurel Herbst of the San Diego Hospice. "We have a much clearer understanding of the physiology of pain. Ninety-five percent of patients stay awake, alert, and pain-free." Prescription painkillers including morphine can lessen physical discomfort; steroids can lift, a bit, the dying patient's profound fatigue. If pain increases as death approaches, morphine may be given in higher and higher doses, easing the slide into unconsciousness.

It was in those last days that hospice was of particular help to me. I had not seen anyone die before; in the most rudimentary sense I did not know what to make of the process, did not know what to do. Use swabs to moisten her mouth, the nurse told me. Hold her hand. That breathing you hear is called Cheyne-Stokes; it tells you life is drawing to a close. Her senses are dimming, but hearing will linger. Tell her you love her.

For hospice advocates, deaths like my mother's are examples of the succor hospice can provide. And at best, they say, hospice can do more than that, making death not just an ending but a kind of culmination. When Byock first began encountering dying patients and their families, he didn't believe this was possible. "But every once in a while a person would tell me, 'This has been the most wonderful time of my life,'" he says. "It took several of those incidents before it finally dawned on me that the universe was trying to teach me something."

Byock's new book, *Dying Well*, tells the stories of a dozen of his hospice patients. Byock doesn't ignore the messy terrifying aspects of death—the IVs, the incontinence, the pain. But he shows how they can be managed and sometime transcended. A brassy hard-living woman reconciles with her estranged sister. Stricken with an inoperable brain tumor, a middle-aged man lets go of his deep-seated anger and expresses love for his wife and children.

"If you control symptoms," Byock insists, "if you provide basic support to people and families, you see enormous growth at the end of life. Erikson, Maslow, Piaget all said human development is a life-long process. We in hospice have shown they are right. Some of us know that end-of-life care doesn't have to be that bad. There are robust alternatives to suicide even at the very end of life."

IF HOSPICE PROMISES COMFORT, dignity, and even growth at the end of life, why don't more Americans embrace it? The nation's 3,000 hospice programs currently tend 15 percent of America's dying—about 390,000 deaths a year compared to the 1.3 million who die in hospitals. Experts like Joanne Lynn believe that hospice programs could well serve twice that number. Indeed, Lynn feels that if hospice developed less intense and less expensive variations, it might be appropriate for *anyone* dying of a chronic illness—about 70 percent of the dying. Meanwhile, polls reveal that most Americans are aware of hospice and support—in theory—its goal of dying at home. So what's holding us back? What's standing between us and the good death we say we want?

The biggest obstacle is one that's existed since the first American program opened in 1974: Many doctors are reluctant to refer patients to hospice, seeing the proposal as a painful admission of defeat. Doctors often suggest more treatment rather than face a patient and his or her family with the news that there's no hope. This tendency is changing as more doctors see hospice's advantages. But even now, says Jennifer Morales of the National Hospice Organization, "We have to get away from the notion that death is a failure for a physician."

Reluctance isn't limited to physicians. Many patients and family members also balk at stopping treatment. Doctors say families frequently hesitate to sign the consent forms required to place someone in hospice, a step that would concede death was on the way. Says Holden, "There is always a certain discomfort patients and families have."

Current Medicare rules are another stumbling block. Medicare will reimburse the costs of hos-

pice care only if a doctor certifies that the patient has less than six months to live. That requirement works fairly well for patients with late-stage cancer, a disease whose course is relatively predictable, and in fact about a third of cancer deaths occur in hospice. But hospice is now stretching to care for patients with emphysema, AIDS, congestive heart failure, and neurological disorders like Parkinson's disease. All of these illnesses progress in less predictable ways, making it difficult for doctors to determine when a patient might die. This year Holden polled local physicians about the biggest problem they experienced in referring patients to hospice. More than 80 percent said it was judging whether a patient had just six months to live.

It hasn't helped that the Department of Health and Human Service's Office of Inspector General is currently auditing hospice programs to see if they have violated Medicare rules. The office charges that some hospices have gotten Medicare to pay for patients' care even when it was clear the patients would not die within six months. The National Hospice Organization counters that most of these cases involve simple differences of medical opinion. Given the timing, hospice administrators find the investigations dispiriting. "It's having a significant chilling effect on extending hospice care," says Byock. Adds Holden, "We've been accused of being cancer focused. But about the time we open up to other illnesses, we get our hands slapped. Right now would be a scary time to start a hospice program."

Combine reluctant doctors and families with hospice directors watching their backs, and the result is that Americans are spending more time in the grips of hospital machinery than makes sense either financially or emotionally. A recent study of 6,500 hospice patients by Nicholas Christakis of the University of Chicago highlighted the scope of the problem. He found that the patients who'd had the longest hospital stay—at least a month—died on average after just a month of hospice. One in seven patients died within seven *days* of moving home. Christakis's overall conclusion was that even among people who do eventually enter hospice, the majority are receiving hospital care long after it has stopped benefiting them. "People are clamoring for better care for the dying," he says. "And hospice offers that. People need to ask for it earlier."

To allow more dying patients to take advantage of hospice, advocates would like legislation to loosen Medicare's six-month limit. Just as much, they'd like a deeper understanding—among physicians and the public both—of the advantages of hospice.

This was not a learning experience. It was no grand reconciliation. **IT WAS JUST THAT FOR ONE EVENING WE COULD ENJOY OUR OLD LIFE TOGETHER.**

And this is why the debate over assisted suicide troubles most hospice professionals. For who can pay attention to hospice when Jack Kevorkian dominates the headlines and talk shows? The controversy may have helped Americans recognize the ways in which medicine fails the dying, but it has also distracted us from the real challenge of providing decent end-of-life care. "In a sense," says Byock, "the attempt to legalize assisted suicide is an extension of our cultural denial about dying."

The hospice establishment has taken a strong stand against assisted suicide. In the cases before the Supreme Court, the National Hospice Organization filed a brief opposing its legalization. After passage of Oregon's Death With Dignity Act, one prominent hospice announced that its staff would not attend patients who wanted to die with a doctor's help.

This antipathy can partly be explained by hospice's roots. Most of the earliest hospices were affiliated with churches, and even today many hospice workers share moral aversion toward the taking of life. Others look abroad with alarm. They note that the Netherlands, a nation where physician-assisted suicide has been decriminalized, has a weak hospice program, and they worry that legalizing suicide for the dying might similarly weaken hospice in the United States. Psychiatrist Herbert Hendin, author of *Seduced by Death,* a report on the Dutch experience, sums up the concern: "When assisted suicide is legalized, assisted suicide becomes the easier option, and hospice is a casualty."

Most hospice physicians and nurses maintain that when a patient asks for help committing suicide, the problem is likely not with the patient but with the nature of care being given. "It's a red flag," says Holden. "In the great majority of times it is a cry for better symptom management and more emotional support. And if, in fact, you address those needs, the person's desire for suicide goes away."

In other cases, caregiver burnout is responsible. "Have I ever wanted to help someone kill themselves?" Byock asks. "You bet. And anyone in this profession who says they haven't is lying.

But it always turned out it wasn't about the patient. It's when *I've* felt overwhelmed, when *I've* felt helpless."

And yet, within the hospice movement there are people who think that assisted suicide and hospice are not mutually exclusive. One is New York internist Timothy Quill, a champion of hospice care who nonetheless argues that for a small percentage of the terminally ill, physician-assisted suicide should be an option. Holden is another. She was one of a group of hospice professionals who filed a brief in the Supreme Court cases arguing in favor of legalization; she believes that even given the best possible care, some patients simply cannot endure their agony. "There are a small number of people who, as they perceive it, are suffering so much they don't wish to tolerate it any longer." When that happens, expediting death may tempt not just the caregivers but the patient, too. "Patients begin hoarding pills, usually sleeping medication," Holden says. "Doctors sometimes prescribe them knowing that's what's going on. It's unreported, it's unregulated, and the fact that suicide is illegal forces everyone to act in secrecy.

"I think hospices sometimes tend to wear rose-colored glasses," says Holden. "I have had deaths in my family that were quite beautiful and gratifying. My father died in a hospice unit, and he had a very peaceful death. I was able to be at his bedside with my two daughters. And we had no desire to hasten it. But for some people, dying is very difficult and quite dreadful."

DIFFICULT AND DREADFUL. That describes my mother's last weeks. Even with the best of assistance, amateur caregivers make mistakes. When the mistakes involve a terminal illness, they can be grievous. Misreading the physician's instructions, my father and I gave my mother far too much morphine. The overdose caused her to hallucinate; we thought we might be killing her. She was rushed back into the hospital for a day and then rushed home with accompanying ambulance sirens in both directions.

Other crises were beyond anyone's control. The electric bed had not been engineered to withstand power failures. When our neighborhood went dark one evening, the bed's air-cushioned mattress deflated, dropping my mother's frail ribs and spine onto a spiky nest of coils and pipes. She screamed while my father screamed into the telephone, demanding that the electric company turn on the power *right now.* It did not.

These were the moments I dwelled on while I stood beside the Pacific Coast Highway, thinking this couldn't go on any longer. These are the moments I relive when I realize that I don't take the strong stand against assisted suicide. I once did.

Serious illness is a journey to a foreign country. You don't speak the language, the inhabitants are strangers, you cannot know how you will behave until you arrive. St. Thomas Aquinas condemned suicide because it violates God's authority over life. I believed that. And one of my favorite writers, Flannery O'Connor—herself the victim of a slow death at a young age—wrote, "Sickness before death is a very appropriate thing and I think those who don't have it miss one of God's mercies." I believed that, too. Now I believe that there is suffering that is ennobling but also suffering that strips the humanity from a person, that is so unendurable you would be wise not to predict your reaction to it until you confront it.

But inner strength, too, is unpredictable. Often during the past few years of heated debate over assisted suicide, I have listened to people plead that they could not possibly endure the final illness of someone they love—or endure their own final illness. And I find myself thinking, Don't sell yourself short. Don't be so sure. It will be bad. But perhaps not as bad as your worst fears. I have

reached an age where people I know—parents of friends, aging relatives—are receiving terminal diagnoses with some regularity. I find that once I hear the grim news, the second or third sentence out of my mouth is "You'll want to find a hospice program."

For after I stopped by the side of the road and thought I couldn't go on, we went on. That could not have happened without hospice. We struggled through a few more very bad days. But later that week we had a good day. It was May in Southern California, with mustard blazing yellow on the hills and the ocean half in mist and half in sunlight. My mother felt better. The hospice nurse had made her comfortable. The nurse's aide had set her hair.

We made a small celebration of this good day. My father barbecued steaks and tossed a caesar salad. I hit every florist in town trying to find a dozen yellow roses, my mother's favorite. My mother didn't eat more than a bite of steak and salad, but she said they looked delicious. She liked the roses. We opened the windows, and you could hear the ocean and smell a breeze that carried the start of summer on its shoulders.

This day was not a learning experience for us. It was no grand reconciliation. It did not offer us any moment of particular insight. It was just that the three of us were home, and for one warm May evening we could enjoy a brief piece of our old life together. It had been for all of us a happy life. The kind of life you would want to hold on to for as long as you could.

Peter Fish is a senior writer at Sunset *magazine.*

How Kids Mourn

Dealing with death: Let children grieve, the experts say. Don't shield them from loss, but help them express their fear and anger. **BY JERRY ADLER**

"THE PAIN NEVER GOES AWAY," says Geoff Lake, who is 15 now, and was 11 when his mother, Linda, died of a rare form of cancer. He is only starting to realize it, but at each crucial passage of life—graduation, marriage, the birth of children—there will be a face missing from the picture, a kiss never received, a message of joy bottled up inside, where it turns into sorrow. His sleep will be shadowed by ghosts, and the bittersweet shock of awakening back into a world from which his mother is gone forever. If he lives to be 100, with a score of descendants, some part of him will still be the boy whose mother left for the hospital one day and never came home.

A child who has lost a parent feels helpless, even if he's a future King of England; abandoned, even in a palace with a million citizens wailing at the gates. But children have ways of coping with loss, if they are allowed to mourn in their own ways. Grief can be mastered, even if it is never quite overcome, and out of the appalling dysfunction of the Windsor family, one of the few positive signs psychologists could point to was the sight of William and Harry trudging manfully behind their mother's bier, both brushing away tears during the service. "There is something very healing," says Catherine Hillman, coordinator of the Westminster Bereavement Service, "about openly sharing pain."

The death of a parent can have devastating psychological consequences, including anxiety, depression, sleep disturbances, underachievement and aggression. But so can a lot of other things, and losing a parent is actually less devastating than divorce. "We know that children tend to do better after a parental death than a divorce," says sociologist Andrew Cherlin of Johns Hopkins, "and that's a stunning statistic, because you'd think death would be harder." Historically, people have always had mechanisms for coping with the early death of a parent, a fairly common event until recently.

As late as 1900, a quarter of all American children had lost at least one parent by the age of 15. The figure today is about 6 percent. A century ago most people lived on farms and died at home, so children had a fairly intimate, routine acquaintance with death. In the genteel, antiseptic suburban culture of midcentury, death became an abstraction for most American children, something that happened on television (and, in the case of cartoon characters, was infinitely reversible). Growing up as what psychologist Therese Rando calls "the first death-free generation," Americans forgot the rituals of grief so ancient that they predate civilization itself. So the mental-health profession has had to fill the gap. In the last few decades more then 160 "bereavement centers" have opened around the country, directed at allowing children to express and channel their grief over the death of a parent or sibling. The one thing they can't do is make the grief disappear, because it never does.

If they could enroll, William and Harry would be prime candidates for bereavement counseling. Experts consider them almost a case study in risk factors for future emotional problems, with the notable exception that, unlike many other children who have lost a parent, their social and financial status is not in any jeopardy. But children who experience "multiple family transitions"—such as a death on top of Charles and Diana's acrimonious and humiliatingly public di-

vorce—"don't do as well as children who experience just one," Cherlin warns. David Zinn, medical director of Beacon Therapeutic Center in Chicago, thinks this may be especially true if there is some casual connection, however remote, between the divorce and the death. It is not such a great leap of logic, for a child, to blame his father for the circumstances that put his mother in the back seat of a speeding car with a drunk at the wheel.

Moreover, the princes are each at an age that has been identified—by different experts—as being at particular risk when a parent dies. An adolescent, such as the 15-year-old William, is already undergoing difficult life changes, says Rabbi Earl Grollman, author of 25 books on coping with loss. "You're not only dealing with the death of a parent, you're dealing with the death of your own childhood," he says. "You thought you were beginning to know yourself, but now the road ahead is uncertain." "I think it's hardest when you're 9 to 12," says Maxine Harris, author of "The Loss That Is Forever." (Harry was just short of his 13th birthday when Diana died.) "You're not a little kid, so you feel more shy about crying or sitting on someone's lap, but you're also not an adolescent, with all the independence that comes with that."

Worse yet, in the opinions of most armchair specialists, is the famously reticent and undemonstrative temperament of the Windsor family. "The way to handle grief is to allow the expression of feelings and the sharing of sadness," declares Dr. Dennis Friedman, a psychiatrist who has written a book on the psyche of the British royal family. "This particular family doesn't allow the expression of grief. . . . There has been a pat-

COURTESY FERNSIDE, A CENTER FOR GRIEVING CHILDREN

Some mourning children draw or paint, others pound a toy in frustration

This is, as it happens, almost the exact opposite of what was accepted wisdom a generation ago, when children were encouraged to get on with their lives and parents advised not to depress them with reminders of the departed. Lori Lehmann was 6 when her mother died of leukemia, 30 years ago. Lori was dropped off at a neighbor's house for the funeral, and afterward her father packed up all her mother's belongings and took down all her photographs, and no one ever talked about her. "He was so sad that you didn't feel like you could ask him about it," she remembers. Her father died himself nine years later, and now she is trying to reconstruct her parents, her mother especially, from relatives' memories. "It's the little things they tell me that I really love," she says. "Like what she cooked for dessert. I don't think my aunts realize how I cling to these things." Of course, by not talking to her, her father was sparing his own feelings as well; men of that generation didn't like to be seen crying.

And it's easy for parents to overlook the grief of young children. A child of 6, says New York psychiatrist Elliot Kranzler, is just on the cusp of mastering the four essential attributes of death: that is has a specific cause, involves the cessation of bodily function, is irreversible and is universal. Before that, children may nod solemnly when told of their father's death, and still expect him to be home for dinner. Young children process their loss a bit at a time; they may be sad for 10 minutes, then ask to go outdoors to play. And they are captives of childhood's inescapable solipsism. "It hits them over the head that they have needs to be met, and one key provider is gone," says Kranzler. "They pretty quickly tell their surviving parents to remarry." That isn't callous, merely practical on the child's part; and, of course, when the parent finally does remarry, it is one of the invariable rules of human psychology that the children will hate the new spouse. "There has not been a person I've interviewed who liked their stepparents when they were children," says Harris.

Children mourn piecemeal; they must return to it at each stage of maturity and conquer grief anew. Over the years, the sharp pang of loss turns to a dull ache, a melancholy that sets in at a certain time of year, a certain hour of the night. But every child who has lost a parent remains, in some secret part of his or her soul, a child forever frozen at a moment in time, crying out to the heedless heavens, as Geoff Lake did, when his mother died just days before his 12th birthday: "Mom, why did you die? *I had plans.*"

With PAT WINGERT *in Washington,* KAREN SPRINGEN *in Chicago,* BRAD STONE *in New York,* PATRICIA KING *in San Francisco,* CLAUDIA KALB *in Boston and* DONNA FOOTE *in London*

tern of deprivation of love beginning with Victoria, then gathering momentum, and ending up with Charles. [The princes] are bereaved not only by the loss of a mother who was very close to them, but also for a father who is quite often unavailable to them because of his duties and temperament."

It will be hardest at night, when the routines of the day wind down and the memories crowd in. Nighttime is when 11-year-old Dennis Heaphy leaves his bedroom and pads down the hall of his home in New York's Long Island to take his place on the floor of the master bedroom. His 7-year-old sister, Catherine, is already sleeping in bed alongside their mother, Mary Beth, who lies awake with her own thoughts of Brian, the husband who died of a brain tumor last January. He was 37, a big, strong man until he got sick. Dennis remembers his father's teaching him to play basketball and the hockey games they would play in the street until 9 o'clock at night. The memories make him miss his father even more, but they are precious all the same. "My sister doesn't remember my dad so well," Dennis says. "She remembers him from when he was sick, when he would get mad at the littlest things and not act like himself. We have to help her out."

Children cling to their memories, try to fortify them against the passage of the years. "They're always afraid they're going to forget how their mother looked, what her voice sounded like, how she smelled," says Debby

Shimmel, a volunteer at the St. Francis Center in Washington. They paint their memories onto the quilts that are ubiquitous at bereavement centers, little shards of a shattered family, sharp enough to pierce the heart: "Mommy read Matty bedtime stories." "Leo and Mommy played Candyland." Or they draw their parents as angels in heaven. Envisioning what heaven is like for their dads, says Stefanie Norris of the Good Mourning program in Park Ridge, Ill., children sometimes draw a giant football stadium. At the end of each eight-week group session, children hold a memorial for their dead parents; they wear something their parent wore, or perhaps make one of their favorite dishes. This is a more concrete form of memorial than a church eulogy, and a lot more meaningful to a 7-year-old.

The other thing children can't do in church is get angry, but bereavement centers provide for that as well. The Dougy Center in Portland, Ore., the model for scores of bereavement houses around the country, includes a "splatter room," where kids throw violent sploches of paint, an innovation suggested by a child who came to the center after his father had been accidentally shot to death in his home by police. And most centers have some variation of the "volcano room," thickly padded with foam and supplied with large stuffed animals that are periodically pummeled into piles of lint. Barney is said to be the favorite of many teenagers.

Unit 5

Key Points to Consider

❖ After having charted your family's health history, what type of future do you see for yourself? What changes do you see yourself making in your life?

❖ What decision have you made about long-term commitments—marriage or some other relationship? How about children? Do you see divorce as a viable option, even before marriage? Do you expect to live "happily ever after"?

❖ In what ways have secrets been integral to your family life? In what ways have you been hurt by family secrets? How have you benefitted?

❖ What is the state of rituals in your family? What rituals might you build in your family? Why?

 **Links** | **www.dushkin.com/online/**

These sites are annotated on pages 4 and 5.

What is the future of the family? Does the family even have a future? These questions and others like them are being asked. Many people fear for the future of the family. As previous units of this volume have shown, the family is a continually evolving institution that will continue to change throughout time. Still, certain elements of family appear to be constant. The family is and will remain a powerful influence in the lives of its members. This is because we all begin life in some type of family, and this early exposure carries a great deal of weight in forming our social selves—who we are and how we relate to others. From our families, we take our basic genetic makeup, while we also learn and are reinforced in health behaviors. In families, we are given our first exposure to values and it is through families that we most actively influence others. Our sense of commitment and obligation begins within the family as well as our sense of what we can expect of others.

Much writing about families has been less than hopeful and has focused on ways of avoiding or correcting errors. The five articles in this unit take a positive view of family and how it influences its members. The emphasis is on health rather than dysfunction.

Increasing evidence of genetic factors in physical as well as mental health serves to promote the need for awareness of our family's health history. "To See Your Future Look into Your Past" considers how charting your relatives' medical history can save your life. Steven Finch provides a useful technique for mapping out your family health history so that you can anticipate, plan, and possibly change your health behaviors. Then, the article "Defining Daddy Down" suggests that for the first time since the baby boom, society is singing the praises of fathers, leading to responsible fatherhood initiatives being set up across the nation. "What's Ahead for Families: Five Major Forces of Change," identifies five societal trends that Joseph Coates believes will have an impact on the future direction of families. Then, "The Power of Secrets" is related to family dynamics and shows the ability of secrets to shape how we relate to others. Concluding this volume, "Rituals for Our Times," by family therapists Evan Imber-Black and Janine Roberts, describes the ways in which rites and ceremonies are used to strengthen families. Through examples, readers see how they might use ritual in their own families.

TO SEE YOUR
FUTURE
look into your past

Tracing your family health history may be the most
important step you ever take toward long life

BY STEVEN FINCH

AS A CHILD Kathi Marangos always found her birthday cake a bit hard to swallow. Each sugary bite reminded her of a mother who gave her up for adoption and of a family she didn't know. But she recalls her 18th birthday as especially bittersweet.

"That's when my mother found me," she says. "She hired a private detective so she could give me information about my family."

Marangos felt at once transformed— into the proud daughter of a ski lodge manager and a Harvard graduate. But at the same instant she felt the chill from her family's dark side: its frightening predisposition for depression, heart disease, and colon cancer.

Today, at 35, Marangos, with her doctor's help, keeps an eye out for any sign of cancer while she makes sure her family sticks to a low-fat diet. "I'm so glad to know my medical history," she says, "to know I can use it to protect myself and my kids from our genetic shortcomings."

If only more Americans would see the light, says Michael Crouch, director of the Baylor Family Practice Residency Program in Houston and a leading expert on inherited risks. Tracing your roots to learn your family's health history may be the single most important thing you ever do to bolster your well-being.

Why? Because any disease that runs in your family puts *you* at risk. And regardless of whether the risks stem from your genetic code or from habits nurtured in your childhood, many family-

linked ills can be kept at bay if you know the right steps to take.

If a woman and her husband both have insulin-dependent diabetes, for example, any child of their runs a one-in-ten chance of getting the disease herself. But she greatly lowers her risk if she eats well, exercises regularly, and maintains a healthy weight. For problem such as alcoholism, the genetic connection is less certain. Children of alcoholics are between two and four times more likely to become alcoholics than other people.

> "People who see illness patterns in their families tend to note the red flags in their own lives; then they seek help."

"People who recognize patterns of alcoholism in their families tend to note the red flags in their own lives and are more likely to seek help or avoid a problem in the first place," says Crouch. What's more, doctors alerted by family histories

can aggressively look for and treat specific health problems.

"Take breast cancer," says Steven Esrick, a family physician who helps direct Kaiser-Permanente's preventive care programs in the northeastern United States. "It's reasonable for most women to start having mammograms at age 50, but I'd want a woman with a family history to start at 40." And many physicians who'd normally recommend counseling for depressed patients, says Esrick, are quicker to consider antidepressant drugs if the family history includes suicide attempts.

"I know one woman who lost her mother and one sister to ovarian cancer at a young age," says Esrick. Because this cancer tends to be fatal and is difficult to detect early, even with frequent screening, the patient chose to have her ovaries removed. Not the decision for everyone, to be sure. "But because this woman knew her risks," says Esrick, "she was better able to weigh the options and to make the right decision *for her.*"

People in this country are hardly strangers to unearthing family history. Nearly half say they've at least dabbled in genealogy, and tens of millions have compiled some kind of family tree.

Still, Crouch and Esrick are amazed by how few people know even the barest details of their relatives' medical histories. Only now, thanks to health maintenance organizations and other managed care groups, is this trend starting to change. Under Esrick, for example, Kai-

Preventable Perils: Are You at Risk?

ONCE YOU FIND OUT which health problems various family members have had, your doctor can help you figure out how that affects your risk—or refer you to a genetic counselor if necessary. Many inherited conditions, alcoholism or obesity for example, are passed on by a mix of inborn tendencies and family habits, such as cocktail hour every night or a love of fried foods. But here's one rule of thumb: The more close relatives who suffered one of the conditions listed below—and the younger they were at the time—the likelier you are to have inherited a predisposition to the illness. Here's how to size up your risk—and improve your odds.

HEART DISEASE
If your father or grandfather had a heart attack or bypass surgery before age 55 or your mother or grandmother before 65, your risk rises significantly, especially if you're African American. *If it runs in your family:* Swear off smoking, and have your cholesterol tested. If it's over 240, you need to have your blood analyzed for LDL, or "bad" cholesterol. An LDL level over 160 will likely prompt your doctor to prescribe cholesterol-lowering drugs and to advise you to exercise and cut back on fatty foods.

HIGH BLOOD PRESSURE
A family history of high blood pressure increases your risk of developing the condition, which in turn boosts your odds of having a stroke sixfold. *If it runs in your family:* Have your pressure checked regularly, watch your weight, exercise, and eat a diet low in fat and high in calcium, potassium, and magnesium. Your doctor may advise you to cut down on salt or to take calcium supplements or blood pressure drugs.

DIABETES
If you have one parent with type I (insulin-dependent) diabetes, you typically have a 4 to 6 percent chance of getting it yourself. If one parent has type II (non-insulin-dependent), your risk is 7 to 14 percent. African Americans, Mexican-Americans, and Pima Indians are at highest risk. *If it runs in your family:* Exercise regularly, lose weight if you're obese, and eat a low-fat, high-fiber diet.

BREAST CANCER
Many women assume they have a genetic predisposition to breast cancer if a family member developed the disease. But only 5 to 10 percent of all breast cancers are inherited. Scientists have pinpointed a mutated gene, BRCA1, linked to both breast and ovarian cancer, and 1 percent of Jewish women carry it. *If it runs in your family:* You may want to start yearly mammograms at 40 instead of 50. If many members of your family developed the disease at a young age, you might ask your doctor about being tested for the mutated form of BRCA1.

COLON CANCER
Ten to 15 percent of all colon cancers are inherited; family genes lead to about 20,000 new cases each year. *If it runs in your family:* Ask your doctor whether you should get a sigmoidoscopy. Regular, low doses of aspirin may offer protection, as does a low-fat, high-fiber diet.

ALCOHOLISM
Thirteen to 25 percent of children of alcoholics are likely to become alcoholics. *If it runs in your family:* You need to be especially vigilant about your drinking habits; dependence develops over time. If you've ever found it hard to keep your drinking under control, or anyone close to you thinks your drinking is a problem, you may want to seek treatment.

DEPRESSION
Some types of depression run in families and occur generation after generation. Not everyone with a vulnerable genetic makeup will develop depression, but stress is believed to trigger its onset. *If it runs in your family:* Your doctor is more likely to suggest early intervention with antidepressants if you become depressed and your family history includes suicide attempts or major depressions requiring hospitalization.—*S.F.*

women whose mothers had breast cancer prior to menopause run a much higher risk themselves. "It's hardly worrisome if several relatives died in their eighties due to heart disease," says Crouch. "But it's a different kettle of fish if they died at 35 or even 55."

Crouch constructs a health history for every patient but tells people not to worry just because a couple of relatives

> "It's not just that family trees prompt more people to come in for tests. The right people are getting the right tests."

have suffered from heart disease or struggled with addiction. "My guess is that there's a genetic component to almost every disease," he says. "But few of them are caused entirely by genetics." In other words, having a diabetic grandfather raises your risk—it doesn't necessarily doom you to the disease.

Neither does a clean record mean you can quit taking good care of yourself, says Bruce Bagley, public health chairman of the American Academy of Family Physicians. "Just because you don't have a history of hypertension or heart disease doesn't mean a doctor won't still urge you to have your blood pressure checked, to eat healthily, and to exercise." But when doctors can tie in family history, he says, blanket health warnings are made personal.

"Sure, no one should smoke," Bagley says. "But if somebody looks at their family history and sees low cholesterol coupled with a two-pack-a-day cigarette habit, they may come to realize it was really Dad's smoking that caused his heart attack. That's a pretty strong impetus for a person to quit."

This type of nudge can be crucial for people with silent conditions like high blood pressure and elevated cholesterol, says Esrick. Why change your habits if the disorder doesn't make you feel bad? "What feels bad," he points out, "is what happened to your parents."

No wonder Esrick often finds that his patients aren't ready to discuss their family's medical past until they're about the same age as a mother or brother was when she or he became ill or died.

ser recently began an ambitious effort to gather family health information from all 114,000 of its patients in New York, Connecticut, and Massachusetts.

"What you're really looking for is patterns," says Crouch. Most crucial, he explains, are cases of cancer, high blood pressure, heart disease, diabetes, depression, and alcoholism—all common, life-threatening hereditary diseases that you can do something about.

"Another important pattern," Crouch says, "is the age at which your relatives developed a disease." For example,

Family Facts: Where to Find Them

FEW AMERICANS KNOW even the highlights of their family's health history, but no group knows less than the 5 million people who were adopted. Confidentiality has been the watchword for adoption agencies since the 1930s. Today only Hawaii and Kansas allow open records. That means someone adopted in any other state has no right to his or her health history—although judges have sometimes ordered records to be opened in emergencies. Of course, you don't have to be adopted to be blind to some bogeyman in your bloodline. The following agencies can help you track down your relatives, research your heritage, and, after you've compiled a health history, gauge your risks or those facing your children.

IF YOU'RE BUILDING A FAMILY TREE

NATIONAL GENEALOGICAL SOCIETY Offers two publications ($6 each) that explain ways to track down family health records. 4527 17th St. N., Arlington, VA 22207.

FAMILY HISTORY LIBRARY OF THE CHURCH OF JESUS CHRIST OF LATTER-DAY SAINTS Houses the world's largest collection of genealogical records (church members are only a fraction of the database), with 2 million rolls of microfilm and 300,000 bound volumes containing 2 billion names. The staff can answer brief questions and refer you to sources. You can also check the databases at more than 1,800 Family Search Centers in the United States and Canada; call for the nearest location. 35 Northwest Temple, Salt Lake City, UT 84150; 801/240–2331.

NATIONAL SOCIETY OF GENETIC COUNSELORS Gives referrals to professionals who flag hereditary illnesses and determine your risks as well as the chances of passing an illness on to a child. Once you've compiled your family health history, send the society a written request. 233 Canterbury Dr., Wallingford, PA 19086.

IF YOU'RE SEEKING YOUR PARENTS

NATIONAL ADOPTION INFORMATION CLEARINGHOUSE Sends important facts on state adoption laws and on searching for birth relatives, including a list of mutual consent registries as well as other organizations and support groups. 5640 Nicholson Ln., Suite 300, Rockville, MD 20852; 301/231–6512.

INTERNATIONAL SOUNDEX REUNION REGISTRY Matches data on adopted children with data on biological parents who have given up a child for adoption (a free service). Call for a registration form. The registry will contact you if the computer turns up a match. P.O. Box 2312, Carson City, NV 89702; 702/882–7755.

AMERICAN ADOPTION CONGRESS Has local support groups across the country for adoptees, birth parents, and adoptive parents. Each group offers psychological as well as search guidance. 1000 Connecticut Ave. NW, Suite 9, Washington, DC 20036; 202/483–3399.

CONCERNED UNITED BIRTHPARENTS Provides support and some search help through a monthly newsletter and 14 local branches around the country. First-year membership is $50. 2000 Walker St., Des Moines, IA 50317; 800/822–2777.

ADOPTEE LIBERTY MOVEMENT ASSOCIATION Holds search workshops at 62 chapters worldwide. Also provides a registry for people adopted from foreign countries who are seeking their biological relatives. P.O. Box 727, Radio City Station, New York, NY 10101; 212/581–1568. —*S.F.*

relatives, both living and dead. Focus first on older family members, since they're more likely to have suffered whatever ailments run in your bloodline. After tracking down information on your parents, grandparents, aunts, uncles, and siblings, you can compile the data for your spouse and children. If you're ambitious, you can even fill in facts on cousins, nieces, and nephews.

> "Some may be afraid of finding an illness in their bloodline. But knowledge is a good thing, even when the news is bad."

Placing a few phone calls is all it takes for some people. Others send out questionnaires or plan a big reunion so family members can swap medical details. Of course, close-knit families have a distinct edge over those separated by geography or personal disputes. But even deep gaps can be bridged. One method is to send any estranged relatives a note describing how a comprehensive health tree will benefit the whole family.

Locating relatives is the easy part, says Crouch. Often tougher, he says, is convincing them to open up about their maladies—and provide details. Health topics are highly sensitive; some are taboo to older people. Remember that not long ago it was the norm in this country to keep mum on miscarriages, mental illnesses, and even cancer.

Ethnicity, too, remains a delicate topic, albeit an important one. "For example, we worry about hypertension in blacks because they suffer more damage from the disease earlier in life. But in the South especially," Crouch says, "if a mother was Creole it's often not talked about because some people don't want to know what the racial background really is."

If one relative is tight lipped, see if your chatty aunt might be more forthcoming. But in the end, says Crouch, don't sweat a few unknown details about an unreachable uncle or long-lost grandparent. Your goal is simply to gather as much information as you can. For all your close relatives, try to find out:

"I had one patient who finally came in because he's 47 and his father had a heart attack at 50," says Esrick. "Now he's taken up walking two days a week, he's reduced his weight, and because he lost someone he cared about, he's agreed to take cholesterol-lowering medication."

Esrick's gospel is steadily sinking in. "A lot more people here are being coun-seled and screened," he says. "And it's not just that more people are getting mammograms and Pap smears and cholesterol tests. It's that the *right* people are being given the *right* tests."

Getting yourself to that stage doesn't have to be difficult, Esrick says, but it does take a little time. An ideal health tree includes details on all your close

- full name and dates of birth, marriages, divorce, and remarriage.
- ethnic background.
- height and weight.
- average amount that he or she drank or smoked.
- any health problems, from recurring headaches and frequent colds to allergies and even limps. Pay special attention to heart attacks, strokes, cancers, diabetes, high blood pressure, high cholesterol, miscarriages, and major surgeries. List the age at which an event occurred or a condition was diagnosed.
- any depression or substance abuse and all suicide attempts.
- date and cause of death. Tease out as much information as you can. If a grandmother died of stroke, was it caused by a blood clot or by bleeding in the brain? Did she also have high blood pressure? If she died of cancer, what kind?

Organize your tree so that you and your physician can easily compare the health histories of two or more family members. The more close relatives you see who developed a hereditary illness and the younger they were at the time they got sick, the more significant your own risk. Some illness patterns—all your aunts had osteoporosis—will be obvious. But your doctor might notice threats that you miss and possibly refer you for tests or even suggest that you see a genetic counselor, who can help gauge your risk of, say, kidney disease or multiple sclerosis.

"Some people will always be worried about finding an incurable disease in their bloodline—though I'm of the school of thinking that knowledge is a good thing even if the news is bad," says Crouch.

Not everyone agrees. Both patients and doctors worry that insurance companies might use this information to deny coverage to high-risk individuals, such as women who carry the gene mutation that raises the odds of breast cancer. Still, 11 states already have laws on the books banning this type of discrimination.

And though there's no advantage to finding out that a relative had an incurable illness such as Alzheimer's or Lou Gehrig's disease, the day will come when doctors can actually repair defective genes. Until then, Crouch says, there's a lot we can do about the big things people die from—heart disease, hypertension, cancer—especially if a family tree leads to an early diagnosis.

"In the balance of things," Crouch says, "learning more about your family history is about as close as you can get to controlling your destiny."

Steven Finch is a writer and research editor for Hippocrates *magazine.*

Defining Daddy Down

By Barbara Dafoe Whitehead
and David Popenoe

FOR the first time since the baby boom, America is making room for daddy. The President and Vice President sing the praises of fathers. Governors set up special task forces on fatherhood. "Responsible fatherhood" initiatives and programs are spreading across the nation. Scholars have discovered fatherhood as an important new (and fundable) field for research. Fatherhood is now a professional social work discipline.

Resource guides and how-to books on fatherhood are more popular than ever before. Nearly 500 books on fatherhood, most published in the past year or two, are listed on Amazon.com. Not so long ago, how-to reading for fathers ran the gamut from greasy copies of Chilton's car-repair manuals to back issues of *Field and Stream*. Now fathers can buy how-to books on everything from cooking a tasty meatloaf to negotiating a joint custody arrangement.

All this attention to fathers must be good news for children, right? Not exactly.

The fatherhood movement set out to improve the lives of children. But powerful political forces are tugging it away from considerations of what is best for children. What began as an effort to improve child well-being by strengthening married fatherhood is becoming a movement focused almost entirely on divorced and unwed fathers who live apart from their children.

The fatherhood movement grew out of a discussion on how to improve child well-being. Its founders included a handful of scholars and policymakers who were concerned about the way rising proportions of fatherless families—created by divorce and unwed childbearing—seemed to be leading to rising levels of child poverty, juvenile crime, and unwed teen parenthood.

We were part of this discussion in the early 1990s. Our group was hardly politically or ideologically monolithic. We had differences —indeed, profound differences—about the best model of contemporary fatherhood and what men and women's family roles should be. But we agreed on one key point: An impressive body of research showed that, in general, children did better when they grew up in households with two married parents. Therefore, we concluded, one way to improve children's lives would be to revitalize fatherhood. Practically speaking, this meant working toward the goal of strengthening marriage and thus attaching fathers to their children.

One outcome of this effort was a crop of books and articles devoted to the problem of father absence. In 1993, Barbara Dafoe Whitehead wrote "Dan Quayle Was Right" for Atlantic Monthly, later expanded into a book, The Divorce Culture. David Blankenhorn published Fatherless America in 1994, a passionate polemic on the problem. In 1996, David Popenoe offered a comprehensive summary of the social scientific evidence on fatherhood, marriage, and child well-being in Life Without Father. This body of literature was controversial at the time, attacked and even ridiculed by liberal pundits and academics, but also influential. It put fatherhood on the political map. Governors and other elected officials came calling.

Another outcome of this early focus on child well-being and fatherhood was the formation of the National Fatherhood Initiative (NFI) in 1994. Led by foundation head and civic activist Don E. Eberly together with Wade Horn, a psychologist and former Commissioner

Reprinted from *The American Enterprise,* September/October 1999, pp. 31-34. © 1999 by the *American Enterprise,* a Washington, DC–based magazine of politics, business, and culture.

for Children, Youth, and Families in the Bush administration, NFI set out to initiate a larger public discussion of father absence and to build a broad coalition to support fathers and revitalize fatherhood. From the start, it paid attention to the plight of single fathers and helped develop strategies to reconnect them with their children. But the organization also steadfastly stuck to the goal of increasing the critical mass of married, two-parent families who raise their own children and serve as a model for children growing up in other family arrangements.

In the last few years, however, new players have begun to march under the fatherhood banner. Though these players are not united around a common set of goals, they share one common feature: They are single-mindedly focused on unwed and divorced fathers who live apart [from] their children.

For one thing, fathers' rights activists have jumped on the fatherhood bandwagon. For the most part, these activists are divorced fathers who believe that the courts and child support system are biased against fathers. Although their numbers are not large, these activists are energized by a deep sense of grievance and a fierce commitment to getting justice from the courts. Their driving mission is to change the laws and the court system in the areas of child support, custody, and the use of restraining orders. Their rhetoric is pro-child (some even say their mission is to ad-

vance "children's rights"), but their agenda is pro-divorced dads.

In addition, state governments are powerful new players in the fatherhood movement. Welfare reform brought special block grants for fatherhood initiatives into the states, and the states responded. According to a study by the National Center for Children in Poverty, 46 states link their fatherhood agenda to welfare reform. These state initiatives are wide-ranging, covering everything from in-hospital paternity-establishment programs, to supervised visitation for fathers accused of abuse or domestic violence, to license-revocation programs targeted at parents who are not paying child support.

Although some state fatherhood programs pay lip service to the goal of strengthening married fatherhood, their first order of business is reducing the welfare caseload. Thus, living-apart fathers—chiefly unwed fathers—are the core constituency for fatherhood initiatives in the states.

Advocates for low-income fathers have joined the cause. They argue that poor fathers, many young and undereducated, are simply unable to take on the economic and emotional responsibilities of fatherhood without some help. Some of these mostly unwed fathers have spent time in jail and are struggling with drug problems. Many are unemployed or intermittently employed. Their advocates claim that you can't get blood from a turnip and poor unwed fathers are society's turnips. Thus, they say, states should reduce child sup-

RESPONSIBLE NON-PARENTHOOD

Ever since Sigmund Freud declared that all young boys secretly wanted to kill their fathers and marry their mothers, the psychiatric community has been waging war on parents. The latest salvo comes from two psychologists in an article entitled, "Deconstructing the Essential Father," in the June issue of American Psychologist, the official journal of the American Psychological Association.

But this time, rather than simply blaming individual mothers and fathers for their children's unhappiness, professors Louise B. Silverstein and Carl P. Auerbach argue that moms and dads as a group are largely irrelevant. And most insignificant of all to children's well-being, say the two researchers, is whether moms and dads are married to each other: "In contrast to the neoconservative perspective, our data on gay fathering couples have convinced us that neither mother nor father is essential."

They concede that kids do need some "responsible, care-taking" adult, but they say "one, none,

or both of these adults could be a father (or mother)." What's more, they don't believe "that heterosexual marriage is the social context in which responsible fathering is most likely to occur."

Silverstein and Auerbach readily acknowledge that "our reading of the scientific literature supports our political agenda," but then so does the neoconservatives' approach. The difference, of course, is that the neoconservative agenda, which advocates the traditional role of mothers and fathers joined in lifelong commitment, is rooted in literally thousands of years of human experience across different cultures.

Researchers like Silverstein and Auerbach clearly want to hasten the demise of the married-couple, two-parent family, while claiming that children won't suffer. That's nonsense. The real casualties in this war on parents won't be mothers and fathers but children.

—excerpted from a syndicated column by Linda Chavez, president of the Center for Equal Opportunity port obligations, forgive arrears, and get disadvantaged fathers into jobs and training programs.

To be sure, each of these new political players in the fatherhood movement has a good reason to be there. Some fathers have been pushed out of their children's lives as the consequence of divorces they didn't want. Other divorced fathers have suffered serious financial setbacks when they lost the economies of scale in marriage. And there is every reason in the world to work for the reduction of poverty, crime, school failure, drug addiction, and the shocking level of incarceration among young, inner-city men.

Nonetheless, all this new-fangled advocacy has had two large affects. First, the action in the fatherhood movement has shifted from civil society to government, with marriage lost in the shuffle. And second, the fatherhood movement has created its own set of victims—and they are not fatherless children. They are dads who live apart from their children.

Another sign of the drift away from marriage and child well-being is the deliberate effort to redefine fatherhood in ways that make no reference to the married, two-parent family. "Words are extremely important. They reveal our beliefs, and conscious use of them can change our beliefs." So writes a divorced father named William Klatte in *Live-away Dads*, one of many recent books targeted at solo dads. And Klatte is right. Words

"RESPONSIBLE FATHERHOOD" CONSPICUOUSLY EXCLUDES THE ONE TYPE THAT IS BEST FOR CHILDREN— MARRIED FATHERHOOD.

THE ESCAPE FROM MARRIED FATHERHOOD

In a single generation, the Bachelor Dream has edged its way from fantasy subculture right into the mainstream. Just from 1970 to 1992 the proportion of men who were unmarried and footloose more than doubled (to 54 percent) among 25-29 year-olds, and roughly tripled among men in their thirties, the U.S. Bureau of the Census reports. Various impermanent forms of sexual cohabitation are at all-time highs, contributing heavily to our frightening level of births to unmarried mothers.

Between a lack of marriages and the ending of marriages, the proportion of children who live apart from their biological fathers has doubled since 1960, accounting now for one out of every three children. —*the editors*

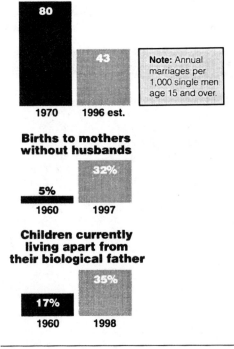

Male marriage rate
80 — 1970
43 — 1996 est.

Note: Annual marriages per 1,000 single men age 15 and over.

Births to mothers without husbands
5% — 1960
32% — 1997

Children currently living apart from their biological father
17% — 1960
35% — 1998

Sources: U.S. National Center for Health Statistics. *The State of Our Unions 1999*, National Marriage Project.

do shape our beliefs and behaviors.

Consider, for example, the term "irresponsible fatherhood." This phrase makes its appearance in the fatherhood movement around 1995 or so. Its exact origin is murky, but a report by the Federal Interagency Forum on Child and Family Statistics attributes the phrase to James Levine, Director of the Fatherhood Project at the Families and Work Institute. According to Levine, a responsible father does not consider conceiving a child until he is emotionally and financially prepared to support a child, establishes legal paternity, shares in the emotional and physical care of his child, and shares in the financial support of his child.

This notion of "responsible fatherhood" is now the accepted definition of fatherhood in the policy world. So, it's worth pausing and thinking about what "responsible fatherhood" includes and what it leaves out. It includes the legal requirements and financial obligations of paternity. And it emphasizes the contemporary notion of co-parental sharing when it comes to providing support for a child; that is, dad and mom both work and pay their fair share.

"Responsible fatherhood" conspicuously excludes the one form of fatherhood that is best for children–married fatherhood. Nowhere does the definition suggest that a "responsible father" has anything more significant than a financial arrangement with the mother of his children.

If words are important, then the successful campaign to edit marriage out of the definition of fatherhood is an important development. It creates a new norm of fatherhood that may fit the requirements of the government and the capacities of living-apart fathers, but doesn't even come close to fulfilling a child's economic needs and emotional hungers. Responsible fatherhood is daddy defined down to his minimum legal requirements: a name on a birth certificate, a signature on a child support check, some unspecified expression of emotional care—a birthday card, weekends together, whatever. Call it daddy lite.

It is a cliché that fatherhood is not simply a matter of biology. It depends heavily on law, religion, culture, and especially the institution of marriage. In virtually every known society, marriage has improved the rearing of children by connecting the father to the mother-child unit. It's not as if we don't know what kind of fatherhood is best for children. That is empirically well established. It is the kind of fatherhood that fuses biological and sociological characteristics; namely, a biological father who is stably married to their mother. This is more important today than ever before, because so many traditional extended-family and community ties have eroded. If this is what's best for children, why is married fatherhood dropped from the definition?

One answer is that "irresponsible fatherhood" is a political accommodation to a growing constituency of unwed and divorced fathers, who are not likely to go away. In fact, male mating patterns are rapidly moving away from monogamous marriage in the direction of serial polygyny, in two forms. Low-status males have serial cohabiting partnerships with women who bear their children or bring other men's children with them into the union. Higher-status males have serial wives. (On weekends, in fashionable city neighborhoods and countryside getaways, it is easy to spot these high-status guys, graying

THIS IS DADDY DEFINED DOWN TO HIS MINIMUM LEGAL REQUIREMENTS. CALL IT DADDY LITE.

and paunchy, pushing a double stroller of twins with their pretty young wives at their side.) And as these forms of fatherhood become increasingly commonplace and as these men and their advocates lobby for rights and privileges, it will become politically unpopular to talk about anything other than "responsibility" as the standard for paternal behavior.

Feminist Barbara Ehrenreich, a long-time observer of fatherhood trends recently offered a forecast of things to come. Marriage, she suggests, will be replaced by a "parenting contract" between a living-apart man and woman who have a child. The twenty-first century family will be stripped down to a mother-child twosome, with a little help from a distant "irresponsible" father. (Of course, for the men with second or third families or children by several women, it will be a bit more complicated.)

We may not have long to wait before this becomes the new standard of fatherhood. Ask today's teenage men what they think should be the best resolution to a pregnancy for an unwed girlfriend. According to findings from the National Survey of Adolescent Men, the percentage of young men who recommended marriage or adoption in such a situation declined substantially between 1979 and 1995, while the percentage suggesting the mother have the baby and the father just help to support it increased from 19 to 59 percent in the same years. Teenage women, too, are increasingly supportive of unwed parenthood.

Is this what Americans want for the next generation of children? We don't think so. Indeed, if responsible fatherhood becomes the sole goal of the fatherhood movement, it will institutionalize the very trends that created the problem of father absence in the first place. The fatherhood movement should be thinking of ways to prevent unwed and divorced fatherhood, rather than advancing efforts to defend and sustain it.

Barbara Dafoe Whitehead and David Popenoe co-direct the National Marriage Project, a research and public education initiative based at Rutgers.

What's Ahead for Families: Five Major Forces of Change

A research firm identifies key societal trends that are dramatically altering the future prospects for families in America and elsewhere.

BY JOSEPH F. COATES

No adequate theory in the social sciences explains how values change, so it is very difficult to anticipate changing social values. On the other hand, the social sciences are outstanding in reporting and exploring historic patterns of social change and in reporting contemporary social values through surveys, opinion polls, and observational research.

Identifying long-term shifts in values is complicated by the great deal of attention given to fads—that is, transient enthusiasms. A good example is "family values," a topic of great interest in recent political seasons. Both the family and values are undergoing shifts, and the challenge for futurists and other observers of social change is to identify the long-term trends and implications in both of these important areas. Social values are slowly evolving trends.

To help you understand the myriad of evolving patterns in families, this article describes several major trends and forecasts in families and values and suggests what they may imply for the future.

TREND 1

Stresses on Family Functions

The family in the United States is in transition. While the forces at play are clear and numerous, the outcomes over the next decades remain uncertain.

Anthropologists agree that the family is a central, positive institution in every society. It performs two functions: the nurturing and **socialization** of children and the regulation of the expression of **sexuality**. In European and North American society, the family serves another basic function: **companionship**. Also important are the **economic** functions of families, such as providing care for the elderly and sick and social support for unemployed members.

All of these family functions are being stressed by structural changes in society. Among the patterns that have long-term implications are:

• Increased life-spans mean that adults live well past the period in which nurturing and socialization of children is central to their lives. In many cases, longevity leads to the death of one spouse substantially before the other, creating a companionship crisis.

• Sexual behavior is increasingly being separated from its procreative function, thanks to reproductive technologies such as artificial insemination and *in vitro* fertilization, as well as contraceptives.

• New patterns of work and leisure mean that people are developing interests and activities that are different from other members of their family. In many cases, this leads to conflicting interests and expectations rather than convergence and mutual support. As a result, the companionship function of families comes under increasing stress.

• Television and magazines create images of lifestyles, which may influence people's expectations of each other and the roles of families.

• The anonymity of metropolitan life eliminates many of the social and community pressures on families. There are no watchful and all-knowing eyes in the big city that compare with those in smaller and more cohesive communities, where "What will the neighbors think?" is a critical socializing factor.

These forces will not wipe out the family or the commitment to family, but they will continue to reshape it.

Implications of Stress on Family Functions:

• **Substitutes for family functions will develop.** As family members seek other sources of companionship, and nurturing children becomes less important in matured families, institutions will have a challenge and opportunity to meet human needs. Already, people are finding companionship and even forming committed relationships on the Internet. Schools, businesses, and governments are all under more demand for meeting human services once provided in families, such as

From *The Futurist*, September/October 1996, pp. 27–25. © 1996 by The World Future Society, Bethesda, MD. http://www.wfs.org/wfs. Reprinted by permission.

About the Report

This article expands on research prepared for "Social and Value Trends," the third in a series of reports by Coates & Jarratt, Inc., on critical trends shaping American business in the next 30 years.

The reports were collected under the general project title, American Business in the New Millennium: Trends Shaping American Business, 1993–2010, which was prepared for and sponsored by 15 U.S. organizations: Air Products and Chemicals, Battelle Pacific Northwest Laboratory, CH2M Hill, Discover Card Services, Dow Chemical Company, E.I. DuPont de Nemours & Company, Eastman Chemical Company, Motorola, Niagara Mohawk Power Corporation, NYNEX Corporation, Ohio Edison, Sony Corporation of America, South western Bell Corporation, Goodyear Tire & Rubber, and U.S. West.

Other reports in the series covered trends in U.S. and world demography, politics, the global economy, science and technology, environment and resources, information technology, health and safety, transportation and habitats, and more.

For more information on the reports, contact: Coates & Jarratt, Inc., 3738 Kanawha Street, N.W., Washington, D.C. 20015. Telephone 202/966-9307; fax 202/966-8349.

health and medical care, child care, retirement care, unemployment compensation, etc.

• **Interest groups will proliferate.** Support groups have burgeoned in recent years to help people with special health or emotional problems. Similarly, special-interest groups such as book-discussion salons, travel and adventure societies, or gourmet dinner circles could see a renaissance as individuals seek others with similar interests outside their own families.

• **"Recreational sex" may become more acceptable** as the connection between sexual activity and child-bearing diminishes. Greater access to information on health and "safe sex" will allow people—including the very young and the very old—to engage in sexual activity more safely, both physically and emotionally.

TREND 2

Economics Drives Family Changes

The greatest changes in families have to do less with the family structure and more with economics. The change richest in implications is the rise of the two-income household. The United States has a way to go. Sweden and Denmark are the standards for mothers participating in the labor force. Sixty-five percent of U.S. mothers with children under age 18 are in the work force, compared with 86% in Denmark and 89% in Sweden. For children under 3, the figures are 53% in the United States, 84% in Denmark, and 86% in Sweden. Among the significant patterns emerging are:

• By 2000, women will make up just under half of the work force.

• Women are older when they marry and have their first child, deferring family formation until after they finish their education and get their first job. In 1988, the median age of mothers of firstborn children was 26, the oldest at any time in U.S. history.

• Although the average income of the family household has stayed relatively flat over the last 15 years, the growth of the two-income household is allowing couples to make a higher average income.

Implications of Changes in Family And Economics

• **Two incomes, two decision makers.** Both breadwinning members of two-income households will have broader opportunities to start a new career or business initiative. Any change of job or relocation offer will thus affect two incomes rather than just one, making life/career planning doubly complicated.

• **Women disappear from the community.** Women's greater commitment to work means a long-term change in their commitment to home and the community. Like male breadwinners of the past, women may be rarely seen in stores, in their neighborhood, at home, and so on. In the shopping mall of the future, for instance, the only daytime customers may be the very old, the very young with their mothers or minders, and after-school teenagers.

• **A masculinization of the home** will spread to the community. Telecommuting allows one or both breadwinners of the dual-income household to work at home. Many

Enduring Family Values

(Percentage of adults saying these values are important)

Respecting your parents	70%
Providing emotional support for your family	69%
Respecting people for who they are	68%
Being responsible for your actions	68%
Communicating your feelings to your family	65%
Respecting your children	65%
Having a happy marriage	64%
Having faith in God	59%
Respecting authority	57%
Living up to your potential	54%
Being married to the same person for life	54%
Leaving the world in a better shape	51%

Source: *American Demographics* (June 1992), from the Massachusetts Mutual American Family Values Study, 1989.

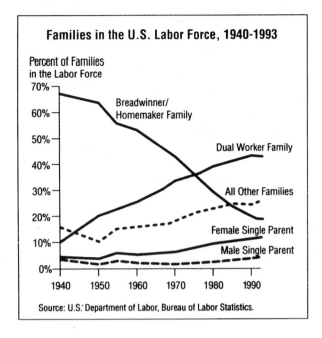

Families in the U.S. Labor Force, 1940-1993

Percent of Families
in the Labor Force

Breadwinner/Homemaker Family

Dual Worker Family

All Other Families

Female Single Parent

Male Single Parent

Source: U.S. Department of Labor, Bureau of Labor Statistics.

men are choosing this option in order to be more available for domestic responsibilities such as cooking, cleaning, and chauffeuring children to various activities. Men may also increasingly become involved in volunteer activities, especially those that directly benefit their own families, such as neighborhood crime-watch groups and the PTA.

• **An economy of convenience will emerge.** A working lifestyle for most families will also continue to shape their preferences in eating, at home, for entertainment, and in shopping. Many families will be willing to pay a premium for convenience in all goods and services they purchase.

TREND 3

Divorce Continues

Divorce may be viewed as a way to correct social mistakes and incompatibility. In the 1940s, for example, there was a surge of marriage in the early 1940s as young Americans went off to war, and at the end of the war there was a surge of divorces in 1945–1947, apparently correcting impetuous mistakes. There was an even greater surge in post-war marriages.

Divorce is seen by many as the death knell of family values. On the other hand, a high divorce rate could be seen as a positive social indicator. It represents an unequivocal rejection of a bad marriage. For the first time anywhere in a mass society, the United States has had the income, the wealth and prosperity, and the broad knowledge base to allow people previously trapped in lifelong misery to reject that state and search for a better marriage. The evidence is clear, since the majority of divorced people either remarry or would remarry were the opportunity available.

Among the patterns emerging in divorce are:

• Divorce rates fell below 10 per 1,000 married women between 1953 and 1964, then surged to a high of almost 23 per 1,000 married women in 1978. Divorces have continued at about 20 to 21 per 1,000 for the last decade.

• Commitment to marriage continues, as demonstrated in the fact that the majority of divorced people remarry. One-third of all marriages in 1988 were remarriages for one or both partners. The average time until remarriage is about two and a half years.

• The shorter lifespans of many families has led to serial marriages. Almost surely there will continue to be people who have three, four, or five spouses, without any intervening widowhood. In the long term, it is much more likely that society will settle down into a pattern of

later marriage, earlier sexual engagement, and much more careful and effective selection of life mates.

• **Marriages and families will be businesses.** Families may increasingly be treated as business units, which form legal partnerships and plan and evolve their own lifecycles as an integrated activity. Families may even incorporate to obtain tax and other benefits. Divorces will be handled as simple business or partnership dissolution. *[Ed. note: The rise of "families as businesses" was predicted by Lifestyles Editor David Pearce Snyder in his article, "The Corporate Family: A Look at a Proposed Social Invention," THE FUTURIST, December 1976.]*

• **Teenage sex—but not pregnancy—will increase.** Teenagers will observe and emulate their parents' distinct separation of sexuality and commitment.

• **Companies will share and care.** Businesses will offer their employees training in household economics and management, as well as family and divorce counseling. These courses could also be marketed as a service to the community.

• **Opportunities for marketing to new families will emerge.** Many of the families in the top income segments will include remarriages and

U.S. Divorce Rate, 1940-1992

Rate per 1,000 married women,
aged 15 and over

Source: National Center for Health Statistics.

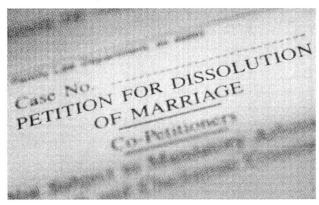

Divorce petition. Author Coates anticipates a movement to improve matchmaking in order to strengthen marriages and families.

second and third families, in which the parents will have a strong incentive to tie together the new relationships. Aiming at this concern could offer opportunities. For example, a new blended family may want financial planning and related services to reallocate its resources. Club memberships for the new family, new homes, etc., all could be important among this group.

• **A "pro-family" movement will take new directions.** One of the most important underlying causes of divorce is that no institution in the United States—school, church, Boy Scouts, or other—teaches and trains people about what it is like to be married, to live in a two-income household, or to share and be involved in a new division of domestic labor. The search for a good marriage is not supported by the right tools to aid that search. Over the next decade, society will focus more on creating more-effective families. A new "pro-family" movement will encourage better and more effective matchmaking, as well as better teaching and training on marriage lifestyles and on economic and household management.

TREND 4

Nontraditional Families Proliferate

A variety of nontraditional family forms are evolving in the United States, shaped by economic and social changes. For example, higher expectations for education mean young people spend more years in the educational system and marry later. The greater tolerance of divorce and remarriage affects how often people dissolve and re-form families. Many people enter long-term cohabiting relationships before marriage. And many single-parent families are being formed among low- and middle-income communities, as a result of divorce, widowhood, or out-of-wedlock childbearing.

The emerging patterns include:

• More couples are cohabiting. In 1988, one-third of all women aged 15–44 had been living in a cohabiting relationship at some point.

• The number of "boomerang" families is increasing. Young people—post-high school or post-college children who would otherwise be on their own—are returning home to live with Mom and Dad. To a large extent, this is a money-saving move more commonly practiced by men than by women.

• Blended families are becoming the norm. Blended families result from divorced parents who remarry, either linking stepfamilies together or linking the children of one partner to the subsequent children of both. It is estimated that, for nearly 16% of children living with two parents in 1990, one of those parents is a stepparent.

• Technology is creating new families. These may involve adopted children matched for similar genetic inheritance, children from surrogate parents, and eventually children from cloned embryos.

• Gay families are surfacing as a result of the new openness in society. Aside from the social approval so valuable to many in the gay community, acknowledgment offers substantial economic benefits in corporate or business health and recreation benefits packages. Time will make family resources available to members of nontraditional families.

• Group living, with or without sexual intimacy, is likely to remain a transitional life stage for an increasing number of people, often as an alternative to living alone.

• Single-parent families are increasingly common across all socioeconomic groups. The unmarried woman who bears a child is one of these family styles. It is unclear what the consequences are for middle- and professional-class mothers and children in these voluntary single-parent households. Evidence is strong that teenage childbearing, particularly

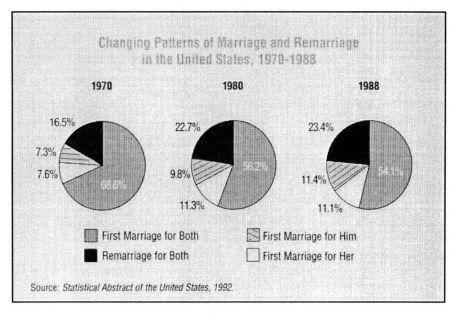

Changing Patterns of Marriage and Remarriage in the United States, 1970-1988

1970
16.5%
7.3%
7.6%
68.6%

1980
22.7%
9.8%
11.3%
56.2%

1988
23.4%
11.4%
11.1%
54.1%

First Marriage for Both
Remarriage for Both
First Marriage for Him
First Marriage for Her

Source: *Statistical Abstract of the United States, 1992.*

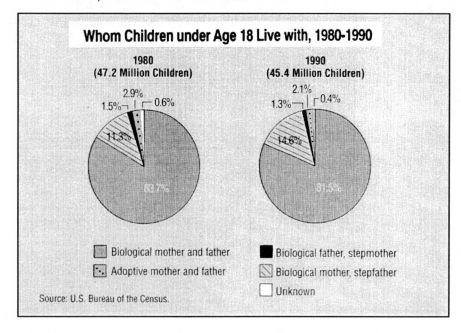

Whom Children under Age 18 Live with, 1980-1990

1980
(47.2 Million Children)

2.9%
1.5%
11.3%
0.6%
83.7%

1990
(45.4 Million Children)

2.1%
1.3%
14.6%
0.4%
81.5%

- Biological mother and father
- Adoptive mother and father
- Biological father, stepmother
- Biological mother, stepfather
- Unknown

Source: U.S. Bureau of the Census.

by unmarried mothers, is socially destructive of the future well-being of both the mother and the child. Some single-parent families are single by divorce or separation.

Implications of the Proliferation of Nontraditional Families

• **Rearranged families will rearrange the workplace.** The work force will continue to be profoundly affected by new family structures. The proliferation of family arrangements will create new pressures on employers to be flexible and responsive in relation to working hours.

• **Businesses will make attitude adjustments.** Employers will be hard-pressed to justify accepting one type of family arrangement among their employees and not another. One company decided to offer benefits to gay couples because they could *not* get married and deny them to male-female couples living together because they *could*. Workers did not accept this justification.

• **"Nonfamily" families will gain in status.** Many groups of people consider themselves families, even though they do not fit traditional definitions (e.g., gay couples, unmarried couples with or without children, foster parents, long-term housemates, etc.). This has implications for business and nonbusiness

issues, for example in marketing, housing codes and covenants, loans, billing, leasing, and so on.

• **Family-oriented organizations will reinvent themselves.** For example, Parent-Teacher Associations may broaden into Family-Teacher or Community-Teacher Associations. Schools may provide more counseling for students in nontraditional families.

• **Flexible architecture will be mandatory.** Housing will become more flexible, with walls that can be easily taken down and rearranged to form new rooms depending on the needs of new family members.

TREND 5

An Aging Society Will Redefine Families

The traditional family in past decades was the nuclear family: a working father, a homemaker mother, and children. As the children aged and left home, the traditional family was two adults with no children living at home; then one or the other died, leaving an elderly single person alone.

Aging creates a crisis in traditional families' lifecyles. The patterns to watch now include:

• Death rates of men are relatively high compared with women. Men also tend to marry women younger

than themselves. As a result, at age 75 and older, 66% of men but only 24% of women are living with a spouse. At age 65, for every 100 men there are 150 women. At age 85, for every 100 men there are 260 women.

• The savings rate among working adults is now just 4.1% of personal income, compared with 7.9% in 1980; this low rate bodes ill for Americans' economic status in retirement.

• Voting rates among seniors are traditionally higher than for younger people (60.7% of those 65 years and older voted in 1994, compared with 16.5% for 18- to 20-year olds and 22.3% for 25- to 34-year olds). It is likely that the baby boomers' influence on public policy will gain strength as they approach retirement years.

Implications of Age and Family

• **The end of retirement?** A combination of several factors may lead to the end of retirement: the emotional need of seniors to feel useful when their families no longer demand their daily attention, the financial needs of seniors who didn't save enough during their working years, the improved mental and physical health of older people, and the need in businesses for skilled, experienced workers.

• **Economic priorities shift away from children.** There is already concern among the elderly about balancing their economic assets against commitments to their children. Personal savings during their working years for their kids' college education may have left them ill-prepared for retirement.

• **Parents will "boomerang" back to their kids.** Just as adult children of the 1980s and 1990s moved back into their parents' home for economic security, elderly parents in the twenty-first century may increasingly move into the homes of their grown children. "Granny flats" and mother-in-law apartments will be common additions to houses.

• **No retirement from sex.** The sexual experimentation characteristic of baby boomers' youth may be brought to their old age. New drugs and therapies, such as penile implants, will help.

• **Elders will have roommates** or form other shared-living arrangements. A substantial increase in cohabitation offers the benefits of companionship without compromising the individual's financial survival or reducing the children's inheritance. We may see some college campuses convert into retirement communities, with dorm-style living.

The Effects of Population Changes on Values

Changes in values in the United States will depend to some extent on demographic change. Social institutions will continue to be stressed when population groups such as the aging baby boomers pass through society.

The baby boomers' children, the echo generation, now number more than 80 million people; they will be an even larger generation and a bigger social force than the baby boom was. They may be expected to stress and reshape education, justice, and work in turn, beginning now and accelerating through 2005, when they reach 20 and are ready to go to work.

Through the 1990s, the young echo boomers will increase school enrollment, then college enrollment. As they reach their late teens and move into their violence-prone years, the United States could experience an increase in violent crimes after the turn of the century. At around the same time there may be some risk of social unrest either in universities or in cities, as the echo boom goes through its years of youthful idealism and discontent.

The aging of the baby boom in the 1990s and 2000s may push the dominant values of U.S. society to be more conservative, more security conscious, and more mature and less driven by youthful expectations. In 2010, the first of the baby boomers turn 65. If the conservatism of their elders becomes repressive, the echo boomers could have more to rebel against.

As the U.S. population grows, if the economy affords only shrinking opportunities, this may promote more conservative views. At the same time, there may be an emerging social activism around worker rights, employment stability, and related issues.

Effects of Shifting Family Patterns

As a flexible institution, the family will continue to accommodate itself to the economy and the values of the Information Age. In many societies, this means an ongoing shift to dual-income partnerships.

It has also meant a shift in what work is available for the family to earn its income—away from agriculture and manufacturing and to information and services. This shift has brought millions of women into the work force because the work now requires education rather than raw physical might—mind, not muscle.

In many societies, men are finding it more difficult to find work unless they, too, can shift to information-based work. It is possible that women will become the higher wage earners in millions of families. It is also possible that as a result child care and family responsibilities will be more equally distributed between men and women.

People will continue to want to be part of families, but for some the economic necessity to do so will be less. For example, young people will need to spend more time in acquiring their education, and they will form their families later. Women with substantial careers will have less economic need to remarry after divorce.

Education, prosperity, and a decline in regard for authority will continue to secularize U.S. society, but concern for the family and community will tend to promote ties with religion. The church will continue to be a source of support for those who feel in some way disadvantaged by current values and attitudes. The other attractions of religion are its rituals, its shared experiences, its mysteries, and its social events. These will continue to bring in and keep people in religious groups, unless urban society develops some alternatives.

Conclusion: Belief in the Family Remains High

Anticipations of family life have not diminished to a significant degree in the last decades. In general, Americans are committed to the family as the core of a successful life. It is particularly gratifying to see this view widely maintained by young people. The percentage of college freshmen saying that raising a family is "essential" or "very important" has been fairly constant in the past quarter century: 67.5% in 1970 and 69.5% in 1990.

Adults' commitment to the family has become somewhat tempered by the higher likelihood of divorce. But most people still agree that being happily married and having a happy family is an important goal.

About the Author

Joseph F. Coates is president of Coates & Jarratt, Inc., 3738 Kanawha Street, N. W., Washington, D.C. 20015. Telephone 202/966–9307; fax 202/ 966–8349.

This article is based on the "Social and Value Trends" section of a major report by Coates & Jarratt for its clients, *American Business in the New Millennium: Trends Shaping American Business, 1993–2010.* The author acknowledges the assistance of Christine Keen of the Domani Group and the team support of Jennifer Jarratt, John Mahaffie, Andy Hines, Andrew Braunberg, Sean Ryan, and Nina Papadopoulos of Coates & Jarratt, Inc.

The POWER of Secrets

They divide people. They deter new relationships. And they freeze the development of individuals.

There's no question that family secrets are destructive. But it matters mightily when and how you reveal them. Resist the temptation to handle them at transition times such as weddings, graduations, and new beginnings.

BY EVAN IMBER-BLACK

As a family therapist, I'm a professional secret-keeper. I'm often the very first person with whom someone risks telling a long-held secret. Several decades of guiding people struggling with secrets have taught me that they have an awesome if paradoxical power to unite people—and to divide them.

From government conspiracies to couples having affairs, secrets permeate every level of society. Secrets have existed throughout time, but the nature of secrets has recently changed in our society. Today's families face special dilemmas about secrecy, privacy, silence, and openness.

We live in a culture whose messages about secrecy are truly confounding. If cultural norms once made shameful secrets out of too many events in human life, we are now struggling with the reverse: the assumption that telling secrets—no matter how, when, or to whom—is morally superior to keeping them and that it is automatically healing. My own experience, however, has shown me that telling secrets in the wrong way or at the wrong time can be remarkably painful—and destructive.

The questions we need to concern ourselves with are: When should I keep a secret? How do I tell a secret without hurting anyone? How do I know the time is right? I've learned the answers as I've witnessed—sometimes with terror, more often with joy, and always with deep respect—families making the courageous journey from secrecy to openness.

Secrets are kept or opened for many complex motives, from self-serving abuses of power to altruistic protection of others. Understanding the best ways and situations in which to reveal a family secret can help you decide when and how to do so.

HOW SECRETS SABOTAGE

Although we encounter secrets in every area of life, they are perhaps most destructive when kept in the home. Families are support systems; our identity and ability to form close relationships with others depend upon the trust and communication we feel with loved ones. If family members keep secrets from each other—or from the outside world—the emotional fallout can last a lifetime.

There are four main ways that family secrets shape and scar us:

• they can divide family members, permanently estranging them;

From *Psychology Today,* July/August 1998, pp. 50-53, 62. Excerpted from *The Secret Life of Families,* by Evan Imber-Black.
© 1998 by Evan Imber-Black. Used by permission of Bantam Books, a division of Random House, Inc.

- they can discourage individuals from sharing information with anyone outside the family, inhibiting formation of intimate relationships;
- they can freeze development at crucial points in life, preventing the growth of self and identity;
- they can lead to painful miscommunication within a family, causing unnecessary guilt and doubt.

A person who seeks to undo the damage caused by family secrets must accept that revealing a secret is not a betrayal but a necessity. Luckily, as you'll see, it's never too late to do so.

SHATTERING THE TRIANGLE

Not all secrets are destructive. Many are essential to establishing bonds between two people. When siblings keep secrets from their parents, for example, they attain a sense of independence and a feeling of closeness. But the creation of any secret between two people in a family actually forms a triangle: it always excludes—and therefore involves—another.

When family members suspect that important information is being withheld from them, they may pursue the content of the secret in ways that violate privacy. A mother reads her daughter's diary. A husband rifles through his wife's purse. Relationships corrode with suspicion. Conversely, family members may respond to a secret with silence and distance, which affect areas of life that have nothing to do with the secret.

Either way, the secret wedges a boulder between those who know it and those who don't. To remove this obstacle, families must break the triangle formation.

Molly Bradley first called me during what should have been a joyous time. She had recently given birth. Her happiness, however, was bittersweet. Molly felt a deep need to surround herself with family but hadn't spoken to her brother, Calvin, in six years. The reason, I discovered, reached back 30 years to a secret made by Molly's mother.

When Molly, Calvin, and their youngest sister, Annie, were teenagers, their grandmother committed suicide. Molly and Annie were told she died from a heart attack. Only Calvin, the eldest, knew the truth. His mother made him promise not to tell. His sisters sensed a mystery, but if they asked about their grandmother, their mother switched topics.

Making secrets soon became the family's modus vivendi. Their aunt committed suicide two years after their grandmother's death. Calvin fathered a child out of wedlock. Each secret was kept from Molly and Annie, amplifying the family pattern of secrecy. Calvin grew distant from his sisters, their relationship weakened by mistrust. Eventually, Molly guessed the truth of her grandmother's death but, in her family's style, told only Annie.

All families have some secrets from the outside world. Yours, no doubt, has jokes and stories told only within.

Secrets between Calvin and his mother were matched by those between Molly and Annie, tightening family alliances.

From the outside, the family looked like two close pairs—Calvin and his mother, Molly and Annie. But the pairs were actually triangles; Calvin and his mother distanced themselves from the girls with their secret, forming one triangle, while Molly and Annie, keeping their own secrets from the rest of the family, formed another.

'DON'T TELL ANYONE OUR BUSINESS'

Molly convinced her two siblings to enter therapy, but each felt that overcoming feelings of alienation was impossible. When I asked Annie if she'd ever considered confiding in Calvin as a child, she told me the thought had never occurred to her. If family members cannot even imagine a different way of interacting, then secrets have truly taken hold of their lives.

In order to bridge the distance between the Bradley children, I asked them to relive their memories of how it felt to keep—and be kept out of—secrets. Molly, Annie, and Calvin each acknowledged that their needs to connect with each other had gone painfully unmet. Calvin explained tearfully that being forced to keep information from his sisters left him unable to relate to them, causing him to withdraw into himself. Molly revealed that watching her infant son each day made her miss Calvin—and the relationship they'd never had—more and more.

The siblings finally began to share long-held secrets, realizing that they were bound and supported by their desire for closeness. After the fourth session of therapy, they went to dinner together for the first time in years. "This was so different from any other family event," Annie reported. "Things felt genuine for the first time."

As a lifetime of confessions and hopes emerged into the open, the triangle of secrecy was replaced by one-to-one relationships. When everyone in a family knows a secret, triangles cannot create barriers between members.

All families have some secrets from the outside world. Yours, no doubt, has shared jokes and stories told only within the family circle. You also have a zone of privacy that demarcates inside from outside, building your family's sense of identity. But if a dangerous secret—one concerning

> **Being the family member who opens internal secrets is difficult. It may seem like an act of betrayal.**

an individual in immediate physical or emotional jeopardy—is held within your house, the boundaries between family and the rest of the world become rigid and impenetrable. Friends and relatives are not invited in, and family members' forays out are limited. "Don't tell anyone our business" becomes the family motto.

BREAKING FAMILY RULES

Some families create inviolable rules to keep information hidden, making it impossible for members to ask for assistance or to use needed resources in the outside world. Even problems that do not touch on the secret may go unresolved if resolution requires outside help.

When Sara Tompkins, 37, first came to see me, she spoke with great hesitation. "If my family knew I was speaking to you, they'd be very angry," she confided. She told me about growing up in a family that completely revolved around her mother's addiction to tranquilizers. "My father is a physician. To this day, he writes her prescriptions. No one was supposed to know. The worst part was, we were supposed to act like we didn't know. Our family invented 'don't ask, don't tell' long before the government ever thought of it."

Even though Sara hadn't lived with her family for 15 years, this was the first time she had ever broken the family rule against speaking about the secret. When Sara left home for college, she was surrounded with new and exciting faces, each seeking lifelong friends and stimulating late-night discussions. But Sara found herself unable to open up, ultimately finding few friends and fewer lovers. She found it difficult to reveal anything personal about herself to anyone, and even suspected others of withholding from her.

Secrets were how she had learned to process and handle incoming information. Sara finally sought therapy when she realized that she had never been able to sustain a romantic relationship past the second date.

When a family's secret is an ongoing condition—such as drug addiction, physical abuse, an illness—then both family relationships and interactions with the outside

world are profoundly affected. In families like Sara's, members must organize their everyday lives around the needs of the secret while performing the breathtaking feat of pretending not to notice anything is out of the ordinary. Conversation is superficial, since what is truly important cannot be discussed. Members become paralyzed, unable to develop relationships with others or to deepen the relationships within the family. Since individual well-being takes a backseat to group fidelity, being the family member who challenges internal secrets is difficult. Taking the risk of opening a long-held secret to friends and loved ones may seem like an act of betrayal. The anticipated catastrophe of exclusion from the family stops many people—often long after leaving home.

But breaking the rules of family secrecy is necessary to ensure the achievement of freedom and honesty crucial to making and sustaining authentic relationships. One of the best ways to ease into revealing long-hidden information is to tell an objective listener, like a therapist.

ROOM FOR REHEARSAL

Only rarely do my clients want their first and final telling to be with me. Making secrets with a professional helper is a double-edged sword. A client's relationship with a therapist, minister, priest, or rabbi can be an excellent arena to dissolve shame, find acceptance and empathy, and seek new resources for support and strength.

At the same time, sharing secrets only with professionals may negatively affect marriage and other relationships. Important issues may be discussed more in therapy, for example, than at home. Instead of being a dress rehearsal for life, therapy becomes the show. Most often, I find that people want a receptive and empathetic context in which to unpack a secret initially, room to explore the consequences of telling others, then the help to do it well.

Imagine if your sister made a secret with you on the eve of your wedding and told you that you must not tell your husband. Or you are dragged into a secret about your parents just when you are taking tentative steps into the outside world. If a secret is made at a key point in development, the natural unfolding of self and relationships may be frozen. The shifting of boundaries that ordinarily would occur is suspended, creating a developmental deep freeze.

FROZEN FAMILIES

Every family experiences developmental stages. These are most evident when someone enters the family by marriage or other committed relationship, birth, or adoption, and when someone exits the family by leaving home or through separation, divorce,

> # Families must open secrets only during a normal time in everyday life, or else resolution can't occur.

or death. Such entrances and exits require that a family reinvent itself in order to accommodate new roles. The stages of development are not discrete events but rather processes that take place over time. When that process goes well, complex adjustments occur in every corner of the family. When a secret is made in the midst of this process, adjustment screeches to a halt.

Samuel Wheeler tried to leave home when he was 19, but his discovery of a central family secret pulled him back and short-circuited his young adulthood. When Sam came to see me, he was 34 and still struggling with the aftermath. Aimless, jobless, and depressed, Sam wondered why he had never really found his focus. As we explored his past, I realized that Sam's life had frozen when his attempts to assert independence were squelched his first year of college.

Early in his first semester, Sam invited his mother to visit. "I was more than surprised when she arrived with a close friend of the family, Duncan," said Sam. Each morning for three days, Mrs. Wheeler left Sam's apartment at five A.M. and returned to have breakfast at eight o'clock. When Sam finally asked what was going on, his mother admitted that she and Duncan were having an affair. She also revealed that his younger sister had actually been fathered by Duncan.

"My mother had kept this secret for years," Sam mused. "Why did she have to put it in my face at that moment?" The ill-timed revelation kept Sam from proceeding with his new life and developing his own identity. While very bright, Sam did poorly his first year in college, dropped out, and went back home. He had subconsciously returned to play watchdog for the family's relationships. His sister was only 15, and he was worried that she would discover the secret. He remained home until she left for college.

RESPECTING TRANSITION TIMES

Giving voice to the developmental deep freeze, Sam said, "Knowing these things about my mother's life has kept me from changing my relationship with her and my dad in ways I would like. I wanted to get closer to my dad, but this secret is like a rock between us."

Pulling Sam into a secret just as he and his family were moving apart also kept him from asserting independence. While there is no such thing as the perfect moment to open a secret, there are better occasions than a life-cycle ritual, such as a wedding or graduation. Because family relationships are already shifting, rituals may seem a perfect time to open a secret. The excitement of a major life change, however, will prevent resolution of the secret. Either the importance of the secret will be lost in the event, or the secret will diminish the importance of the ritual.

For family members to have the strength to handle a life-altering secret, it should be told during a normal time in everyday life. Otherwise, development linked to a life passage will stop in its tracks.

When secrets are as much a part of families as birthdays, it may seem impossible to extricate them from the daily routine. But I know it can be done. Each time I meet with a new client, I'm moved by the courage people bring to this endeavor, by the human desire to heal and to connect.

Rituals

FOR OUR TIMES

Evan Imber-Black
and Janine Roberts

Evan Imber-Black is the director of the Family and Group Studies program of the Department of Psychiatry at Albert Einstein College of Medicine. Janine Roberts is the director of the Family Therapy program of the School of Education at the University of Massachusetts.

EVERY FOURTH OF JULY, PAUL and Linda Hoffman pack their three children and their dog into the station wagon and drive 250 miles to Paul's sister's home, where all of the Hoffmans gather. The event is fairly unpleasant. The women spend the day cooking, which Linda resents, while the men watch sports, an activity Paul doesn't care for. The young cousins spend most of the day fighting with one another. In the evening, Grandpa Hoffman sets off fireworks, but no one really pays attention. On the fifth of July, Paul and Linda drive home, wearily vowing that this is the last year they will spend their holiday this way.

The following June, however, when Paul and Linda dare mention that they are thinking about doing something different for Independence Day, Paul's sister calls and tells them how upset their parents will be if the couple and their children don't come this year. Alternate plans fall by the wayside, and on the Fourth of July into the car they go.

How today's families are developing innovative rites and ceremonies to ease difficult transitions, heal relationships, and celebrate life.

Does this story sound at all familiar to you? Because of experiences like the Hoffmans', in which celebrations are static and meaningless, many of us have minimized the practice of rituals in our lives. One woman we know who grew up in a family whose rituals were particularly confining put it this way: "I don't want any rituals in my life. Rituals are like being in prison!"

Yet in these times of rapid and dramatic change in the family—with more children being raised by single parents, more mothers working outside the home, fewer extended families living in close proximity—rituals can provide us with a crucial sense of personal identity as well as family connection. Despite the changing status of the family, membership within a family group is still the primary way that most people identify themselves. Rituals that both borrow from the past and are reshaped by relationship needs of the present highlight for us continuity as well as change. A family in which ritual is minimized may have little sense of itself through time. Everything simply blends into everything else.

As family therapists who have been working with and teaching the use of rituals since the late '70s, we have encountered an increasing number of people who are longing to revitalize the rituals in their lives. They just don't know how. Rituals surround us and offer opportunities to make meaning from the familiar and the mysterious at the same time. Built around common symbols and symbolic actions such as birthday cakes and blowing out candles, or exchanging rings and wedding vows, many parts of rituals are well known to us.

A ritual can be as simple as the one that sixty-two-year-old Eveline Miller practices when she needs to sort things through. She goes to her grandmother's rocking chair, sits, and rocks. When she was a child and needed comfort, this was where she used to go to lay her head upon her grandmother's lap. Her grandmother

From *New Age Journal*, September/October 1992, pp. 70–73, 140. Excerpt from *Rituals for Our Times: Celebrating, Healing, and Changing Our Lives and Relationships* by Evan Imber-Black and Janine Roberts. © 1993 by Evan Imber-Black and Janine Roberts. Reprinted by permission of HarperCollins Publishers, Inc.

would stroke her hair and say, "This too will pass." Now, as Eveline rocks and thinks, she repeats those words to help calm herself and provide perspective.

Rituals also can be more elaborate and creative, such as one that Jed and his wife, Isabel, a couple in their early twenties, designed for Jed's brother. Several months after Jed married Isabel, his mother died suddenly, leaving Jed's nineteen-year-old brother, Brian, orphaned. Brian came to live with Jed and Isabel. The young couple thus found themselves not only newlyweds but also new "parents." One day Brian told them, "You know, I feel like I don't have a security blanket. My friends at school, other people in my classes—most of them have at least one parent still alive. Their parents can help them if they're having trouble in school, or if they need a place to stay, or can't find a job. And I don't have that security blanket because both of my parents are dead."

What Brian had said seemed so important to him that Jed and Isabel talked about it between themselves and eventually came up with an idea: They would make Brian a quilt—a security blanket. Jed's sister had an old nurse's uniform of their mother's that they could use for material. An older brother had a Marine camouflage shirt of their father's. They found some other old fabric among their mother's things. Then, as they began to cut the material into squares, they realized that they would need help sewing them together into a quilt. Jed thought of his maternal grandmother, who had sewn a number of quilts for other family members.

The siblings and the grandmother began gathering in secret to sew the quilt and share memories of Brian's parents and their earlier life. And when the family gathered to celebrate the grandmother's eightieth birthday, Brian was given the quilt—a blanket that symbolized both the ability of Jed and Isabel to "parent" in creative ways and the new network of contact that had been built between the siblings and their grandmother. Together,

these family members had proved to be Brian's "security blanket."

The symbols and symbolic actions of rituals embrace meaning that cannot always be easily expressed in words. Eveline Miller's rocking chair, for example, was much more than a place to sit; it evoked safety, reassurance, and the memory of her grandmother. Brian's quilt was not just a cover; it represented the interconnected people in his life—from the past and the present—whom he could carry with him into the future. The textures, smells, and sounds of ritual symbols—an heirloom rocking chair, a family-made quilt—can be powerful activators of sensory memory. Family members may recall scenes and stories of previous times when similar rituals were enacted or some of the same people were together. Rituals connect us with our past, define our present life, and show us a path to our future.

FAMILY RITUALS TAKE A VARIETY OF forms. There are daily practices, such as the reading of a child's bedtime story or the sharing of a mealtime. There are holiday traditions, some celebrated with the community at large (seasonal events such as the solstice, religious events such as Passover, national events such as the Fourth of July) and others exclusive to a particular family (birthdays, anniversaries, reunions). Then there are life-cycle rituals, which mark the major transitions of life.

All human beings throughout the world and throughout time are born, and all die. All of us experience emerging sexuality. And most create sustained adult relationships to form new family units and new generations. Such changes are enormously complicated, involving both beginnings and endings; holding and expressing both pain and joy. They may shape and give voice to profoundly conflicting beliefs about our personal existence and our relationships. It's little wonder that every culture in the world has created rituals to celebrate and guide our way through these life-cycle passages.

The truly magical quality of rituals is embedded in their capacity not only to announce a change but to actually create the change. Given that volumes have been written advising people how to change, and that people spend countless hours in therapy, often agonizing over their inability to make needed changes, it is easy to see why rituals exist in all cultures, to ease our passage from one stage of life to another. Using familiar symbols, actions, and words, rituals make

---

A family in which ritual is minimized may have little sense of itself through time.

---

change manageable and safe. Simply knowing which rituals lie ahead during a day, a year, or a lifetime stills our anxiety. Change is *enacted* through rituals and not simply talked about—couples don't change from being single to being married by talking about marriage, but rather by participating in a wedding ceremony. Teens don't graduate from high school when a teacher says "you're finished now"; they attend proms, picnics, and the graduation ceremony itself.

As families have changed, life-cycle events have changed too, and there are many crucial transitions for which there are no familiar and accepted rituals in our culture. Changes that often go unmarked include divorce, the end of a nonmarried relationship, adoption, forming a committed homosexual relationship, leaving home, pregnancy loss, and menopause. Since life-cycle rituals enable us to begin to rework our sense of self and our relationships as required by life's changes, the lack of such rituals can make change more difficult.

Rituals tend to put us in touch with the profound circle of life and death, so it is not surprising that healing moments emerge spontaneously during these celebrations. If you keep that in mind when changes are occurring in your life or in the lives of those close to you, you can plan a ritual to specifically generate healing.

Healing a Broken Relationship

The crisis of shattered trust and broken promises can lead to genuine atonement, forgiveness, reconciliation, and relationship renewal or, alternatively, to chronic resentment, bitterness, parting, and isolation. Since rituals are able to hold and express powerful contradictory feelings, such as love and hate, anger and connectedness, they enhance the possibility of relationship healing.

For Sondra and Alex Cutter, ritual provided a way to bury that past. The Cutters had spent seven of their twelve years of marriage in bitter arguments about a brief affair Alex had had just before their fifth anniversary. Sondra didn't want to leave her marriage, but she felt unable to let go of the past. Alex, in turn, had become extremely defensive about his behavior and was unable to genuinely show Sondra that he was sorry. In couple's therapy, Sondra and Alex were asked to bring two sets of symbols of the affair. The first set of symbols was to represent what the affair meant to each of them at the time it occurred. The second set was to symbolize what the affair had come to mean in their current life together. As a symbol of her feelings at the time of the affair, Sondra brought a torn wedding photograph to show that the affair meant a break in their vows. Sondra

was surprised by Alex's symbol: an old picture of his father, who had had many affairs. "I thought this was just what husbands did," said Alex. "I thought this was what made you a man, but I found out quickly that this didn't work for me and for what I wanted my marriage to be. Then we couldn't get past it." Sondra had never heard Alex speak about the affair in this way. Her belief that the affair meant he didn't love her and that he loved another woman began to shift for the first time in seven years.

As a symbol of what the affair meant currently, Alex brought the wheel of a hamster cage, remarking, "We just go round and round and round and get nowhere." Sondra brought a bottle of bitters, and said, "This is what I've turned into!" After a long conversation engendered by their symbols, Sondra said quietly, "This is the first time in seven years

(UN photo/John Isaac)

Rituals shape our relationships and give us a basis for a healthy society. Simply having a family meal together helps establish a stronger sense of self.

that we've talked about this without yelling and screaming." When the therapist asked if they were ready to let go of the past, both agreed that they were. They decided to revisit a favorite spot from early in their relationship and to bury these symbols there. During the ceremony, Alex cried and for the first time asked Sondra to forgive him, which she readily did. They followed this with a celebration of their anniversary, which they had stopped celebrating seven years earlier.

This healing ritual was created as part of couple's therapy, but you don't need the help of a therapist to create rituals to effect healing. Common to all healing rituals is a dimension of time—time for holding on and time for letting go. Selecting symbols to express painful issues generally allows for a new kind of conversation to emerge. Taking some joint action together, such as symbolically burying the past, can impart a new possibility of collaboration. Creating a ritual together can help you to rediscover the playful parts of your relationship, such as the couple who "put an affair on ice," placing symbols in their deep freezer and agreeing that they could only fight about the affair after they had thawed these symbols out!

A Ceremony for Grieving

There is no life that is lived without loss. We all experience the death of people we love and care for deeply. When healing rituals have not occurred, or have been insufficient to complete the grief process, a person can remain stuck in the past or unable to move forward in meaningful ways. Even the unhealed losses of previous generations may emerge as debilitating symptoms in the present. When this happens, new rituals can be created to address the need for healing.

Joanie and Jeralynn Thompson were identical twins who had a close and loving relationship. They went away to the same college and planned to graduate together. During their junior year, however, Jeralynn developed

Rituals connect us with our past, define our present life, and show us a path to our future.

leukemia. She died within the year. Before her death, Jeralynn talked with Joanie about how important it was that Joanie continue college and graduate. Joanie did go back to school after her sister's funeral, but she found it impossible to study. At the urging of friends, she took a year off in order to be with her family and begin to deal with the terrible loss of her sister. But a year turned into two years, two years into three. Finally, her family insisted that she go back to college. Joanie returned to school and finished all of her courses, but remained unable to do her senior thesis. She didn't graduate that June. "I don't know how I can graduate without Jeralynn," she told her mother. "It'll mean that she's really gone." Once her mother began to understand what was stopping Joanie from finishing, she talked with her daughter about how they might honor Jeralynn's life while still celebrating Joanie's entering adulthood with her college graduation. After developing a plan with her mother, Joanie finished her thesis in time to graduate the following December.

Joanie and her mother planned a special ceremony to be held two nights before graduation. They invited extended family and close friends, asking them to bring symbols of Jeralynn and to speak about her openly. During a very moving ceremony, many people spoke about what they thought Jeralynn would have wished for Joanie. One aunt made a video

that showed places the two sisters had both loved, and after showing it told Joanie, "These places still belong to you." Joanie's father brought photographs of several pets the twins had raised, carefully pointing out the individual contributions each twin had made to these animals. Then, in a five-minute talk, he highlighted the strengths and gifts of each young woman and gave Joanie permission to be her own person. People grieved the loss of Jeralynn openly and then embraced Joanie for finishing school and going on in life.

Several months later, settled in a new job as a teacher, Joanie talked about this ceremony and her graduation: "They all helped me to graduate. If we hadn't had our memorial first, I know all I would have been wondering about on graduation day was what my family was feeling about Jeralynn's death. Instead, all of it was out in the open. We could be sad together and then we could be happy together on my graduation day. They call graduation a commencement, an ending that's really a beginning, and that's what mine was. I miss my sister terribly—I'll always miss her—but my family and friends helped me take the next step in my life, and Jeralynn's spirit was right there with me."

Celebrating Recovery from Illness

Sometimes very important changes take place but remain unacknowledged. This may be because the changes are difficult to talk about, because they bring up the pain of how things used to be, or because no one had thought about how to mark the change. In our experience, recovery from medical or psychiatric illness is an aspect of change that is seldom marked by a ritual. Families, relationships, and the individual's own identity remain stuck with the illness label, and behavior among family members and friends remains as it was when the person was ill.

Adolescents who have recovered from cancer or adults who are now healthy after heart surgery often maintain an "illness identity," and others treat them accordingly. A ritual can declare in action that a person has moved from illness to health. Such a ritual might include a ceremony of throwing away no-longer-needed medicines or medical equipment, burning or burying symbols of a long hospital stay, or writing a document declaring new life and health.

After recovering from breast cancer, Gerry Sims had a T-shirt made that read HEALTHY WOMAN! She wore this T-shirt to a family dinner and announced to everyone that they were to stop treating her as a patient, and that, in particular, she wanted people to argue with her as they had before she became ill. Then she handed out T-shirts to her husband and children that read HUSBAND OF A HEALTHY WOMAN, CHILD OF A HEALTHY WOMAN. Everyone put on his or her T-shirt and for the first time spontaneously began to talk about what they had been through together during Gerry's year-long illness. They cried out loud to each other. Following this, Gerry's teen-age daughter picked a fight with her, just as Gerry had hoped!

A Rite of Passage

Like many life-cycle passages, a child leaving home is an event that carries deeply mixed feelings, including a sense of joy and accomplishment, fear regarding what lies ahead, sadness over the loss of relationships in their present form, and curious anticipation about what life will look like next. This life-cycle passage of leaving home may be even more difficult when the leaving is unanticipated or when the child has grown up with a handicap. Creating a leaving-home ritual whose symbols and symbolic actions speak to the many contradictory issues can ease this passage for everyone in the family.

Jennifer Cooper-Smith was born with some severe disabilities that affected her capacity to read, write, and speak. During her childhood she took the handicap in stride despite the cruel teasing of other children and de-

spite coming from a family where high academic achievement was the norm. Through it all she taught her family a lot about perseverance in the face of enormous struggles and about building on strengths rather than focusing on weaknesses.

When Jennifer reached nineteen, since her disabilities would preclude her going to college, it was clear that high school graduation was to be her rite of passage. The family wanted to create a ritual that would both honor all that she had accomplished and send her forth into the adult world with confidence.

Jennifer wanted a party at a Chinese restaurant with her favorite festive food. Her mother and stepfather invited people who were important to Jennifer—extended family who lived far away, friends who had supported her, special teachers and co-workers from her part-time job. The invitation included a secret request for special items—poems, letters, photos, stories, drawings, and so on—to help make a "becoming an adult woman" album for Jenni. During the weeks before the party, her mom worked secretly to construct the album, which began at the time Jennifer joined the family as an adopted infant and included sections that marked significant stages of her development. Although the handicaps had sometimes made it difficult for both Jennifer and those around her to notice her growth and changes, this album recorded them for all to see.

When Jennifer arrived at the party, the album was waiting for her as a special symbol of her development. What she still didn't know, though, was that the album was open-ended, and a new section, "Becoming an Adult Woman," was about to be added during the party. After dinner, when people were invited to give their presentations to Jennifer, a moving and unexpected ceremony unfolded. Person after person spoke about how they experienced Jenni and what she meant to them, and they gave her their own special brand of advice about living.

Her grandma Dena gave Jenni a photograph of Dena's late husband— Jenni's grandfather—down on his knees proposing marriage. She spoke about enduring love and her wish that Jenni would have this in her life. Her aunt Meryle Sue read an original poem, "Portrait of Jenni," and then spoke through tears about what this day would have meant to Jenni's grandfather and how proud he would have been of her. Her cousin Stacey wrote a poem that captured who Jenni was to her and offered words about Jenni's future. Advice about men and what to beware of was given by Jenni's step-grandfather and received with much laughter. Photographs of strong women in history were presented.

Person after person spoke with grace and love and special stories about Jennifer's strengths. Her mother watched as Jennifer took in all that she was to people and the sometimes unknown impact that her own courage had had on family and friends. And then all who gathered witnessed the emergence of Jennifer, the adult woman, as she rose from her seat and spoke unhaltingly and with no trace of her usual shyness, thanking each person in turn for what they had given her in life, and talking about the loss of her grandfather and her wish that he could be with her today. She ended with all that she anticipated next in her life.

The weeks and months following this ritual were perhaps even more remarkable than the ceremony itself. Her family experienced a changed Jennifer, a Jennifer who moved from adolescence to young womanhood— starting a full-time job, auditing a community college course, traveling by herself, making new friends, and relating on a previously unseen level.

AS ALL OF THESE EXAMPLES ILLUSTRATE, rituals ease our passage through life. They shape our relationships, help to heal our losses, express our deepest beliefs, and celebrate our existence. They announce change and create change. The power of rituals belongs to all of us.

AE Article Review Form

We encourage you to photocopy and use this page as a tool to assess how the articles in **Annual Editions** expand on the information in your textbook. By reflecting on the articles you will gain enhanced text information. You can also access this useful form on a product's book support Web site at **http://www.dushkin.com/ online/.**

NAME: _____   DATE: _____

TITLE AND NUMBER OF ARTICLE: _____

BRIEFLY STATE THE MAIN IDEA OF THIS ARTICLE: _____

LIST THREE IMPORTANT FACTS THAT THE AUTHOR USES TO SUPPORT THE MAIN IDEA:

_____

WHAT INFORMATION OR IDEAS DISCUSSED IN THIS ARTICLE ARE ALSO DISCUSSED IN YOUR TEXTBOOK OR OTHER READINGS THAT YOU HAVE DONE? LIST THE TEXTBOOK CHAPTERS AND PAGE NUMBERS:

_____

LIST ANY EXAMPLES OF BIAS OR FAULTY REASONING THAT YOU FOUND IN THE ARTICLE:

_____

LIST ANY NEW TERMS/CONCEPTS THAT WERE DISCUSSED IN THE ARTICLE, AND WRITE A SHORT DEFINITION:

_____

ANNUAL EDITIONS revisions depend on two major opinion sources: one is our Advisory Board, listed in the front of this volume, which works with us in scanning the thousands of articles published in the public press each year; the other is you—the person actually using the book. Please help us and the users of the next edition by completing the prepaid article rating form on this page and returning it to us. Thank you for your help!

ANNUAL EDITIONS: Marriage and Family 00/01

ARTICLE RATING FORM

Here is an opportunity for you to have direct input into the next revision of this volume. We would like you to rate each of the 45 articles listed below, using the following scale:

1. Excellent: should definitely be retained
2. Above average: should probably be retained
3. Below average: should probably be deleted
4. Poor: should definitely be deleted

Your ratings will play a vital part in the next revision. So please mail this prepaid form to us just as soon as you complete it. Thanks for your help!

RATING	ARTICLE
	1. A New Focus on Family Values
	2. The Intentional Family
	3. African American Families: A Legacy of Vulnerability and Resilience
	4. Boys Will Be Boys
	5. Sex Differences in the Brain
	6. Flirting Fascination
	7. Back Off!
	8. Protecting against Unintended Pregnancy: A Guide to Contraceptive Choices
	9. The Brave New World of Parenting
	10. Pregnant Pleasures
	11. Fetal Psychology
	12. Maternal Emotions May Influence Fetal Behaviors
	13. Fertile Minds
	14. The Cost of Children
	15. Our Babies, Ourselves
	16. The Science of a Good Marriage
	17. The Healing Power of Intimacy
	18. Men, Women & Money
	19. Parental Rights: An Overview
	20. Father Love and Child Development: History and Current Evidence
	21. Parents Speak: Zero to Three's Findings from Research on Parents' Views of Early Childhood Development
	22. Do Parents Really Matter? Kid Stuff

RATING	ARTICLE
	23. Anatomy of a Violent Relationship
	24. Helping Children Cope with Violence
	25. Resilience in Development
	26. Sex & Marriage
	27. Shattered Vows
	28. The Politics of Fatigue: The Gender War Has Been Replaced by the Exhaustion of Trying to Do It All
	29. A Progressive Approach to Caring for Children and Community
	30. Do Working Parents Make the Grade?
	31. Balancing Work and Family
	32. Should You Leave?
	33. Divorce Reform: New Directions
	34. Is Divorce Too Easy?
	35. Smart Plan to Save Marriages
	36. The Children of Divorce
	37. After Divorce
	38. Hard Lessons
	39. A Harder Better Death
	40. How Kids Mourn
	41. To See Your Future Look into Your Past
	42. Defining Daddy Down
	43. What's Ahead for Families: Five Major Forces of Change
	44. The Power of Secrets
	45. Rituals for Our Times

(Continued on next page)

We Want Your Advice

ANNUAL EDITIONS: MARRIAGE AND FAMILY 00/01

BUSINESS REPLY MAIL
FIRST-CLASS MAIL   PERMIT NO. 84   GUILFORD CT

POSTAGE WILL BE PAID BY ADDRESSEE

Dushkin/McGraw-Hill
Sluice Dock
Guilford, CT 06437-9989

NO POSTAGE
NECESSARY
IF MAILED
IN THE
UNITED STATES

ABOUT YOU

Name _____   Date _____

Are you a teacher? ☐   A student? ☐
Your school's name

_____

Department

_____

Address _____   City _____   State ____   Zip ____

School telephone # _____

YOUR COMMENTS ARE IMPORTANT TO US !

Please fill in the following information:
For which course did you use this book?

_____

Did you use a text with this *ANNUAL EDITION*? ☐ yes ☐ no
What was the title of the text?

_____

What are your general reactions to the *Annual Editions* concept?

_____

Have you read any particular articles recently that you think should be included in the next edition?

_____

Are there any articles you feel should be replaced in the next edition? Why?

_____

Are there any World Wide Web sites you feel should be included in the next edition? Please annotate.

_____

May we contact you for editorial input? ☐ yes ☐ no
May we quote your comments? ☐ yes ☐ no